Anthropological research

Anthropological research

The structure of inquiry

Second edition

PERTTI J. PELTO

Professor of Anthropology and Medicine
University of Connecticut

GRETEL H. PELTO

Assistant Professor of Nutritional Sciences and
  Anthropology
University of Connecticut

CAMBRIDGE UNIVERSITY PRESS

Cambridge
London   New York   Melbourne

Published by the Syndics of the Cambridge University Press
The Pitt Building, Trumpington Street, Cambridge CB 2 1RP
Bentley House, 200 Euston Road, London NW1 2DB
32 East 57th Street, New York, NY 10022, USA
296 Beaconsfield Parade, Middle Park, Melbourne 3206, Australia

First published by Harper and Row, Publishers, 1970
Second edition by Cambridge University Press 1978

Printed in the United States of America
Typeset, printed, and bound by Vail-Ballou Press, Inc., Binghamton, New York

Library of Congress Cataloging in Publication Data
Pelto, Pertti J.
Anthropological research.

Includes bibliographical references and index.

1. Ethnology – Methodology.   2. Anthropological research.
I. Pelto, Gretel H., joint author.   II. Title.
GN345.P44 1977   301.2'01'08   76-62583
ISBN 0 521 21673 7 hard covers
ISBN 0 521 29228 X paperback

Contents

v

Preface to the second edition

In the six years since the first appearance of this book the trend toward greater interest in methodological issues has continued. Most graduate programs in anthropology now include training in the structure of scientific research; training in statistics and computer use has increased steadily, and several books devoted to research paradigms and statistics-for-anthropologists have appeared.

The growth of interest in methodology has sharpened certain longstanding philosophical and theoretical issues in anthropology. The central methodological debate of the 1970s continues to be the conflict between quantitative methods and the supposedly more personalized and humanistic qualitative scholarship. Closely linked to this issue is the continuing discussion about emic versus etic data. Contrary to our earlier expectations, that anthropological conversation remains lively today and attention to the emic-etic issue has livened other disciplines as well.

Reflecting on these issues, we find that our views about them are not much changed from six years ago. Then, as now, we argue for a judicious mixing of quantitative and qualitative research. The problem is not *which* mode of data gathering to use *but how to integrate both* to build credible and effective anthropological knowledge. The goal of research is to develop *useful and credible* information. Credibility, in matters of human behavior, can never rest finally on purified numerical analysis. Nor can it depend wholly on rich verbal description that ignores underlying questions of quantity and intensity. As we examine some of the most refined statistical or mathematical analyses of anthropological data, we often find them losing their anchorage to live, human subject matter.

In the past ten years of anthropological research we have seen the demonstration that the complexities of human thought and behavior are extremely difficult to quantify in entirely rigorous ways. Random-sampling strategies are beset with many practical obstacles; and attempts to standardize field observations fall short in many social settings. Sometimes we are tempted into relatively trivial topics of observation simply because quantifiable data are more accessible there. Thus overquantified, computerized anthropology quickly reaches the point of diminishing returns in both credibility and usefulness.

ix

The "old-fashioned" qualitative-descriptive modes of research have often been extolled as preserving a personalized ingredient essential to understanding human behavior (cf. Honigmann, 1976). Whenever we step into field work, we are reminded of the significance of the human factor in all our observations. More than other behavioral scientists, we anthropologists find that a personalized, qualitative-descriptive research period is essential to discovering *what the fundamental questions* (hence variables and hypotheses) really are, even when we approach the field with clear theoretical ideas.

Without denying the importance of our preestablished conceptual frameworks, we feel that anthropology is the most fundamentally inductive of the sciences. The personalized discovery of "the way it really is" in human communities is only a first step, however. Much of the glamour and mystique of anthropology is found in that emotional experience, but the commitment and emotional understanding that grows in the course of field research is not enough to assure that resulting data will be either useful or credible. The personal factor that seems crucial in the *discovery* phases of work must be brought under control (not eliminated) in the later phases of research. The recent history of debates and discourse on human behavior and history have continued to strengthen the significance of Francis Bacon's assessment, that the human mind "as an uneven mirror distorts the rays of objects according to its own figure and section, so the mind . . . in forming its notions mixes up its own nature with the nature of things" (Bacon, 1960:22; first published, 1620).

In the last analysis we can of course do nothing to eliminate entirely the distortions of the uneven human mirror. The challenge is to *control* our own subjective and personalized feelings and impressions. To do this the researcher, provides to his/her audience the information about *specific observations*, the evidence on which descriptive generalizations are based, to the fullest extent possible. Does an ethnographic "fact" arise from first-hand observation of a given behavior – once, twice, ten times? Or is it based on informants' statements? On how many such statements does it depend? How were the statements made?

The emic-etic controversy has further heightened our awareness of the fundamental elusiveness of definitions and concepts. Overreliance on the personal factor in research can mean that the anthropologist, a stranger to the local community, has imposed his or her definitions and feelings about reality on behaviors and events that may have quite a different significance from the emic, insider's point of view. On the other hand, a people's emic point of view may be of limited usefulness (or even limited accuracy) depending on one's focus of research. An insider can be just as biased or unaware as an outsider concerning aspects of local behavior and culture.

The first step toward adequate credibility of anthropological data still depends on clear definitions of basic concepts, the fundamental units or building blocks around which our observations are organized. Sometimes these items and observations need to be *counted*; often the variations must be recorded and to some extent *measured*. This methodological process is often such a thorough mixture of qualitative and quantitative aspects that the distinction becomes meaningless. Furthermore, even the most refined numerical observations must be fitted into a matrix of human behavior (and a broader theoretical framework) that is fundamentally nonquantitative for all practical purposes.

In the past few years, since the first edition of *Anthropological Research*, there has been considerable soul searching concerning applied or action anthropology. With more experience in applied research, we now feel that the methodological requirements of applied work are not always the same as in academic anthropology. Practical, community-oriented action research often has severe time constraints; applied projects in the inner cities, in health care systems, in schools, or in various economic development programs often do not stand still for long-term research. In order to be useful, data are needed right away – within a few days or weeks.

Many anthropologists will balk at the idea of "quick and dirty" research. Some action anthropologists see their roles in organizing the action rather than in providing useful research data. However, all applied projects must have some minimum of concrete information; all projects and programs modify their scope and style in response to feedback from their environments (social and physical); and *somebody* must provide these data during the continuing lifetime of any project. The whole process of intelligent data utilization – supposedly the hallmark of the human animal – calls for much more anthropological attention. And some of that attention takes the form of direct action research in a variety of practical projects.

Action anthropology often includes another significant feature – that the *questions* to be studied arise from a particular, localized context, and if the project is *for* some community group, members of the group may be the chief sources of the questions. That is very different from the scholarly situation in which the research questions and strategies arise from the established anthropological culture – the books and journals and academic seminars.

To explore fully the methodological ramifications of these differences would call for an entire volume devoted to applied anthropology. We have only touched on these points in this new edition, but Chapter 10 is intended to point out the great importance of further methodological exploration in applied contexts.

The earlier edition of this book was already a joint product in many respects. Since then the research and thinking leading to a revised edition have involved a team effort that we feel fully justifies joint authorship. At the same time, we have discussed methodological issues with a great many people, including a new generation of graduate students. Only a few of these contributions can be recorded here, and we owe large debts of scholarly gratitude to many others besides these: Billie R. DeWalt, Allen and Orna Johnson, Marvin Harris, William Dressler, David Spain, Ralph and Charlene Bolton, and Roger Sanjek. These newer intellectual debts do not lessen our appreciation for those mentioned with gratitude in the first edition of this book.

P. J. P.
G. H. P.

Storrs, Connecticut
April 1977

Preface to the first edition

When I embarked on my first major anthropological research venture – the field work for my Ph.D. dissertation – I had had no formal training in the logic and structure of social sciences research. Many of my peers have described a similar lack of methodological preparedness in the years of their doctoral candidacy. Our generation of anthropologists, trained in the 1950s, learned the descriptive and theoretical contributions of our predecessors, but not how these anthropological contributions were achieved. We were not unconcerned about how field research is carried out – in fact we were almost frantic to find out – but we were assured by our teachers that we could learn the mysteries of field work only through personal immersion in the practically indescribable but romantically alluring complexities of the field. Much of the lore about field research that we picked up informally in our graduate-student days was concerned with the gentle arts of rapport building and role playing in field situations. We were not so much concerned, nor were our mentors, with rules of evidence, questions of "representativeness," "validity," "reliability," and the many other related elements of scientific inquiry with which our friends in other social sciences seemed to be preoccupied. I can recall no discussion or even mention of the idea of "operationalizing variables" in those halcyon days.

As I took up my first position of teaching anthropology to a newer generation, I developed an interest in teaching research methods to graduate students. I quickly found, however, that discussions of anthropological methods were few and far between in our professional writing and that to examine many problems of the social sciences it was necessary to turn to a fairly voluminous literature in sociology and psychology, much of which had to be reinterpreted to fit the context of our cross-cultural research interests. In recent years there has been a steady increase in the amount of anthropological discussion of research methods. This accumulating literature includes many personalized accounts of field experiences that provide useful information about what anthropologists do in field research and how they collect specific types of information. There still seems to me, however, to be a serious shortage of material concerning the logical steps and requirements whereby ethnographers convert the stuff of raw observation

xiii

into abstract anthropological conceptual structures. This is the domain of methodology, as contrasted with the concrete, how-to-do-it realm of field techniques.

In this book I focus my discussion on what I consider to be the essential elements of preparing and manipulating the supporting evidence from which generalizations about human behavior are derived. At some points this discussion of research logic must touch base in the relatively concrete details of specific tools of observation – for example, informant interviewing, observing ceremonial behavior, and survey research. But my main intention is to examine the details of particular research instruments only to the minimum extent necessary for looking at how these basic observations can be systematically translated into sociocultural generalizations.

Most of the principles of research methodology that I incorporate into this book have been around in the social sciences for a long time, and they have been successfully utilized by a number of anthropologists. Thus, in writing this book I have tried to serve mainly as a compiler of methodological principles and techniques.

In general, the reader of these pages will note that my point of view is quite eclectic; I put strong emphasis on quantification and statistics, but I also feel strongly that many of the more qualitative aspects of anthropological working styles are essential to effective research. If I were to pick out some main themes of my argument, the following working principles would receive special emphasis:

1   Anthropological generalizations and more complex theoretical structures can be built up only through careful operationalizing of basic concepts – the building blocks of all theory.
2   Successful description and hypothesis testing depend on the judicious mixing of quantitative and qualitative research materials.

Many people helped me write this book. At various stages in its preparation portions of the manuscript were read and commented on by Harold Driver, Theodore Graves, Myles Hopper, James Jacquith, Philip Kilbride, Robert Maxwell, Raoul Naroll, Philip Newman, Richard Pollnac, Michael Robbins, Ronald Rohner, and Douglas White. I owe them all many thanks for their suggestions.

The research projects that provided much of the experience on which this book depends involved many graduate students, some of whose research contributions are discussed in the text. Of these, I am particularly grateful for the excellent field work and critical discussion of John Lozier, J. Anthony Paredes, John Poggie, Jr., Stephen Schensul, and Barbara Simon.

Over the past few years I have had innumerable conversations with anthropologists, sociologists, psychologists, and other social scientists about methodological problems. Of these people I am particularly indebeted to Gerald Berreman, Fernando Cämara, Robert Flint, Luther Gerlach, Eugene Hammel, William Lambert, Luis Leñero, Frank Miller, Paul Mussen, Rafel Nuñez, John M. Roberts, Murray Straus, Arthur Wolf, and Frank Young, and many others who contributed directly and indirectly to the writing of this book. To all these people and to those I have not mentioned, I would like to acknowledge a large debt of gratitude.

My wife, Gretel, has read all parts of this manuscript several times and has been my chief assistant, adviser, and editor. Many aspects of my treatment of methodological issues were developed in discussions with her. I have occasionally incorporated passages into this book over her objections but, for the most part, she shares fully in whatever credit and criticism may come from this work.

Among the many other people who contributed time and thought to the preparation of the manuscript I owe grateful thanks to Ellen Kinberg, who had the difficult chore of translating my drafts into cleanly typed copy.

P. J. P.

Storrs, Connecticut
January 1970

1 The domain of methodology

In simple, personalized terms the essence of research methodology lies in seeking answers to the following basic question: How can we find "true and useful information"[1] about a particular domain of phenomena in our universe? This fundamental question involves two closely related problems.

1 How can we personally investigate some domain of phenomena in order to obtain true and useful information?
2 How can we know, with some assurance, what other persons (researchers) mean when they assert propositions about information, and how can we judge whether to believe them?

The first problem directs our attention to the techniques and conditions necessary for exploration of our phenomenal world. If we wish, for example, to gain some new information about stellar bodies and their behavior, it is likely that a telescope would be a handy tool in this search for information. The many different domains of phenomena in our universe each require their special tools and techniques for gathering knowledge about them. The study of bacteria and other microorganisms requires a microscope; the examination of electrical circuitry requires various meters and other devices; getting knowledge about the anatomical characteristics of animals requires surgical techniques and tools for looking at features that are generally hidden from view.

When it comes to studying human behavior, the matter of research instruments is a little different. Most primary data in the social sciences come from three sources: (1) directly observing human behavior, (2) listening to and noting the contents of human speech, and (3) examining the products of human behavior – particularly those products found in archives, museums, records, and

---

[1] We use the expression "true and useful information" in quotation marks in order to indicate that, although we generally assume the presence of a concrete, real world, "the truth" or "the facts" about the real world are always seen and interpreted by means of our observational equipment, our conceptual categories, and our general theoretical outlook. Hence we can never establish any final "absolute truth." On the other hand, scientific information varies with regard to its degree of approximation to some postulated absolute truth. In general, though, the truth value of our information is best measured by criteria of usefulness – in predicting and explaining our experience in the natural world. Criteria of usefulness are derivable both from theoretical domains of science and from people's practical experiences and problems.

libraries. For example, in the study of economic behavior the significant data may be in the form of prices of goods, volume of goods (e.g., numbers of cars, bushels of wheat), costs of production, and related numerical information. Research in economics, then, may be carried out without special instruments of observation and measurement, but the researcher must be able to go to sources of already-recorded information (governmental statistical records, record systems of individual manufacturing enterprises, etc.). The monetized structure of economic behavior in our society provides built-in observational units. In nonmodern societies without cash economies, on the other hand, economic research involves primary observations of behavior and goods; hence techniques of data collection must be quite different. In general, the social sciences differ from other scientific fields in that primary data gathering is usually possible without the aid of highly specialized instruments.

An untrained person looking into a microscope or telescope learns practically nothing from the use of the powerful instrument. Similarly, a nonspecialist presented with lists of prices, costs, and other numerical data can make little sense of this pile of economic data. Without some kind of additional experience and information, the novice has no framework and no rules for interpreting what he or she sees. Novice microscope users need to acquire conceptual frameworks for differentiating living from nonliving forms; they need a set of definitions concerning types of organisms, parts of organisms, and their relationships. Novice economists are equipped with at least commonsense definitions of "price," "cost," and so on; but they cannot make sense of a mass data without some logical rules for plotting curves, indices, and other relational statements. Ethnographic observations, similarly, make little sense unless the observer has a general conceptual framework for sorting out and organizing behavioral elements.

Thus, in addition to the basic tools and instruments of observation and measurement, a scientific researcher must have, at the very least, sets of procedural rules (including concepts and definitions) for transforming sensual evidence into generalizations about phenomena. It is one of the goals of all scientific disciplines to link together low-order generalizations, or propositions, into larger networks of propositions that will make possible the prediction and explanation of phenomena within the given domain. Such networks of propositions are generally called *theories*. The relationships among the several elements of scientific work can be diagramed as in Figure 1.1.

Methodology, then, refers to the structure of procedures and transformational rules whereby the scientist shifts information up and down this ladder of abstraction in order to produce and organize increased knowledge. At the point of primary observation, as the bacteriologist peers into the microscope, he *must* have available some conceptual tools – definitions of things seen and experienced – for giving form and description to observations. The primary descrip-

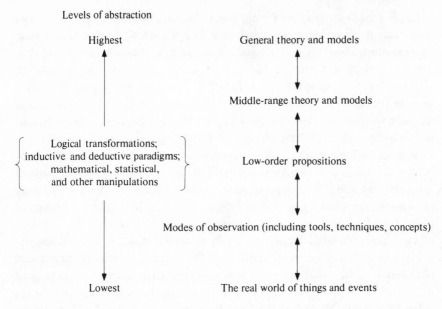

Figure 1.1. The domain of methodology.

tions, in turn, are related to more abstract propositions – to general theory about microorganisms – by a progression of logical steps that must be very clearly understood and agreed on by fellow scientists in the profession. This progression through levels of abstraction is not a one-way process, however. The bacteriologist does not select objects for observation randomly. The general, theoretical framework is a prime source of ideas and predictions in terms of which particular foci of observation are selected.

Thus defined, "methodology" can be distinguished from "research techniques" in that the latter term is useful for referring to the pragmatics of primary data collection, whereas methodology denotes the "logic-in-use" involved in selecting particular observational techniques, assessing their yield of data, and relating these data to theoretical propositions. In practice, the practical problems of using particular techniques of data gathering cannot be entirely separated from the examination of their logic-in-use. Any methodological discussion, then, must include some reference to techniques.

In Chapter 5 we will examine methodological problems related to interviewing key informants. Whole books have been written about *techniques* of interviewing, for the yield of data by this process can vary greatly depending on the skill, tactics, and other characteristics of the interviewer. On the other hand, our concern in this book will be mainly with the *logical manipulations* whereby we use interview data to accomplish theoretically important (and valid) results.

Let us turn to an example from anthropological research in order to explore some basic issues of research methodology. Suppose we are interested in finding out something about the cultural and social characteristics of relatively isolated, nomadic groups of hunting peoples. If we want to get firsthand information about such groups, we must arrange for a field expedition to a region where they may be found. On the other hand, because there are published accounts of nomadic societies, we can begin our analysis with these materials. We could start with a systematic collection of relevant literature under the rubric *nomadic hunting-gathering societies*. Notice that our opening move – a search of the literature – is impossible without some definitions. We need at least tentative definitions of "nomadic," "hunting-gathering," and "societies." Since the literature contains reports from a great many different ethnographers, general agreement about definitions and concepts is of great importance. Thus even the most elementary conceptual tasks depend on a larger, more abstract, theoretical system.

Having set out our tentative definitions of the research domain, we obtain a set of materials dealing with a number of hunting-gathering peoples in various parts of the world. Suppose one of the research reports about nomadic societies is Allan Holmberg's *Nomads of the Long Bow* (1969), an account of the Sitrionó people of eastern and northern Bolivia. As we turn to an examination of that work, we learn that "besides being a member of a nuclear family, every Sitrionó also belongs to a larger kin group, the matrilineal extended family" (p. 128). Our first problem is to determine what Holmberg means by the expression "matrilineal extended family." Fortunately, he provides a definition that is quite explicit: "An extended [matrilineal] family is made up of all females in a direct line of descent, plus their spouses and their unmarried children." This definition is, in effect, a *rule* for grouping information. That is, the concept of matrilineal extended family allows Holmberg to state a number of generalizations that apply simultaneously to several different actual groups of persons. Holmberg's monograph, like all such works, is full of terminology that, in essence, permits the clustering, or abstracting, of information into shorthand form in terms of transformational rules.

We are faced, however, with the problem of knowing how Holmberg obtained the information contained within the expression "matrilineal extended family." From the monograph and other sources it is clear that he lived with the Siatonó for a number of months, so that the possibilities for gaining the information were clearly present. Perhaps during this time he asked one of the Siatonó about his kinsmen. His informant might have replied, "I, like all Siatonó, belong to a matrilineal extended family, which may be defined as. . . ." Such a response is unlikely, however. It is much more likely that Holmberg's informant would have answered with a series of statements concerning his most important kinsmen, or perhaps with statements about the people with whom he shared food and other items. After further questioning, he might have told the ethnographer that everybody belongs to or has a group of kinspeople with whom food and other items are shared and that these groups are always the same in that membership in them is traced through female links in a particular way.

Holmberg may also have obtained the information by direct observation. It turns out that members of the extended families "cooperate to build that portion of the dwelling which they occupy. They sometimes plant gardens in common" (ibid., 128). Also, "the distribution of food rarely extends beyond the extended family." Because Holmberg lived among the Sirionó and because each band lives in a communal house, we expect that he had ample opportunity to observe that certain individuals were regularly grouped together in terms of key activities.

Without asking about kin groups from the people themselves, Holmberg may have noted that whenever a certain individual A returned to the communal house with some meat, he distributed it to persons B, C, D, and E, but never to any of the other persons in the band. In addition, he may have noted that A, B, C, D, and E worked together to build a portion of the communal dwelling, after which they were usually to be found in that portion of the house – sleeping, eating, or resting – if they were present in the band area. He would, of course, need verbally produced information about the presumed kinship relationships linking the persons in the observed groups.

Typically, anthropological fieldworkers combine the data from personal, eyewitness observation with information gained from informants' descriptions. Holmberg's statements about matrilineal extended families among the Sirionó undoubtedly were based on both kinds of information. Unfortunately, Holmberg's description, like practically all other ethnographic descriptions, rarely makes clear exactly what kinds of observations formed the basis for particular generalizations.

Like most ethnographers, Holmberg intended to collect a wide range of information about his chosen research people in order to present a holistic portrait of their way of life. That is, the theoretical orientation of cultural anthropology has for the most part encouraged a very eclectic view with regard to the selection of relevant data. In a summary section of his book, Holmberg drew together the wide range of primary observations about the Sirionó into a series of generalizations about them. On the whole, he felt, these people are rather unsuccessful in their food quest, and they live under conditions of perennial food insecurity and hunger frustration. From another complex array of primary observations, he came to the conclusion that the Sirionó are uncooperative vis-à-vis one another, greedy about food, uncaring about one another's welfare, and generally quarrelsome and suspicious.

From these descriptive field data Holmberg suggested a series of middle-range generalizations "for further refinement and investigation in other societies where conditions of food insecurity and hunger frustration are comparable to those found among the Sirionó." The following is a sampling from his list of propositions:

1   Such societies will be characterized by a general backwardness of culture.
2   Aggression will be expressed largely in terms of food.
3   Positions of power and authority will be occupied by individuals who are the best providers of food.
4   There will be a tendency to kill, abandon, neglect, or otherwise dispose of the aged, the deformed young, and the extremely ill.
5   Prestige will be gained and status maintained mainly by food-getting activities.

These middle-range theoretical propositions were advanced by Holmberg as derivatives from a very general psychophysiological theory of human behavior. Thus the low-order descriptive generalizations about the Sirionó were combined with elements from much higher levels of abstraction (general psychological theory) to form a series of potentially researchable statements about "societies with high food insecurity."

There are several points of methodological interest in this research example. First, it is clearly recognized by the researcher himself that the data from a single society can only be used for *suggesting* higher-order relationships; establishing more abstract theoretical propositions depends on the transformation of primary descriptive data from many different societies.

Also, it is important to keep in mind that the successful testing of Holmberg's research hypotheses can be carried out only if available descriptive data from other "hungry societies" contain the same kinds of observations and descriptive generalizations as those available for the Sirionó. Even if such data are available, there may be some serious problems in making systematic comparisons, because of the difficulty of establishing cross-culturally usable definitions of terms such as "backwardness of culture," "aggression," and "positions of power and authority." Even seemingly obvious concepts, such as "best providers of food" and the "extremely ill," require definition; and, more importantly, for each of these basic terms in Holmberg's propositions there must be specification as to the methods of data gathering by means of which the concepts are operationalized. That is, from the variety of *possible* ways to obtain the needed comparative information, some *one* method should be selected if these cross-cultural data are to be strictly comparable.

It is instructive to note that Holmberg's propositions have not been tested in any definitive way, although *some* individual cases of other hungry societies have been described as providing refutations of the hypotheses. Since the Sirionó data and accompanying research suggestions were originally published about three decades ago (1950), why have these rather important ideas remained untested?

The answer to this question takes us to the heart of some methodological dilemmas of contemporary anthropology. As has already been suggested, cross-cultural testing of anthropological hypotheses requires standardization of research procedures in such a manner that operationally equivalent observations can be selected and compared. At the very least, research reports would have to include enough information about research procedures so that an investigator seeking to compare information from a number of societies can make informed judgments concerning the comparability of descriptive statements. Thus Holmberg's hypotheses have remained untested at least partly because of the methodological difficulties involved.

In this review of Holmberg's research on the Sirionó we see an illustration of the fact that the expression "true and useful information" in our original methodological question refers to a wide range of different kinds of statements, at different levels of abstraction. At a relatively low level of abstraction we have information such as: "The Sirionó are frequently hungry." At the level of middle-range theory Holmberg suggests a series of propositions about societies with high "food insecurity and hunger frustration." These statements (hypotheses) relate to very general theoretical propositions such as: ". . . the human organism is stimulated to behave by what are known as drives. . . . They are of two kinds: primary (basic or innate) and secondary (derived or acquired). The primary drives are those which result from the normal biological processes . . . such as hunger, thirst, sex, fatigue, and pain" (ibid., 244).

There is no essential logical difference between the low-level generalizations and those at the most abstract levels. Description and theory *are not different kinds of logical processes*. The congruence of these forms is apparent in the following transformations (arranged in descending order of abstraction):

1　Noun phrase / verb phrase.
2　The human organism / is stimulated by what are known as drives.
3　Societies high in food insecurity and hunger frustration / allocate prestige and status largely in terms of food-getting activities.
4　The Sirionó / allocate prestige and status largely in terms of food-getting activities. "If a man is a good hunter, his status is apt to be high" (ibid., 145).
5　Enía (brother-in-law of Chief Eantándu) / was of low status until Holmberg taught him to use a shotgun, and Enía began to bring in lots of game. "Needless to say, when I left Tibaera he / was enjoying the highest status" (ibid., 146).

This set of transformations of data statements, based on the logical patterning of Holmberg's statements about the Sirionó, suggests a series of questions for special methodological attention.

1　*What kinds* of primary observations of Sirionó individuals are necessary and sufficient for establishing useful statements about, for example, allocation of prestige and status?

Closely related to this first question are the following:

2   *How many* observations (based on what criteria of selection) are needed to establish the generalization(s) about prestige and status?
3   *How* can societies characterized by high food insecurity and hunger frustration be identified and contrasted with other societies in order to test propositions about allocation of prestige and status?
4   Holmberg assumes that characteristics of the individual human organism (drives) can be transformed directly into *group,* or societal, characteristics (allocation of prestige and status). Many anthropologists (and others) would disagree, maintaining that individual organic processes and societal behavior norms represent two distinct *levels of phenomena,* so that transformations between the two levels cannot occur in the form implied by Holmberg. How can this general methodological conflict be resolved? Stated in more general terms, what are the rules for transformations of data *across* supposed levels of phenomena?
5   The informational statements in the preceding paradigm are highly subject to modification (or even total negation) by other factors affecting human behavior. What rules and procedures can be used to express the interrelationships among a large number of interrelated factors affecting social events and processes?
6   Theoretical propositions derived from other domains and "schools" of the social sciences may be equally efficient sources of higher-order statements that can be transformed into the lower-order information about the Sirionó. That is, a number of other kinds of statements could be substituted for some of Holmberg's statements. How can the *most effective* general theoretical propositions (or systems of general theory) be selected from among competing alternatives?

If one became involved in actual research on Holmberg's propositions, a large number of additional methodological issues would have to be faced. This discussion is intended to set forth only the outlines of problems concerning anthropological methodology. Additional details about these problems, as well as some proposed solutions to them, will be discussed in relation to specific research cases in later chapters.

Elements of research methodology

The discussion about the Sirionó and about Holmberg's theoretical statements is intended as an illustration of the main elements of research methodology. These elements make up the research language, the logical framework, in terms of which anthropological investigations (and other scientific studies) are carried out. At this point it would be useful to clarify some of our assumptions about these methodological elements.

Concepts and definitions

The language of anthropology, like that of every science, consists mainly of concepts, propositions, models, and theories. Concepts are the basic elements – the building blocks of anthropological research. Familiar anthropological terms, such as "family," "digging stick," "peasant," "hunter," "slash-and-burn agriculture," and "religion," are all examples of concepts, though these examples differ considerably in degree of abstraction. The point to emphasize is that concepts are abstractions from concrete observations. The term "digging stick," for example, is an abstraction that refers to a variety of pointed (usually wooden) objects by means of which horticulturalists in various parts of the world carry out some of the essential acts related to crop growing. This statement (which is not a definition) is constructed from a string of abstract concepts. Nonetheless, the term "digging stick" is much less abstract than, for example, the term "religion," which does not refer to a particular type of object, but rather to a domain of widely varied beliefs, objects, and actions.

Whole books in the philosophy of science have been devoted to examining the fundamental logic and relationships among scientific concepts. We will not explore this vast area of discourse here, but certain fundamental assumptions must be made clear. First, it should be emphasized that concepts are arbitrary selections from the universe of experience. Goode and Hatt, in discussing the arbitrariness of definitions, make the following significant points:

1 "Concepts develop from a shared experience."
2 "Terms used to denote scientific concepts may also have meanings in other frames of reference."
3 "A term may refer to different phenomena."
4 "Different terms may refer to the same phenomena."
5 "A term may have no immediate empirical referent at all."
6 "The meaning of concepts may change." (Goode and Hatt, 1953:44–8.)

For this last point it is instructive to take an example from the physical sciences. Ernest Nagel, in his discussion of the structure of science, points out that the definition of the concept *electron* has changed as theoretical physics has developed:

What is to be an electron is stated by a theory in which the word "electron" occurs; and when the theory is altered, the meaning of the word undergoes a modification. . . . though the same word "electron" is used in prequantum theories of the electronic constitution of matter, in the Bohr theory, and in post-Bohr theories, the meaning of the word is not the same in all these theories. (Nagel, 1961:88.)

Propositions

Propositions are statements about interrelationships among concepts. The statement "Peasants are pragmatic" is a proposition whose relative truth value depends on the effectiveness of the researcher's manipulations of the concepts *peasant* and *pragmatic*. Propositions often have a two-part, subject-predicate form, in which one concept involves the definition of the given population (of objects, persons, events) about which a measurement or judgment of qualities (e.g., pragmatic, joyous, intelligent, homogeneous, well organized, effective) is to be made.

In all cases the definitions of particular concepts as subjects of research involve explicit or implicit contrasts between the concept under consideration (e.g., peasants) and the set of all other possible subjects chosen from the same universe. Thus *peasant* is defined as a type of person (or community) having particular characteristics that contrast with *urban dwellers, hunters,* and other possible members of this particular domain of discourse (human groups categorized in a subsistence-based typology). Since the conceptual domain of *humans* (*people, human societies, cultures*) can be differentiated in terms of a great number of different characteristics, it follows that each anthropological researcher establishes a typology within this conceptual domain in terms of assumptions (stated or unstated) about important or theoretically significant distinctions among types of *humans*. Theories are constituted of *systems* of concepts (typologies and taxonomies), propositions about concepts, and the assumptions that underlie such propositions.

Theories and hypotheses

Theories, as systems of interrelated concepts and propositions, can be "grand theories" that attempt to fit together in logical pattern vast areas of human behavior. On the other hand, a theoretical system can be much more modest in scope, involving only a small number of concepts and propositions.

Theories as such are never "proved." Rather, they differ with regard to their effectiveness as sources of propositions that can be tested by means of empirical research, and they also differ with regard to the numbers of empirical observations that support the propositions of which the given theoretical system is constituted. Thus the general theoretical system usually called the "theory of biological evolution" is supported by a very large array of empirical observations, whereas in the social sciences theoretical systems of similar scope can boast of far fewer supporting empirical observations.

When an individual says, "I have a theory about that," he frequently means that he has a proposition about certain phenomena that (presumably) could be put to empirical test. Such a proposition is usually referred to as a *hypothesis*. Theoretical systems are often the sources for researchable propositions (hypotheses). On the other hand, hypotheses are also derived from individual empirical observations of phenomena.

Successful verification of propositions (hypotheses) always has implications for the theoretical system to which it relates. Each such verification helps to build theory. This is the case even when the researcher is unaware of the set of theoretical assumptions from which the hypothesis was derived. Theories and elementary concepts are thus inextricably interrelated, and debate about which of these comes first is beside the point.

Models

The term *model* is sometimes used as simply another synonym for the term *theoretical system*. However, Kaplan has argued that

. . . a more defensible usage views as models only those theories which explicitly direct attention to certain resemblances between the theoretical entities and the real subject matter. With this usage in mind, models have been defined as "scientific metaphors." A metaphor, like an aphorism, condenses in a phrase a significant similarity. When the poet writes "the morn, in russet mantle clad, walks o'er the dew of yon high eastern hill," he evokes awareness of a real resemblance, and such awareness may be made to serve the purpose of science. When they do serve in this way, we are likely to conceptualize the situation as involving the use of *analogy*. The scientist recognizes similarities that have previously escaped us, and systematizes them. Electricity exhibits a "flow," there is a "current" exerting a certain pressure (the voltage), having a certain volume (the amperage), and so on. Analogies, it has been held, do more than merely lead to the formulation of theories, so that afterwards they may be removed and forgotten; they are "an utterly essential part of theories, without which theories would be completely valueless and unworthy of the name." (Kaplan, 1964:265, ending with a quote from N. Campbell.)[2]

When the essential elements and relationships in a theoretical system can be made isomorphic with a set of arithmetic notations and the tautological relationships involved in the arithmetic notations, a particularly powerful kind of model becomes possible. The logical properties of the arithmetic system can then be used to generate new propositions and hypotheses. The theory of games and probability theory are two such mathematical models that are now widely used in social sciences and related areas. Davenport (1960) has applied the game-theory model to an analysis of Jamaican fishing, and aspects of probability theory are rather widely used in all the social sciences. However, major problems are

[2] From *The Conduct of Inquiry* by Abraham Kaplan published by Chandler Publishing Company, San Francisco. © 1964 by Chandler Publishing Company. Reprinted by permission.

generally encountered in meeting the informational requirements of these mathematical models.

It is also useful to apply the term "model" in a more modest fashion to those theoretical systems for which scientific metaphors or analogies can be rendered in the form of diagrams, flow charts, or other pictorial and physical representations. In anthropology the standard rendering of kinship charts is a frequently encountered type of model, but more comprehensive systems, such as the interrelationships in complex ecological interactions, can often be made more clear and explicit by means of some kind of pictorial representation. Figure 1.2 is the theoretical model in terms of which the psychologically oriented Six Cultures project was conceptualized (Whiting, 1963).

When a set of theoretical relationships has been expressed in some kind of pictorial representation (or even in a physical structure, such as the models of molecules one often sees in general-science laboratories, or the model cities displayed in schools of architecture), the discovery of new relationships and research directions is often facilitated. It becomes possible to experiment with the model itself, to see if changes in some parts of the structure force predictable modifications in other portions. Such experimentation is often greatly enhanced if at least some of the relationships among the parts of the model can be expressed in mathematical terms.

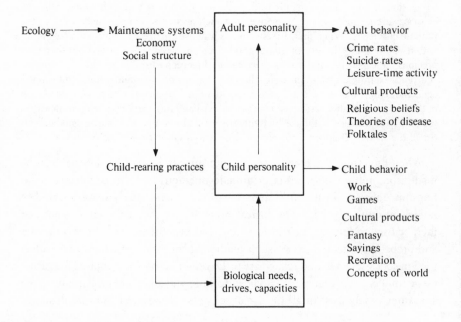

Figure 1.2. The relation of personality to culture (adapted from Whiting, 1963).

The question of the validity and usefulness of particular theoretical models is an empirical one, and the conclusions derived from mathematical computations or other manipulation of models must be examined by means of research in the real world. Some schools of social theory have been justly criticized for their nearly exclusive concentration on models, unsupported by any program of empirical research. In Chapter 11 we will return to a discussion of the importance of models in guiding and organizing research.

Assessing the usefulness of definitions

Every concept, however concrete in appearance, implies a typology or categorization of the conceptual domain from which the particular concept is derived. It is our position that concepts are arbitrary selections from the vast range of things and events in the universe. Anthropological literature is full of examples that illustrate the arbitrariness of concepts. For example, the categories of color that we take to be natural are organized differently among various cultures. The Navajo, like many other people in the world, do not distinguish terminologically between green and blue, whereas their neighbors, the Zuñi, do not have separate words for red and orange. The Navajo and the Zuñi have different (probably implicit) theories about color as a conceptual domain, and the results are typologies that differ from the color system common in Euro-American culture.[3] It can be suggested that among Euro-Americans, males and females have different theoretical systems with regard to color. At least it appears that many females in our society recognize colors such as "holiday gold," "plum," "charice," "fuchsia," "magenta," and "emerald green," which have little functional significance for most Euro-American males.

Categorizations of illnesses and symptoms provide another example. In many Latin American communities when a child displays general lassitude, headaches, and a loss of appetite, it is likely to be diagnosed as *susto* or "magical fright" (Clark, 1959; Rubel, 1960). The same symptoms in other societies might be diagnosed as illness due to sorcery, whereas North American physicians may label them as psychological complaints or a vaguely defined cluster of allergies. Furthermore, conditions and behavior that are considered illnesses in some societies are regarded as within the range of normal health in others.

Even though we pay lip service to the idea that definitions, concepts, and typologies of phenomena are arbitrary slices from the world of experience, it goes against the grain to accept the idea that *all* definitions and typologies are equally valid. We feel intuitively that the Linnaean system of classifying plants and

---

[3] This does not mean that Navajo and Zuñi *perceptions* of color are necessarily different from those of Euro-Americans.

animals is natural and correct; some other classifications would seem "wrong." But what distinguishes correct or significant classifications from those we feel to be wrong? Abraham Kaplan, in *The Conduct of Inquiry* (1964), states the case as follows:

What makes a concept significant is that the classification it institutes is one into which things fall, as it were, of themselves. It carves at the joints, Plato said. Less metaphorically, a significant concept so groups or divides its subject matter that it can enter into many and important true propositions about the subject matter other than those which state the classification itself. Traditionally, such a concept was said to identify a "natural class" rather than an "artificial one." Its naturalness consists of this, that the attributes it chooses as the basic classification are significantly related to the attributes conceptualized elsewhere in our thinking. Things are grouped together because they resemble one another. A natural grouping is one which allows the discovery of many more, and more important, resemblances than those originally recognized. Every classification serves some purpose or other (the class-term has a use). It is artificial when we cannot do more with it than we first intended. The purpose of scientific classification is to facilitate the fulfillment of any purpose whatever, to disclose the relationships that must be taken into account no matter what.

Plainly, the significance of a concept in this sense is a matter of degree. Even an artificial classification is not wholly arbitrary if it really serves its own limited purposes. A classification of books by size and weight is not "as natural," we feel, as one based on their content. But the printer and the freight agent have claims as legitimate as the librarians. The point is that the former stand nearly alone in their interests; the librarian is joined by every reader, by everyone else who is concerned about his reading. Whether a concept is useful depends on the use we want to put it to; but there is always the additional question whether things so conceptualized will lend themselves to that use. And this is the scientific question. (Kaplan, 1964:50–1.)[4]

Inductive and deductive approaches

The logic in use of scientists is far from being a unidirectional process. Generally, scientific hunches and ideas arise somewhere in the realm of models and theories, but some researchers generate new research ideas by concentrating on the characteristics of their observational tools and techniques. Again, a relatively atheoretical observation of events or things in the real world can provide the stimulus for a new hypothesis. Successful testing of the hypothesis adds to a body of theory or an elaboration of a model, which in turn leads to reexamination of the real world *and* the techniques of observation. It is unlikely that any one pattern of interaction among these elements is the highroad to successful science; on the contrary, insistence on a single mode or pathway of research work can lead to stultification of creative effort.

Sir Francis Bacon is often credited with the definitive statement of an induc-

[4] Kaplan, op. cit.

tive approach to scientific effort. In his *New Organon* (1620), Bacon contrasted the deductive and inductive methods and cast his ballot for the latter:

There are and can be only two ways of searching into and discovering truth. The one flies from the senses and particulars to the most general axioms, and from these principles, the truth of which it takes for settled and immovable, proceeds to judgment and to the discovery of middle axioms. And this way is now in fashion. The other derives axioms from the senses and particulars, rising by a gradual and unbroken ascent, so that it arrives at the most general axiom last of all. This is the true way, but as yet untried. (Bacon, 1960:43.)

A generally accepted modern view of scientific procedure holds that effective theory construction depends on *both* inductive and deductive procedures. That is, solid foundations for scientific propositions often depend on a painstaking accumulation of, and generalization from, basic observations of the real world; but, just as often, theoretical systems provide the frame of reference and basic assumptions in terms of which relevant hypothesis-testing observations can be pursued. In any case, a random gathering of facts cannot by itself result in an increase of scientific understanding. Bacon phrased a useful simile to illustrate this aspect of science:

Those who have handled sciences have been either men of experiment or men of dogmas. The men of experiment are like the ant, they only collect and use; the reasoners resemble spiders, who make cobwebs out of their own substance. But the bee takes a middle course; it gathers its material from the flowers of the garden and of the field but transforms and digests it by a power of its own. Not unlike this is the true business of philosophy; for it neither relies solely or chiefly on the powers of the mind, nor does it take the matter which it gathers from natural history and mechanical experiments and lay it up in the memory whole, as it finds it, but lays it up in the understanding altered and digested. (Bacon, 1960:93.)

Method and theory building

In our examination of the general paradigm of research methodology, the point has been made in a number of ways that atheoretical description is not logically possible – that all research is structured in terms of theoretical constructs, however implicit and unrecognized by the researcher. In spite of the ubiquitous presence of theory, anthropologists (and other researchers) vary a great deal in the extent to which they organize research in terms of explicit theoretical systems.

In Chapter 11 we will turn our attention to the matter of theory building in relation to methodology and methodological problems. Here, as we begin our examination of the structure of research, we want to point out our general position. Regardless of what particular theory or set of theories serves as the framework for any given study, the main pathway to eliminating anthropological credibility gaps is to concentrate methodological attention at the relatively low-abstraction end of the research paradigm. The most pressing problems in anthropological research design lie in the structure of primary data gathering – in the actual field-research operations. Once the procedures and concepts of primary anthropological descriptions have been systematized, rigorous controlled comparisons can be developed, and theory building can proceed on firmer foundations.

The logic in use of anthropological data-gathering operations is essentially the same as that of all scientific endeavors. Therefore, our examination of methodological principles does not depend on any particular theory. Research examples in later chapters represent a number of different theoretical positions, but their logical structures belong to a general scientific realm that embraces at least all of those disciplines concerned with human behavior.

2 Science and anthropology

When we try to establish a useful definition of *science*, we immediately encounter the basic problem of all definitions: Different people use the term in quite different ways and contexts, and it is often loaded with a considerable freight of value judgment. We have only to listen to the outpouring of claims in the mass media for "scientifically proved" products to see the term's range of usage and implication. Consider also the problems raised by the following expressions: "Christian Science," "scientific haircuts given here," "library science," and "scientific bridge playing."

The word *science* is derived from the Latin word *scientia* (*sciens*, the present participle of *scire*, "to know"), and *Webster's Collegiate Dictionary* gives a series of definitions for it, including:

1. Knowledge; 2. Any department of systematized knowledge; 3. Art or skill – chiefly humorous or sporting; as, the *science* of boxing; 4. A branch of study concerned with observation of facts, esp. with the establishment of verifiable general laws. . . . 5. . . . . accumulated knowledge systematized and formulated with reference to the discovery of general truths or the operation of general laws.

A widely accepted way of defining *science* is to equate the term with the concept of methodological rigor. For example, after combing a wide range of literature about science, Carlo Lastrucci suggests that there exists something like a "consensus among authoritative writers with regard to the essential attributes or processes of science. According to such a consensus, *science may be defined* quite accurately and functionally as: *an objective, logical, and systematic method of analysis of phenomena, devised to permit the accumulation of reliable knowledge*" (Lastrucci, 1963:6; his italics). By this definition, science becomes a particular mode of investigation rather than a body of knowledge, a quest for knowledge, or a search for nomothetic generalizations.

Lastrucci's definition appears to imply that anyone who is not systematic or personally objective is ipso facto not part of, or contributing to, the development of science. He appears to leave little room for the work of persons who are, for example, impelled to scientific inquiry by passionate, subjective motives of nationalism or by a fanatic desire to save lives. Also, such a definition places scientists' intuitions, theoretical speculations, and serendipitous discoveries outside the realm of scientific enterprise; or at least it shunts these elements into a devalued limbo.

W. I. B. Beveridge, in his suggestively titled book *The Art of Scientific Investigation*, has given us rich illustrations of some apparently unsystematic and disorganized aspects of research. Strict methodological procedures seem notably lacking, for example, in the case of von Mering and Minkowski (1889 in Strasbourg), who accidentally discovered the importance of urine-carried sugar (and related facts about diabetes) when they noticed the swarms of flies attracted to the urine of a dog from which they had removed the pancreas. The discovery of penicillin by Fleming appears to have been facilitated by the dust and dirt in his antiquated laboratory, where some colonies of staphylococci were accidentally contaminated and killed by a theretofore unknown substance.

One of the most striking anecdotes in Beveridge's recitation is about the pharmacologist Otto Loewi at the University of Graz. Loewi awoke in the middle of the night with a brilliant idea. He reached for a pencil and paper and jotted down a few notes. On waking the next morning, he was aware of having had an inspiration during the night, but to his consternation he could not decipher his notes. During the next night, to his great joy he again awoke with the same flash of insight, which he carefully recorded before going to sleep again. "The next day he went to his laboratory and in one of the neatest, simplest, and most definite experiments in the history of biology brought proof of the chemical mediation of nerve impulses" (Beveridge, 1957:95).

The German chemist Kekulé is described as having developed the idea of the benzene ring (which revolutionized organic chemistry) during a dream as he sat napping in front of his fireplace. He described how the atoms "flitted" before his eyes:

Long rows, variously, more closely, united; all in movement wriggling and turning like snakes. And see, what was that? One of the snakes seized its own tail and the image whirled scornfully before my eyes. As though from a flash of lightning I awoke; I occupied the rest of the night in working out the consequences of the hypothesis. . . . Let us learn to dream, gentlemen. (Quoted in Beveridge, 1957:76.)

These examples suggest that any useful definition of science should be based on the general premise that "science is whatever it is that is happening when scientists are productive." Thus if we include these cases in the realm of science, our definition should be broad enough to include, at least tacitly, some nearly random scanning of phenomena (with or without microscopes, etc.); seizing upon accidents, exceptional events, and other chance circumstances for generating new research ideas; and engaging in a fair amount of simple but inspired day- (and night) dreaming. A caution should be introduced, however: These are illustrations of the unpredictable and intuitive nature of the origins of scientific ideas;

processes of systematic verification of hunches and hypotheses are much more subject to objective description and codification.

Ernest Nagel alludes to the same problem when he states in *The Structure of Science:*

There are no rules of discovery and invention in science, any more than there are such rules in the arts. . . . Nor, finally, should the formula be read as claiming that the practice of scientific method effectively eliminates every form of personal bias or source of error which might otherwise impair the outcome of the inquiry. (Nagel, 1961:12–13.)

Thus although the scientific method Lastrucci describes is important in identifying *some* aspects of science, it should not, in our opinion, be taken as synonymous with science, for that leads to a disregard of the less systematic, emotionally flavored search for ideas and theoretical insights. In the history of science there have been important events that can only be described as wild speculation about relationships and forces and concepts, some of which may never be definable in terms of empirically observable phenomena.

Science and history

In earlier decades of this century it was fashionable to divide scholarly research into two realms: history and science. In terms of this dichotomy, history is ideographic research, in which the aim of investigation is to give concrete descriptions of particular events, things, and peoples, located in time and place. Science, on the other hand, is the search for the nomothetic laws or principles that apply to a particular domain of phenomena without regard to specific times or locations. Thus basic principles of chemistry and physics are highly nomothetic, whereas descriptions of the Battle of Waterloo or the aboriginal cultural patterns of the Mandan-Hidatsa Indians are ideographic studies.

Many anthropologists, including Radcliffe-Brown (1952), Kroeber (1952), and Hoebel (1966) have made use of the history-versus-science dichotomy in discussing the nature of anthropology and its relationships with other fields of study. This dichotomy has a certain heuristic usefulness, but when it is used to characterize entire disciplines, it asserts a distinction between description and theoretical work that is no longer generally accepted. Historical description has come to be recognized as a highly selective process in which observations are ordered in terms of some theoretical frame of reference, however implicit, even when the researcher claims that he is "only giving the facts" (cf. Nagel, 1961:79–152; Lastrucci, 1963). Maintaining the distinction appears to be increasingly impractical in discussions about the nature and objectives of scholarly research.

Those who have argued that anthropology is mainly a historical or humanistic discipline, basically different from "real" science, have often taken physics and chemistry as their points of comparisons and have perhaps oversimplified their conceptualization of science. In the first place, it should be recognized that a number of respectable scientific propositions in the physical sciences involve particularistic observations; note the number of scientific statements that include particularistic references to the sun, the moon, and other stellar bodies.

In general, limiting science to examples drawn from physics and chemistry produces an extremely narrow view of the scientific enterprise, for this is to ignore important areas of research in geology, biology, paleontology, and many other established disciplines that are frankly particularistic in important respects. Few people claim, for example, that the geologist is not scientific, even though his aims may be the study of particular features of the Cambrian age or descriptions of some glacial sequences of northern Europe.

Just as scientists in other disciplines are not always concerned solely with nomothetic generalizations, historical researchers are far from being totally ideographic. Historians and anthropologists are frequently concerned with describing human behavior in specific times and places, but it is not in principle impossible to find nomothetic propositions applicable to large classes of historical cases, and many writers (Toynbee, Spengler, Kroeber, others) have generalized about broad features of civilizations, the fall of empires, and other nomothetic topics.

Nagel, in The Structure of Science, lists four principal modes of explanation employed in scientific discourse: (1) deduction from known and lawlike principles; (2) probabilistic statements, in which the "explanatory premises do not formally imply their explicanda"; (3) functional or teleological explanations, in which statements are made about the "functions (or even dysfunctions) that a unit performs in maintaining or realizing certain traits of a system to which the unit belongs, or of stating the instrumental role an action plays in bringing about some goal" (Nagel, 1961:24); and (4) genetic, or historical, explanations, "which set out the major events through which some earlier system has been transformed into a later one" (p. 25). A glance at parts of biology (embryology, the study of evolution, etc.) and astronomy (study of the history of the universe) reminds us that this fourth mode of explanation is not uniquely a property of those disciplines that study human history and behavior.

If we accept Nagel's four types of explanation as valid parts of science and scientific inquiry, we may suggest that different sciences exhibit different mixtures of these four logical models, without thereby departing from membership in the scientific community. The kinds of explanations sought by some historians, anthropologists, and others who reject the label of science are not different in kind from the types of explanations of interest to other scientists, but the traditional patterns of research and use of evidence make their pursuits seem radically different from those of the sciences. The logic of scholarship is the same for both, but canons of evidence are different.

For example, much has been written by scholars in diverse fields about the so-called national character of the Germans, Russians, Japanese, Americans, and other large national groups. The explanations have traversed the spectrum of viewpoints from psychological (including psychoanalytic) theory through geographical, historical, and biological theories to complicated models of structural functionalism. Each such study seeks to produce "truths" based on explicit and implicit propositions about character and personality formation, and each is naturalistic in that supernatural causation is not assumed. Yet some of these studies involve relatively careful data gathering and rules of evidence, with accompanying statistics, whereas others present their arguments in a broad-brush, vividly anecdotal fashion, leaving key terms and concepts undefined, and employing verbal eloquence, rather than tightness of data handling, as their chief means of enhancing credibility.

Science and controlled experiments

Some of the people who have argued that anthropology, and the social sciences generally, cannot really be scientific disciplines make much of the fact that controlled experiment is nearly impossible in the study of human behavior. If "controlled experiment" is used to mean only those situations where *all* supposedly relevant variables are controlled and manipulated by the researcher, then we would have to agree that anthropologists cannot make use of controlled experiments in any useful sense. However, we must ask whether all the so-called "hard sciences" rely upon controlled experiment as the principal method of research. We have already pointed out that there are numbers of sciences that depart from the model of science offered by physics and chemistry. Geology and astronomy can again be cited as examples of scientific inquiry in which the methods of observation frequently do *not* involve controlled experiment but which, nonetheless, have produced reputable bodies of theory and explanation.[1]

Science: a definition

From all the foregoing, it appears difficult and misleading to maintain any narrow definition of science, either as a particular commitment to strict methodology

[1] It should also be pointed out that the experimental sciences can only claim to control all or most known variables. Because the presence of additional, unknown, variables is logically possible in all experimental situations, the control of variables is a matter of degree rather than an absolute criterion for differentiating one type of research from another. In chemistry and physics it would appear that relatively high levels of control are possible; in the biological sciences the problems of control are much greater; even the most strictly controlled experiments in psychology involve problems of unknown factors that may seriously influence research results (cf. Blalock, 1964).

or as a nomothetically oriented search for laws and basic general principles. This leads us to propose a broader, more diffuse definition: *Science* is the structure and the processes of discovery and verification of systematic and reliable knowledge about any relatively enduring aspect of the universe, carried out by means of empirical observations, and the development of concepts and propositions for interrelating and explaining such observations.

We suggest that science includes a large component of searching, speculating, and discovering – a whole set of activities that cannot be easily codified and systematized. Serendipitous discoveries and inspired daydreaming are part of this aspect of science. The institutional organization of science – the schools, laboratories, journals, and other communications channels – are also included within the bounds of this definition. Furthermore, there are large areas of science in which complex value judgments rather than strict methodological criteria form the basis for action. The decisions about *which* topics are to be given research priorities, *where* the money for investigation comes from, and *who* shall carry out research activities are part of the institutional structure of science. A further large component of value judgment enters at the output stage – in the articulation to practical applications. Who will receive the scientific information? Who will apply the knowledge, and in what situations? In some areas of science the people who call themselves scientists work actively in the practical applications of the scientific endeavor. In other domains of research the investigators keep themselves far removed from the engineers and administrators whose job it is to apply available knowledge to practical human needs and activities.

Science is a very broad spectrum of scholarly activity. No sharp lines can be drawn to differentiate the so-called hard sciences from other disciplines, and no strict methodological canons can clearly distinguish the work of the scientific Nobel Prize winners from that of a host of unknown research assistants. Science has many facets that articulate with philosophy, the performing arts, and ethical judgment. But somewhere in the middle of this conceptual domain is the matter of methodological verification – the sets of rules whereby useful knowledge can be accumulated and pyramided into a more powerful understanding of the universe.

The position taken in this book is that anthropology can be considered a science because it involves the accumulation of systematic and reliable knowledge about an aspect of the universe, carried out by empirical observation and interpreted in terms of the interrelating of concepts referable to empirical observations. Anthropology includes within its broad domain the search for panhuman generalizations about behavior and human adaptive processes and cultural products. The accumulated knowledge also includes historical description and analysis of particularistic phenomena. The fact that a great deal of anthropological research includes value decisions on the part of the researcher and intuition in the gathering of basic information does *not,* in our opinion, make the discipline *ipso facto* unscientific. If the "personal factor" in anthropology makes it automatically unscientific, then much of medical science, psychology, geography, and significant parts of all disciplines (including chemistry and physics) are unscientific. However, we do need to look closely at some of the reasons why progress in the accumulation of a useful body of anthropological theory appears to be disappointingly slow and uneven.

Anthropology and problems of methodology

From the perspective on the nature of science and scientific method adopted in the preceding section, all anthropologists are "doing science" whenever they are actively engaged in accumulating raw data or in putting together generalizations based on observational data in a search for reliable knowledge about human behavior. It is beyond argument that anthropologists, like all other scholars, are trying to be systematic, and that they are generally favorably disposed toward reliable information rather than error and falsehood.

The conflict begins when we take up the subject of the effectiveness of particular methods of research and scholarship. It is in the matter of evidence and the believability of anthropological research results that we find the focus of controversy. Those outside the field who say that anthropology is not a science probably intend to say that anthropologists accept generalizations on the basis of evidence that will not stand up under close logical scrutiny. Further, these outside critics can probably make a strong claim that anthropologists frequently present a prima facie case for a proposition and then move on to some other area of study, leaving the generalization to be debated pro and con in a speculative manner, rather than proceeding with careful examination of empirical evidence. Anthropologists are lax in their theory-building habits.

One well-known instance of unresolved theoretical debate in the anthropological literature is the Oscar Lewis–Robert Redfield controversy about life in the Mexican village of Tepoztlán. Redfield had studied the community in the 1920s and described the people as living in harmony with their universe. Seventeen years later, Oscar Lewis and his associates studied the same community and reported a quite different picture. Lewis summed up the differences between the two research reports in these words:

The impression given by Redfield's study of Tepoztlán is that of a relatively homogeneous, isolated, smoothly functioning and well-integrated society made up of a contented and well-adjusted people. His picture of the village has a Rousseauan quality which glosses lightly over evidence of violence, disruption, cruelty, disease, suffering and maladjustment. We are told little of poverty, economic problems, or political schisms.

Throughout his study we find an emphasis upon the cooperative and unifying factors in Tepoztecan society.

Our findings, on the other hand, would emphasize the underlying individualism of Tepoztecan institutions and character, the lack of cooperation, the tensions between villages within the municipio, the schisms within the village, and the pervading quality of fear, envy and distrust. (Oscar Lewis, 1951:428–9.)

Redfield replied with an admission that

. . . Lewis established the objective truth of certain of the unpleasant features of Tepoztecan life. He has shown that more than half of the villagers did not own land at the time that he studied the community; that many were in serious want; that stealing, quarreling, and physical violence are not rare in Tepoztlán. . . . It is true that the two books describe what might almost seem to be two different peoples occupying the same town. (Redfield, 1960:134.)

He adds, however: "The greater part of the explanation for the difference between the two reports on this matter of Tepoztecan life and character is to be found in differences between the two investigators. . . . I think that it is simply true that . . . I looked at certain aspects of Tepoztecan life because they both interested and pleased me" (Redfield, 1960:135).

Another instance of this kind of anthropological debate concerns the character of life among the Pueblo Indians of the Southwest. The story begins in 1934, when Ruth Benedict published her characterization of the Pueblo Indians in *Patterns of Culture*. In this work she described the Pueblos as "Apollonian" – restrained in emotions, avoiding violence, quarrels, or warfare and given to moderation in all things. Other writers, notably Laura Thompson, have given similar portraits of the integrated qualities of Pueblo culture.

This "Apollonian" ethos of the Pueblo peoples is supposedly so pervasive that alcohol has never become a problem among them. "Drunkenness is repulsive to them," Benedict wrote. "In Zuñi after the early introduction of liquor, the old men voluntarily outlawed it and the rule was congenial enough to be honored" (ibid., 1934:82). Similarly, all types of emotional and violent display were said to be entirely inconsistent with Pueblo attitudes.

On the other hand, Esther Goldfrank and Dorothy Eggan (among others) have described some aspects of Pueblo lifeways (particularly among Zuñi and Hopi) as traumatic, violent, and repressive (see especially Eggan, 1943; Li An-Che, 1937; Goldfrank, 1945.) In support of her argument, Esther Goldfrank offered, for example, the following quotation from H. R. Voth's observations of the Oraibi Powamu ceremony:

With the crying and screaming of the candidates, men and women mingle their voices, some encouraging them, others accusing the Katcinas of partiality, claiming that they whip some harder than others; in short, pandemonium reigns in the kiva during this exciting half hour. But the scene has not only its exciting, but also its disgusting features. As the whips are quite long, they frequently extend around the leg or hip of the little nude boys in such a manner that the points strike the pudibilia, and the author noticed on several occasions that the boys, when being placed on the sand mosaic, were warned to protect these parts, which they tried to do by either quickly freeing one hand and pushing the pudenda between the legs or by partly crossing the legs. It was also noticed on several occasions that some of the boys, probably as a result of fear and pain, involuntarily micturated and in one or two cases even defecated. (Quoted in Goldfrank, 1945.)

Concerning the Pueblo people's alleged aversion to alcohol, Barnouw (1963) gives a considerable list of evidence to the contrary, including the information that "Matilda Coxe Stevenson, whose report on Zuñi was published in 1904, also described prevalent drinking, particularly around the time of the Shalako festival" (Barnouw, 1963:45). Thus on the liquor question the empirical facts seem to be contrary to what was claimed by Benedict, and have been so at least since the turn of the century.

John Bennett examined the two versions of Pueblo culture and concluded:

The differences in viewpoint, therefore, cannot be explained entirely either on the basis of scientific goodness or badness, nor on the basis of publication differentials. Underneath both these factors lies what I have already suggested may be a genuine difference in value orientation and outlook in the feeling about, the reaction toward, Pueblo society and culture in the light of values in American culture, brought to the scientific situation by the anthropologist. (Bennett, 1956:211.)

According to Bennett's analysis, Thompson and Benedict stressed (and showed approval of) the organic unity and "logico-aesthetic integration" of Pueblo culture as an admirable end product, whereas Goldfrank, Eggan, and other observers have concerned themselves with the means (painful initiation and other social control mechanisms) by which the supposed integration of Pueblo life is maintained. Thus "scientific anthropology is . . . implicated in an on-going process in our own culture, and from this level of observation it is "nonobjective" and "culturally determined" (Bennett, 1956:212).

From the point of view of scientific method in anthropology, we can summarize the situation as follows:

1　All of the anthropologists cited appear to have been sincerely concerned with presenting systematic, reliable information. All were trying to be scientific (in terms of our earlier definition).
2　All of the materials in these cases were derived from, or purported to be derived from, empirical observation.
3　Each of the authors attempted to set forth propositions about particular, definable communities, using terminology that implied a naturalistic and an objective orientation rather than metaphysical or supernatural speculation.
4　In each case the method of the author was to present a general, unified (but somewhat vague) hypothesis about very general and abstract conditions of life in particular communities, around which he accumulated a series of sketches, anecdotes, quotations, and other bits and pieces that formed a network of evidence in favor of the hypothesis.

5   In each of these cases the necessary conditions for *negation* of the hypothesis were notably lacking.

6   In each of the cases, types of societies were postulated – for instance, "Apollonian," "peaceful peasants," "hostile peasants" – that were treated as real categories. The ensuing debates centered on the question of whether the particular societies conformed to the ideal types.

7   In each of the cases the main hypothesis was at such a high level of abstraction (the configuration of a culture; the ethos of society) as to be nearly unresearchable for practical purposes.

8   However, none of these research ideas appears to be *in principle* unresearchable, even though serious problems of definition would be encountered before a systematic research methodology could be constructed.

Given these conditions of scholarship, it seems intrinsically likely, as Bennett observes, that the general value preferences of the anthropologists have had an important, if covert, role in shaping the directions of argument and description. Redfield openly admits this in his reply to Lewis.

The cases of Tepoztlán and the Pueblos are only the most famous of a long series of instances in which anthropologists have strongly disagreed concerning theoretical constructs and the interpretation of masses of objective (or potentially objective) data. In most such debates the language of dispute is at such a high level of abstraction (so far removed from the concrete observations themselves) that their resolution continues to be in terms of emotional and literary persuasiveness, frequently backed by the weight of "authoritative opinions" of leading scholars rather than in any systematic analysis of evidence.

What, then, is missing in these studies, and in contemporary anthropology, generally, that causes them to be lacking in scientific rigor? Some people will here call out "quantification." The position taken in this book, however, is that quantification is but one aspect of a more complicated problem. In his short but excellent statement of *The Scientific Approach*, Carlo Lastrucci outlines what appear to be the basic elements of the scientific method. Abstracting from his work and similar discussions, we offer the following list of essential ingredients that should be present or accounted for in any sound piece of scientific work, however intuitive the sources of the original hypotheses or propositions:

1   The problem, the aim, of the particular work should be stated, and that problem should be researchable, at least in principle. The statement of the problem may be simply a hypothesis to be tested, an event to be described, or any of a number of other possible types of research aim. (Hypothesis is here defined as "a tentative theory or supposition provisionally adopted to explain certain facts and to guide in the investigation of others.")

2   The essential elements, or terms, of the problem must be defined. Definition may involve simply identifying elements or units that are common knowledge among researchers, stating operational definitions (measurements, types of observations, etc.), or referring to previously established definitions of a particular researcher or school of

researchers. All the terms in the stated problem must relate to observable natural phenomena of the universe, however indirect the paths of abstraction involved. THE SINGLE MOST SERIOUS PROBLEM IN ANTHROPOLOGICAL RESEARCH IS THE FAIL- URE TO PAY CAREFUL ATTENTION TO DEFINITION OF UNITS AND VARIABLES.

3 The procedures of observation related to the essential, defined elements must be de- scribed in enough detail so that another anthropologist (or other scientist) reading the work can evaluate the adequacy of the research observations and can clearly under- stand what steps would be necessary to replicate the observations involved in the piece of research.

4 The step-by-step analysis of these observations must conform to the usual canons of logic employed in the sciences. The logic involved in anthropology is in principle the same as in all other scholarship.

5 Steps 2, 3, and 4 must be so constituted that it is possible to see what data would con- stitute a negation of the results described by the researcher. That is, the work must be falsifiable.

Some comments should be added here about this tentative model for evalua- tion of research works. First, Statement 2, concerning definitions, should not be construed to mean that all the concepts employed in anthropology (or any other science) must have direct and accessible empirical referents. Lastrucci (p. 115) lists terms such as "force," "symbiosis," "intelligence," and "social mobility" as "having no apparent empirical qualities." The anthropologist could easily add to this "culture," "evolution," "acculturation," and "personality." Second, what- ever abstract, relational terms of this sort are employed in research, the research design must nonetheless make clear to the reader just what observational proce- dures will be taken as evidence supporting a proposition involving the abstract concept.

When we look at the published works of anthropologists, we note first that there are many to which application of the "yardstick of scientific method" will be fairly difficult. Ethnographic descriptions generally consist of great numbers of both descriptive and analytic statements; frequently, objective and simple descriptions are interspersed with statements referring to abstract relationships.

Here are some examples from Clyde Kluckhohn's work among the Navajo. (We use these materials here simply for illustrative purposes and not because they represent as far as we know any notable departure from what is usual in eth- nographic descriptive works.) In discussing the social relationships among pa- tients, assistants, and others at Navajo curing ceremonials, Kluckhohn noted that:

The singer usually has a first assistant and several other helpers. The relationship of the first assistant is significant in respect to the singer rather than to the patient. Sometimes the singer takes with him to the ceremonial a member of his extended family group who has had some experience and training. Dick . . . and Jake . . . are quite occasionally ac- companied by their sons-in-law. These two men are not trying to learn the ceremo- nials. . . .

Those present (other than patient, singer, and necessary assistants) until the final day of a ceremonial are almost invariably limited to members of the patient's immediate family group and perhaps a few neighbors. Spectators gather during the final day, reaching a maximum during the concluding all-night singing. Studying the lists of those present suggests that kinship and geographic propinquity are the two principal determinants of attendance. Only one fact that is at all remarkable emerges – namely that paternal relatives are about fifteen per cent more numerous in the lists than maternal relatives. Since this is true in spite of the fact that the residence system is still more matrilocal than patrilocal, it may be significant. At the very least, it affords demonstration of the bilateral character of kinship reciprocities. (Kluckhohn, 1962:119.)

Farther along in the same article, Kluckhohn noted that: "Many statements make it clear that there is social pressure upon brothers and sisters, uncles and aunts, and other relatives of the patient to aid by their presence and by gifts of food and money" (p. 120). "Becoming a singer is probably the principal mechanism for the 'circulation of the elite' (in the Paretian sense) in Navajo society as a whole" (p. 121).

In this section, as in many other descriptions about Navajo ceremonial patterns, Kluckhohn referred to some individual cases, lists of people present at ceremonials he had witnessed or for which he had obtained information, and it is clear that he is describing patterns for which he has a great deal of primary data. At some points his generalizations apply to a particular set of Navajo ceremonials to which he had access (the geographic and time range of these materials is unclear); but at other points his generalizations are clearly intended to apply to Navajo society as a whole. Nonetheless, we do not have much difficulty imagining the *kinds* of data that would be relevant for the generalizations he made. The data in those passages involve behavior that any normally competent anthropologist or other observer should be able to report fairly accurately. There would seem to be no problems about the definitions of terms and the logic of explanation.

In another section, however, Kluckhohn discussed Navajo morals at a much more abstract level, and the relevant data are not as apparent:

The Protestant virtue of care of possessions (though not the frequently paired one of cleanliness) is shared by the Navajo: destructiveness, waste, carelessness, and even cleanliness are disapproved of. Gambling is wrong "if you lost your mother's jewelry. . . ." Games must not interfere with work. One must not even attend ceremonials too often lest this become a way of loafing. Knowledge, including ceremonial knowledge and sound judgement, are good because they are conducive to health and long life. . . . Sobriety, self control, and adherence to old custom are valued . . . drinking is wrong if it results in loss of superego control, if one becomes "wild and without sense." One should talk "pretty nice" to everyone . . . (ibid., p. 170).

Here we are involved in descriptive statements that are far from simple. Moral values are extremely difficult to generalize about, as it is nearly impossible to disentangle people's statements of Utopian ideals from their pragmatic "rules for real life."

It is clear from the context that Kluckhohn was referring to "traditional Navajo codes of conduct before Western influence became maximal." Can we assume, though, that all Navajo agree with these kinds of statements? Given the large amount of time that traditional Navajo people have spent in attending ceremonials, we are surely justified in asking "How often is too often?" if indeed the people are afraid it could lead to loafing. What kind of talk is "pretty nice"? Do Navajo define "pretty nice" the way that Harvard University people would define that expression?

All of the concepts and relationships in the quoted passages are definable, but the anthropologist did not give us the definitions. Some of the generalizations appear to be based on direct statements of informants; others refer to observed individual events; still others are derived from stories and myths; and some seem to be shaped from an analysis of language usage. In any case, we are given little information about how the data specific to each generalization were obtained.

Clyde Kluckhohn was unusual among ethnographers in the large amount of time he spent immersed in data gathering with one particular people. He was well aware that individual Navajo differ from one another in behavior and interpretations of Navajo culture. He felt that "in part, the disagreements relate to the fact that Navajos of different regions have had their main historical contacts with different tribes of other Indians. It is also true that Indians in general have not troubled to create systematic and completely congruent theologies . . ." (ibid., 140).

In most respects, Kluckhohn's discussions about Navajo culture, social organizations, and behavior do not differ significantly from other ethnographic accounts, whether written by British social anthropologists, French structuralists, or anthropologists of other schools of thought. Various explanations are given by anthropologists to account for our usual styles of ethnographic discourse. Many anthropologists would probably admit to some methodological problems in this kind of data management, but reactions differ:

1   Some anthropologists would say that the passages cited are lacking in scientific rigor but would assert that the problem is unavoidable because the description of a culture or community in all its aspects involves so much information that strict research operations (and the reporting of them) cannot be adopted because of time and space limitations.

2   Some anthropologists would feel that there are no serious problems posed by the previous passages, because the accuracy and effectiveness of anthropological research operations depend on *building into the anthropologist* certain standard techniques of observation that result in accurate reporting, even though the processes of combined intuition and observation are too complicated to be included in a description of the data.

3   Some anthropologists feel that anthropological field techniques must be more carefully structured (and described) than they have been in the past. For complex holistic
studies it is impossible (and unnecessary) to develop rigorous methods for documenting *every* piece of information that makes up a monographic description; nonetheless,
a *framework* of carefully operationalized evidence is necessary. Methods for the study
of complex values, attitudes, and cognitive orientations must be developed that will
make possible the objective, replicable testing of the hunches and intuitions of fieldworkers. Furthermore, readily observable data such as houses and furnishings, animals, and other material possessions, occupations, and many aspects of social relationships should be studied with carefully constructed sampling procedures that can
provide quantifiable bases for empirical generalizations.

A study by Edward Banfield in southern Italy (1958) is interesting as an ethnographic description because he appears to satisfy certain important criteria for
effective field methodology, including the use of a structured research instrument (Thematic Apperception Test), as well as clear descriptions of his principal theoretical terms. Banfield's monograph is quite clear in its theoretical intent and is focused on a particular aspect of the cultural system rather than on
seeking to describe "everything" in the local system. In the *Moral Basis of a
Backward Society* Banfield seeks to explain why a particular southern Italian
community, Montegrano, is extremely poor and "backward." His general thesis
is that this community (and by extension others like it in southern Italy and elsewhere) is incapable of improving its political and economic position because of
an ethos he calls "amoral familism," a pervasive system of beliefs, values, and
sentiments. Understanding this ethos will "enable an observer to predict how the
Montegranesi will act in concrete circumstances. The hypothesis is that the
Montegranesi act as if they were following this rule: maximize the material, short
run advantage of the nuclear family; assume that all others will do likewise"
(Banfield, 1958:85).
    The hypotheses Banfield tested in his research are:

1   The ethos of amoral familism is a dominant tendency in Montegrano.
2   It is a cause of the continuing poverty and generally undesirable political and eco-
    nomic situation of these people.

Banfield presents extensive quotations from people's responses on the research
instrument, and he reproduces much of the raw data in order to make clear his
research methods and definitions. At the same time, problems in his field work
are readily apparent. Although he has some fairly systematic behavioral evidence, there are several broad, inferential leaps necessary to arrive at generalizations such as "In the Montegrano mind any advantage that may be given to
another is necessarily at the expense of one's own family. Therefore, one cannot
afford the luxury of charity . . . toward those who are not of the family the reasonable attitude is suspicion . . . he must therefore fear them and be ready to do

them injury in order that they may have less power to injure him and his" (ibid., p. 116).

Banfield's assertation that the Montegranesi's belief system is the primary *causal* factor for their social and economic conditions cannot be demonstrated with the kind of data he collected. Even if he had documented a pervasive ethos, it cannot be concluded that the belief is *causally responsible* for the economic conditions. A second major problem with his hypothesis, as with any hypothesis concerning qualities or characteristics of a particular group of people, is that it *implies* comparison with other groups – yet he does not carry out such comparisons. Banfield's ideas about "amoral familism" are meaningless as a causal explanation if it turns out that families in practically every society are also characterized by a strong tendency to look after intrafamilial interests first, with considerable suspicion about relationships to more distant kin. Amoral familism cannot be an all-or-nothing quality; the generalizations about a community in southern Italy are only relevant if those people have a *degree* of amoral familism that is quite contrastive with other types of societies.

Banfield did not give any statistical or other systematic comparison of southern Italians with peoples he would characterize as not amoral familists. In the same vein, Kluckhohn's generalization that Navajo people "are against drinking if it results in loss of superego control" would become more meaningful if a contrast could be demonstrated with people who value such loss of superego control. Often the implicit basis of comparison is "modern, middle-class North American society." At this point it is fair for the reader to ask: Do Americans approve of drinking to the point of loss of superego control? Can the behavior of American family heads be characterized as amoral familism? What kinds of comparative information, with what checks and controls, would be necessary to establish these points?

Some of Banfield's generalizations have been put to systematic testing by another researcher. The generalizations in his book are defined clearly enough that another person can seek to replicate the results. In this case the reexamination of amoral familism was carried out by Roy A. Miller in Terrone, a town in the same region of southern Italy as Montegrano. Miller acknowledges that it is not strictly comparable to Montegrano in all respects. Nonetheless, Terrone would seem to be comparable enough in its poverty, seclusion, and location so that the results of the research have some relevance to Banfield's hypothesis.

As Miller points out, "In order to test the hypothesis that southern countrymen are amoral familists, it was necessary to conceptually and operationally define 'amoral familism' . . . an amoral familist was conceived to be a man who was not morally inhibited from approving of *any* prescription for the performance of family-serving acts" (Miller, 1974:253).

In our opinion, the advantage of Miller's study over Banfield's is that Miller assumed from the beginning that there might be some variation among males in Terrone with regard to attitudes and beliefs and that his data gathering should reflect such variation. His research methods included a structured interview technique, which compares favorably with Banfield's use of the structured Thematic Apperception Test. Miller's amoral familism scale contained twelve items, which he administered to "fifty male residents of the village . . . ranged in age from seventeen to seventy years . . . their occupations ranged from agricultural and unskilled industrial laborers, through skilled laborers, small farmers and shop owners, to clerical, technical and professional workers" (ibid., p. 525).

Of the twelve basic questions that Miller asked, there were a few statements that 90 percent of his informants agreed with. Some statements were approved by about 50 percent of the men, and one statement was approved by *only 4 percent of the people*. The latter statement, which sounds like the hallmark of amoral familism, was: "There are times when a father has to do things that might hurt a fellow townsman if it would help his own family." The Terronese were divided about half and half in responding to the following: "There are times when it is necessary for a father to cheat or swindle the others a little."

In contrast to Banfield, who used the results of the structured research instrument to make generalizations about the whole community, Miller's data demonstrate the range of variation *within* the community in the matter of beliefs related to amoral familism. On the basis of these results there is no justification for suggesting that these southern countrymen structure their lives in terms of an amoral familistic ethos. While a few men in the community did endorse most of the statements that were intended to measure this ethos, many men did not respond as they should have if they believed in the ethos, and some were strongly opposed to the sentiments expressed in the amoral-familism scale.

There are, of course, aspects of Miller's research that can be criticized. One can question the meaning of the key items in his scale for people in southern Italy, and his sample of informants was not strictly random, so that a question about its representativeness can be raised, even though his sampling is much more impressive than the typical case in ethnographic reporting. Nothing in Miller's research can satisfy us about the causal force of this constellation of beliefs, but his more refined study gives us an understanding of the range of variation in a very complex domain of ideas, rather than a labeling of an entire community or an entire culture as adhering to a particular uniform traditional trait.

There are some similarities between the Banfield–Miller "debate" on amoral familism and the earlier and much better known Redfield–Lewis disagreements. In each case the focus is on community studies of agricultural populations, and the ethnographers intended to present some rather broad generalizations about life style and ethos. In some respects, though, there is marked improvement from the earlier to the later example. (We must keep in mind, however, that we do not have an answer from Banfield to Miller's presentation.) Both Redfield and Lewis were aiming at sweeping generalizations that would be extremely difficult to narrow down to clear-cut and definable research operations. Furthermore, there could be no resolution of a debate in which it appears that the two researchers were looking at different data, with different standards and values affecting their data gathering.

It is important to make research propositions more specific, and where possible the methods should be more available to criticism. Banfield's research on amoral familism was sufficiently precise to enable other researchers to focus on approximately the same target. We cannot claim that Miller has unambiguously proved that amoral familism is *not* the social and cultural factor Banfield claimed it to be. On the other hand, the research in both studies gives the reader a fairly clear idea of the way the data were collected and assembled, and (especially in Miller's work) it is possible to see what the evidence looks like. Another researcher could take the information from both Banfield and Miller as a guide for retesting the hypothesis in other southern Italian villages in order to refine further or to replicate the studies.

Validity and reliability

The problems of anthropological credibility just reviewed embody two important concepts that are commonly encountered in methodological discussions. "Validity" refers to the degree to which scientific observations actually measure or record what they purport to measure. For example, we all understand the validity of the temperature as measured by thermometers and the measures of distance we can gauge with yardsticks and rulers. In anthropology, and the social sciences generally, there is a great deal of debate over the validity of particular observations of culture and behavioral concepts. Is the display of food for a guest really a measure of friendship and hospitality? Are the answers given to door-to-door interviewers, and duly recorded in their notebooks, valid expressions of people's opinions and attitudes? Are differences in material wealth and other possessions in a community valid indicators of *social* inequalities? In their field research anthropologists have invested much effort to achieve validity, for we generally assume that a long-term stay in a community facilitates the differentiation of what is valid from what is not, and the assembling of contextual supporting information to buttress claims to validity.

"Reliability" is often closely related to the matter of validity; it refers to the repeatability, including interperson replicability, of scientific observations. When we buy a good thermometer, we expect it to demonstrate a high degree of reliability in repeated measurements. Certain types of interview procedures used by sociologists, anthropologists, and others have been demonstrated to produce approximately the same range of responses on repeated trials, even with different interviewers. On the other hand, there are types of materials and situations in which structured interviews produce quite varied data depending on the style and tone of the interviewer and the context in which interviews take place. For this reason questions can easily be raised about the reliability of these techniques of verbal observation.

To return for a moment to the Redfield – Lewis controversies, the arguments involve both validity and reliability. Lewis claimed that Redfield's "measurements" of particular dimensions were inaccurate, because they were grossly different from his own observations of the same general set of phenomena. The problems of defining just what it was that was being measured, however, loomed very large in that whole business.

In the case of Kluckhohn's descriptions of the Navajo, there are problems with both the reliability and the validity of his statements about abstract moral rules. Most important, perhaps, is the lack of specification of research *operations* that another investigator could use to replicate the data. Definitions of key terms are lacking, and the precise modes of observation (interviewing format, selection of behavioral scenes for participant observation, etc.) are not generally specified by the ethnographer. At other points, however, in generalizing about certain aspects of Navajo ceremonialism, Kluckhohn did specify the data-collection procedures that another might use to replicate his results.

Miller's study of amoral familism among the Terronese has some advantages of replicability, because he gave a very clear description of his methods, including the key questions. There would appear to be a fair degree of reliability in his research methods. On the other hand, critics could suggest that the townspeople might not answer truthfully the kinds of questions he asked, and hence one might question the validity of the results. The fact that Miller found quite consistent *patterning* in the people's answers to his questions is evidence on his side of the matter, that is, in the form of "pattern validity."

Anthropological researchers have usually tried to maximize validity and, to some extent, reliability through the use of an eclectic mix of research operations. The blending of relatively nonstructured, long-term observations and interviews (high validity) with more structured interviews, psychological tests, and other more formalized procedures enhances reliability and replicability. The tradition of relatively long-term field work enhances the possibility for putting such eclectic methodology to sound use.

Interpersonal replicability

In their book on anthropological methods, Brim and Spain have commented that "an essential characteristic of science, perhaps the most crucial one, is that *the procedures used to make observations and test hypotheses are described objectively and in detail so that another investigator may repeat and independently verify the results.* This characteristic we may call *replicability"* (Brim and Spain, 1974:26; emphasis in original).

Anthony P. Glascock and Robert Kimble have recently examined anthropological journals to determine "to what extent research designs and methodologies are reported in the literature most closely associated with anthropology." They examined the content of over 400 anthropological publications and found that "less than 3% reported research designs and methodology to a degree that allowed replication . . ." (Glascock and Kimble, personal communication).

Glascock and Kimble were not evaluating the *effectiveness* of anthropological research methodology in this study but were only asking the question: Do anthropologists describe their research procedures so that others can try to repeat, or at least reevaluate, the results? Their findings were disappointing.

None of the methodological critics of the anthropological enterprise intends that all of our research methods used heretofore should be relegated to the scrap heap. Nor is it claimed that all past research is useless. The more modest points raised in these discussions are concerned with ways that we can make progress toward the building of solid theoretical frameworks in anthropology – a process that is often very slow, sometimes painful, but in the long run rewarding for the profession and for us as individuals.

Falsifiability

Philosophers of science remind us that, strictly speaking, we cannot *prove* hypotheses and theoretical propositions. The business of science, rather, is the gradual elimination of less credible alternative explanations and propositions, and the accumulation of evidence favoring the probability of those hypotheses and theories that continue to merit our support. Mere accumulation of *positive* support of a theoretical position is not enough, however. Truly credible support of theoretical propositions comes only when the researcher places a theoretical proposition in jeopardy – that is, he or she sets up conditions whereby a hypothesis can be *disproved*. Researchers should establish conditions whereby their hypotheses and theoretical positions are exposed to *falsification*. The greater the number of situations in which hypotheses have been exposed to falsification and survived the test, the greater the credibility of the theoretical model. Confidence increases that the theoretical model is highly probable, even though we cannot, in principle, ever be sure that a new situation will not arise that will require a revision of the position.

In earlier phases of anthropological research a great many propositions and hypotheses were advanced that had a certain semblance of probability, usually with descriptive supporting evidence, but they were not presented or researched in a manner permitting falsification. In general, falsification is not possible if we do not define our terms and make clear the basic elements in our theoretical statements. The tasks of anthropological research, then, include the development of clearer standards for potential falsification – including the possibilities of replication by other persons who may not have as much fondness and emotional concern about our theoretical ideas as we have.

Conclusions

From the lessons of the Redfield – Lewis debates about Tepoztlán, and the disputes concerning the interpretation of Pueblo culture, it appears that anthropologists need to develop research methods that protect the researchers from their own subjective assumptions and value judgments. Contrary to some earlier opinions, training in anthropology does not rid the investigator of conscious and unconscious cultural biases, but methodological training can provide ways of minimizing the researcher's personal biases by means of systematic, objectifiable research tools.

Quantification and statistical analysis may aid significantly in objectifying anthropological research, but a most important first step toward rigorous methodology lies in careful definition of the focus of research, with specification of the empirical observations that will be used as evidence for *and against* the propositions to be tested.

The methodological requirements suggested here do not in the least suggest that anthropologists give up the time-tested general procedures of participant observation and informal interviewing. These traditional anthropological techniques are indispensable for identifying the significant questions, as well as for finding out how these questions can be studied in terms of the local setting. The intuitive observations of the sensitive fieldworker are essential to the general tasks of anthropological research, particularly in the discovery of significant patterns in cultural behavior. Once the anthropologist begins to lay hold of significant cultural relationships through intuitive hunches, the next essential step is to devise means to test and verify these hunches through systematized research routines.

The archempiricist Sir Francis Bacon observed:

. . . for let men please themselves as they will in admiring and almost adoring the human mind, this is certain: that as an uneven mirror distorts the rays of objects according to its own figure and section, so the mind, when it receives impressions of objects through the sense, cannot be trusted to report them truly, but in forming its notions mixes up its own nature with the nature of things. (Bacon, 1960:22.)

The task of the anthropologist is to reduce to a minimum the distortions of "this uneven mirror" by a careful definition of concepts and a specification of research operations, so that the powers and vagaries of the human mind work to our advantage – without reducing anthropological research to the level of "count 'em" mechanics.

3 Operationalism in anthropological research

As has been frequently pointed out, a main requirement of the scientific method is that the procedures of the researcher should be clearly (and publicly) specified, so that other scientists can understand *how* particular results were produced and can replicate the research when they should wish to do so. In *The Structure of Science* (1961) Nagel states:

If . . . theory is to be used as an instrument of explanation and prediction, it must some-how be linked with observable materials. The indispensability of such linkages has been repeatedly stressed in recent literature, and a variety of labels have been coined for them: coordinating definitions, operational definitions, semantic rules, correspondence rules, epistemic correlations, and rules of interpretation. (Nagel, 1961:93.)

He adds that "the ways in which theoretical notions are related to observational procedures are often quite complex, and there appears to be no single scheme which adequately represents all of them" (ibid., p. 94).

Operationalism and intersubjectivity

Examination of the pages of typical scientific reporting provides us with indications of what operationalism is all about. Descriptions of research in the pages of *Science,* for example, are full of information such as the following (all examples are from *Science,* May 12, 1967):

Calves were lightly anesthetized with thiopental and then given continuous intravenous infusion of succinyl choline. (ibid., p. 827.)

A hyper-transfused-polycythemic (HP) state was induced by intraperitoneal injections of 0.5 ml of washed, packed, homologous red blood cells on 3 consecutive days and again on day 5. (ibid., p. 832.)

Five cocks received alcohol (9 ml/kg body weight, of 33 percent grain alcohol administered orally) and five cocks received an equal amount of water without alcohol 30 minutes before the initial exposure to newly hatched chicks. (Ibid., p. 836.)

It is evident from these examples that the "operations," as given in scientific journals, are often set forth in highly technical codes that refer to established research procedures that are standard practices of particular sciences. Much of undergraduate and graduate training in these sciences involves laboratory practice with the standardized operations.

All of the examples just given refer to laboratory experiments. The descriptions deal with the experimental manipulations by means of which the effects of selected variables can be observed and measured. In laboratory sciences, procedural descriptions such as the ones just given provide a guide or "recipe" whereby another scientist in another laboratory can repeat the experiment to see if the results agree with those reported earlier. However, in many types of research this repeatability of observations is not strictly possible. Behavioral scientists observing an unusual and aperiodic event – a natural disaster, a riot, or a nonrepeatable ceremony such as the crowning of a particular king – cannot provide for repeatability of the observations, no matter how completely they describe the research operations. Similarly, astronomers often report observations of cosmic events that are nonrecurring.

Aperiodic, nonrecurring events require accurate description just as much as do experiments – in order that other scientists may ascertain the extent to which the researcher's procedure was objective. In such a case the main question to be asked is: If another observer *had been* at the particular event, and if he *had used* the same techniques, would he have obtained the same results? This is a question of intersubjectivity. Research methods and descriptions that fail to provide sufficient operational description to satisfy the requirements of intersubjectivity are extremely common in the social sciences and are an indicator of disciplinary immaturity.

The philosopher Herbert Feigl states the basic issue as follows: "There are two questions with which we are (or at least *should* be) concerned in any cognitive enterprise: *'What do we mean by the words or symbols we use?'* and *'How do we know that what we assert in these terms is true (or confirmed to some degree)?'* " (Feigl, 1945:250; his italics).

Operationalizing of research procedures is not carried out simply for the edification and information of other scientists, however. The scientist tries for better and better research operations in order to generate more accurate observations, hence more effective theory building and testing. Specification of operations enhances control of extraneous variables, increases the precision of basic measurements (or other types of observations), and provides the framework of information that permits the researcher to retrace his or her steps mentally in order to understand both predicted and unpredicted results.

The process of operationalizing research is in some ways analogous to using a recipe for baking a fancy cake. The recipe provides the following advantages:

1 It can be given to someone else, and that person can produce the same result by following the recipe point by point.

2   The recipe provides for accurate measurements of variables and makes clear which variables are the most important to measure accurately.

3   By stating a list of essential ingredients, the recipe by implication makes clear which kinds of variables are to be controlled, or kept out of the procedures. (E.g., in beating the egg whites for a cheesecake, any oil or grease in the mixture would ruin the cake.)

4   The recipe provides a clear series of steps that can be retraced to find one's mistake if something goes wrong and the cake turns out badly. Also, the clever baker can examine the recipe to find ways in which the procedures can be improved. Significant innovations can be made at certain points only.

5   The recipe provides explicit operational definitions for important concepts that are often left vague and undefined in ordinary discourse. (For example, "bake in a hot oven" becomes translated into "place in oven set at 450°F for 30–35 minutes.")

Our analogy is also useful for pointing out the ways in which scientific operations *are not like* cooking with recipes. The model has definite limitations. A cookbook recipe is usually used in a situation in which one wishes to produce an already known end product. This, of course, is not the case in scientific research, especially in the social sciences.

Unlike the cookbook recipe for a cake, the operationalizing of research must always provide for a careful assessment of the adequacy of the end product. The "cookbooks of science" focus attention on the procedures whereby the results are examined in terms of their relevance for scientific theory.

Lest the reader misconstrue this discussion as a plea for a sterile, mechanical, cookbook mode of anthropological research, let us hasten to point out another element in the analogy. Expert cooks do not slavishly follow the dictates of recipes! Recipes provide general sets of guidelines, in terms of which the *chef de cuisine* experiments with new combinations and innovative procedures in the manner of a creative artist. Scientific investigation is similarly a highly creative art, as made clear by W. I. B. Beveridge (see Chapter 2). The creative scientist, like the creative cook, can be highly innovative in the production of new knowledge because of intimate acquaintance with standard ingredients and techniques. Perhaps the scientist differs most from the cook in the attention paid to the procedures used in verifying results.

Operationalism and operationism

From the foregoing discussion the idea of operationalism that is essential to effective scientific advance may be defined as follows: *Operationalism* is a research strategy in which primary elements (terms) of descriptions and theoretical propositions are structured, *wherever possible*, in forms that prescribe, or otherwise make intersubjectively available, the *specific acts of observation* that provide the primary transformations from raw experience to the language of theoretical systems. Furthermore, the strategy provides that higher-level theoretical propositions and models be constructed, whenever possible, by means of intersubjectively specified transformational rules that set standards of sampling, definitions, and logical fit whereby low-level descriptions and generalizations are sorted and organized. The intention of this rather abstract statement will, we hope, become more clear as we take up some concrete examples later in this chapter.

While there is no serious disagreement concerning the proposition that any science, to be effective, must employ sets of correspondence rules and operational definitions, some complexity has been added to discussions of methodology by those social scientists who have insisted on a radical-empiricist research strategy known as *operationism*. According to their thinking, concepts in theoretical systems *have no meaning independent of the particular research procedures* in which they are used. Thus the term "intelligence" can mean only "that which is measured by a particular intelligence test," and nothing more. (By this same logic, a distance measured with a calibrated tape and a distance measured by a process of triangulation are *two different concepts* of distance.)

The attitude of strict operationism may be useful in some areas of science, but it is far too restrictive to be useful in anthropology. Insistence on fully operationalized research methods appears to arise in part from a misunderstanding of the structure of research operations in the so-called hard sciences. The advanced state of the procedures of physics has led some people to believe that the correspondence rules and operations of physics are clear, direct, and fully operationalized. Such, however, is not the case.

Feigl (1945) has pointed out that the various sciences have two general kinds of theoretical structures, which he labels neutrally "theories of the first kind" and "theories of the second kind." Theories of the first kind are those in which the constructs "are homogeneous with the operationally defined terms in the empirical laws of the given fields." Type I theoretical systems include those of chemistry (with its elements, compounds, compounding weights, affinities, etc.), classical thermodynamics, and, in psychology, Hullian and Skinnerian behaviorism. Type II theoretical systems are made up of heterogeneous constructs for which transformational rules are often somewhat vague. Atomic theory, statistical thermodynamics, and the neurophysiological theories of Sherrington and Köhler are examples, Feigl says, of theoretical systems in which there are some "gaps." They include hypothetical constructs and rough-and-ready transformations linking one construct level with another.

Ernest Nagel has examined this matter of the correspondences of theoretical ideas with experimental observations in some detail. Like Feigl, he characterized some areas of theoretical physics by saying that "rules of correspondence for connecting theoretical with experimental ideas generally receive no explicit formulation; and in actual practice the coordinations are comparatively loose and imprecise" (Nagel, 1961:99). Nagel's example is that of Niels Bohr's (in its time) relatively successful atomic theory, which was "an eclectic fusion of Planck's quantum hypothesis and ideas borrowed from classical electrodynamic theory" (Nagel, 94).

Nagel comments: "But how is the Bohr theory brought into relation with what can be observed in the laboratory? On the face of it, the electrons, their circulation in orbits, their jumps from orbits to orbits, and so on, are all conceptions that do not apply to anything manifestly observable" (ibid., p. 95). He notes that the Bohr atomic theory was usually not presented "as an abstract set of postulates, augmented by an appropriate number of rules of correspondence," but rather as a model expounded "in relatively familiar notions, so that instead of being statement-forms the postulates of the theory appear to be statements, at least part of whose content can be visually imagined" (ibid., p. 95). As a result of this kind of theory presentation, "despite the use of a model for stating a theory, [it should be clear] that the fundamental assumptions of the theory provide only implicit definitions for the theoretical notions employed in them" (ibid.).

Feigl points out:

The prototype of an operational definition such as we can advance for directly measurable magnitudes should not mislead us into banishing all concepts which do not come up to this high level of methodological aspiration. Even in physics we have to define many concepts (not only highly indirectly but) sometimes only very partially. Before any theory of x-rays was developed, x-rays were simply "what you got when cathode rays impinged on metal surfaces," and "that which produced photographic images of a certain kind." Only as we advance in discovery and technique such very sketchy definitions are supplemented by fuller qualitative, quantitative, and far-flung relational characteristics. Operationism wisely understood and applied must take account and render account of the level of precision, completeness, and fruitfulness reached at the given stage of concept formation. (Feigl, 1945:256.)

These comments about operationism and the differing degrees to which theoretical terms are (or can be) operationalized may be summed up as follows:

1   It appears to be generally agreed among scientists and philosophers of science that, wherever feasible, concepts should be given meaning (in terms of their relationships to other specified concepts) by means of repeatable methods of observation and experimentation that give them empirical content.

2   Whereas some people have taken a position of radical operationism, insisting on full operationalizing and empirical definition of *all* scientific terms, a more widely held, and more moderate, view accepts the prospect that even in well-developed sciences there are frequently elements of terminology that are only loosely tied to empirical observations.

3   It would appear that in some cases scientific concepts have proved useful and productive even when the technology of the time offered little possibility of operationalizing the variables. In Feigl's words: "Concepts of atomic structure were very far beyond practical testability only forty years ago. Concepts regarding the nature of cerebral

memory traces are in the promissory-note stage today. Scientific research as an ongoing process involves a continuous scale of degrees of technical testability" (ibid., p. 253).

4   When we survey the great welter of anthropological work that is produced without any semblance of operationalism, we can be assured that most of the anthropological enterprise would experience a drastic slowdown if *complete operationism* were to be insisted on. On the other hand, it would seem justified to suggest that anthropologists develop operational definitions for concepts in common use. In theory it would appear that much of the work of anthropologists is easier to operationalize than some of the obscure constructs with which physiologists, for example, struggle in their laboratories.

5   The fact that anthropology is not a laboratory science in no way detracts from either the importance of or the possibilities of operationalizing the elements of our theoretical systems.

Operationalism in anthropology

Judging from the examples of anthropological literature reviewed in Chapter 2, operationalism is not highly developed in anthropology. Statements of ethnographic "fact" are often given without any mention of the research techniques used to derive them. Just as often, the anthropologist reports in a general way that the data were gathered by means of interviewing and participant observation, but the *particular observations* on which key generalizations are based remain unreported. There are exceptions, of course. To an increasing degree interview schedules and other structured techniques are used to collect certain kinds of information, and these procedures provide at least minimal operational definitions of important concepts.

The ethnographer often makes some general introductory statements about his research procedures (with gracious acknowledgments of the invaluable help provided by informants, etc.), but particular fact statements in the ethnography are not accompanied by information concerning *how* the fieldworker made these particular observations. Since field-work observations generally consist of complex mixtures of interviewing and direct observation, laced with variable quantities of other more specialized procedures, it is frequently impossible to separate data that are operationalized in the form of informants' statements from those that were based on the anthropologist's direct observations.

Some writers have discussed the lack of scientific rigor in anthropological research as arising from a "mystique of field work." Field research in non-European cultures has been referred to as a mysterious "rite of passage," in which the most significant ethnographic information is obtained through an intuitional "experience" – a process that is basically indescribable to outsiders (including graduate students of anthropology). Morris Freilich has suggested that secretiveness concerning field-work techniques has developed because of the serious difficulties (and occasional failures) encountered in the field situation, the admission of which is not encouraged in the profession, because success in field work is thought to reflect one's personal character and professional adequacy (Freilich, 1970).

Part of the reason for the relatively carefree attitude toward operational specificity in anthropology probably stems from an earlier day when both lay and professional opinion held that most cultural customs (among "primitive" peoples) were clear, observable entities, requiring no concern with sampling, sophisticated interview procedures, or other specialized modes of observation. This complacency has largely disappeared, and most schools of anthropology are showing a rapidly increasing concern about methods and techniques of research. The problem then arises – what kinds of techniques, or research operations, can succeed in the complicated business of observing the day-to-day behavior of human groups? It seems clear that the time-tested techniques of interviewing and participant observation are still the mainstays of field procedure, but how can these procedures be systematized for those portions of ethnographic observation that call for stricter operationalism?

Strict operationalizing of *all* field observations would be almost impossible to achieve, and would be extremely slow, cumbersome, and wasteful of effort. Many observations in field work appear to require little in the way of procedural support. Statements about usual crops grown, distance to other settlements, materials from which tools are made, locations of water, supplies, and so on, could in many cases be self-evident and would not require operational definitions. Also, statements about events – such as "The weekly market was held on Saturday," "The Ravens beat the Wolves by a score of 29–17" – appear to be unambiguous.

The need for operationalizing descriptive constructs in research depends on the level of use of particular types of information. Data statements that are given in a general way as part of the descriptive background may be exempted from the requirements of operationalization, but the same descriptive constructs, when they appear as central terms in general hypotheses or propositions, require more careful specification. For example, "distances to other settlements" given as approximations may be perfectly adequate as informational background to a descriptive ethnography, but the data require greater specificity when they become part of a statement such as "Rates of intervillage marriages decline sharply as the distance between settlements increases." In this statement it is important to know whether "distance" means "as the crow flies"; along footpaths or roads; whether it is by land or by water; whether it is measured, estimated, or extrapolated; by whom it is measured; and so on.

The more complicated, abstracted, statements that fill our descriptive ethnographies pose much more serious problems of operational definition, however. From a recent anthropological journal, we culled the following:

Social atomism is evidenced by a characteristic weakness of formal organic bonds between individuals or subgroups in the kinship, economic, political, or religious fields of activity.

Feelings of hostility and repulsion – in the common forms of backbiting and evil gossip . . . are so prevalent as to form a social pattern.

The overt expression of either hostility or intimate friendship is rarely seen in [the community].

The Italian male must be *maschio* at all times.

The alignment of lineages is relevant only in certain situations, of which the most important are fighting, marriage and ritual.

Much of the struggle for headship of the lineage is played out during the dying elder's last hours.

Winter affords more leisure time than any other season of the year.

Relations between a mother and her sons are in general warm and affectionate.

In each of these ethnographic statements we can recognize two main procedural problems: (1) What kinds of behaviors or things are to be grouped together conceptually to "mean" organic bonds, feelings of hostility, backbiting, alignment of lineages, struggle for headship, leisure time, warm and affectionate relations? (2) How does the fieldworker amass sufficient observations of these particular behaviors (and things) so that he can reasonably make such descriptive statements?

Some possible methodological solutions to these problems can be examined by a review of anthropological handling of a widely used construct. For this purpose we will take the problem of *status inequality*, which is frequently a central concern in community descriptions and has received considerable attention in the methodological literature.

One of the major studies in which status inequality is a focus of interest is Marshall Sahlins's *Social Stratification in Polynesia* (1958). He noted that "an egalitarian society would be one in which every individual is of equal status, a society in which no one outranks anyone. But even the most primitive societies could not be described as egalitarian in this sense. There are differences in status carrying differential privilege in every human organization" (Sahlins, 1958:1).

The most general element in Sahlins's conception of status, therefore, is the matter of "differential privilege" in whatever terms privileges are allocated in particular societies. The various elements in terms of which privilege and prestige are allocated include: economic (material) advantages, such as food, land, and other resources; political power; religious privileges and prerogatives; and social ratings of valor, bravery, patriotism, effectiveness in combat, wisdom, and other "virtues," the meanings and contents of which vary markedly from one society to another.

In spite of the differences in *contents or criteria* of stratification, Sahlins felt that comparisons could be made among societies concerning the degree of stratification because certain general features of stratification are broadly similar in human societies. The least stratified human societies, Sahlins contended, are those such as the Australian aborigines, in which the only qualifications for higher status are those that practically every society uses to some extent, namely, age, sex, and personal characteristics.

Sahlins has suggested that any society in which these universals are the only criteria of rank allocation can be designated "egalitarian," because such a society exhibits the minimal level of stratification found in human societies. Any society that is stratified beyond the theoretical minimum Sahlins referred to as a "stratified society," but he quickly noted that societies vary a great deal in the degree to which they are stratified.

One society may be considered more stratified than another if it has more status classes, restricted by principles other than the universals, or if high rank bestows greater prerogatives in economic, social, political, and ceremonial activities. Criteria for estimating stratification . . . are thus divisible into "structural"; the degree of status differentiation, and "functional"; the degree to which rank confers privilege. (Ibid., p. 2.)

As Sahlins and numbers of other researchers have pointed out, the relative importance and extent of correlation among economic, sociopolitical, and ceremonial (and other) elements in stratification can vary from society to society, although these functional aspects of stratification tend to be highly interrelated.

Given these preliminary observations about the general definition of social stratification, we can pass on to the problem of operationalizing the concept for given theoretical purposes. In Sahlins's own monograph the data are drawn from the available ethnographic descriptions of various Polynesian societies, and these sources usually provide information in the form of *assertions about stratification*, rather than systematic presentation of the relevant evidence.

In spite of many differences in the specific contents and forms of social stratification in the several Polynesian societies, Sahlins was able to group these ethnographic materials into four classifications for purposes of theoretical analysis. For example, his Group I (Hawaii, Tonga, Samoa, Tahiti) is characterized by the following features:

Structurally complex ranking systems, usually with three status levels; preeminent stewardship by high chiefs; severe punishments and dispossession of those who infringe chiefly decrees on land or sea use; control of communal production by high and middle levels; direct supervision of household production by chiefly and middle levels, including inspection and ability to apply secular sanctions for failure to plant; complex redistributive hierarchy of three levels; ability of chiefs to confiscate goods of others by force in some cases; divorce of upper level, and perhaps middle level, from subsistence production; large range of clothes, ornaments, etc., serving as insignia of rank; arbitrary despotism described in general statements by observers; control of socioregulatory processes by high chiefs; marked difference by status in ability to inflict secular punishments on wrongdoers including ability to kill or banish those who infringe chiefly rights; close-in marriages among chiefs strictly enforced; very complex mana-tabu system concerning upper status level; elaborate obeisance postures and other forms of respect including developed chiefs' languages and carrying of chiefs on litters, etc.; unique rites for all life crises of high chiefs, held on a spectacular scale, (Ibid., p, 11.)

These very abstract descriptive statements, and other similar materials employed by Sahlins in his theoretical analysis, suggest some of the kinds of direct observations in terms of which these data about social stratification were obtained.

The elements from which ethnographic descriptions have been made in the area of social stratification (in Polynesia and elsewhere) include:

1 *Statements* by informants as to the existence of different, named groups in the society, accompanied by statements that such groups have differential powers and prerogatives.
2 *Statements* by informants as to differential decision-making powers of various individuals in their communities.
3 *Statements* by informants concerning the ritual meaning of ceremonial performances and rules (reflecting differential prestige).
4 *Observations* of ceremonial performances in which elements of the rituals reflect inequalities through either universalistic symbolism, or symbolic interpretations provided by members of the local community.
5 *Observations* of differences in access to the favors of supernaturals or in access to esteemed ritual performances.
6 *Observations* of differences in decision making among different individuals in the community.
7 *Observations* of differences in possession of, or access to, scarce economic resources, for example, land, among the populace.
8 *Observations* of differences in possession of significant (and presumably desirable) consumable goods.
9 *Observations* of inequalities in access to differentially valued occupations of the community.
10 *Observations* of inequalities of access to other scarce resources, such as sexual favors (and marriage partners), freedom of travel, and access to public and ceremonial places, and so on.
11 *Observations* of dress, ornaments, insignia, speech, and so on.
12 *Observations* of gestures of respect and other differential behavior.

As a general rule, we can say that observations by the researcher (or his agents or assistants) are of higher value than the (essentially hearsay) evidence provided by informants' statements. Hearsay evidence provided by informants is much used by anthropologists and is rendered valuable whenever independent statements of several informants can be cross-checked for reliability. Anthropologists usually (though not always) take into account the possibilities of prejudicial interests of given informants. The anthropologist, like the court of law, is especially suspicious of evidence against Smith introduced by his known enemy, Brown. By the same token, Smith's best friends and kinspeople cannot be regarded as unbiased reporters of Smith's behavior either.

Social ranking by informants

The method of ranking social *categories* by pooling the responses of a panel of local informants was used by Stanley Freed to obtain a ranking of castes in a village in India (1963). Freed asked twenty-six males in the village of Shanti Nagar to rank all the local caste groups (their names were written on slips of paper) in a single hierarchy of prestige. Median rank scores were then calculated in order to determine the consensus of the panel. While there were interesting discrepancies among the rankings given by the informants, the results indicated a high degree of consensus in the local community.

Paul Hiebert (1967) examined the caste rankings of another village in India, using methods similar to those just described. However, in addition to the caste rankings, Hiebert also obtained rankings of a series of *individuals* in terms of their relative prestige. He found that the prestige positions of individuals were not isomorphic with the caste rankings, thus reflecting the fact that caste membership is only one of the determinants of relative prestige in Indian villages (although it is a powerful factor in most cases).

Prestige ranking by informants in caste-structured communities appears to work well because the concept of a hierarchy of status is so pervasive in local social action. In other types of societies prestige ranking may be more difficult, particularly in communities in which there is an ideological commitment to the idea of equality and classlessness. In American communities Warner and his associates (1960) found that informants were quite willing and able to make status distinctions in terms of "classes" and hierarchies, even though there is thought to be a strong commitment to egalitarianism in American cultural traditions. In

Table 3.1. *Class stratification in the Deep South*

Social classes	As seen by upper-class people
Upper upper	"Old aristocracy"
Lower upper	"Aristocracy, but not old"
Upper middle	"Nice respectable people"
Lower middle	"Good people, but 'nobody'"
Upper lower	Poor people
Lower lower	Poor people

Source: Adapted from Warner et al., 1960:19.

several different American communities, Warner found that the status hierarchies were conceptualized in terms of upper, middle, and lower classes, each of which could be subdivided into two parts. The conceptualization of class stratification in the Deep South, for example, was depicted by Warner as in Table 3.1.

In midwestern communities, such as "Jonesville," Warner found that an upper upper class was typically lacking. "Such communities usually have a five-class pyramid, including an upper class, two middle, and two lower classes" (Warner et al., 1960:17).

Index of status characteristics

The categories of general prestige ranking obtained by Warner and associates, as well as similar data obtained by sociologists working in the area of status inequalities, were quite closely related to certain socioeconomic variables that are simultaneously indicators of relative social ranking *and* elements in the differential distribution of scarce resources. The most significant and useful indicators of status in North American communities, in the work of Warner and many other researchers, are occupation, income, education, housing, and dwelling area – in various combinations. Upper-class people generally live in exclusive residential areas, and the opulence of their houses provides material indication of presumed "social merit."

Many anthropologists have noted differences in housing styles in their research communities, but the possibility of using house style and furnishings as indicators of status gradations has not been systematically explored in non-Western ethnographic contexts. (This is surprising, because archeologists have used these indicators with considerable success.) Frequently special domiciles such as palaces of kings, large houses of chiefs, and the like, are mentioned in ethnographic literature as symbols of high status; on the other hand, the lowest social rungs in many societies are at least partially identifiable by their housing styles, which receive labels such as "hovels," "shacks," "slums." Homelessness is often (but not always) an indicator of lowest social position. The relationships of domicile to social ranking are empirical problems that require different solutions in different societies.

Rating by symbolic placement

Of course the suggested status indicators are all symbolic in significant respects, even though houses, occupations, and income have their important pragmatic aspects as well. Some societies – perhaps those that seek to deny *utilitarian* differences in social status, as well as those in which social differences are pervasively salient – provide systems of nonutilitarian symbols in terms of which prestige inequalities are expressed. In some communities in Mexico (particularly in the Mayan areas) a series of religious offices – called *cargos* – with their attendant obligations, including financial expenditures, provide the calculus in terms of which social excellence is measured.

Frank Cancian (1965) has written a detailed analysis of the *cargo* system of the community of Zinacantan. He presents statistical and other evidence for the prestige ranking of the various *cargos*, from the lower level of *mayordomos* and *mayores* (thirty-four different positions) to the three highly prestigious *alcaldes* (Cancian, 1965:29).

Although the *cargos* are ideologically considered equal in that "all *cargos* are in service of the saints, and all service of the saints is equally virtuous," Cancian was able to produce evidence for a close interrelationship between a man's general prestige ranking and the specific *cargo* levels he had served. With this evidence as background, it becomes valid to use the data on "*cargos* served" as a direct, symbolic index of a man's relative social worth in the community. Cancian also demonstrated that his indicator of relative prestige is related positively to socioeconomic status as measured in other ways. Thus socioeconomic privileges tend to follow the lines of differential religious excellence.

Our task at this point is not to provide an exhaustive critique of studies of stratification but to examine *status inequality* as a complex social variable that has been operationalized in several different ways. Following the leads provided by the foregoing examples, a fieldworker who wishes to examine social stratification of status inequalities has several different strategies from which to choose:

1   Ask informants to rank members of the local populations in terms of relative merit, prestige, or social worth.
2   Seek out objective socioeconomic indicators, such as housing style, control of scarce resources, and other significant material possessions, in terms of which to differentiate people.
3   Examine important ritual events for evidence of status differences (e.g., differential roles in religious observances).

The particular combination chosen for intensive work depends on other characteristics of the research situation.

In each of the studies described previously the fieldworker defined a *standardized information-getting system* that provided the socially differentiating *indicators* for a series of individuals and groups in the community. These primary data on differentiation were then organized in terms of scores, index numbers, average ranks, or other means of analysis in order to set out the actual social positions of the research subjects. Although the precise steps have not been given in full detail here, the research procedures of Warner, Freed, Hiebert, and Cancian provide the recipes by means of which other researchers could go to the same communities and establish (with a high degree of probability) the same social hierarchies as those described in the original studies.

In all human societies differential prestige and privilege take manifold forms. Differences in socioeconomic status are expressed in myriad small and large symbolic events, inequalities of action, and status-revealing possessions. Many books have been written about the uncountable ways in which Americans, for example, make evident their status differences. Private schools, expensive summer camps, special license plate numbers, titles, habits of speech, dress fashions, hair styles, body markings, and modes of entertainment (e.g., formal parties) are part of our code of invidious distinctions.

It follows that any operational definition of social stratification represents only a *sample*, at one point in time, of the complex, multidimensional domain intended by the theoretical cover term "social stratification." The researcher selects a small segment of behavior from this general semantic domain and announces that this segment stands for the general theoretical construct that carries the same label. Naturally, the researcher intends the sampling process to be fair or representative.

The word *indicator* has been used here a number of times. This label, too, carries the meaning of sampling from the large, usually unmeasurable universe encompassed by a theoretical concept. Thus footsteps in the snow are operational indicators that "someone went that way"; it takes only a whiff of a peculiar odor to operationalize a danger signal concerning a leaky gas main; the election totals are interpretable as indicators of relative popularity of the candidates, and so on. In each case, the sample or indicator selected should be as nearly as possible an irrefutable surrogate for the concept it represents.

Theory versus reality: the operational compromise

As we emphasized in Chapter 1, our methodological tactics, including various modes of operationalization, provide us with rules and manipulations for transforming low-level observations into theoretical propositions of varying degrees of abstraction. Frequently, a set of theoretical propositions *suggests* a new theoretical relationship, which can be verified only through some kind of empirical investigation. The terms of the theoretical statements provide the concepts that must be operationalized. At this point the realities of the "world out there" strongly affect our selection of research operations; hence specific research techniques represent a compromise between the ideals of theory and the practicalities of given research contexts.

In Cancian's research on economics and prestige in Zinacantan, his theoretical concerns with the matter of prestige probably would have been best satisfied if he could have obtained direct statements about the relative social worth of all adult persons in the community, together with similar rankings of the relative merit attached to each of the religious offices. But the Zinacantecos either would not or could not make such direct prestige ratings for Cancian. Their behavior, however, indicated that they had an organized set of ideas of relative prestige that applied to both persons and religious offices. This difficulty forced Cancian to look for indirect roads to his theoretical goal. The chronicles of field projects can be profitably conceptualized as the often frustrating, trial-and-error searching for adequate research operations that reflect theoretical concerns. Indeed, sometimes theoretical goals are changed because no means of adequate operationalization of the relevant concepts is possible.

Sometimes events and observations in a field-work situation suggest new theoretical propositions to the researcher in such a way that the means for systematic observation become apparent at the same time. Thus the theoretically significant observation that "it looks like most of the vendors in this market are out-of-towners" contains within its logic the research tactic of counting the local vendors and out-of-towners (perhaps by asking them where they have come from), to provide empirical support of the generalization.

Any theoretical hunch that arises during field work takes on meaning only because of a vast, complicated network of social metatheory in terms of which the researcher sees and interprets his world. At the same time, it is useful to admit that the intuiting of new propositions and concepts from the raw materials of field experience can produce important contributions to anthropological theory without in the least resembling the careful theorem testing of classical deduction. Even though field-grown theoretical contributions depend for their structuring on a complex of concepts (often unrecognized) from previous anthropological history and experience, the immediate process at work can be labeled *induction*. And the transformational rules of observation – in the operationalization of variables – are not logically different from those employed in the deductive style of research.

While it is important to note that research operations make sense only in terms of the particular theoretical constructs for which they provide supporting evidence, it is equally relevant to keep in mind that the tasks of operationalizing theoretical concepts are often crucial in sorting out the useful from the meaningless in theoretical discourse. Contentless tautologies and vague confusions of abstract discourse are often best exposed through examination of their operational implications. If a theoretical proposition eludes any sensible pattern of empirical testing, the chances are that the proposition does not make sense, however elegantly phrased. Anthropology, like many other young sciences, includes a number of theoretical disputes for which there are no solutions because the arguments are meaningless.

Summary and conclusions

Anthropologists are certainly among the most eclectic of all social scientists in modes of research. Out of the complex, buzzing confusion of life in human societies the fieldworker picks out *indicators* and traces of behavior complexes in a great many forms. Sometimes an informant's whole lifetime of worldy experiences is operationalized in the form of a few hours of mechanically recorded utterances on magnetic tape. A few days' worth of observations in the cornfields jotted down in field notebooks stands for the thousands of hours of the people's horticultural activities, which are then compressed into one chapter of the ethnographic monograph. For some activities a small amount of direct observation suffices, because the activities are highly patterned and repetitious.

Thus watching (like a human camera) and listening (like a tape recorder) constitute the core elements of practically all operationalized definitions in anthropology. But operationalizing requires specification of *what* was watched or *who* was listened to, under what circumstances. Sometimes a special, standardized stimulus is presented to an informant in order to promote a stream of verbal material that will be interpreted in terms of personality characteristics, cognitive style, or social position.

The products and effects of human behavior are a special and very important set of materials that can be observed systematically as surrogates for conceptual domains. Roads and paths mutely testify to volume of traffic; cartloads of produce stand for economic productivity; rows of lighted candles represent operationalized religion.

In later chapters an inventory of the varieties of field research tools will be presented. This is done so that their respective advantages and disadvantages can be discussed. Special problems of operationalization arise when cross-cultural comparative research is carried out by means of the systematic use of data from a number of different ethnographic sources. Operational definitions then become transformational rules whereby pieces of information from ethnographies are selected in a standard, intersubjectively replicable manner.

Before we move on to a discussion of various field research tools and techniques, one very general, all-encompassing methodological question should be examined. Much discussion has taken place in recent years concerning the relative validity and methodological usefulness of the insider's (native's) view versus the outsider's (the objective scientist's) categorizations as main organizing principles of cultural behavior. Chapter 4 is devoted to this special problem.

4 Units of observation: emic and etic approaches

In anthropology we want our concepts to be useful in the construction of more and more inclusive and successful theoretical systems. The success of both concepts and broader theoretical structures is measured in terms of their efficacy in explaining human behavior. In recent years there has been a growing feeling among anthropologists that our science has been progressing too slowly toward successful explanation of human behavior. As a result, critical attention has been focused on aspects of anthropological method.

One diagnosis that has been offered for the theoretical and methodological crisis in anthropology is that our problems grow out of a particular kind of weakness in the strategy of conceptualization used in most ethnographic descriptions. According to this view, cultural behavior should always be studied and categorized in terms of the inside view – the actors' definition – of human events. That is, the units of conceptualization in anthropological theories should be "discovered" by analyzing the cognitive processes of the people studied, rather than "imposed" from cross-cultural (hence ethnocentric) classifications of behavior. This point of view has been variously referred to as "the New Ethnography," "ethnoscience," or "ethnosemantics."

The contrast between ethnosemantics and other anthropological methodologies has often been expressed as the opposition between "emic" and "etic" approaches to classification. The terms appear to have been coined by Kenneth Pike. He stated the idea as follows:

In contrast to the Etic approach, an Emic one is in essence valid for only one language (or one culture) at a time. . . . It is an attempt to *discover* and to describe the pattern of that particular language or culture in reference to the way in which the various elements of that culture are related to each other in the functioning of the particular pattern, rather than an attempt to describe them in reference to a generalized classification derived in advance of the study of that culture. (Pike, 1954:8.) . . .

An etic analytical standpoint . . . might be called "external" or "alien," since for etic purposes the analyst stands "far enough away" from or "outside" of a particular culture to see its separate events, primarily in relation to their similarities and their differences, as compared to events in other cultures, rather than in reference to the sequences of classes of events within that one particular culture. (Ibid., 10.) . . .

Etic criteria have the appearance of absolutes, within the range of sensitivity of the measuring instrument (or the expertness of the analyst); emic criteria savor more of relativity, with the sameness of activity determined in reference to a particular system of activity. (Ibid., 11.)

The emic approach

The development of an emic approach to anthropological methods owes its origins to certain important features of the Boasian historical school. Much of Franz Boas's teaching of ethnological methods emphasized the importance of collecting data in the form of verbatim texts from informants in order to preserve the original (i.e., "native") meaning of the information. The emicists' view of anthropological classification is clearly stated by Boas:

In natural sciences we are accustomed to demand a classification of phenomena expressed in a concise and unambiguous terminology. The same term should have the same meaning everywhere. We should like to see the same in anthropology. As long as we do not overstep the limits of one culture we are able to classify its features in a clear and definite terminology. We know what we mean by the terms family, state, government, etc. As soon as we overstep the limits of one culture we do not know in how far these may correspond to equivalent concepts. If we choose to apply our classification to alien cultures we may combine forms that do not belong together. The very rigidity of definition may lead to a misunderstanding of the essential problems involved. . . . If it is our serious purpose to understand the thoughts of a people the whole analysis of experience must be based on their concepts, not ours. (Boas, 1943:314.)

Edward Sapir expressed approximately the same point of view:

It is impossible to say what a person is doing unless we have tacitly accepted the essentially arbitrary modes of interpretation that social tradition is constantly suggesting to us from the very moment of our birth. Let anyone who doubts this try the experiment of making a painstaking report of the actions of a group of natives engaged in some form of activity, say religious, to which he has not the cultural key. If he is a skillful writer, he may succeed in giving a picturesque account of what he sees and hears, or thinks he sees and hears, but the chances of his being able to give a relation of what happens in terms that would be intelligible and acceptable to the natives themselves are practically nil. He will be guilty of all manner of distortion. His emphasis will be constantly askew. He will find interesting what the natives take for granted as a casual kind of behavior worthy of no particular comment, and he will utterly fail to observe the crucial turning points in the course of action that give formal significance to the whole in the minds of those who do possess the key to its understanding. . . . Forms and significances which seem obvious to an outsider will be denied outright by those who carry out the patterns; outlines and implications that are perfectly clear to these may be absent to the eye of the onlooker. (Sapir, 1927, reprinted in Mandelbaum, 1949:546–7.)

Sapir's statement is similar to the position of some later emicists in that it involves an apparent denial of the idea of definitional relativity in adjudging the correctness or adequacy of concepts. Instead of assessing conceptual categories in terms of their relevance for theoretical problems, he adopts the assumption that the *native's categorization of behavior is the only correct one.*

Some of the more important programmatic statements concerning an emic approach to ethnography have been made by Frake (1962), Gladwin and Sturtevant (1962), Goodenough (1956, 1970), and Sturtevant (1964). Frake has outlined the basic assumptions and methods of a thoroughly emic approach to ethnography. "The basic methodological concept advocated here – the determination of the set of contrasting responses appropriate to a given, culturally valid, eliciting context – should ultimately be applicable to the 'semantic' analysis of any culturally meaningful behavior" (Frake, 1962:76). As a first step, the anthropologist must identify particular "segregates" – the meaningful behavioral items that are grouped together as sets of contrasting responses. Frake suggested that such forms will be found by observing verbal behavior, particularly in bounded sociolinguistic contexts. To illustrate he suggested that observations at an American lunch counter are likely to result in an identification of segregates such as "ham 'n cheese sandwich," "hamburger," "cheeseburger," and "hot dog." Identifying all the segregates that are substitutable for one another (the alternatives within a given type of "something to eat") results in the production of a "contrast set." The construction of logically arranged hierarchies of terms related to a given semantic domain (e.g., "something to eat") results in a taxonomy. Frake's illustrative taxonomy from the lunch counter is shown in Figure 4.1:

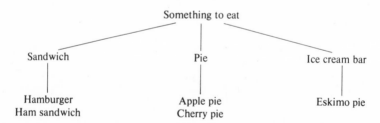

Figure 4.1. Something to eat (adapted from Frake, 1962:80).

After the anthropologist has identified this kind of taxonomy of segregates in a contrast set, it is essential to find the relevant "attributes" that distinguish the items from one another. As Frake pointed out, a hamburger can vary a great deal in a number of characteristics yet still be identifiable as a hamburger. Addition of a piece of cheese, however, changes it into a cheeseburger. Analysis of the attributes that distinguish segregates at particular levels of contrast permit the ethnographer to identify the dimensions of contrast that supposedly have semantic and cognitive significance. The systematic study of semantic domains is often called "componential analysis."

For Frake this method of analysis has as its goal the development of an "operationally explicit methodology for discerning how people construe their world of experience from the way they talk about it" (Frake, 1962:74). The method has been most frequently used in the analysis of kinship systems (Goodenough, 1956, 1965; Wallace and Atkins, 1960; Wallace, 1965; etc.), but it has also been utilized for describing color categories (Conklin, 1955), weddings (Metzger and Williams, 1963), religious behavior (Conklin, 1964), firewood (Metzger and Williams, 1966), ingredients for beer making (Frake, 1964b), and many other semantic domains.

The method, as applied to a specific field problem in another culture, is well illustrated by Metzger and Williams's (1966) report on the study of native Tzeltal categories of firewood. From systematic interviewing the researchers found that the Tzeltal speakers of Tenejapa (Mexico) conceptualize "the things of mother-earth" to be divisible into "people," "animals," and "trees-and-plants." One sub-category of "trees-and-plants," that of "trees/wood," was examined (Metzger and Williams, 1966:394) in terms of the contrast set of mutually exclusive uses consisting of:

1 house-(building) wood
2 axe handle
3 pruning-fork handle
4 hoe handle
5 dibble
6 (forked stick suspended from ceiling on which clothing, etc., is hung)
7 bench
. . .
18 bridge
19 firewood
20 charcoal

The category *firewood*, it was found, can be internally differentiated by a set of criteria referring to "good" and "poor" firewood, as shown in Table 4.1.

Table 4.1. *Criteria of firewood evaluation*

Lek ("good")	*Ma Lekuk* ("poor")
"hard wood"	"soft wood"
"be hard"	"be (middling) soft"
"burns strongly"	"burns quickly"
"burns strongly" (an alternative form)	"burns quickly" (an alternative form)
"dries rapidly"	"dries slowly"
"its fire is hot"	"its fire is only little hot"

Source: Adapted from Metzger and Williams, 1966.

The grounds for these differential evaluations of good versus poor firewood were discovered through the systematic application of "frames" (questions) in the form of "Why is————good (as firewood)?" and "Why is————not good (as firewood)?"

Additional information about the domain *firewood* was structured in terms of "consequences of burning certain varieties of wood," "lengths" and "dimensions" of firewood, and so on. Metzger and Williams were able to show by means of this systematic questioning technique that each of three cultural groups – the Tzeltal-speaking Indians, their Spanish-speaking *ladino* neighbors, and the Tzotzil-speaking Indians in the neighboring *municipio* of Chamula – has a somewhat different system for classifying and evaluating firewood, even though there are no differences in the kinds of wood/trees available to the groups. For example, the Spanish-speaking informants "are able to name or recognize fewer varieties, differentiate among fewer varieties, and in some instances make different allocations of class membership" (p. 402).

It is important to consider the methodological and theoretical issues involved in the emic method of research because at least some of the practitioners appear to claim that it is the only sound basis for progress in cultural anthropology. Sturtevant (1964:101) stated, for example, that "ethnoscience shows promise as the New Enthnography required to advance the whole of cultural anthropology," adding that it "raises the standards of reliability, validity, and exhaustiveness of ethnography." A pessimistic note is added by Sturtevant's admission that:

One result is that the ideal goal of a complete ethnography is farther removed from practical attainment. The full ethnoscientific description of a single culture would require many thousands of pages published after many years of intensive field work based on ethnographic methods more complete and more advanced than are now available. (Ibid., 123.)

Considering our earlier analysis of the relationships between theory and method in anthropology (and science generally), we should raise this question: What theoretical problems are the "emicists" attempting to solve? It would appear that the method has some pertinence to the general problem of describing folk taxonomic systems. However, as proponents of a new kind of taxonomic system for the analysis of *all* human behavior, the emicists have thus far provided little in the way of a general theoretical framework.

Although the ethnoscientists have offered no comprehensive statement of theory in connection with their methodological practices, we can nonetheless look at some of the pieces of theory, explicit and implicit, imbedded in their works. They are explicit in pointing out that their main assumptions are derived from linguistics. This theoretical model is one that generally assumes formal patterns or "mechanical models" of behavior rather than probabilistic or statistical patterning. It is usually assumed that there *is one "right" description of, or logical organization of, a given semantic domain* (say, kinship or plants) and that all or most of the members of a given society know that particular system. The ethnoscientists, therefore, have tended to be unconcerned with intracultural variations in peoples' uses of taxonomic categories.

A comprehensive criticism of the emicist approach has been presented by Marvin Harris (1964, 1968, 1974). Concerning the general assumption of cognitive or semantic homogeneity of populations, Harris described his own experience in eliciting puzzling variations of kin terms among the Bathonga:

What I encountered in some of my "ill-informed informants" was an even greater measure of confusion. Thus, while Junod attributed the substitution of the grandfather term (*kokwana*) for mother's brother (*malume*) as a dialect difference, I kept running across people who insisted that both *malume* and *kokwana* were appropriate! . . . It may be that these variations can be handled as subcultural or dialect differences taking place inside different heads. On the other hand, it is equally plausible that these variations take place inside the same head. Indeed, this is true for many Bathonga in the modern situation. If that is the case, then an "adequate" ethnography must express the ambiguity of the system, and it must do so statistically. (Harris, 1968:586.)

He makes a similar critique of Goodenough's (1965) (and others') analyses of "the American kinship system."

Goodenough's assumptions need to be tested against sample population responses under standardized conditions. . . . None of the attempts to define the basic cognitive features of American kinship terminology has thus far made concessions to the possibility that ambiguity is one of the salient characteristics of this domain. (Ibid., 587.)

In the area of nonverbal behavior the assumptions of cultural homogeneity and unambiguity become strained even more than they were in the matter of folk taxonomies.

If permitted to develop unchecked, the tendency to write ethnographies in accord with the emic rules of behavior will result in an unintentional parody of the human condition. Applied to our own culture it would conjure up a way of life in which men tip their hats to ladies; youths defer to old people in public conveyances; unwed mothers are a rarity; citizens go to the aid of law enforcement officers . . . television repairmen fix televisions sets . . . [etc.]. (Ibid., 590.)

Granted that Harris's caricature is not altogether fair to the methods and assumptions of the ethnoscientists, it nonetheless clearly points up a central problem – that of intracultural variations, which requires answers to questions of representativeness of informants, statistical examination of data, and a host of related methodological issues.

In addition to the matters of homogeneity versus heterogeneity of cultural behavior patterns, many of the emicists appear to assume an excessively idealistic theory of human behavior. They place strong emphasis on the power of ideas and language forms as causal factors in human affairs. This tendency is evident in the frequent statements by the emicists that equate understanding of native categories of thought with predictability of cultural behavior. The importance of idea systems – for example, ideologies and religious-belief systems – cannot be denied, but any adequate description of human cultural behavior must surely involve careful consideration of nonlanguage factors, such as material conditions, social relationships, and technological equipment as part of the explanatory frame of reference.

The eticists

Marvin Harris: observing the stream of behavior

The problems that have been raised by the emicists are thrown into sharper relief when we examine the methodological suggestions of the eticists. As the most outspoken critic of the emicists, Marvin Harris has proposed a "new ethnography" of his own.

Harris's point of departure for studying human behavior is the classification of body motions, in terms of the effects these motions have on the environment. Hence his minimal unit of analysis is the "actone," which "is a behavioral bit consisting of body motion and environmental effect which rise above the threshold of the observer's auditory and visual senses" (ibid., 37). In beginning his observations with these relatively microscopic units, Harris admits that "when the observer is confronted by a multi-actor situation, there will be many intervals during which he will be unable to note the actones of all the people within his field of vision. Recourse to a second or third observer and to motion picture cameras and tape recorders will solve part of this problem" (ibid., 45).

Table 4.2 is a sample list of actone classes (actonemes) suggested by Harris. In

Table 4.2. *Actone classes*

Actoneme	Body part	Body motion	Environmental effect
carry	hand	hand moves horizontally while fingers grasp	object moves horizontally
drink	mouth	mouth opens	liquid disappears inside mouth
drop	fingers	fingers open	object falls
pick up	hand	hand elevated while fingers grasp	object is raised
poke	hand	hand moves down rapidly, fingers grasping	object moves down rapidly

Source: Adapted from Harris, 1964:47–9

giving these examples, Harris notes that there are a great many words in ordinary language that are relatively specific in meaning (hence operationalizable) as contrasted with other classes of words that are useless for precise description (e.g., *beautify, celebrate, betray*).

Harris suggests that "episodes" can be built up from chains of actones. These consist of the combination of actone with information about actor-type, object-type, time, and place (the "stage coordinates" of analysis). Such episodes can, by observation, be linked in "episode chains," in which certain episodes may be analyzed as "nodes" because they are the "logico-physical functional requisites" of the given chain. Such functionally requisite behaviors are identifiable in cases in which "one may retrospectively assert, on the basis of simple logico-physical principles, that the later episodes could not have occurred unless the antecedent episodes had occurred" (ibid., 78).

The next higher taxonomic levels in Harris's methodology are nodal chains, mono- and multi-actor "scenes" and then "serials." At this point, Harris is able to bring his detailed microobservational terminology to bear on the identification of operationally valid groups, in terms of which he can discuss social structure, social relations, and other larger questions.

In his criticism of the emic analysis of behavior, Harris, as we have noted, is insistent that verbal behavior requires a style of treatment different from the analysis of nonverbal behavior. Most important, he feels that the actors' verbal descriptions should *not* be used as the main evidence for actual behavior, though he points out that actors' verbal descriptions are useful sources of information about where to look and what to expect in observations of complex scenes.

As for the more detailed noting of language behavior, Harris feels that verbal analysis of scenes makes possible the separation of these observational units into subtypes. For example, two closely similar scenes identified as academic "classes" can be distinguished as "class on Chaucer" and "class on social stratification" on the basis of verbal content.

From the point of view of Harris and other theorists a truly etic research methodology must be based on intensive, first-hand observation – eyewitnessing – of human behavior. Some researchers have introduced videotape procedures in order to record actual behavior for later analysis. In the most ambitious of these videotape projects, Harris and associates contracted with families in New York to set up TV cameras in their homes, in order to observe the day-by-day actions of selected families far more intensively than would be possible by live, flesh-and-blood field observers. The raw data of this project consist of hundreds of hours of videotaped action. (It is noteworthy that the volunteer families soon got used to the omnipresent electronic surveillance and carried on their daily rounds with little apparent deviation from their usual patterns.)

DeHavenon (1975) analyzed authority relationships and other dimensions of behavior in the New York videotapes and found, for example, that assessments of authority could be made from the ways that family members interact in relation to food. She also noted that family members, when interviewed about their eating habits, were quite inaccurate about details of their food-use behavior. They may have some expectations of norms or standards of eating, but these expectations are frequently modified by external contingencies. There have been a number of other studies that have employed detailed, etic analyses of ongoing behavior (Erickson, 1975; O. Johnson, 1975; Silverberg, 1975). Invariably these intensive research efforts have demonstrated that:

1 There are, indeed, significant discrepancies between what people do and what they say they do (hence between more-or-less emic and strictly etic observational results).
2 Fully etic research requires inordinate time commitments, so that the payoff in terms of completed research has been slim thus far. (The same generalization applies, of course, to carefully constructed emic work.)

Emic, etic, and the goals of anthropology

The basic differences in methodology and theory between emic and etic approaches can be generally summarized as follows (allowing for some discrepancies introduced by differences in definitions of those elusive terms):

	Emic	Etic
1	Primary method is interviewing, in depth, in the native language.	Primary method is observation of behavior.
2	Intent is to seek the categories of *meanings*, as nearly as possible in the ways "the natives define things."	Intent is to seek patterns of behavior, as defined by the observer.
3	The people's definitions of meaning, their idea systems, are seen as the most important "causes" or explanations of behavior.	Impersonal, nonideational factors, especially material conditions, are seen as significant movers of human action.
4	Systems and patterns are identified through logical analysis, especially by a quasi-linguistic analysis of contrast sets.	Systems and patterns are identified through quantitative analysis of events and actions.
5	Cross-cultural generalizations must wait for the *conversion* of culturally specific patterns and meanings into more abstracted, intercultural categories.	Cross-cultural generalizations *can* be made directly, by applying the same methods of observation, with the same outside-derived concepts, to two or more different cultures.
6	The methodological strategy is fundamentally inductive, for research cannot proceed until the "natives' categories of meaning" have been *discovered*.	The methodological strategy can range from "pure induction" to various mixtures of inductive and deductive research.

The contrasts between emicists and eticists have been examined at some length in order to put into perspective what is probably the single most important theoretical disagreement in cultural anthropology – one that involves the foundations of all our methodological procedures. If either the emic or the etic side of the argument is overwhelmingly correct in its assertions, the work of the other must be regarded as nearly worthless. The main directions of future anthropological strategy are clearly involved in the controversy.

Most anthropologists do not consider themselves to be either completely emic or unalterably etic, although many researchers see themselves as adhering to Malinowski's directive "to grasp the native's point of view, his relation to life, to realize *his* vision of *his* world" (Malinowski, 1922:25). But that is not the only task. Having grasped the "native's point of view," most anthropologists also go on to study actual behavior in relation to more general theoretical problems.

To some extent the degree of emicism of method that a particular researcher uses reflects the degree of abstraction or generality of his or her theoretical perspective. Grand theorists, working for an all-encompassing view of human evolution, do not linger long over specific behavioral or cultural details, whether emically or etically derived. On the other hand, field anthropologists usually find that they need a wide variety of methods in order to acquire enough information to present a well-rounded account of the community, society, or other unit of study. This applies even in the case of problem-oriented research, for in most cases the testing of specific hypotheses requires a descriptive, ethnographic context within which the focus on a small number of key propositions can be made meaningful.

For some anthropologists a crucial difference between emic and etic data is identifiable from the researcher's *purposes*. When the intention is to identify the peoples' cognitive, *ideational categories*, the data from a structured interview are emic. When the structured interview is intended as an approximation of *real behavior* and materials (e.g., Who are the members of this household? What are the sources of income in this household?), the data are incorporated in a basically etic research strategy.

The variations, ambiguities, and gradations in definitions of emic and etic are particularly apparent in the case of structured interview schedules, which are increasingly common in contemporary field work. Because any structured interview depends on people's verbal responses (rather than direct observation), it may be considered emic according to the definition used by Harris. But structured interviews are frequently devised by fieldworkers from their own (observers') theoretical perspective and are interpreted according to anthropological (rather than "native") categories. Such is the case, for example, when the researcher derives indices of modernization, "cosmopoliteness," or other theoretical dimensions. These categories are hardly native definitions of reality, and from the perspective of Kenneth Pike (see earlier) structured interviews could be regarded as fundamentally etic in nature.

If the fieldworker has elicited the local terminology and categories of some domain through intensive interviewing, and then incorporated these emic data, along with etic constructs, in a comprehensive interview schedule, the resulting data would appear to be a thorough mixture of emic and etic. Many field researchers test hypotheses by using combinations of emic and etic data. For example, in research on the effects of technological change in a rural Mexican village, B. R. DeWalt (1975) ranked a series of households in terms of their material possessions (an etic measure of stratification). He also obtained a wealth ranking of the same households from two key informants (an emic method). These two measures correlated with one another. DeWalt felt that the two somewhat different indices of socioeconomic stratification were both significant expressions of the underlying differentiation, so he combined these measures, along with cash income, to create a composite measure of stratification.

Intracultural variation in emic categories

Much of the ethnosemantic work of the 1960s was based on intensive interviewing of a few key informants, which produced taxonomic systems that were conceptualized as *the* cultural system, applicable to the entire community or population speaking that particular language. This uniformist presentation of peoples' cognitive styles has been significantly modified by demonstrations of intragroup variations in many contexts. Stanley and Ruth Freed (1970) reported significant variations in Navajo versions of kinship terminology; Sankoff (1971) found that the Buang people of northeastern New Guinea assigned individuals to specific kin groups in different ways, and there were also differences of opinion with regard to the assignment of land plots to particular kin groups. Stephen Tyler demonstrated variations in kin term usage among the Koya people of India, depending on "social setting, audience composition, sex and age of speaker/hearer, linguistic repertoires of speaker/hearer, and – most difficult of all – something that might be called the speaker's intention" (Tyler, 1966:704–5).

One of the most comprehensive studies of intracultural diversity to date is Richard Pollnac's work among the Baganda. Examining variations in color terminology, he found it was possible to divide the 180 respondents into no fewer than eight different subgroups on the basis of similarities and differences in cognitive categories. These differences reflected variations in education, sex, residence, frequency of travel, and other social factors (Pollnac, 1975).

Since Pollnac's work among the Baganda was based on a large sample, a skeptic might suggest that the variability of responses was due to variations in interviewing. In any case, skeptical or not, we might ask, what kinds of intragroup variation are found through *intensive* ethnosemantic analysis? Terence Hays (1974) studied the ethnobotany of the Ndumba people of highland New Guinea, using the intensive methodological procedures of ethnosemantics. His informants were five men and five women, each of whom possessed a lexicon of over 1,000 plant names! A core lexicon of 971 named plants was more or less shared by the ten informants, while another 311 plants were variable in name, taxonomy, modes of use, and other information. Sex differences accounted for some of the diversity, but Hays felt that a dichotomy of "male" and "female culture" would be an oversimplification; hence "a significant proportion of Ndumba plant names can be judged referentially ambiguous for the informants as a group" (Hays, 1974:2). Hays's research is especially significant because his field techniques were fully *emic* in the sense intended by Pike, Goodenough, and other ethnosemanticists.

The *intra*cultural variations now coming to light have introduced a new, dynamic dimension into *emic* studies, at the same time introducing significant modification of the earlier monolithic view of cultural causation. With the demonstration that peoples' cognitive maps are affected by a variety of economic and social factors, the older assumption that cultural ideas shape (cause) behavior is no longer tenable in most contexts, and the once clear differences between emic and etic assumptions are somewhat blurred.

Conclusions

Anthropologists are frequently in a position where they must ask questions, and note information about research communities, in terms derived from cross-cultural ethnological theory and from their own special research hypotheses. In these cases fieldworkers do not wait to extract native categories of experience through full emic processes. They assume that for purposes of testing theory and hypotheses, *some* of the outsiders' definitions of significant actions or cultural categories are useful. They do not, on the other hand, ignore completely the question of the local insiders' definitions and categorizations of behavior.

The test of correctness of field research strategies is the same – its empirically determined productivity. The complete outsider's set of survey questions put to a sample of the local populace is often empty of meaning and devoid of predictive utility – the questions are out of touch with the definitions of reality operative in the local scene. But the local people are not invariably better than the ethnographer in categorizing their own social reality, for the simple reasons that: (1) they are not social scientists and (2) their (arbitrary) categorizations were not constructed for the purpose of cross-cultural study of behavioral systems. When we keep in mind that no one taxonomy of cultural behavior (or any other semantic domain) can be inherently correct, and when we note that componential analyses and other ethnoscientific styles of study have often demonstrated that *several alternative interpretations or taxonomic styles are possible* (Goodenough, 1956; Burling, 1964; Wallace, 1965), we are in a position to adopt a freewheeling pragmatism in our modes of categorizing cultural observations. Following Kaplan, the only useful test of our classifications is in the successes and failures of hypothesis testing and theory building.

This is the strategy that will be adopted in our examination of research methods. Neither the insider nor the outsider in the cultural scene has the final answers for appropriate categories and definitions of behavioral facts. The appropriate categories depend on their predictive consequences in research. But the fieldworker must be able to judge – and his critics must be able to interpret – the consequences of conceptual strategies. Hence one must operationalize definitions of cultural terms in such a manner that hindsight can adjust for misjudgment. When the fieldworker needs to examine precise details of behavior in a number of action settings, he will find the suggestions of Harris and other eticists extremely useful. When theoretical tasks require careful analysis of the natives' categorization of behavior, and of the world around them, then the techniques of the ethnosemanticists will be of great importance. Many research questions require both techniques for their solution.

On the other hand, most important theoretical questions in anthropology involve cross-cultural comparison, and such comparisons by definition require etic categories and styles of data gathering. While emic studies, through componential or other semantic analysis, often provide significant guides to realistic native definitions of units of observation, these must be fitted to the researcher's cross-cultural (etic) concepts in order to test general propositions about human behavior.

5 Tools of research – I

For every scientific concept there are likely to be a number of alternative procedures available for observing, or operationalizing, the relevant phenomena. For example, the concept *strength of electrical current* can be operationalized in measurements of heat change, intensity of light, electrical shock felt by a person, changes in speed of a motor, changes in magnetic fields, and so forth. The same idea applies in anthropology, and it is often useful to employ more than one measure or mode of observation in the study of particular cultural institutions. This is the principle of multi-instrument research. The anthropological fieldworker, therefore, must have a number of different research tools in his or her field kit. Unlike the situation in the laboratory sciences, research tools in anthropology involve relatively little in the way of hardware and gadgetry but require great sensitivity and self-awareness on the part of the investigator. The fieldworker is the principal research instrument, and the various methods of investigation are alternative techniques for objectifying and standardizing the fieldworker's perceptions.

The research tools to be discussed in this chapter and the following one are the most frequently encountered techniques of anthropological investigation. It is not a complete inventory, however, and every fieldworker should be constantly alert to the possibilities of developing new modes of observation to supplement the standard items. Usually, new field-work techniques are refinements or modifications of one or the other of these main techniques. A corollary of this statement is that in practically every instance of field research, the techniques employed – whether questionnaires, projective tests, specialized behavioral observations, or modes of informal interviewing – must be adapted by the fieldworker to the special requirements of the local scene. There are no ready-made instruments.

Participant observation

Soon after I had established myself in Omarakana Trobriand Islands, I began to take part, in a way, in the village life, to look forward to the important or festive events, to take personal interest in the gossip and the developments of the village occurrences; to wake up every morning to a day, presenting itself to me more or less as it does to the natives. I would get out from under my mosquito net, to find around me the village life beginning to stir, or the people well advanced in their working day according to the hour or also the season, for they get up and begin their labors early or late, as work presses. As I went on my morning walk through the village, I could see intimate details of family life, of toilet, cooking, taking of meals; I could see the arrangements for the day's work, people starting on their errands, or groups of men and women busy at some manufacturing tasks. Quarrels, jokes, family scenes, events usually trivial, sometimes dramatic but always significant, form the atmosphere of my daily life, as well as of theirs. It must be remembered that the natives saw me constantly every day, they ceased to be interested or alarmed, or made self-conscious by my presence, and I ceased to be a disturbing element in the tribal life which I was to study, altering it by my very approach, as always happens with a newcomer to every savage community. In fact, as they knew that I would thrust my nose into everything, even where a well-mannered native would not dream of intruding, they finished by regarding me as a part and parcel of their life, a necessary evil or nuisance, mitigated by donations of tobacco.

Later on in the day, whatever happened was in easy reach, and there was no possibility of its escaping my notice. Alarms about the sorcerer's approach in the evening, one or two big, really important quarrels and rifts within the community, cases of illness, attempted cures and deaths, magical rites which had to be performed, all these I had not to pursue, fearful of missing them, but they took place under my very eyes, at my own doorstep, so to speak. And it must be emphasized whenever anything dramatic or important occurs it is essential to investigate it at the very moment of happening, because the natives cannot but talk about it, are too excited to be reticent, and too interested to be mentally lazy in supplying details. Also, over and over again, I committed breaches of etiquette, which the natives, familiar enough with me, were not slow in pointing out. I had to learn how to behave, and to a certain extent, I acquired "the feeling" for native good and bad manners. With this, and with the capacity of enjoying their company and sharing some of their games and amusements, I began to feel that I was indeed in touch with the natives, and this is certainly the preliminary condition of being able to carry on successful field work. (Malinowski, 1961:7–8.)

Malinowski's famous statement illustrates the central role of participant observation in effective field work. Participation is, of course, a matter of degree; even the casual adventurer or traveler participates, if only momentarily, in the lives of local people. The anthropological fieldworker, Malinowski stressed, should totally immerse himself in the lives of the people; and that can only be done through months of residence in the local community. Whenever possible the fieldworker should master the language of the people, though much of the behavior available for observation is nonverbal. Residence in the research community ensures, as Malinowski suggests, that the fieldworker observes details of daily life and activity enacted by people who have become relatively indifferent to, and unabashed by, the presence of a foreigner. The fieldworker sees elements of daily life repeated over and over again; they become commonplace.

Part of the fieldworker's ethnographic knowledge becomes imbedded in his or her own daily routines. Many of the habits and concerns of the local people are internalized. Fieldworkers differ a great deal in the extent to which they take on local cultural characteristics, as "going native" has its disadvantages as well as advantages for effective research. But it is difficult to overestimate the importance of the information that the anthropologist accumulates through direct participation.

The relatively unsystematized scanning of information through participant observation is basic to all the other, more refined, research techniques. Preliminary data from participant observations provide the fieldworker with insights and clues necessary for developing interview questions, psychological tests, or other more specialized research tools. Participant observation also provides the further checking and monitoring of field information that is necessary for evaluating data gathered by the specialized techniques. The chronicle of a field project usually consists of the interplay between participant observation and the other modes of data collection.

Every individual is a participant observer – if not of other cultures, then at least of one's own. But the typical nonanthropological resident in a foreign community usually returns to his native haunts with a very unsystematic and incomplete picture of the scene he has observed. Field work requires much more than simply being there and passively watching what people are about. Often the fieldworker, in observing a particular pattern of behavior or an event, must find out a great deal more about that event than can be observed firsthand. His personal theoretical frame of reference suggests questions to ask; relationships of this event to other types of data must be explored; and a host of other materials must be considered in order to make individual observations useful. In cases in which the fieldworker feels that a significant block of information is available simply through observation of a particular type of event, he may nonetheless need to devise ways of ensuring the representativeness and objectivity of the observations in a series of repetitions of the given event. By structuring observations and systematically exploring relationships among different events – through interviewing, meticulous eyewitnessing, and perhaps administering "tests" – participant observation can be converted to scientific use.

Another important difference between field work and casual observation is in the recording of what is seen and heard. Memory cannot be trusted. Often the meticulous recording of observations, during and after they occur, can take nearly as much time as the events themselves.

Some individuals are keen observers, whereas others fail to notice or remember many of the details to which they are exposed. Some individuals are excellent witnesses and can provide detailed play-by-play descriptions of actions at which they were present. People differ with regard to which aspects of scenes and events most capture their interest and are thus subject to clear recall. For example, American women seem better than men at recalling details of clothing, colors, and features of decoration and adornment. Professional cooks notice food and cooking equipment that escape the eye of the novice, and farmers notice details of agricultural technique that city people miss. Every individual has areas of special interest and expertise that affect habits of observation.

Each anthropologist needs to become aware of his or her own strengths and weaknesses in observational style. One should practice observing and recording events in order to discover observational biases and to develop more systematic techniques of recall. One should find out how extensive note-taking must be in order to ensure accuracy of recall. One must learn to direct attention to features that tend to be neglected. Habits of participant observation are, of course, closely nterrelated with theoretical orientation. An anthropologist trained in ecological theory will certainly view a feast or ceremonial action differently than would the anthropologist who is concerned with processes of symbolic analysis.

Theoretical systems provide the concepts and frames of reference for pigeon-holing observations. The fieldworker must examine with great care the nature of the classifications and concepts employed in field observation. A constant danger is the quick leap to abstraction. Primary reporting of concrete events and things in field work should proceed at as low a level of abstraction as possible. Thus observational statements such as, "The two men were very hostile toward one another" or "The building was rather dilapidated," are overly general statements; they may seem perfectly adequate to the fieldworker at the time one writes them, but they will be difficult to interpret in later months when the fieldworker sits down to sort out and analyze these notes.

Language of observation in field work

The following paired comparisons of (hypothetical) field-note entries illustrate some differences between overgeneralized reporting and notes that preserve the sense evidence on which descriptive generalizations are based:

	Vague notes	Concrete notes
1	A showed hostility toward B.	A scowled and spoke harshly to B, saying a number of negative things, including "Get the hell out of here, Mr. B." He then shook his fist in B's face and walked out of the room.
2	The boy was very uneasy in the presence of the strangers.	In the presence of these strangers, the boy appeared to be very uneasy. He shifted from one foot to the other, stammered while he spoke, and his voice was so low he could hardly be heard. He kept picking at a scab on his left arm. When the strangers began to walk toward the house, he ran behind the house and disappeared.

3 The house was very dilapidated in appearance.	Compared to many houses in the community this house appeared quite dilapidated. The part of the roof that was covered with tar paper had a number of large rips in it. The corrugated iron sheet on the part of the roof closest to the road was awry, with part of it hanging down over the eaves. The log foundations of the house leaned markedly toward the west. Two windows were broken, and there were several holes in the floor of the main room where rotted floor boards had been broken in and not replaced (etc.).
4 The child was angry because the neighbor children would not let him play with them.	The child told me he was angry because the neighbor children would not let him play with them. He said he had gone toward the X (neighbor's) house with his bows and arrows, but K and L (neighbor's children) had chased him away shouting insults at him.

These examples direct our attention to some points that fieldworkers must keep constantly in mind in the course of their research.

1   Our language in both ordinary usage and theoretical terms is full of concepts that are used as "cover terms" for a wide range of different specific actions and conditions. The observations to which cover terms such as *hostile, uneasy, indifferent, hospitable,* and so on, refer may range from simple verbal statements or paralinguistic hints to violent overt action.
2   These general cover terms have very little meaning except as qualities assessed in relation to other events of the same type. Thus it is extremely easy for an individual fieldworker to be misled by personal cultural biases in judging whether a particular action is hostile, indifferent, and so on.
3   When judgments in terms of vague categories are inserted into field-work reports, the standard of comparison on which the judgment is based should also be inserted. Thus if one judges that a particular house is *dilapidated,* it is important to note whether the judgment is in relation to other houses in the immediate neighborhood or whether the fieldworker is using his own society as a reference point.
4   A commonplace that is often ignored by fieldworkers is the fact that a statement by an informant should not be accepted at face value as a statement of truth. Even if the informant's statement seems plausible, it is best to record the observation simply as, "The informant said that. . . ."
5   Thus in every case the fieldworker should describe *the observations themselves* rather than the low-level inferences derived from the observations.

Key-informant interviewing

One of the mainstays of earlier anthropological work was the use of key informants as sources of information about their cultures. This methodology has been, of course, indispensable for recovering information about ways of living that have ceased to exist, or have been sharply modified, by the time the fieldworker arrives on the scene. Thus most of the available descriptions of American Indian culture were reconstructed from informants' statements about a past way of life that was no longer in existence at the time of the anthropologist's field work. Direct observation was not possible, so the remaining source of available information was the recall of individuals who *had* been participants in the given culture.

From our experience with our fellow humans we know that individuals vary a great deal with regard to their knowledge and interpretations of their own social and cultural systems. People differ greatly in the extensiveness of their vocabularies; some of our peers appear to be walking books of etiquette, whereas others blunder about through ignorance of accepted practice. In the great variety of adaptive techniques and tools, some individuals are widely knowledgeable, whereas others seem dependent on their fellows for information concerning routine things. Most important, we notice that humans differ in their willingness as well as their capabilities for verbally expressing cultural information. Consequently, the anthropologist usually finds that only a small number of individuals in any community are good key informants.

Some of the capabilities of key informants are systematically developed by the fieldworkers, as they train the informants to conceptualize cultural data in the frame of reference employed by anthropologists. This is especially true in the case of linguistic and sociolinguistic field work, but the point applies to all anthropological interviewing. The key informant gradually learns the rules of behavior in a role vis-à-vis the interviewer-anthropologist, and, if the interaction lasts long enough, the informant may begin to employ the anthropologist's theoretical concepts in the analysis of his own culture. Thus in some studies that have involved great dependence on key informants over long periods of time the possibility cannot be ruled out that the interpretations of cognitive structuring, basic postulates, or functional relationships that appear to emerge naturally from the key informants were in fact shaped to a considerable extent by the anthropologist.

Frank and Ruth Young carried out an analysis of the degree of agreement among key informants from their field work in Mexico (Young and Young, 1961). They found that key informants were most reliable (in terms of interinformant agreement) in giving information on subjects such as:

1   Physical geography and public buildings (e.g., "Is there a church here?")
2   Institutions and institutional roles ("Do you have a doctor here?")
3   Dates of important community events ("When did you get electricity in this town?")

On the other hand, they found that evaluative questions such as, "Has there been any change in religion in this community in the past ten years?" or "What percentage of the people here customarily eat eggs?" or "How friendly are people here?" show a much lower degree of agreement (hence reliability) among informants.

John Poggie (1972) followed up the Youngs's study in the same region in Mexico, with some further refinements. He compared key informants' reports with the results of a survey data in seven communities. The results, shown in Table 5.1, speak for themselves.

The key informants in both the Youngs's and Poggie's research were prominent local leaders with presumably extensive knowledge of their own communities and fellow citizens. The most seriously damaging finding (damaging to key-informant data) was Poggie's discovery that when he used the key-informant and the survey data to *rank order* the seven communities, *agreement* between the two rank orders fell below 50 percent on fully half the questions. Months of intensive field work, and other evidence, supports the strong presumption that the survey data are much more accurate than the key-informant responses in those many areas of discrepancy.

From these materials we might be tempted to conclude that key informants will be accurate in reporting about *their own daily behavior*, which they know about firsthand. However, people are not necessarily aware of all the mundane details of their own routine behavior. DeHavenon queried the New York families whose behavior was videotaped (see Chapter 4) about their food habits and found marked discrepancies between their accounts and what she observed directly on the videotapes. Similarly, Diamond and Schein (1966) questioned New York waste collectors about their job performance and found a variety of discrepancies between self-reports and actual, observed behavior. For example, members of the waste-collection crew stated that it took them one-half to three quarters of an hour to complete the work between Amsterdam and Broadway. Actual observation showed that this segment of work required from six to fourteen minutes.

It has been frequently noted that different interviewers can elicit different

Table 5.1. *Comparisons between key informants and survey data in Mexico (data for town of Benito Juarez)*

Question	Key informants	Survey
Number of men from this town who work in the nearby factory city?	100%	152%
Percent of houses of adobe in this town?	75%	77%
Percent of families with radios?	50%	78%
Percent of people who eat eggs regularly?	100%	15%
Percent of people who would want to live in the factory city?	20%	44%

Source: Adapted from Poggie, 1972:26–8

kinds of answers from the same informants. The social characteristics, the style of presentation of self, and other qualities of the interviewer have important effects on the persons interviewed. This is not the place to go into great detail about interviewing techniques, good and bad, but it must be remembered that the interaction between fieldworker and informants is a complex social process. The data that are entered into a fieldworker's notebooks or interview schedules may differ markedly, depending on how one managed the interview scene.

It is often claimed that fieldworkers can trust key informants because of their long-term friendly relationships with them, but it must be kept in mind that the long-term, friendly relationship will inevitably create a style of interaction and a shared set of attitudes and tendencies that may significantly color the information given by the informant. A fieldworker who is especially interested in people's negative characteristics – their fears, hostilities, aggressions, and deviant behaviors – is likely to elicit descriptions of behavior from informants that include a liberal sprinkling of such negative attributes. The fieldworker who dwells on the positive side of things may evoke information of a somewhat "pollyanna" quality as friendship and interaction with key informants progress.

Aside from interviewer effect on the quality of key-informant responses, there are numbers of other problems in the interpretation and analysis of verbal data from selected individuals. Every individual human being has a particular image of himself and his position in the world of people and things – an image he endeavors to maintain as a consistent presentation of self to fellow human beings. His verbal statements to anthropologists are affected by this tendency.

Key-informant interviewing is used to best advantage when it is closely integrated with participant observation. This is the point made by Malinowski when he emphasized that "whenever anything dramatic or important occurs it is essential to investigate it at the very moment of happening, because the natives cannot but talk about it, are too excited to be reticent, and too interested to be mentally lazy in supplying details." Whenever the fieldworker has observed an event and has command over a considerable portion of the relevant information, he or she is in a position to vastly improve the data by systematic checking with informants. Their recall of details is sharpest during an event and immediately after it. Their interest in talking about significant events is likely to be highest at the time of the event or just before (and after) it.

Also, through participant observation, the fieldworker notes *which* persons are most involved in the actions – they are usually the ones with the greatest amount of firsthand information. Furthermore, one learns about informants' particular "stakes" in social actions, so that one can assess the likelihood that any given informant might distort information to maintain self-respect or for other reasons. If we have observed the battle, we are less likely to be led astray by the distorted accounts of either the winners or the losers – we can interview both, or, better yet, we may be able to locate neutral spectators of the action. Participant observation is essential for checking and evaluating key-informant data.

A fieldworker's most important informants are frequently persons who occupy specialized positions in the local society. Often the anthropologist hopes to have special relationships with political leaders, skilled craftsmen, and other important persons. Thomas Rhys Williams (1967) relates:

In Sensuron we identified and selected a girl of 16 for our household assistant. Her grandmother was one of the leading female ritual specialists of the Tambunan area. The girl had been trained as a ritual specialist. In addition, she was closely related to six persons holding key positions in the community. She served as a key informant in Sensuron. Her special ritual knowledge and her ability to give meaningful and accurate details of widely shared aspects of her culture were invaluable. (Williams, 1967:29.)

Such close social contact with a specialized key informant has disadvantages as well as advantages. Many anthropological reports include useful discussion of the selection and utilization of special persons as key informants in field work.

So much of anthropological field work is composed of participant observation and key-informant interviewing that a large portion of methodological writing in anthropology is devoted to these aspects of research procedures. Some of the autobiographical accounts of anthropologists are especially interesting and informative in this regard. Hortense Powdermaker has presented a lucid account of her own field-work experiences (Powdermaker, 1967); John Beattie's *Understanding an African Kingdom: Bunyoro* (1965) gives much insight into the elements of anthropological method; and there is much excellent information about field interviewing and related techniques in *Marginal Natives* (Freilich, 1970), *Women in the Field* (Golde, 1970), and *Being an Anthropologist* (Spindler, 1970). The *Handbook of Method in Cultural Anthropology* (Naroll and Cohen, 1973) contains more detailed discussion of these same topics.

Collection of life histories

As suggested, key-informant interviewing frequently becomes so important in anthropological field work that extensive personal documents are collected from a small number of persons with whom the anthropologist has especially good rapport. The anthropologist may then collect extensive materials about persons who are unusually eloquent and sensitive in their presentation of personal and cultural data. Thus, in most cases, life histories represent the lives of exceptional rather than representative or average persons in the community. In spite of this fact, the richness and personalized nature of life histories afford a vividness and integration of cultural information that are of great value for understanding particular lifeways.

Some life histories of anthropological importance have been collected by individuals who were not themselves anthropologists. One of the most famous of these is the narrative of John Tanner, written and edited by Dr. Edwin James in the 1820s (James, 1956). Tanner was a skilled raconteur whose recall of the details of day-to-day activities among his Indian companions was little short of phenomenal. He lived a life of such varied adventures that his narrative is frequently cited as data concerning the conditions of life among Obijwa peoples in northern Minnesota in the early nineteenth century.

Life-history materials are often collected and presented by anthropological researchers in an attempt to relate the abstractions of ethnographic description to the lives of individuals. The aim of Paul Radin's biography of a Winnebago Indian was, in his own words, "not to obtain autobiographical details about some definite personage, but to have some representative middle-aged individual of moderate ability describe his life in relation to the social group in which he had grown up" (Radin, 1920:384).

L. L. Langness (1965) has discussed the uses of life histories in anthropological research and examined problems of rapport, translation, reliability, and sampling. To the objection that life-history data frequently cannot be checked against objective observations of real behavior, he replies that very frequently a chief anthropological concern is the patterning of peoples' beliefs and conceptualizations of past events, rather than the truth or falseness of these accounts. From that point of view, life-history materials may be more useful for examining the patterning of general values, foci of cultural interests, and perceptions of social and natural relationships than as true histories. This point is well illustrated in the book *Cheyenne Memories* by John Stands-in-Timber and Margot Liberty (1967). Stands-in-Timber presented in great detail a Cheyenne version of the Custer fight. His version of this famous battle is different from other accounts. Although it is of importance for historians and others to use this information as they attempt to piece together the story of what probably happened on that day in June 1876, Stands-in-Timber's narrative is of greater anthropological significance as evidence concerning the beliefs and views of modern Cheyenne Indians, who experience economic and cultural difficulties as a reservation enclave within American society.

One of the most ambitious studies to date involving life-history materials is Cora DuBois's study, *The People of Alor* (DuBois, 1960). She collected eight personal biographies from the Alorese, supplementing them with collections of dreams, results from Rorschach tests, and other psychological materials. DuBois collected the life-history materials mainly for analyzing the Alorese personality, but the narratives are rich in cultural information as well. The psychiatrist Abraham Kardiner examined the individual life narratives and derived personality sketches for each of the eight individuals. Generalizations about the personalities of these individuals were also obtained in a separate analysis of the Rorschach protocols. The considerable congruence in these personality descriptions provides some prima facie evidence for the validity of these methods of psychological study, though the results were not subjected to statistical analysis. DuBois's monograph includes description of her data-collection methods and is therefore valuable as a guide for other fieldworkers.

The People of Alor brings into focus a central issue in the use of life histories as data about cultures. The problem is the matter of representativeness. In most cases persons who willingly narrate their life histories for ethnographers appear to be atypical members of their communities. DuBois, in fact, makes it very clear that her eight informants were in no sense a representative sample of the local community. Thus the data from the eight life histories can be generalized to the entire local population only if assumptions are made about the homogeneity of personality characteristics among these people. These same problems of representativeness are encountered in all studies involving life-history materials. One way of overcoming these problems is to use life histories as explanatory and illustrative materials in connection with other kinds of data that have been collected in a more representative manner.

Structured interviews and surveys

Participant observation and key-informant interviews have generally formed the core of anthropological research, but, taken by themselves, these methods have exposed anthropology to some serious criticisms, some of which have already been mentioned earlier.

1 *Quantification.* Although Malinowski and other leading anthropologists insisted that the fieldworker should count events and measure things as much as possible, quantification has been notably lacking in most research reports.
2 *Representativeness.* In those cases where data have been collected from a number of different informants or from numerous personal observations the researcher has generally not specified the total population or universe from which these observations are a sample, and steps were not taken to ensure that the sample was representative of the population.
3 *Specificity of research procedures.* In many cases anthropologists give no information about the research methods underlying particular descriptive generalizations. References are generally made to participant observation and interviewing, but for specific pieces of field information the supporting data are usually not given. That being the case, the critical reader usually has no way of evaluating the reliability and validity of the information.
4 *Lack of comparability.* Often the very excellence of vivid, personalized ethnographic reporting produces an overwhelmingly unique description, making comparisons with other ethnographies difficult.

In recent times anthropologists have developed a number of refinements in field techniques, which are designed to offset these criticisms. In practically all cases these techniques are outgrowths and modifications of the basic field-work tools of observation and interviewing. For example, the use of an interview schedule is simply a formalization of basic interviewing techniques.

Much has been written, especially by sociologists, concerning the design, administration, and processing of interview schedules and other survey research instruments. Anthropologists are well advised to turn to those sources of advice and information when preparing to carry out structured interviewing. It will be sufficient, therefore, to take up only a few main points here. Goode and Hatt (1952), Madge (1965), Bernard S. Phillips (1966), and Festinger and Katz (1953) all carry excellent treatments of the steps and problems in questionnaire and interview schedule construction. Glock (1967) edited a collection of inventory papers, *Survey Research in the Social Sciences*, in which an article by Bennett and Thaiss summarized main lines of anthropological use of these data-collection methods.

One standard and highly practical use of interview schedules is in the preparation of a basic census of a research population or community. In some cases such census taking is restricted to a simple enumeration of household composition, with very little additional data other than perhaps occupation, marital status, age, and place of origin. On the other hand, census procedures are often expanded in order to gather much more comprehensive data from the households in the research population.

Elizabeth Colson described a rather extensive interview schedule used in connection with her enumeration of persons among the Plateau Tonga (Colson, 1954). The data she collected for each household included names, clan affiliation, ethnic affiliation, and birthplace of parents; data on siblings, spouses, and children; names, alternative names, place of birth, approximate date of birth, ethnic affiliation, and clan of household head; previous residences, labor history, details of puberty ceremony (for women only); marriage payments, religious affiliation, fields and crops, inherited succession, number of persons in household, and kinship category of ancestor to whom the household was dedicated. These data were, of course, checked by means of other types of field observations in the course of her research. Extensive, quantified data collection as part of census taking appears to have been particularly characteristic of the research of Audrey Richards and her colleagues at the Rhodes-Livingstone Institute in Africa (Mitchell, 1967). A basic interview schedule of the type described by Colson ensures adequate quantification of a large array of materials for which the field-worker otherwise can assemble only informants' generalized statements and his own, far from random, observations in a complex scene of social action.

An important use of structured interview schedules in field work is for cross-checking key-informant data, as Poggie did in the work cited earlier. The alert fieldworker will, of course, test all data with as many different kinds of validity checks as possible. Colson gave some interesting examples of the utility of checking informants' statements against survey data:

I originally assumed that the period of seclusion for girls at puberty had been progressively diminished by mission and school influence. When I compiled material on the length of seclusion, classifying the material according to the decade in which the woman had been born, I found that there had actually been a progressive increase in the length of time of seclusion in all areas, but that this trend had been reversed for the last group of women to reach puberty. I now suspect that the increased prosperity of the Tonga . . . enabled more families to indulge in the status-producing practice of lengthy seclusion. . . . (Colson, 1954:58.)

Colson also found that informants' statements about the age of women at marriage were at variance with the data from her interview-schedule materials. She notes that "today I find that when I make a statement about the Tonga I am inclined first to check it against the material drawn from the census to see whether or not I am coming anywhere near the facts of the case. Impressions can be thoroughly wrong; so can the statements of informants" (Colson, 1954:58).

Use of an extensive interview schedule requires fairly thorough knowledge of local cultural patterns and social groupings. When several different cultural groups are present in a region, it is important to obtain approximate population data so that stratified samples can be drawn. Patterns of land tenure, ownership of material goods, kinship relations, religious activities, and recreational practices cannot be effectively quantified in an interview schedule until fieldworkers have identified the potentially significant questions by means of participant observation and key-informant interviewing.

In a multicommunity study in rural northern Minnesota, our fieldworkers carried out informal interviewing and other preliminary work for several weeks in order to identify significant questions for structured interviewing. We found, for example, that many of the households of the area had more than one source of income. Farmers usually had part-time employment in construction jobs, pulp-cutting, and various other occupations. It became clear that our interview schedule needed to provide for complex questioning concerning occupations. For the Indian subgroups, on the other hand, preliminary work pointed to importance of information about wild-rice harvesting, participation in summer powwows, and attendance at Indian council meetings. Initial data gathering also established some of the terminology that was appropriate for interviewing in the region.

Preparing interview schedules

The major problem in constructing any interview schedule is phrasing the questions that elicit the information the researcher is seeking. Questions should always be pretested on pilot samples (not part of final research sample), and translation from the local language or dialect to the researcher's language should be double-checked by means of back translation. Ronald Cohen's research on the causes of divorce among Kanuri people in Nigeria involved an elaborate set of questions, which was pilot-tested, revised, and then

. . . the revised version was taken back to Bornu and a two-man team of Kanuri assistants translated the questionnaire, then back-translated it into English. These operations were continued through several rounds until everyone connected with the project was satisfied that the Kanuri words and phrases were in fact denoting, and as nearly as possible connoting, the meaning we had originally written into the English version after the 1964 pilot study. (Cohen, 1971:16.)

Cohen described his problems with the seemingly simple query, "Do you have a horse?" "There was nothing particularly wrong grammatically or semantically with my own phrasing, but the native Kanuri speakers simply felt more at ease with this second choice [more informal phrasing]." The next question, "Where did you get it?" was more of a problem, for it was perceived as impolite. Cohen rephrased it to ask "Who gave it to you?" To this polite question, 76 percent of the respondents replied that the horse was not a gift and proceeded to explain how they had obtained it: "Thus, what a Westerner would consider a 'leading question' seems to have been a perfectly neutral and indeed a more polite way of speaking." Cohen concludes that "no foreigner should ever construct a questionnaire without the help of a group of native speakers . . ." (ibid., p. 16).

Types of questions

For many situations fieldworkers should devise questions concerning concrete events, behaviors, and possessions, instead of asking questions involving vague generalizations. Compare and contrast the following:

Q. Do you often visit other communities?
Q. When did you last visit Community A? Community B? Community C? Are there any other communities you have visited recently? (Questions are based on the assumption that preliminary field work has established a tentative list of important communities with which the people have contact.)

Whereas the first question requires the respondent to interpret the word "often," which is highly ambiguous, the second question refers to specific actions requiring only that the respondent remember the specific occasions of visits to other communities. Gathering data in this form allows fieldworkers to make their own decisions about the meaning of "often" or "seldom."

Questions in interview schedules also differ in terms of whether they are relatively closed or open ended. An open-ended question allows the respondent to give any type of answer he or she wishes, long or short. On the other hand the closed or fixed-alternative question requires the respondent to choose from a set of categories. Examine the following:

Q. If one of your children wished to marry a Protestant, how would you feel about it?
Q. If one of your children wished to marry a Protestant would you
       Object somewhat
       Object strongly
       Not object
       (Other answer)

In the first case the open-ended question makes it possible to obtain a wide variety of reactions from respondents. Also, the responses will be shaped by what the people consider to be important rather than by the categories provided by interviewers. But open-ended questions require considerable work in the form of coding and content analysis before quantified analysis is possible. Also, the answers to open-ended questions may fall into several different domains of discourse so that comparability among different respondents is sacrificed. Sometimes open-ended questions give respondents the opportunity for evasion through vague and indefinite answers.

If an investigator is quite clear about the range of specific responses that will be most useful, fixed-alternative questions may be the most appropriate, and they are certainly much easier to tabulate and analyze. Effective interview schedules often contain a mixture of both types of questions.

Questionnaires

Strictly speaking, questionnaires are distinguished from interview schedules in that the *respondent* fills out the answers to the questions on the form provided by the investigator. In complex societies questionnaires are often sent by mail to respondents, and return of the answers is voluntary. Questionnaires are not satisfactory as primary census-taking devices, because of the unevenness of returns. In any study involving statistical analysis, questionnaire responses are open to objection because of the nonrandom character of the sample. Where statistical analysis of materials is secondary to the gathering of general descriptive information, questionnaires can be quite useful, and once the schedules have been prepared, very little time is sacrificed in administration. If a researcher wishes to examine the general validity and representativeness of data gathered by means of a mailed questionnaire, interviewers can be sent out to a sample of persons who did *not* return the original questionnaires, so that the characteristics of nonresponders can be ascertained. If the nonresponders appear to be distributed randomly throughout the population, no serious problems arise in use of the questionnaire data. On the other hand, if the nonresponders are predominantly from a special segment of a population (e.g., higher socioeconomic groups), then the interpretation of the results must take this into account.

Anthropologists have developed many specialized questionnaires and interview schedules designed to explore particular domains of cultural and social behavior. Whiting and associates have developed a specialized interview for the study of child training and socialization (Minturn and Lambert, 1965); Landy used a carefully constructed schedule in interviewing mothers in a Puerto Rican village (Landy, 1965); The Cornell Medical Index has been used to assess levels of physical and mental health (Ness, 1975); Graves and associates have used a long interview schedule (approximately two hours) in exploring drinking and deviant behavior among Indians, Spanish-Americans, and Anglos in a community in the Southwest (Graves, 1967; Jessor, Graves, Hanson, and Jessor, 1968); a variety of techniques has been used in the study of socioeconomic stratification, as mentioned in the preceding chapter (e.g., Warner et al., 1960); and sociologists, of course, have developed specialized interviewing materials on practically every conceivable subject, as this is a main methodological strategy in that discipline.

Ratings and rankings

Fieldworkers often ask their informants to group or rank a series of fellow villagers, caste groups, occupations, or other kinds of items. Silverman used this technique to study stratification of prestige in an Italian community (1966, 1975). During her early months of field work, she found evidence (through observation and key-informant interviewing) that the people of the community exhibited deference to one another according to essentially occupational criteria but that other, unknown, criteria affected the ranking in particular cases. She pursued the matter further with a selected list of key informants.

Each informant was presented with a number of cards naming various members of the community and was asked to try to sort them out as "higher" and "lower." No indication was given of the dimensions of hierarchy that I wanted, for my explicit aim was to permit the informant to establish the terms in which "higher" and "lower" are meaningful to him. . . .

Each informant indicated that there are various possible ways of distinguishing a person as "higher" and "lower" (such as financial position and values attached to occupations). However in each case *rispetto* was soon mentioned. This concept . . . seemed satisfying to the informants and they readily returned to it.

In addition to suggesting the relevant questions to be put to informants, the preliminary interviews yielded other information that affected the way in which the sorting task was set up. First, it became evident that *rispetto* regulates relations only outside the household; it is adjudged for the family group as a whole and (with a few exceptions) at the common level of all members. The unit taken in subsequent interviews, therefore, was the family (household) rather than the individual. It was also determined that in Colleverde assessments of the level of *rispetto* correspond to a discrete, small number of categories, rather than to a continuum of graded rank or a very large number of levels. Therefore, informants could be asked to sort families "into groups." Moreover, since these categories are correlated with objective attributes, it seems possible to identify these attributes by referring to a sufficiently large representative part of the population, after which the level of others who shared these attributes could be predicted.

The sorting task was carried out in two two hour interviews with each informant. The informant was given one hundred and seventy five cards, one for each family in the village and for a selected sample of the countryside families. He was asked to sort all the cards into groups, as many or as few as he wished, according to the level of *rispetto*. It should be noted that the special task I set did not force the informant to behave in ways that do not occur in natural events; rather, it was a stimulus for the informant to simulate his normal behavior, to make the same judgments as those required of members of the community in everyday situations. (Silverman, 1966:903–4.)

It is interesting that Silverman's informants did not produce identical groupings of families in terms of the concept *rispetto*. She reports that "there were discrepancies in the number of groups (Renaldo recognized six groups, Gianni four groups, and Alberto seven groups) and in the points at which groups were cut off one from another, although there was high agreement in the relative rank of most persons" (Silverman, 1966:905).

Having established the hierarchy of *rispetto* by means of the sorting operation, Silverman turned to further informal interviewing and participant observation to provide further validation and behavior description of this prestige system. She felt that her research strongly supported a social-ranking model, as shown in Table 5.2.

Table 5.2. *Rank "rispetto" groups in an Italian village*

Landowners (those who live off their land income)
Professionals
White-collar workers and merchants
. . . .
Village artisans, "civilized"
Village artisans, "noncivilized"
Unskilled nonagricultural laborers, village residents
Unskilled nonagricultural laborers, country residents
. . . .
Peasant proprietors and farm tenants
Agricultural wage laborers
Mezzadria peasants
Drifters

Note: Dotted line indicates a minor line of differentiation; solid line indicates a major point of differentiation.

A major point of procedure stressed by Silverman is that it is important to allow the informants to devise their own categories and criteria for categories – particularly in initial stages of this kind of sorting operation. Once major dimensions, such as *rispetto,* have been established, it is then possible to ask informants to use this dimension in their ranking operations. Simon has used the same procedure in studying social stratification in a Mexican rural community (1972). She found that the major dimension used by Mexican villagers was referred to as *categoría.* Several points should be noted in this kind of methodology:

1   The structured ranking task should be preceded by a considerable amount of work, so that the researcher can give a preliminary structuring to the situation from firsthand information.
2   Although the fieldworker may have hypotheses concerning the nature and dimensions to be ranked, it is extremely important to avoid forcing a particular structure on the informants.
3   Reasons and comments provided by the informants in the course of their ranking operations are a valuable source of additional data. Simon used a tape recorder to record her informants' responses; content analysis of the informants' comments added greatly to the understanding of the data.
4   Participant observation and informal interviewing should be used as a follow-up to this structured procedure, to obtain further validation of the ranked results and to fit the rankings and ratings into the context of day-to-day behavior in the community.

Anthropologists have devised other kinds of rating and ranking tasks for specialized purposes. For example, Ralph Bolton (1973) asked Qolla informants in an Andean community to rank people from high to low in aggressiveness, a concept that the people readily understood in that hostility-ridden village. DeWalt (1975) secured rank ordering of Mexican villagers on drunkenness, socioeconomic status, and industriousness. A number of researchers have asked people for rank orders of food (e.g., taste preferences). Not all native classifications of persons or groups of other units must be in the form of hierarchies, however.

Listing, selecting, and sorting

One technique for mapping a behavioral, social, or material domain is simply to ask individuals to list items or categories. Sanjek, working in a multiethnic neighborhood in the city of Accra, Ghana, asked respondents to enumerate all the different "tribes" (ethnic groups) in the city. While the usual answer produced between eight and twelve "tribes," one informant listed over fifty different groups (Sanjek, 1975).

Asking people to create lists not only produces a working inventory of names and categories, but it can also be considered a trial exploration of peoples' taxonomic systems – their ways of organizing information. Some researchers have

Table 5.3. *Rank ordering of salience of ethnic groups by frequency of mention*

Ethnic group	Number of mentions	Percent (of 58 respondents)
Ewe	50	86
Fanti	42	72
Ga	40	69
Ashanti	39	67
Kwawu	34	59
Hausa	30	52
Nzima	25	43
Dagomba	24	41
Akan	18	31
Akwapim	18	31
Krobo	18	31

Source: Sanjek, 1975.

also suggested that the order in which items are mentioned reflects the *salience* or importance of those items – highly salient items occur early in the list, while those of lesser significance for the individual are likely to be mentioned later. Romney and D'Andrade (1964) obtained lists of kin terms from high school students and identified the following ordering of salience/importance:

mother
father
brother
sister
aunt
uncle
cousin
grandfather
grandmother
grandson
granddaughter

The ordering of the list appears to reflect an organizing principle of grouping kin terms in opposite-sex pairs. Other principles of grouping or organization may be reflected through the listing procedure. As shown in Table 5.3, Sanjek identified the rank ordering of salience of ethnic groups (top eleven only) based on frequency of mention.

Triad sorting

The triad-sorting technique is another means of collecting systematic information on a people's idea systems. The technique will be familiar to most people from primary school days when you were asked to "Pick out the picture that does not fit." The respondent is presented with items (kin terms, diseases, plants, tribes, etc.) in groups of three and is asked to "Pick out the one that is the most different from the others." Lieberman and Dressler (1977) used triad sorting to study disease categories of people in St. Lucia. The triad responses of average individuals looked something like this:

More alike	Most different
worms, vomiting	high blood pressure
diarrhea, worms	high blood pressure
high blood pressure, diabetes	worms
diabetes, asthma	diarrhea
high blood pressure, asthma	cold
diarrhea, worms	cold
diarrhea, cold	high blood pressure

In this example worms, vomiting, and diarrhea seem "close together" in relation to the more distant items such as high blood pressure, which seems to be "close to" asthma and diabetes. To obtain a satisfactory mapping every possible combination of three should be included in the responses. Lieberman and Dressler computed the "average distance" of each disease from every other and plotted a map for their English-speaking St. Lucian respondents (Figure 5.1).

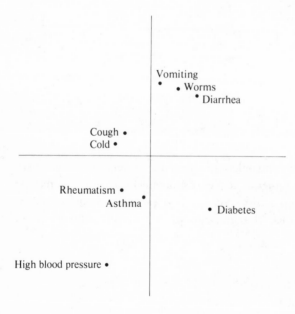

Figure 5.1. Partial "map" based on triad sorting of disease categories among English-speaking St. Lucians (from Lieberman and Dressler, 1977).

Sorting and arranging objects

All of the special interview methods described so far require reactions to verbal cues, usually with verbal output. Frequently, it is possible to ask for people's responses to actual objects. Berlin and Berlin (1975) used a set of forty-five objects to study the color terminology of Aguaruna (Jivaro) people. The objects they used included felt-tip pens of various colors, a dark-green soap wrapper, a yellow cup and a light-blue plate, red chili pepper, a dark-green leaf, a red shotgun shell, and a blue dish sponge. They also used painted strips coded according to a standardized system (the Berlin–Kay Munsell color array).

In the Aguaruna study fifty-five respondents were asked the question: "What stain does it have?" for each of the forty-five items.

The final task required of all informants was the mapping of the terms which each informant had individually volunteered in the object-and-painted-strips-naming-tasks onto the standardized Berlin and Kay Munsell color array. Mapping was carried out by placing the mounted color array (which had been out of sight during the other naming tasks) before the informant, generally on the floor in front of him in the open doorway of our house covering the chips with a clear piece of acetate. Each informant was presented with a black felt marker pen and asked . . . "draw a big wall around all of the _____ [a particular color] and subsequently . . . "where is the strongest _____ [the color]?" . . . Each informant's acetate mappings and naming responses were immediately coded on individual 8½ × 11 inch code sheets. . . . (Berlin and Berlin, 1975:66, 83.)

Berlin and Berlin found that their informants differed in their color terminology systems and that the differences were related to individuals' acquisition of Spanish as a second language.

Studying people's cognitive mapping of color is perhaps unique in the degree to which physical materials can be used in the interview process. Nonetheless, fieldworkers should always be alert to ways in which physical materials, or pictures of them, can be used to make interviewing more realistic, and often more interesting, for informants. For example, Marvin Harris (1970) and Roger Sanjek (1971) used drawings of people to explore systematically the meaning of different "racial" terms among Brazilians.

The semantic differential technique

Charles Osgood and associates have developed a technique for investigating the *connotational* dimensions of people's cognitive worlds by means of a systematic interviewing procedure.

In the typical semantic differential task, a subject judges a series of concepts (e.g., *my mother, Chinese, modern art,* etc.) against a series of bipolar, seven-step scales defined by verbal opposites (e.g., *good–bad, hot–cold, fair–unfair*, etc.). The concept is given at the top of each sheet, and the subject judges it against each successive scale by putting his checkmark in the appropriate position, e.g., +3 *extremely good*, +2 *quite good*, +1 *slightly good*, 0 *equally good and bad or neither*, −1 *slightly bad*, −2 *quite bad*, and −3 *extremely bad*. (Osgood, 1964:172–3.)

Respondents' ratings on the various scales can be averaged in order to explore the range of "semantic space" assigned to a particular concept; these can then be compared with other concepts in the same semantic domain. It is also possible to compare the patterns of response among various groups – for example, cultures and subcultures – in order to examine differences in the assignment of adjectival qualities such as "good" and "bad." Using factor-analytic techniques, Osgood and his colleagues found evidence that adjectival judgments in all societies tested tend to cluster into three main domains of connotational meaning. They labeled these semantic dimensions *evaluation, potency,* and *activity*. This led them to suggest that "human beings share a common framework for differentiating the affective meanings of signs."

The semantic differential technique can be used in a variety of ways for making comparisons of people's cognitive worlds. Schensul (1969) has used a modification of this instrument for comparing rural peoples of Ankole (Uganda) and northern Minnesota in terms of definitions of the "rural–urban continuum." He had the respondents rate concepts such as "my village," "the market town," "the city," "the best life," and "myself" on a series of dimensions including "religious–irreligious," "clean–dirty," "much money–little money," "hospitable," and so on.

To facilitate administration of the semantic differential Schensul prepared a wooden board with seven indentations corresponding to the seven-point scale. (This semantic board was modeled upon a board game that is popular in East Africa.) Concepts were represented by small cards with symbols on them – for example, "farmer" was represented by a banana tree for the respondents in Ankole. The respondent was given oral instructions about the appropriate terms for each end of the scale (e.g., inhospitable–hospitable) each time he was asked

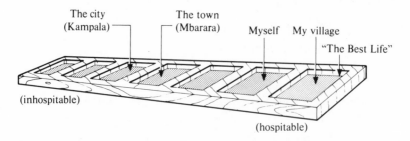

Figure 5.2. Semantic differential "board" used by S. Schensul in Uganda, with pattern of responses of a typical villager.

to consider a new dimension of meaning. Figure 5.2 illustrates the semantic differential board and a typical Banyankole response pattern for the hospitable–inhospitable dimension. Schensul was able to show that the rural people of northern Minnesota and Ankole had many similarities in the way significant geographical and social concepts are arranged in multidimensional semantic space.

Projective techniques

The concept of *projection* involves the assumption that humans have a basic psychological tendency to project their personal needs, inclinations, and themes into their verbal responses and behavioral styles. Artists project psychological features into their paintings; writers project something of themselves into their poems and stories; and drivers express certain personality tendencies in the way they drive automobiles.

This Freudian assumption, now generally accepted as common sense, is the basis for a wide variety of personality tests, ranging from the well-known Rorschach ink-blot test to various picture tests (Thematic Apperception Tests), sentence-completion tasks, and other research techniques. Most of these tests, originally developed for diagnostic use in clinical psychology, have been adapted for cross-cultural research by anthropologists, psychiatrists, and psychologists.

Both the Rorschach ink-blot test and the Murray TAT (Thematic Apperception Test) materials were originally designed to be quite vague and ambiguous in content, in order to allow individuals an opportunity to use their imagination in responding to the stimulus pictures. Such projective tests are not, in essence, logically different from standard interviewing situations. The basic procedure involves asking informants to respond verbally to *something* (oral, written, pictorial, other) presented to them by the researcher.

The Rorschach ink-blot test

The Rorschach ink-blot test was developed by the Swiss psychiatrist Hermann Rorschach immediately after World War I. The standardized test consists of ten pictures in the form of symmetrical ink blots. Half of these are polychrome; the other half are composed of various shades of gray and black. The cards are presented to the respondent in a standardized order, and the subject reports what the figures resemble or suggest.

A number of different systems of scoring have been developed for the Rorschach test. The system devised by Klopfer (1956) has been the most frequently used. Scoring Rorschach responses involves considerations of "location," "determinant," and "content." "Location" refers to whether the subject responds in terms of the whole ink blot (W) or to some detail (D) within the blot. These in turn can be subdivided into categories of "small" (Dd) and "rare" (Dr). "Determinants" refer to whether the subject's association is primarily in terms of form or shape (F); color (C); movement (M) (an element within the ink blot is perceived as moving); or whether the response is determined by shading in the pictures (kk). Mixtures or blends of determinants can be expressed in terms of combinations, such as CF, in which color and form are both important, with color predominating as an influence; or the opposite situation, in which form plays the predominant role (FC).

Content of responses is scored in terms of human (H), nature (N), animal (A), abstract responses (Abs), and so on. Also responses are scored in terms of whether they are common or popular (P) or, on the other hand, original (O). Popular responses are those that have been found to occur very frequently among many different populations of subjects.

The scoring categories such as "whole responses," "small detail," "animal movement," "human detail," and so on, are but a first step to interpreting the Rorschach protocol. These response categories are translated into personality characteristics following "transformation rules" that have been developed from clinical experience among American and European populations. The quantified indexes provide a background against which the trained Rorschach clinician makes global assessments about personality characteristics in terms of a wide range of experience with Rorschach protocols. It is common, therefore, for anthropologists using the Rorschach test to have the protocols scored by clinical psychologists with extensive experience in scoring of these materials.

George and Louise Spindler's study of personality characteristics related to acculturation among the Menominee provides a good example of the use of the Rorschach instrument in testing a hypothesis (Spindler, 1955; Spindler and Spindler, 1958). On the basis of religious affiliation and other social characteristics, the investigators divided the Wisconsin Menominee into five groups as follows:

1 Native-Oriented group (Medicine Lodge-Dream Dance group) – least acculturated.
2 Peyote Cult group – transitional in acculturation.
3 Transitional group – characterized by little participation in any religious activity.
4 Lower-Status Acculturated group – associated with the Catholic Church.
5 Elite Acculturated group – associated with the Catholic religion.

These groups were shown to differ one from another in terms of income, group affiliations, use of Menominee language, and other characteristics. Twelve white subjects living on the reservation were included as a control group.

The Spindlers divided the scores on each of the Rorschach items into the "highs" and "lows," and compared each of the social groups to every other group in terms of their scores on the twenty-one Rorschach indexes. They found that the two extremes of the acculturation continuum (the Native-Oriented compared with the Elite Acculturated) showed significant differences in eight of the twenty-one Rorschach variables. They also found that the Peyote group was the most different from all the others in psychological characteristics.

Bert Kaplan (1955) used the Rorschach test to examine differences and similarities among Zuñi, Navajo, Mormon, and Spanish-American subjects. He examined a total of 170 responses. By means of chi-square statistical tests, Kaplan found that there were significant differences among these four groups, particularly on five of the Rorschach scoring categories. He also examined these data by means of an analysis of variance and found that there was *much greater within-group variance than between-groups variance*. This finding throws considerable doubt on the usefulness of the personality descriptions that have been used to demonstrate alleged differences between cultures. As Kaplan has noted, "A very high degree of overlap among the groups is present, and this, coupled with the small size of the differences that do appear, indicates the variability of individuals in any one culture is greater than the variability between cultures" (Kaplan, 1955:18).

Thematic Apperception Tests (TAT)

The Thematic Apperception Test was originally developed by Henry A. Murray and associates in the 1930s (Morgan and Murray, 1935). Murray's TAT consists of twenty pictures with a variety of content, including a small boy looking at a violin; a farm scene with a man plowing, watched by a woman and a girl; a man and a woman in a semiembrace, in which the woman appears to be restraining the man; an elderly man and a younger man apparently in conversation; a woman and a child; a woman and a young man (frequently interpreted as mother and son); a pastoral scene with a boat moored under a tree, no persons visible; and a number of other pictures, most of which suggest some kind of social interaction.

These pictures are presented to the subject one at a time with the request that he or she invent a narrative to account for what is in the picture. Questions are asked about what led up to the scene in the picture, "how the people feel about it," and what will happen afterward. The story told by the subject is recorded nearly word for word if possible. It is desirable that the investigator not interfere with or prompt the subject.

There is no single standardized scoring procedure for TAT responses. Analysis of responses has been carried out in two main styles. Clinically oriented researchers, both psychologists and anthropologists, have examined the themes and styles of action in TAT stories in order to make inferences about characteristics such as aggressiveness, dependence, sex conflict, and other general personality traits. In this clinical mode of TAT analysis researchers sometimes mention counting of particular thematic elements and even of ratios among these elements, but the procedures of content analysis are usually not made specific, and no statistical analysis of elements is given.

William Henry's (1947) comparison of Hopi and Navajo children's TAT responses was the first significant cross-cultural use of the instrument, and his monograph provides a clear and thoughtful account of the procedures and results. TAT responses had been collected in the course of the Indian Education Research project, conducted jointly by the U.S. Bureau of Indian Affairs and the Committee on Human Development of the University of Chicago. The children ranged in age from six to eighteen and were selected in such a manner as to provide a reasonable representative sampling from the different levels of acculturation in these groups. Henry collected 104 responses from Navajo children and 102 from the Hopi.

As is commonly done in cross-cultural use of TATs, special pictures were drawn so that the facial features and the cultural elements in the pictures would be congruent with Indian life in the Southwest.

The following are some examples of Hopi children's responses to these TAT pictures:

1   The man is talking. He is their father. He tells them he wants help. They will help him in the field.
2   Some mother is taking care of the baby. The little boy and girl playing with the turtle. They found it.
3   This man wants to sell his horse to him. He will take it. He is a white man.
4   The little boy is crying because his father scold him.
5   This man is talking to these two men. These are listening to him. They are his friend. They are talking about animals, sheeps. He wants them to herd his sheep. They will do it.
6   These two children are playing with the turtle. This turtle is going toward that boy. This lady is watching them. She is nursing the baby. These two are playing and talking to each other.
7   Somebody hurt him and he is crying. He is crying on the rock. When he got through crying, he went home. (Who hurt him?) A little boy hurt him. He (the other boy) does not like this little boy. He (the other boy) is a bad boy and too mean.

In seeking validation for psychological constructs derived from the TAT responses, Henry and his colleagues compared TAT interpretations with data from Rorschach tests, life histories, free drawing, and other materials. They found that there was a fairly high degree of agreement in psychological content from these different data sources, but Henry noted that "it is clear that the validating techniques were subjective in nature and some were of unknown validity themselves" (ibid., 81).

Comparisons of James Lake Indians and white respondents in psychological characteristics (G. Pelto, 1967)

In this research project the TAT was administered to randomly selected samples of thirty white and thirty Indian respondents in the community of James Lake in northern Minnesota. Since the Indians and whites in the sample live in the same community and experience the same general natural environment, comparisons between the two groups might reveal something about the nature of cultural/psychological differences in this region.

Much has been written about the alleged introverted character of the Chippewa Indians; examination of the general personality dimension "introversion – extraversion" was therefore a central concern of this research. Eysenck has described extraverted and introverted personality tendencies as follows:

The typical extravert is sociable, likes parties, has many friends, needs to have people to talk to. . . . He craves excitement, takes chances, often sticks his neck out, acts on the spur of the moment, and is generally an impulsive individual.

The typical introvert, on the other hand, is a quiet, retiring sort of person, introspective . . . he is reserved and distant, except with intimate friends. He tends to plan ahead. . . . He keeps his feelings under close control, seldom behaves in an aggressive manner and does not lose his temper easily. (Eysenck, 1965:59–60.)

This description of extraversion–introversion, and descriptive remarks from Barnouw, Hallowell, and others concerning the introversive character of Chippewa personalities, afforded the basis for establishing a systematic content analysis. The responses of the subjects to each of eight TAT cards were examined for presence of extraversive and introversive thematic content. Thus if an individual gave extraverted content in every card, he would have a total extraversion score of eight. The following kinds of content were considered to be indicators of extraversion:

1 In the narrative, participation in group behavior is reported with enjoyment, including mention of friendship, parties, and so on.
2 The subject's narrative involves studying for, or occupying, a job that implies or involves service to others or frequent involvement with others.
3 The subject's response tells of interaction, or attempts to interact, with others.
4 The subject mentions loneliness or feelings of "being left out" (includes going out and looking for somebody).
5 The person in subject's story is asking for help.
6 The narrative includes expression of grief for another person.
7 Persons in the story express concern for, interest in, and attention to others.

An individual's introversion score was derived in essentially the same manner. An introversion – extraversion ratio was then calculated for each of the Indian and white respondents. It was found that Chippewa subjects were not significantly more introverted than white persons in the community of James Lake:

. . . what is most striking in these results is that differences in introversion – extraversion are much more marked when we turn from inter-ethnic comparisons to an examination of contrasts between males and females. When the Indians and Whites are grouped together, males are more introverted than females. Also it is important to note that among female respondents, Indians are more introverted than Whites. (Pelto, 1967.)

The finding that the Indian males are not significantly more introverted than white men living in the same community reminds us of the Spindlers' white control group in the Menominee study mentioned earlier. They, too, found that the white men living in the *same environment* were not substantially different in personality from the transitional and acculturated Menominee group. (They were, however, psychologically different from the Native-Oriented and Peyote groups.)

All studies that involve detailed rating and ranking for purposes of cross-cultural or intracultural comparisions run the risk of contamination through subconscious distortions in favor of the hypotheses being tested (or overreaction *against* the hypotheses being tested). For this reason, content analysis of TATs and other projective tests should be carried out by persons who are unaware of the hypotheses being tested. Sometimes the same kind of protection from rater contamination can be achieved by disguising the identities of the individual protocols.

The sentence-completion test

While the Rorschach and TAT projective tests (and a number of other instruments modified from these prototypes) involve presentation of some kind of visual or pictorial stimulus to subjects, a variety of analogous procedures has been explored using *verbal* stimuli. The most common verbal projective instrument is the *sentence-completion test*, in which standardized sets of incomplete sentences or stems of sentences are presented and the subjects are asked to complete the statements in any way they like. Thus the procedure resembles the word-association test and in fact can be considered a variant type of word-association task. (A variant of this *verbal-completion* projective technique is the *story-completion test* [Murray, 1938].)

Personalities of cane cutters and fishermen in a West Indies community (Aronoff, 1967)

Joel Aronoff used the sentence-completion technique in a sophisticated study of personality characteristics related to occupational choices in the little community of Dieppe Bay in the West Indies. The investigator and his wife carried out several months of field work in the research region, during which they developed hypotheses about the importance of personality variables in explaining why some individuals remain cane cutters while other individuals choose fishing as an occupation (a much more desirable and monetarily rewarding occupation, according to Aronoff). Relying on his firsthand acquaintance with individual cane cutters and fishermen, Aronoff constructed a sentence-completion test to test his hypotheses. He also devised a series of projective questions, another variant form of *verbal* projective technique. An interesting problem in his field work developed when Aronoff found that the people of Dieppe Bay did not conceptualize verbal patterns in terms of sentences. Following are some examples of his sentence-completion items:

1 Money is. . . .
2 Food. . . .
3 I am proud of. . . .
4 A friend. . . .
5 A father. . . .
6 I get vexed when. . . .
15 I am sad because I. . . .
21 I am good at. . . .
28 The people around here. . . .

Some of his projective questions included:

1 If you were given two thousand dollars, what would you do with it?
2 What kind of friend would you choose?
3 What should be done with people who ride bicycles carelessly?
5 What is the worse thing that could happen to you?
6 What is the nicest thing that could happen to you?
11 What is the best thing about women?
12 What should be done with people from another island who do rudeness?

The psychological characteristics that Aronoff examined in his sentence-completion protocols were derived from the personality theory of Abraham Maslow and associates. In this body of theory, concepts such as *self-esteem, self-image, concern with physiological problems* (e.g., hunger and food), *concern about safety, capacity for love and belongingness,* and *self-actualization* are seen as important variables in terms of which "more successful" personalities can be distinguished from those that are "less successful."

Some of the aspects of Aronoff's study that deserve special attention include the following:

1 The fact that his hypothesis testing involves comparisons between groups living in the same community makes the comparisons more credible than those involving distinctly different cultures.
2 Construction of the sentence-completion instrument was carried out *after* extensive field work in the research community.

3 Methods of content analysis were specified in detail.
4 The reliability of scoring techniques was tested by comparing Aronoff's own ratings with those of an independent rater.
5 The results of comparison were subjected to statistical analysis.
6 The data from the psychological tests were related to behavioral data concerning activities of fishermen and cane cutters – for which extensive observations and interview data were available.
7 Some alternative hypotheses concerning the research findings were examined statistically and rejected.

Other projective techniques

Many other projective techniques have been used in anthropological research. Some of these have been directly borrowed from the research kit of clinical psychologists, whereas others have been developed by anthropologists themselves in their particular field-work contexts. Doll-play techniques were used by Henry and Henry (1953) to examine psychological characteristics of Pilagá Indian children. The Goodenough test, the Machover test, and other drawing tests have been used by numbers of anthropologists for the collection of psychological materials. Probably there are scores of collections of children's drawings in the files of anthropological fieldworkers that have never been published or even mentioned in research reports; but a number of selections of drawings have been subjected to detailed psychological analysis by anthropologists and their collaborators. Children's drawings were an important adjunct to DuBois's study of the Alorese; free drawings were part of the psychological data collected in the research project on Indian education (mentioned earlier in connection with Henry's TAT analysis of Hopi and Navajo children); and many other anthropologists have used drawings as projective tests.

Auditory-perceptive techniques (involving music and other sounds) have sometimes been employed by clinicians and experimental psychologists, but they have not been employed very much in anthropological research, although data about music preference has occasionally figured in anthropological hypothesis testing. This is but one example of the many relatively unexplored areas of human behavior that may offer significant possibilities for research.

Administering projective tests

Projective tests and other psychological instruments were, for the most part, developed in the context of psychological laboratories and clinical situations. Under those circumstances the methods of administration were fairly carefully standardized in order to ensure comparability of the stimulus situation. Administration of projective tests in field work, on the other hand, involves presenting and administering materials in an unpredictable variety of contexts. Frequently, projective tests are presented to respondents in their homes, under circumstances where it is extremely difficult to prevent other members of the family, particularly the children, from interfering. Tests have been administered by fieldworkers in the field where farmers were working, in the kitchen as a housewife prepared a meal, in the shade of a tree in the village square, with children playing about, and in many other situations.

In some cases fieldworkers can find temporary quarters in which to conduct their interviews, but usually they must meet respondents on their home grounds. Interviewing respondents in their homes or fields has some advantages, however. It can be argued that the respondent is more natural and relaxed in familiar surroundings and that he may therefore be more expressive and cooperative in the task set by the psychological instruments. This probably varies from one society to another.

Although the fieldworker may be faced with the problem of variations in the test settings, procedures should be standardized as much as possible. The following items provide a partial framework for this standardization:

1   The opening explanation of the test should be presented in the same manner to each respondent. Instructions should be (as nearly as possible) the same, word for word, to each subject. For instance, "I would like you to tell a story about what you see in this picture. It can be any kind of story that you wish to tell, and you can let your imagination roam as freely as you like. Tell what is happening in the picture, what led up to this scene, and then what will happen afterward."
2   Questions asked during administration of the instrument should be standardized so that every individual is asked the same set of "probes."
3   The pictures (or other stimuli) should be administered in the same order to every individual in the sample (or else in randomized order).
4   If the fieldworker makes comments to individuals concerning their stories, such as, "That's fine, let's go on to the next one," the same comments should be used for each person tested.
5   Researchers should become aware of mannerisms and other paralinguistic communications through which they may be influencing respondents to answer in a particular manner. Recent studies in social psychology have demonstrated that test administrators can exert significant influence on persons being tested in extremely subtle and subliminal ways (Rosenthal, 1966).
6   Fieldworkers should suggest to respondents that they not discuss the nature of the test with other persons in their community until the data gathering is finished. That is, the aim is to get each person's *own* individual response, unaffected by suggestions or influences of kinspeople, friends, or other persons.
7   In some cases the researcher may wish to point out some feature in a picture that is intended to serve as a standardized stimulus to the respondent. For example, in research with TATs in northern Minnesota, respondents were instructed that one of the

persons in a particular picture was an Indian and the other a white man. This instruction was intended to ensure high salience of the interethnic component in the picture. Special information or instructions should be presented in a neutral tone, unless the test administrator has very special purposes in mind in arousing emotional reactions.

8   In some cases TAT responses (or other projected materials) are collected by a number of different fieldworkers in the course of a project. In such cases, comparisons between groups may be contaminated by the fact that different persons (with possibly different stimulus characteristics) carried out the research in the different groups to be compared. More effective research design to guard against this kind of investigator effect would divide up the administration of tests in such a way that *all* workers collected tests in *all* of the groups to be compared. That is, if comparisons are to be made between village A and village B, and four fieldworkers are available to collect the psychological responses, it would be best if the four fieldworkers all worked in village A and then moved to village B. Even more effective controls on investigator bias would be ensured if assignments of particular researchers to particular respondents were randomized by means of coin tosses or tables of random numbers.

Nowadays, fewer researchers use the standard forms of TATs or other projective tests, preferring to design materials specific to their own research topics and populations.

Other psychological research instruments

A number of other psychological tests and measurements have been used in cross-cultural and anthropological research. Most of these are not usually regarded as projective techniques, though the distinction is often difficult to maintain.

Perception of illusions

Segall, Campbell, and Herskovits (1966) have devised a test involving several simple optical illusions for examining differences in perception related to differences in types of environment. The investigators found support for the hypothesis that people who live in "carpentered environments" (with rectangular buildings, right-angle street intersections, and other angular features) tend to be more deceived by optical illusions, such as the Müller-Lyer illusion (Figure 5.3), than people who live in environments less dominated by man-made angularities.

Figure 5.3. The Müller-Lyer illusion.

Acuity of perception

Winter (1964) tested Kalahari Bushmen, African laborers, and a white population to determine their accuracy in perceiving relative sizes of discs at various distances. The Bushmen proved to be superior to the other groups in this perception task. Robbins and collaborators examined perceptions of time lapse as well as perceptions of perspective in a standardized picture test among Ganda peoples. These techniques were used to test hypotheses about perceptual correlates of acculturation and urbanization (Robbins and Kilbride, 1968, 1973; Kilbride et al., 1968). The psychologist Doob used a picture test among African peoples in his research on eidetic imagery. This perceptual phenomenon involves the experiencing of visual images "persisting after stimulations relatively accurate in detail, colored positively, and capable of being scanned." Like most other studies of differences in styles of perception, the matter of eidetic imagery is of theoretical importance in relation to problems of acculturation (Doob, 1964, 1965).

Judgments of esthetic qualities

Irvin Child and colleagues (social psychologists and anthropologists) used pictures of art objects to elicit opinions concerning esthetic excellence from "art experts" in New Haven (Child and Siroto, 1965), mask makers in Africa, Fiji carvers (Ford et al., 1966), and Japanese potters (Iwao and Child, 1966). The techniques involved in this kind of research are similar to the ranking and rating of social position and prestige tasks described earlier. That is, selected informants are asked to sort, group, rank, or otherwise differentiate a series of items (art pictures in this case). Average ratings or rankings of the individual items are calculated statistically, and degrees of consensus among the expert raters are compared. In these cross-cultural studies Child and associates found evidence of panhuman similarities in esthetic judgment. They emphasize that these agreements in esthetic judgment are found among "experts"; artistic judgments of ordinary lay persons in different societies do not seem to demonstrate these similarities.

Psychomotor skills

Robert J. Maxwell has used pursuit-rotor tests and manual-sorting operations (such as block sorting) to examine the psychomotor characteristics of Samoans. Differences in performance and in persistence in these psychomotor tasks are thought to be related to extraversion – introversion, as well as to other personality qualities.

Games people play

John M. Roberts and associates have suggested that people's recreational games are significant expressions of cultural and psychological processes. Thus they report that simpler societies, such as hunting-and-gathering peoples, do not generally have games of strategy but find their off-hour enjoyments in games involving physical skill and chance. Games of strategy, apparently, are found in more complex societies and seem to reflect psychological conflicts over mastery of complex social relationships (Roberts, Arth, and Bush, 1959; Roberts and Sutton-Smith, 1962).

Content analysis of games in terms of chance, physical skill, and strategy (or combinations of these), or any other distinctive features provides yet another projection domain for developing quantifiable reflections of the psychological, cultural, and social attributes of peoples. For example, girls' games in a Mexican village have been found to dramatize conflict with sexually predatory males, whereas game playing among boys reflects their ambivalent reactions to authority figures. Part of the research technique in a study by Maccoby, Modiano, and Lander (1964) included the experimental introduction of new games to the Mexican villagers. Because games are usually considered to be harmless pastimes, introducing a new game provides significant information about community behavior without disrupting normal social life. (It may even help to increase the fieldworker's rapport!)

A game as a laboratory device

Murray and Jacqueline Straus (Straus, 1968; Straus and Straus, 1968) have developed an experimental game for the cross-cultural laboratory study of family interaction and problem-solving behavior. The game is played on a 9-by-12-foot court, with wooden targets at one end toward which the subjects push colored balls, somewhat after the manner of shuffleboard. The problem-solving feature of the game is that the players (a husband, wife, and child) must infer the rules of the game from the informational feedback of red (error) and green (correct play) lights. The laboratory setup is shown in Figure 5.4.

The rules the family must learn in order to solve the puzzle are quite simple:

1   The *color* of the pusher, the ball, and the subject's armband must all match.
2   The ball must hit the wooden target.
3   The ball must not roll out of the court after hitting the target.

The game is reported to be quite enjoyable by most participants, even though there is marked variation in the participants' success in solving the problem. This research technique was used with subjects in San Juan, Puerto Rico; Bombay,

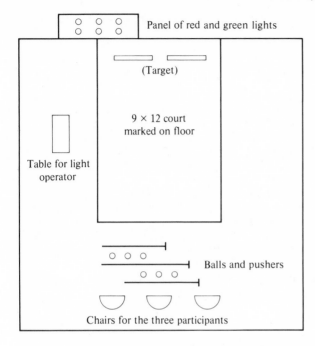

Figure 5.4. Laboratory game for the study of family interaction patterns (adapted from Straus and Straus, 1968).

India; and Minneapolis, Minnesota, in a study of middle-class versus working-class differences in family problem-solving styles. It is important to note that the logic of the research design was based on *intrasocietal* comparison, with cross-cultural replication. In all three areas the middle-class families demonstrated greater game-solving success than the working-class families. Communication patterns as well as individual creativity (in suggesting and trying out various tactics and solutions) were related to these socioeconomic differences.

One of the most important methodological features of this laboratory game is that a number of different measures of behavior can be effectively observed. All interaction (conversation, gestures, etc.) of the participants can be recorded; also, the scores of the player groups provide a quantified measure of success in problem solving. Total number of shots attempted provides a measure of activity level; and various other elements, including "creativity," can be given quite precise operational meanings.

There is no reason why anthropologists cannot develop experimental games (or other situations) that will permit controlled testing of theoretical propositions. Such games need not be elaborate, and they could be quite entertaining for the respondents. The apparatus in the Straus research requires an electrical system; hence it is not easy to carry into remote areas, but innovative anthropologists could develop simpler analogues for controlled observation of interaction styles in small groups, reactions to authority, intersex behavioral patterns, modes of verbal and nonverbal communication, and so on. Such games could be modeled upon locally prevalent pastimes, games, or work arrangements.

Interactional research tools

The research tools described in this chapter are all based on *interaction* between observers and the people in their research locations. Moreover, most of the interaction is verbal, and the materials are therefore correspondingly *ideational* in basic form. All such direct-action data are subject to the criticism that they are to some extent "unnatural," because they intrude the observer into the action space of the people observed. Most anthropologists seek other, less directly confronting data techniques, at least as supplementary sources for these obtrusive observations. Less obtrusive, or at least less directly question-and-answer modes of research will be discussed in the next chapter.

6 Tools of research – II: nonverbal techniques

Research techniques employing questionnaires, interviews, and psychological tests all involve confronting individuals with situations that are, to a considerable extent, outside their daily rounds of living. Thus the researcher interposes some kind of stimulus – whether a set of questions or a performance task – assumed to be in some way an *analogue* of ordinary behavior. The researcher assumes that habitual behavioral tendencies of subjects will be reflected in reactions to the situations structured by the anthropologist. Even informal conversations between anthropologists and research subjects are "obtrusive" in that the anthropologist is to some extent an outsider in the research community. On the other hand, anthropological field work involves observation that is "unobtrusive" whenever the anthropologist watches ongoing behavior – feasts and festivals, daily work, meetings and discussions, recreation, and other habitual activities.

Under the heading of "participant observation" we generally include a wide range of informal and formal materials, which often makes up a large portion of the fieldworkers' field notes. A frequent complaint about ethnographic reporting is that direct eyewitness information is completely mingled with secondhand, hearsay data (cf. Silverberg, 1975). Marvin Harris's discussion of etic ethnography (Chapter 4) represents an attempt to systematize observational data gathering in order to overcome this weakness.

Anthropological fieldworkers would do well to study the increasingly sophisticated modes of observation used by ethologists in studying the behavior of nonhuman primates and other animals. In recent times a large number of new studies of apes and monkeys, herds of deer, wolf packs, field mice, and many other animal groupings have demonstrated carefully defined procedures for observing (and counting) behavioral elements. A most significant aspect of observations among animal groups is the matter of physical location. A great amount of information concerning the social organization of baboon troops, for example, has been inferred from observations of physical spacing (Kummer, 1971; J. Goodall, 1971). Edward T. Hall (1966) has explored what he calls "the hidden dimension" – patterns of interpersonal spacing. It appears from his discussion that observers of human behavior have thus far been relatively unsystematic and impressionistic in observing social spacing in human interaction.

The importance of physical position in human social organization is dramatically illustrated by events and discussions concerning integration, segregation, and related interracial problems in the United States. Seating patterns on buses (Jim Crow laws), restrictions concerning residence (segregated housing practices), de facto segregation in schools, and a number of other highly controversial social practices in the United States demonstrate how physical spacing relates directly to social facts. Campbell, Kruskal, and Wallace (cited in Webb, et al., 1966) studied the seating of blacks and whites in classrooms as indicators of racial attitudes. Classes in four schools were studied, in which there were significant variations in degrees of mixed seating; investigators took this as a presumptive index of the degree to which acquaintance, friendship, and social preferences were influenced by race.

Practically every fieldworker has made significant use of data on physical locations (distances between households; seating arrangements; and other positioning) as important clues concerning community behavior. In ritual events – weddings, funerals, festivals, sacred ceremonies, and so on – the positioning of persons in the scene practically always reflects important social information. Important persons are frequently at the head of the table; seating at feasts often reflects extended kinship relations; and social inferiors are often identifiable because of their locations at the margins, back in the shadows, away from the center of social attention.

The stream of behavior and measurement of social interaction

Closely related to observations of physical location and spacing are the fieldworker's systematic recording of social behavior of individuals and the social contacts among different kinds of individuals. Here again, recently developed techniques in the naturalistic study of animal behavior might prove useful to anthropological fieldworkers. Two of the most important problems facing the fieldworker in his recording of behavioral observations are:

1 Ensuring representativeness when his observations can encompass only a small fraction of all the booming, buzzing confusion of events in a human community.
2 Defining useful behavioral units or inherent segments for identification and observation. Earlier, in the discussion of etic research strategies, we examined the methods suggested by Harris for coping with the problem of obtaining systematic behavioral observations. Painstakingly complete behavioral observations of the type suggested by Harris are feasible only for highly selected aspects of social life in human communities. Fieldworkers must be guided by their own theoretical concerns, plus scientific hunches and intuitions, in selecting certain behavior settings for intensive study, leaving other social scenes for less systematic modes of space observation.

Ecological psychologists, such as Roger Barker and his associates, have perhaps done more systematic field behavioral observations than any other social scientists. Barker argues that it is possible to identify natural behavioral units:

Behavioral units are natural in the sense that they occur without intervention by the investigator; they are self-generated parts of the stream of behavior. . . . There are . . . two grounds for identifying and classifying behavioral units. One ground is their structural-dynamic characteristics; the other is their material-content properties. (Barker, 1963:1–8.)

We note that these assumptions about observational units are not significantly different from Harris's ideas.

To illustrate his method of analysis Barker gives a portion of a record of behavior concerning "Brett Butley, 7 years 2 months of age on July 5, 1957 . . . member of the Upper Infants Class of the Yoredale (England) County School." Some of the behavioral segments observed are (simplified) as follows:

> Eating orange.
> Watching cricket.
> Noting hurt child.
> Brett glanced at (girl).
> 10:40 Brett walked over to the boy who had been batting.
> He took the bat that was handed to him as though this was expected by both of them.
> He stood quietly with the end of the bat resting on the ground as he waited for the bowl.
> Orin bowled.
> Brett struck at the ball rather awkwardly though he failed to hit it.
> It was difficult for Brett to swing the bat.
> The ball was thrown back to Orin and he bowled again.
> This time Brett succeeded in hitting the ball.
> It went a short distance and was thrown back to Orin.

From this record (continued at some length) the observer identified the following behavioral units: eating orange, noting hurt child, watching cricket game, noting hurt child, playing cricket, waiting for boys to move away, and so on (ibid., 10). Barker argues that "playing cricket" is the size of unit that is most useful for descriptive analysis, though the smaller units of observation are important for identifying the boundaries of the natural units.

In addition to this plan of behavioral observation, Barker and associates are much concerned with the delineation of natural behavioral settings – the environmental contexts within which particular sequences of behavior regularly occur.

Because the list of settings which we have identified reads, for the most part, like a common sense directory of town's businesses, organization meetings, school classes, and so forth, it is sometimes overlooked that their identification involves highly technical operations and precise ratings of interdependence . . . the precise quantitative criterion which we have used to establish the limits of behavior settings . . . was selected so that the settings would fall within the usual range of laymen's discrimination. Nevertheless, the criteria for their identification are not lay criteria. (Barker and Barker, 1961:467.)

The study of interaction, in terms of frequencies of dialogue and nonverbal interaction, energy levels, response patterns, dominance in interaction, and so forth, has been highly systematized and mechanized by Elliot Chapple with his "interaction chronograph" (Chapple, 1949). His device for measuring interaction was developed particularly for studying factory social systems and other communities within American society, but the general idea embodied in this research technique can provide the fieldworker (equipped with only notebook, pencil, and watch) with ideas for observations of great value in the field context. In drawing on the interaction chronograph model of research – for example, in studying a meeting — the fieldworker might concentrate on some of the following questions:

1   What are the physical locations of the different persons (and groups) in the meeting?
2   Who initiates major segments of the action?
3   Who speaks? For how long?
4   Which speakers respond to what other speakers?
5   What kinds of reactions are observable in the nonspeakers?
6   What kinds of spaces (pauses) segment the interaction?
7   Do different kinds of persons specialize in different aspects or topics in the meeting (e.g., finances, procedural rules, entertainment, lines of authority)?

The Six Cultures study

The Six Cultures study, inaugurated in the 1950s by John and Beatrice Whiting, William Lambert, and a group of fieldworkers, is the most ambitious cross-cultural project to date in which behavioral observations were systematically planned, executed, and coded. A complete field guide (Whiting et al., 1966) for observing behavior was developed before the research teams set out for their respective assignments in East Africa, Okinawa, Mexico, North India, the Philippines, and New England. The resulting general ethnographies, and some of the more significant research results, are now well known (cf. B. Whiting, 1965; Minturn and Lambert, 1966; Whiting and Whiting, 1975), but the detailed behavioral observations have received less attention – partly because their coding and analysis have been a long and tedious process, with corresponding delays in publication.

In each location the researchers picked two samples of children – three- to six-year-olds and seven- to eleven-year-olds, a total of twenty-four in each community. Taking a key idea from the Barkers, the Six Cultures researchers were instructed to develop lists of behavioral settings and to sample the behavior in these settings in a representative manner, in segments of five-minute observations.

As planned, the observers first mapped the daily routine of boys and girls in the two age groups. They followed the children around, noting their presence in different settings at different times of the day. They recorded the activities in progress in these settings and supplemented their observations by interviews with the adults and the children. (Whiting and Whiting, 1975:40.)

Preliminary identification of these daily routines allowed the field researchers to focus attention on their sample children in a systematic manner. Each time a child selected for observation was encountered in a selected setting, the field-worker noted the time, place, and persons present, recorded all the stimuli that impinged on her or him, and the resulting behavior of the individual. "The observations were recorded in English nouns, verbs, and pronouns with a minimal number of interpretive qualifiers" (Whiting and Whiting, 1975:41).

Each child in the sample (in each of the six settings) was observed at least fourteen times in five-minute segments. A bilingual assistant was present in each situation to translate verbal interaction. The protocols (written descriptions of observations) were mailed back to headquarters (Harvard) from the field sites and were then coded into behavioral categories by carefully trained research assistants. Coding included a series of behavioral categories thought to have universal, cross-cultural meaning. For example, "dominance" was defined as follows:

In a relation with another person or group, dominance consists of tendencies to demand that the other person act in certain ways, to attempt *direction* of the other person's responses without making formal demands, to enforce demands, or to attain a social position which will increase facilities for enforcing demands. (Ibid., p. 60.)

Some examples of behavioral items and how they were subsequently coded will help to illustrate the steps from observation to processed data:

Behavior	Coded
Ombasa is on the path between her mother's house and the co-wife's house with baby brother. *Nyanchama:* "Look for the kitten and we'll tie him up" (p. 190).	"acts sociably"
Romulo and friend wrestle; both laugh (p. 193).	"assaults sociably"
Shirley to girl next to her, "Move over."	"seeks dominance"
Joseph's brother is fighting and playing lightheartedly with a friend. Throughout, *Joseph* is watching them closely, laughing and smiling but not participating.	"offers support"
Barbara to the observer: "I have a pad that's way bigger than that one!" (Adapted from Whiting and Whiting, 1975:187–196.)	"seeks attention"

Table 6.1, showing children's behavior categories in the six communities, further illustrates this mode of data analysis.

Table 6.1. *Frequencies of acts: Six Cultures children*

Act	Nyansongo (Africa)	Mixtec (Mexico)	Tarong (Philippines)	Taira (Okinawa)	Khalapur (North India)	Orchard Town (New England)
Acts sociably	247	432	971	324	236	558
Insults	159	96	451	205	104	133
Offers help	156	148	280	97	60	86
Reprimands	222	64	185	112	67	102
Offers support	106	110	251	73	33	37
Seeks dominance	29	71	123	133	128	125
Seeks help	28	91	127	87	122	148
Seeks attention	62	69	100	89	57	226
Suggests responsibly	171	93	138	69	47	38
Assaults sociably	48	52	237	95	38	59
Touches	21	78	136	17	19	15
Assaults	66	45	45	50	36	21
Total acts coded	1,342	1,349	3,044	1,351	947	1,548

Source: Adapted from Whiting and Whiting, 1975: 64.

The figures in Table 6.1 should be used with due caution, as the Whitings point out. Differences in total numbers of coded behaviors may be due to real differences, or they may reflect different intensities of observation by the research teams. Nonetheless, these relatively simple frequencies are very interesting. Do North American children seek attention (proportionately) more than most other children in the world? Why are the East African children so high on reprimanding? Do they have more responsibilities?

This ambitious project illustrates several significant points about behavioral observations, including:

1 Behavioral observations, to be representative, should be focused on a sample of persons, *and* rigorous procedures of sampling time and place must also be maintained.
   Problem: If the sampled time segments are short, one gets little in the way of continuity or developmental sequences.
2 Actual behavior should be recorded as fully as possible.
   Problem: At what level of abstraction? (E.g., in the examples, do we really know what it means to say that "Romulo and friend wrestle"?)
   Problem: So much of the behavior is verbal – how can we record the tone of voice? (E.g., what was Shirley's *tone* (earlier) when she said "Move over." Was it playful? Threatening? Cajoling?)
3 Interaction among children and adults is extremely complicated, so that description must focus on one individual, the sample person.
   Problem: In some situations the real meaning of behavior may depend on the interaction among several different key persons, but how does one document this when observations focus on only the sample person?
4 The "raw protocols" describing behavior must be transformed into countable units – types of acts – through application of systematic, operationalized criteria.
   Problem: If the types of acts are defined in advance, observers can focus more carefully and specifically on the most significant behavior; but what about all the other behavior that is thus neglected? When *should* operationalized definitions be worked out? (In the Six Cultures research most of the behavioral definitions appear to have been worked out *after* field work had begun.)
5 The raw protocols should be coded by someone who does *not* know the actors and is unaware of any research hypotheses, as such foreknowledge could lead to biases in coding (e.g., tendency to code Barbara, Pete, and Carl as aggressing frequently, because we know they are aggressive little scamps from long months of interaction with them).
   Problem: The coders have a difficult time interpreting behavior because they have so little to go on, and they do not "know the culture."

The problems with systematic behavioral observations are such that the rigorous data must be supplemented with general participant observation, interviewing, and other supporting materials. The Six Cultures project was, in fact, very strong in that regard because the behavioral observations and coding were buttressed with a rich variety of qualitative, contextual information.

The use of carefully programmed behavioral observation as a research tool is becoming more frequent in anthropology. For example, in a highly sophisticated study relating verbally expressed attitudes to behavior, Nancy Graves (1970) observed mother-child interaction among Anglos, and Spanish-Americans in the Southwest, and Baganda families in East Africa. Graves was interested in the extent to which mothers' conceptions about "locus of control" ("the degree to which one believes that what occurs is a result of one's own actions or of forces external to oneself") were reflected in child-rearing techniques. In addition to extensive interviews with mothers, Graves observed each mother in her sample for at least three hours in interaction with her preschool children. The observational data were then coded for content such as mother "explains," "teaches," "suggests," "commands," "demands," and so on. Graves used statistical techniques to examine the relationship of mothers' attitudes about the locus of control and social situations (e.g., rural vs. urban residence, education, etc.) to child-rearing behavior.

Behavioral observation was used by Gene and Marjorie Muehlbauer (1975) to study political factionalism. Noting the frequent occurrence of avoidance behavior between persons meeting on the street outside the window of their research residence, they converted their casual impressions into a careful "actonic" system of observation with time-sampling and an operationalized definition of what constituted avoidance. They were able to analyze statistically the relationships between avoidance behavior and "inter-party encounters."

In research in Australia, Woodrow Denham (1973) spent many hours observing behavior in an aborigine community from a distance and systematically recording pieces of information such as the composition of interacting groups, group size, length of time particular activities were engaged in, and so on. The heavy focus on observation may seem strange to the typical anthropologist, but, together with interview data and more usual ethnographic material, Denham was able to develop some important insights that might not have been possible had he played a more obtrusive, *participant*-observer role.

Proxemics, kinesics, and videotape research

Most of the behavioral observations we have discussed here involve more-or-less commonsense categories of actions at the most overt, explicit levels of analysis. The units of description are relatively broad, such as "help," "hit," "wrestle," "greet," "avoid," and so on. Some anthropologists have focused on the less conscious and overt expressive bodily behaviors and on symbolic use of spatial relationships. The focus on details of bodily movement is often referred to as *kinesics*; the study of social symbolic uses of space was labeled *proxemics* by Edward T. Hall.

Proxemics and kinesics involve such fineness of observational detail that special training is required in the terminology and notational systems by which gestures, postures, touches, and other bodily motions can be recorded. Edward T. Hall (1963, 1975) and O. Michael Watson (1970, 1972) have described these observational techniques in detail. The research of psychologists Robert Sommer (*Personal Space*, 1969) and R. G. Barker (*Ecological Psychology*, 1968) is also relevant to this methodological domain.

Watson and Graves (1966) tested some of Hall's earlier generalizations about differences between Arab and North American proxemic behavior by analyzing the pair-wise intracultural interactions of sixteen male Arab students and sixteen male North American students. Using Hall's system of detailed notations, they coded:

1 *Sociofugal-sociopetal axis* (interrelations of shoulder alignments).
2 *Kinesthetic factors* ("potential to strike, hold, caress or groom" [Hall, 1963]).
3 *Touch code* (from holding and caressing to "no contact").
4 *Visual* (eye contact).
5 *Voice loudness.*

Their results strongly supported Hall's generalizations about Arab-American cultural differences. "Arabs confronted each other more directly than Americans when conversing . . . they sat closer to each other . . . they looked each other more squarely in the eye . . . they conversed more loudly . . . and *no overlapping* is to be found between the distribution of mean scores . . ." (Watson and Graves, 1966:977).

Anyone who has watched instant replays in the Sunday afternoon TV sports spectaculars can appreciate the potential significance of videotape recording as a technical aid to proxemic and kinesic research. Too often when we watch the raw action we pause in puzzlement, pondering: "What happened?" Videotaping of social interaction has become increasingly common, especially in the 1970s with the advent of relatively inexpensive portable cameras. Lyn Miles (1976) used videotape to examine the sign-language performances and other behaviors of chimpanzees at the University of Oklahoma Primate Center. Most of the research by R. and B. Gardner, Roger Fouts, and others on chimpanzee sign language has been accomplished without much technical equipment, and critics have often questioned the accuracy of the observational techniques. Filmed scenes (used mainly for teaching, reporting research, and publicity, rather than as a primary research tool) often left viewers debating over whether they had actually seen a chimp make the signs identified by the researchers. Miles found that playing and replaying several hours of videotaped materials of chimpanzee-human interaction produced a richness of behavioral data that had been overlooked in previous work. The complexities of sign language, chimp gestures and vocalizations (mixed with the verbal and postural outputs of the humans in the scene) are well beyond the record-keeping capacities of even well-trained observers.

Here is a segment (a few seconds) of complex interactions between the chimp, Ally, and a human, as transcribed from videotape:

Human researcher	Ally (chimpanzee)
What do you want?	
	(Play posture).
What?	
	Tickle me (sign).
Who?	
	You tickle me (sign).
(Tickles Ally).	
	(Looks at the teddy bear).
	That baby (sign).
Tickle baby.	
	(Tickles the teddy bear).
	(Play posture) me (sign).
Now what?	
	Tickle Ally (sign).

Many researchers who use videotape equipment have focused on theoretical questions at a more abstracted level than the body-language analysis of Hall, Watson, and Miles. DeHavenon (1975) and others have concentrated on coding of "authority," "compliance," "food access," and a variety of dimensions of behavior that require operational definitions at a different level of complexity than that of proxemics.

Videotaped analysis of behavior in non-Western settings has been carried out by Allan Hoben in Ethiopia, Orna Johnson in South America, and others. Johnson (1975) videotaped Machiguenga intrahousehold behaviors in order to examine co-wife interaction and spouse behavior in polygynous families. She found that, despite the supposed cultural ideals of co-wife equality, there were significant differences in tasks, time spent outside the house, and other activities of co-wives. This research was different from some videotape observations in that data analysis involved *both* filmed scenes and nonfilmed activities.

The great advantage of videotaping as a technique for getting detailed protocols of behavior suggests a major problem in this kind of research. The very fullness of the information on videotape makes it an extremely slow and tedious process to make the transition to coded, usable data. The transformation of 15 hours of Miles's videotaped chimpanzee behavior required at least 300 hours of very tiring, ofttimes discouraging, viewing, reviewing, coding, and checking. In the archives of various research projects there are undoubtedly many reels of film and videotape (as well as audiotape recordings) that have never been fully analyzed because of the tedium and difficulties involved in the process.

Content analysis of folktales, myths, and other literature

Most of us engage in informal content analysis of literary or dramatic materials from time to time. Driving home after viewing a Japanese movie, we may comment, "The Japanese seem extremely concerned with family relations." Such a comment arises from inferences about the relationships between artistic productions and the lifeways and personalities of the people who create them. In more guarded moments we would state such generalizations as hypotheses "requiring further research."

The folktales and myths of nonliterate and literate societies constitute an archive of thematic materials that have been a rich mine of information for various kinds of analysis. Sometimes these archives are used to infer psychological characteristics of people; they are often invoked for the analysis of religious beliefs; and they also serve as evidence concerning the transmission of information (diffusion) from culture to culture. Songs, proverbs, riddles, jokes, and other standardized verbal lore are a significant adjunct to them. Benjamin Colby used a complex statistical method in analyzing the contents of folktales and other text materials in several societies:

By using a revised set of word-groups . . . and by dividing a collection of Eskimo folktales . . . and Japanese folktales . . . into sections, an unexpected number of statistically significant patterns emerged. Each tale was divided into nine equal parts. These were then grouped into nine sections. All the first parts of the folktales were put into section one, the second parts into section two, and so on up to section nine. The word group frequencies of these sections were then graphed and tested for statistical significance. Out of 195 independent word-groups counted for the Eskimo material, forty five or 23% were statistically significant at the .01 level using a chi-square test for "flatness." For the Japanese material, 23% were also statistically significant at this level. (Colby, 1966a:382.)

Table 6.2 details the patterning of the words *fight* and *death* in a sample of Eskimo folktales. From these tabulations it would appear that the theme of fight-

Table 6.2. *Patterns of occurrence of "fight" and "death" in Eskimo folktales*

1	1- -(2)
2- - -(3)	2
3-(1)	3- - -(3)
4-(1)	4- - - -(4)
5- - - - - -(6)	5
6- - - - - - - -(8)	6- - - - - -(6)
7- - - - - - -(7)	7- - - - - - - -(8)
8- - - - -(5)	8- - - - - - - - -(9)
9-(1)	9- - - - - - - - - -(10)
Fight	Death

ing reaches a climax shortly after the midpoint of Eskimo tales, and tapers off at the end. Death, on the other hand, shows a steady increase from the beginning to the end of these tales, so if only one death occurs in an Eskimo folktale, one would be fairly safe in predicting that it comes near the end of the tale. By comparing Eskimo and Japanese folktales, Colby has demonstrated that the patterning in these archival materials varies significantly in ways that are congruent with other aspects of these cultures. Thus, "the pattern of the concept of death in the Eskimo tales . . . reflects the continual preoccupation with life and death of people in a difficult environment. It illustrates the Eskimos' inevitable concern with such basic matters as food, hunting, maintaining physical strength, and staying alive. The Japanese, on the other hand, are more concerned with subtle social situations and strategies than with human survival." (Colby, 1966b:796.)

Hypotheses about differences in social stratification, male–female roles, warlike tendencies, concern with magic, and a wide variety of other elements have been defined and enumerated in cross-cultural folklore samples. These processes of content analysis are very similar to the analysis of themes and elements in TAT materials, sentence-completion projections, and other personality data. Folklore, however, is thought to be the property of an identifiable cultural *group* – hence patterns of social content are said to characterize a population (or time period) rather than individual persons.

The analysis of narrative materials should take account of the following methodological cautions:

1   The body of materials should be assembled with care so that items from different time periods and different regional subgroups are identified.
2   The materials to be analyzed may be defined as *all* myths and tales from a particular people and period or else as a *representative sample* of those.
3   Procedures for scanning and abstracting from the texts should be clearly described.
4   Components such as themes, progressions, motivations, deep structures, opposites, and structural levels must be defined so that other researchers can test their applicability.
5   Where numerical statements of "more than" or "frequently" or "related to" are used, some form of quantification of the relevant categories or features is useful.
6   The reliability of content analysis can often be checked by having two different "coders," working independently, apply the analytic system to the same materials. If two independently working analysts cannot obtain approximately similar results, the content analysis is indeed, a "myth about myth" (C. Levi-Strauss's comment about his own work).

Beyond mere counting of themes or features of myths, movies, or other narrative materials, and testing of hypotheses about these units, various more complex kinds of analysis have been developed, in which the basic structures are identified. Colby (1975) referred to these studies as the search for "cultural gram-

mars." Such grammars, from Colby's point of view, are not simply static structures, but "strategies for solving problems, systems for telling stories, production
procedures for iconic representations, rules of architectural composition, and ritual systems" (1975:914). He gives the example of "African school children pick-
ing up strategies for taking IQ tests similar to the strategies used by American
school children, so that both groups perform certain tasks better than do their un-
tutored peers. . . ." The plots and sequences of folklore embody cultural
strategies, or grammars, so that the purpose of analysis is to transform the raw
materials into more abstract and theoretically significant forms.

Unfortunately, the arena of thematic analysis, of myths and other materials, is
crowded with exciting and provocative essays and interpretations, few of which
are ever subjected to scientific testing. The fascinating writings of Levi-Strauss
have dominated this domain of research, even though many of his structural
analyses are not testable and can be regarded as myths about myths. Colby commented that Levi-Strauss's works "seem to have been produced with an eye to
Parisian intellectual appetites rather than to scientific canons. Thus, attempts at
describing the symbolic component are still in the prescientific stage . . ."
(Colby, 1975:914).

Physical traces: erosion and accretion

In their field work, anthropologists have a long history of Sherlock Holmes-like
acuity in deriving data from physical traces. A well-worn path provides excellent,
though incomplete, evidence concerning the volume of traffic between two
communities; the different states of disrepair of buildings provide possible indexes of relative affluence; the extensiveness of refuse heaps gives testimony to
durations of occupation – a type of evidence that has been raised to full professional status by archeologists. On a more mundane note, numbers of liquor bot-
tles in garbage cans (and other places) have been used as evidence concerning
differential alcohol consumption. The extensive research by William Rathje and
associates on the contents of people's garbage in Tucson has resulted in a number
of impressive discoveries, including measures of wasted foodstuffs and differences
in dietary patterns, related to social class.

These are examples of fairly obvious unobtrusive measures. The imaginative
fieldworker will find many other possibilities for inferring social information
from the physical marks of wear and tear (and pollution) people habitually im-
pose upon their physical environments. Air photos, too, have been used by
archeologists, geographers, and occasionally by social anthropologists to examine
the physical traces of human cultural behavior.

Archives and other written records

In most parts of the world nowadays governments and their agents maintain a variety of records concerning population sizes, births and deaths, crimes, marriages, and other social statistics. These kinds of data are of relatively recent origin in many parts of the world, and anthropologists carry out field research among many peoples for whom no such records exist. Nonetheless, fieldworkers should make every attempt to obtain official archival data whenever possible, even though these materials frequently are incomplete or distorted for particular communities.

In many areas of the world, churches and other private organizations have been more important than governmental agencies in the maintenance of records concerning vital statistics. Subject to their own particular kinds of distortions, church records may be very important sources of data on genealogies, ritual relationships (such as godparenthood), as well as on religious activities and practices.

Another significant archival data source is the local cemetery, whose monuments give information about kinship groups, birth and death dates, and relative social importance as reflected in the size and elaborateness of tombstones and the quality of upkeep. One of the most extensive uses of the archival material of cemeteries is that of Warner (1959) in his monograph *The Living and the Dead*. Warner consulted official cemetery documents to establish a history of the dead and through interviewing, observation, and trace analysis added further data to his description of graveyards. The archeologist Deetz has made an extensive investigation of cemeteries in New England in studying problems related to archeological theory (Deetz and Dethlefsen, 1967).

Records of court cases are important archival sources, not only for people studying legal systems, but for a variety of other purposes as well. While court records are in written form in many parts of the world, "court records" for nonliterate groups are available only through detailed interviewing of specially knowledgeable informants – judges, lawyers, and other practitioners. In many cases, even in modern communities, examination of legal archives requires an interplay between written and oral sources. Other archival sources of potential usefulness include medical records at local hospitals and clinics, shipping and receiving logs at transportation terminals, newspaper collections, high school and college yearbooks and other commemorative publications, and land office records.

Frank Cancian (1965) based an important part of his study *Economics and Prestige in a Maya Community* on the archival information concerning *"cargo careers"* in the community of Zinacantan (see Chapter 4). To test propositions about the functioning of the system Cancian needed to have information about all the *cargos* held by the people in his sample. He describes his collection of the total career sample as follows:

The total career sample includes all recorded cases of men who have passed more than one *cargo*. Only name, hamlet of residence, and *cargos* passed are included. These cases were taken from several sources. All of the cases from the Hteklum and Apas censuses and the Paste economic sample are included. In addition there are several cases that Juan was able to remember in the course of doing the Paste census. All the cases recorded in interviews on diverse subjects and in casual conversations are also included. A major source of information about *cargo* careers was the responses of informants to open ended questions like: "Name all the people you know who have passed an Alferez *cargo.*" Manuel produced the overwhelming proportion of the answers elicited by this method. This method of questioning produced more information on people who had passed prestigious *cargos* than on people who had passed lesser *cargos*. This is a defect in the sampling, but I have no reasons to believe that this defect significantly affects the results of the analysis of the total sample. (Cancian, 1965:203–4.)

Cancian also had available to him one significant written archival source concerning the *cargos*. Sometime during the 1940s, the people of Zinacantan began keeping waiting lists of people who had requested particular *cargos* for the future. "The lists are kept in hard-cover notebooks, and a page or more is devoted to each year in the future to the last year for which there is a *cargo* requested" (Cancian, 1965:176). This data archive was of crucial importance to Cancian in his analysis of the functioning of the *cargo* system.

Technical equipment in field work

Compared with many other sciences, methods of observation in anthropological work generally require very little in the way of specialized measuring and observing devices. The fieldworker is the main instrument of observation, and most of the tools of research discussed in this incomplete inventory are simply methods for sharpening his perceptions and standardizing the recording of observations. Interaction chronographs are not generally taken out into the kinds of communities that anthropologists most frequently study. Recent developments in recording devices and photographic equipment have provided some important supplemental items to the anthropological fieldworker's kit, however.

Tape recorders

Mechanical recording devices were already being used by anthropologists in field work in the late nineteenth century (Rowe, 1953), particularly for recording folktales and other oral literature, but the old Gramophones and other recording devices were too cumbersome for most field purposes. When magnetic tape recorders came into use after World War II, it became feasible for ethnographers to record relatively large amounts of conversation and other aural materials in the field.

During the 1960s tape recorders became extremely compact, portable, reliable, and therefore invaluable as field-work equipment. Life-history materials and other longer narratives from key informants are frequently tape-recorded in order to ensure accuracy and completeness. It is advisable that whenever possible respondents' replies to TATs and other psychological instruments be recorded fully on tape. The ethnographer with pencil and notebook is physically incapable of recording verbatim the statements of respondents when these are given in a natural manner. Improved microphone equipment makes it possible for the fieldworker to record all of the verbal transactions in meetings, conferences, and other important events.

Because the tape recorder as note taker is far superior to the paper-and-pencil ethnographer in most instances, fieldworkers are sometimes tempted to try to "get everything on tape." This strategy is ill advised, however. Transcribing materials from tapes into typewritten notes is an extremely tedious and time-consuming task at best; one suspects that there are great numbers of untranscribed tapes in the files of those ethnographers who have been most avid in the use of this equipment. Also, there are many contexts in which presence of a tape recorder – even a small one – is resented by the people in the research community; or at least it introduces a foreign element into social action and may seriously interfere with the naturalness of the people's behavior. Fieldworkers should therefore use tape recorders with discretion and should seek to minimize the intrusive effects of mechanical recordings. It is of great importance that the fieldworker be so familiar with the tape-recording equipment that it can be operated with a minimum of distractions and uneasiness. The flustered fieldworker fiddling with tape-recording equipment has little chance of maintaining the naturalness of conversational flow.

Cameras and photography

It is rare indeed that an ethnographer goes into the field without a camera. Also rare in anthropological fieldwork is the conscious and carefully planned use of photography as a research tool. An important exception to this generalization is the work by Bateson and Mead (1942), who made an extensive study of the Balinese by means of photography as a central observational technique. Mead also collaborated with MacGregor (1951) in a photographic study of Balinese childhood based on photographs by Gregory Bateson. In recent years John Collier, Jr., has been an outstanding advocate of the use of photography in anthropological research. His book, *Visual Anthropology: Photography as a Research Method* (1967), is a must for all anthropological fieldworkers. Collier has described some of the routine uses of photography in providing general orientation to research sites, in surveying and mapping, and in documenting complex events such as festivals and celebrations. He has also pointed out important possibilities for using photographs in interviewing. Respondents' reactions to photographs can be an important projective technique. Collier described his own research project, in which a sample of twenty-two Indian households in the San Francisco Bay area were studied photographically.

After contact and sufficient rapport had been established by one of the project interviewers, each of the families . . . was photographed on a single visit with consent and by appointment. The fieldworker was present as well as myself, the photographer. In all cases living rooms and kitchens were thoroughly photographed. In all but four houses one or more bedrooms were also covered. The focus was chiefly upon the contents of the household and its arrangements, with wide angle shots to show placement of the various items and furniture and the relationship between rooms, and with close-up shots to show areas of particular interest such as mantels and bureaus and the tops of television sets where small but presumably valued objects were collected. (Collier, 1967:82.)

The analysis of the data

. . . consisted of an inventory of the objects in each of the houses, a comparison of the inventories, with each other, and a comparison of the inventories with what was known about the families from the interview and questionnaire data. Finally there was an attempt to bring these together with the general concerns of the project. This was done by indicating how the houses reflected the attitudes toward "Indianness" and the attitudes toward the dominant culture, and by attempting to identify the value systems by which the various families operated in the urban settings. (Ibid., 83–4.)

Although Collier did not employ any complex statistical analysis, the definitions of observational elements are relatively clear and objective. Collier's monograph includes important technical information concerning photographic equipment.

Cinematography in anthropological research

In *Visual Anthropology* Collier also gave attention to the use of cinematography in anthropological research. He pointed out that, in addition to their pioneering work in use of still photography, Margaret Mead and Gregory Bateson also carried out research using films. Movie film as a research tool should not be confused with the making of ethnographic movies such as Flaherty's *Nanook of the North* (1925) or more recent classics like *The Hunters* by John Marshall and Robert Gardiner (1956). These ethnographic movies are much more pertinent as educational and informational devices than as research materials.

Collier noted that

> . . . film is *the* tool for analysis of process where technological innovation or subtle abstraction on technological change is needed. In anthropology film is not only the complete way of recording choreography but also the most direct way of analyzing dance or ceremony, where so many elements are in motion together. In this situation human memory in notebook recordings becomes wholly inadequate and highly impressionistic.

> . . . *only* the moving picture film can record the realism of time and motion, or the psychological reality of varieties of interpersonal relations. As an example, it is hard to evaluate the character of love between children and parents from still photographs, whereas film can record the family tempo, the nature of touching, how long, how often, and the way an older expresses fondness for a younger brother. (Ibid., 128.)

Gregory Bateson made an observational training film for psychiatrists consisting of two sequences of behavior – giving the baby his bath and feeding the baby – in three families. Collier himself has produced an experimental film, called A *Family's Day,* that was made with a total budget of only $400.

Sorenson and Gajdusek (1966) have made extensive use of cinema for recording behavior – especially children's behavior – and socialization scenes among a number of New Guinea peoples. These researchers are particularly interested in detailed study of development of motor patterns in children, especially children raised in distinctly non-Western social environments. They note that the opportunities for studying relatively "untouched" peoples is rapidly drawing to a close, and the research film is one important way to preserve these "nonrecurring ethno-environmental data."

> We may look at fondling, close bodily contact, nursing, feeding, carrying postures, swaddling, rocking, sleeping, grooming, sucking, genital handling, pacifying, attention to crying, encouragement of walking or talking, enforcement of modesty, language and gesture, singing, associated movement of speech, styles of sitting and gait, mannerisms associated with emotional tension, modes of skilled motor performance, and many other aspects of behavior in a culture and study the range of style manifested by the culture or even by single individuals in it. This we can often do as well from extensive photographic records as while in the field and, in some cases, even better than in the field . . . similarly, we can capture the components of motion in rapid complex movements as in gestures or gesticulation; climbing trees, vines or ladders; tumbling or falling; jumping and running; and quarreling or fighting and find standardized styles or unusual components differentiating the actions as performed by children of one culture from that of another. . . . At present we are only learning to look – slowly discovering what to see. To do this successfully we find that the ability repeatedly to review photographic data on child behavior with convenience, and to look at it in the various frame per second partitioning provided by cinema – returning to the same sequences time and again, continually comparing and contrasting – is of utmost importance, and is an advantage often totally unavailable in the

study of the fleeting unrecapturable events and moments often witnessed while in the field. (Sorenson and Gajdusek, 1966:156–7.)

A number of research films are available from Gajdusek and Sorenson at the National Institutes of Health. This fact illustrates an important point about research films, namely, that they provide a form of data easily lent by one researcher to another so that independent studies can be made of the same materials. Production of useful research films is clearly an expensive process, and requires expertise on the part of the movie maker. On the other hand, the films do not require much editing and finishing, for ideally, research films are assembled with as little editing as possible in order to preserve the original raw data intact and in correct chronological sequence.

Multi-instrument research

Each of the research tools and techniques mentioned in this chapter and the previous one has serious limitations. Interviews, questionnaires, tests, and many other instruments involve confronting individuals with somewhat artificial stimuli, and the awareness of being studied may produce distortions in people's responses. On the other hand, various unobtrusive observations often have a contrived and an indirect character. Therefore, examining cultural behavior with a *variety of different approaches* greatly enhances the credibility of research results.

Webb, Campbell, Schwartz, and Sechrest (1966) have discussed this point in terms of the concept of *outcroppings*, based on an analogy from geology. The physical phenomena pertaining to the different ages and stages of the earth's crust are for the most part buried deeply in the ground. However, the warping and folding of the earth's crust, and erosion by glaciers, winds, and streams, have exposed numerous *outcroppings* – traces or samples from which inferences about the geological phenomena can be made. These outcroppings vary in their structural relationships to other features of the earth's crust, and various tools of observation are combined in examining them. Similarly,

. . . it can be noted that a theory predicting a change in civic opinion, due to an event and occurring between two time periods, might be such that this opinion shift could be predicted for many partially overlapping populations. One might predict changes on public opinion polls within that universe, changes in sampled conversation on commuter trains for a much smaller segment, changes in letters mailed to editors and the still more limited letters published by editors, changes in purchase rates of books on relevant subjects by that minute universe, and so on. In such an instance, the occurrence of the predicted shift on any one of these meters is confirmatory and its absence discouraging. If the effect is found on only one measure, it probably reflects more on the method than on the theory . . . a more complicated theory might well predict differential shifts for different meters, and again the evidence of each is relevant to the validity of the theory. The joint confirmation between pollings of high income populations and commuter train conversations is much more validating than either taken alone, just because of the difference between the methods in irrelevant components . . . any given theory has innumerable implications and makes innumerable predictions which are unaccessible to available measures at any given time. The testing of the theory can only be done at the available outcroppings, those points where theoretical predictions and available instrumentation meet. Any one such outcropping is equivocal, and all types available should be checked. The more remote or independent such checks, the more confirmatory their agreement. (Webb, Campbell, Schwartz, and Sechrest, 1966:28.)

Anthropologists have practically always used a multi-instrument and multioutcropping approach, checking the statements of one informant against another, and comparing both with direct experiences in the field community, then digging into the archives for supporting evidence. Adding specialized tools such as structured surveys, rating and ranking tasks, even videotaping, should not lead the researcher to abandon the strategy of the qualitative-quantitative mix in research operations. Some outcroppings can be quantified and analyzed numerically; other outcroppings related to the same basic sociocultural phenomena may be essentially noncountable, but their richness and concreteness lend special credibility that is lacking in the more structured observations. The multi-instrument approach to the study of outcroppings in human behavioral systems implies not only the testing of hypotheses in a number of different ways but also a continued shifting back and forth between qualitative and quantitative observations.

7 Counting and sampling

In earlier chapters, particularly in the discussion of operationalism, we noted the importance of "counting things" in field work and other anthropological research. Anthropological research reports always include statements that *imply* counting, even when quantification was not consciously and systematically carried out. Thus the typical monograph includes statements such as, "Most of the people participate in the festival"; "Very few of the people can avoid paying their taxes to the chief"; "They often work as much as ten to twelve hours a day"; "Very little in the way of news or other contact reaches the village from the outside world"; and so on.

The ubiquity of such quantitative statements in anthropological literature stems, perhaps, from basic processes of human psychological functioning. In fact, not only humans but also other animals are constantly counting things in the process of adapting to their environments. Basic processes of learning, as described by experimental psychologists, most often imply some kind of counting or measurement that permits an animal (human or other) to distinguish between one condition and another as a relevant stimulus for appropriate action. In the simplest experimental situation with animals, the subject (e.g., a rat or monkey) can quickly learn that pressing a bar rewards it with food, even when the reward does not occur every time the bar is pressed. The animal is able to make some approximation or estimate of the *correlation* between pressing the bar and the appearance of food. If the "correlation coefficient" between bar pressing and food pellets falls below certain limits, however, the animal may decide that there is no relationship between its bar pressing and the food. Extinction of the response results.

Similarly, a hunter may, through long years of experience, accumulate a store of information concerning the habits of animals based on frequencies of particular behaviors, without, however, consciously totaling up the instances in favor of his inferential knowledge, as compared with the instances in which his inferred correlation does not hold true. Charles Erasmus, in his book *Man Takes Control*, noted:

Cognition as a causal factor in cultural behavior takes the form of probability predictions – frequency interpretations derived from inductive inference. Experience or observation is the raw material from which frequency interpretations are inductively derived. Tossing a coin, for example, provides experience or observation from which it can be inductively inferred that the frequency of occurrence of each face is the same. It can be predicted, then, that in repeated throws the coin will land heads up 50% of the time. Human knowledge, on which cognition builds, is made up of predictions, which are simply tentative probability statements – never final truths.

Frequency interpretation is not an exclusively human phenomenon. Experiments have shown that birds have a number sense which enables them to select boxes with the same number of spots (never more than seven) as those presented on a cue card. Even in simple trial-and-error learning among animals, certain positive associations are built up when successful choices frequently lead to a reward. The experimental animal is clearly anticipatory in its actions; and as successful responses grow more strongly motivated, one might even consider the animal's behavior "predictive." . . . (Erasmus, 1961:22–23.)

Frequency interpretation may be arbitrarily divided into correlation (simple or sophisticated) and the derived causal assumption that serve as a basis for action. The latter are essentially predictions, which, like probable knowledge, are never final and never foresee all the consequences of action.

Compared with other animals, humans are peculiarly and richly endowed in the extensiveness of their ability, through language and other symbolic systems, to pass on to their fellow humans the accumulation of probability inferences that form the essence of human cultural knowledge. Thus we do not expect every child in our society to learn completely on his own the probabilities of being hit by automobiles in the street, burned by hot stoves, or made ill by eating contaminated materials. These and thousands of other pieces of cultural-probability knowledge are taught to individuals in verbal form without the necessity of direct personal experience. The knowledge pools of various cultures, even in the simplest of societies, are extensive bodies of information, representing stored probability inferences that would appear to be far beyond the learning capability of a single individual in a single lifetime.

When the anthropologist goes into the field to do research, his or her processes of learning are substantially the same as those just described. At first tentatively, and later with greater assurance, one makes probability inferences about various forms of behavior in the community under observation. These probability inferences are accumulated and organized into what we call "culture patterns." The logic of probability inference is not different when the anthropologist shifts attention from the culture patterns of one society to the search for cross-cultural regularities.

Counting in ethnographic reports

Ethnographic reporting in recent decades has shown a great variation in sensitivity to the matter of counting and numerical analysis. It is instructive, for example, to compare the two books on Tepoztlán by Robert Redfield (1930) and Oscar Lewis (1963). Redfield's monograph contains very few instances of numerical description. Lewis, on the other hand, gives table after table of information on the population of Tepoztlán and surrounding villages, sex and age distribution, birth and mortality rates, language and literacy, family size, hours spent by women of a family at various activities, frequency distribution of age at marriage inter- and intrabarrio and intervillage marriages, occupations in 1926 and 1944, and so on, throughout the monograph. Anyone returning to Tepoztlán today would be able to make useful quantified assessments of culture change if statistical data similar to Lewis's materials were collected.

The growing interest among anthropologists in the study of culture change and the advantages of numerical data for analyzing changes over time have probably contributed to the increase in quantified work among cultural anthropologists. Other factors, too, are undoubtedly involved in the trend toward more quantification in field work. In 1969–70, as part of a study of North American ethnographers, we obtained responses from a random sample of fifty-two anthropologists concerning the degree to which they collected quantified data in their most recent field work. In this group nineteen people reported that they invested a great deal of field-work time to the collection of census materials, formal interviews, questionnaires, tests or other quantified data. An additional nineteen reported *some* collection of quantified material, and only thirteen ethnographers reported no time spent in quantitative data gathering (Pelto and Pelto, 1974).

The increase in statistical analysis is also reflected in anthropological literature. Surveying major journals from 1900 to 1970 David Hurst Thomas (1976) found that until 1950 there was virtually no use of statistics in ethnographic papers. Since the early 1960s about 12 percent of ethnographic articles contain some statistical treatment. Archeology and linguistics are less quantified, showing relatively less change over the past twenty years, whereas the use of statistical inference in articles in physical anthropology has increased from about 5 percent in 1940 to over 25 percent in 1970. A marked increase is reflected in most recent volumes. Thus a survey of the cultural anthropology articles printed in the *American Anthropologist* in 1972 showed that 31 percent included quantified materials; 42 percent of papers in *American Antiquity* and 86 percent of the articles in the *American Journal of Physical Anthropology* for that year had statistical analyses (Thomas, 1976:3–4).

British social anthropology, too, exhibits a wide range of variation in the use of quantification in ethnographic materials. The earlier structural-functional studies of Radcliffe-Brown, Evans-Pritchard, and others were usually concerned more with abstract patterns of social groupings than with numerical analyses of observable behavior. In a review of quantification in social anthropology, Mitchell (1967) has suggested that the main stimulus for numerical analysis in ethnographic reporting probably came from Malinowski, although his own works show little evidence of the quantification he advocated. Several of Malinowski's students have made extensive use of quantitative data, especially Firth in his field work in Tikopia (1959) and Richards (1939 and 1940) in her description of Bemba economic organization and marital patterns.

Mitchell feels that counting elements of social behavior is particularly notable in the work of the Rhodes-Livingstone Institute:

Godfrey Wilson, the first Director of the Institute, set the tone thereafter to be followed by making extensive use of quantitative data in his study of Broken Hill in 1939–40 (1941–1942). Subsequently, Gluckman and the anthropologists who worked among the Plateau Tonga of Mazabuka, quantified their analysis of land-holding and usage (Allan *et al.*, 1948). The practice of gathering full data in quantifiable form was established particularly in a field-training trip to the Lamba near Ndola (Mitchell) and (Barnes, 1950), where quantitative information was collected on population characteristics, kinship and plan composition of villages, marriage and divorce, labor migration and family income and expenditure. (Mitchell, 1967:19.)

In his own work, Mitchell has made extensive use of quantification, particularly in a survey of Copper Belt mining towns in Rhodesia. He gathered statistical information on occupations, religion, tribe, marital status, education, wages, and length of residence in the mining towns. A 10 percent random sample of houses in the four towns was used to represent the population. Intensive anthropological studies were then conducted on a selected subsample of the households from the larger survey (Mitchell, 1954). This study also illustrates the usual anthropological pattern of combining qualitative investigation with numerical analysis.

John Beattie (1965) has described the rather extensive quantitative techniques that he employed in research on the Bunyoro kingdom of Uganda. He sent questionnaires to chiefs and headmen at all levels of administration. He also gathered quantified data from 369 private estates in the Bunyoro territory, in addition to which he administered a complicated interview schedule to 100 percent samples of households in his three research communities (Beattie, 1965:39).

There appear to be three principal research situations that have encouraged numerical analysis by anthropologists:

1   *Large and heterogeneous populations.* Anthropologists have turned in increasing numbers to the study of relatively complex societies, many of which are experiencing rapid social change, including urbanization, industrialization, and nationalization. The growing interest in study of American metropolitan populations illustrates this trend. The complexities of research in these situations have forced anthropologists to develop new field techniques to supplement the face-to-face methods appropriate to the study of small communities.
2   *Comparative studies of social change.* The increasing focus on cultural and social change, in place of the earlier concentration on supposedly stable social systems, leads

anthropologists to seek quantifiable measures of social developments such as migration rates, acculturation, changes in family stability, and so on.

3 *Hypothesis testing in research.* A number of field studies in recent times have been directed to the testing of specific hypotheses, often by means of specialized research instruments developed in other areas of the social sciences. In field work involving psychological tests, specialized interview schedules, and other intruments, anthropologists have become increasingly sensitized to the need for numerical analysis.

While there are clear trends toward increased use of quantification in ethnographic reporting, as well as in other kinds of anthropolgical research, not all researchers accept the usefulness of these techniques. John W. Bennett and Gustav Thaiss have suggested that a main reason for anthropological resistance to quantified research procedures has been a commitment to what they call "holistic depiction." This style of field work is generally exploratory and highly flexible. The investigator adjusts his or her activities to the pace of community life rather than to the requirements of the research instruments. Techniques of participation, open-ended interviewing, and keeping up with the daily activities of the people are attuned to a personalized form of investigation in which laboratory procedures and door-to-door surveying appear to be foreign intrusions. Bennett and Thaiss feel that the older techniques of field work "should not be viewed as 'traditional' or 'imprecise,' as some social scientists have done, but rather as simply another approach to the gaining of knowledge of social behavior" (Bennett and Thaiss, 1967:273).

Problems of representativeness: sampling

When we as anthropologists decide to quantify some of our observations of social behavior, we are faced with the problem of defining the universe of observation and devising ways of ensuring that observations fairly represent that universe. Counting is relatively useless, or even misleading, if there are no provisions against biased selection of the observations (units of study) that are to be quantified.

In some cases researchers may find it convenient to include all the people of a research community in a numerical analysis. For example, in small communities it is a common anthropological practice to make a complete census of households. In this situation information on family size and composition, average size of landholdings and other data are based on a 100 percent sample.

Often, however, the anthropologist is confronted with research populations or communities whose size makes the prospect of 100 percent sampling too costly and time consuming. In a town of 4,000 or 5,000 people it is neither necessary nor practical to interview everyone in order to make legitimate generalizations.

In dealing with relatively large populations, anthropologists have sometimes sampled the range of variation by means of a small number of selected typical cases. For example, Manning Nash, in his monograph *Machine Age Maya* (1958), contrasted workers and farmers of Cantel by presenting extensive information about one worker household and one farmer household. His generalizations about family interaction, spending patterns, religious activities, and other characteristics were, of course, based on observation of, and interviews with, a number of families within the community (a population of about 1,700).

In selecting informants and in presenting typical cases, the anthropologist often uses unstated, intuitive criteria as a guide to the sampling. An improvement on this intuitive approach to sampling is evident in David Landy's study of child training in a Puerto Rican village (1965). Landy completed a full census of the community of El Camino (113 families), obtaining many categories of demographic, sociological, and psychological data. He felt that the survey procedure was very useful for developing relationships with all the resident households. From these census data he then selected eighteen lower-class families for intensive study. His selection criteria included geographical representativeness, consideration of family size and composition, father's occupation, and other aspects that he felt were important for their effects on socialization practices. Landy's procedure may be considered a special kind of *quota sample* (see below).

A rather unusual variation in sampling techniques is presented by Gladwin and Sarason in *Truk: Man in Paradise* (1953). In this case the researchers sought to obtain a wide range of contrast in personality types. Gladwin, the anthropologist, obtained ratings from the Trukese concerning the most liked and the most disliked persons in the population. From these preliminary categories,

> . . . six of the most "liked" and six of the most "disliked" of each sex were set apart, and three were selected by chance out of each such group for intensive study; there were thus six persons of each sex in our sample who were putatively "unusual." Of those remaining in the middle range, five of each sex were again selected by chance for inclusion in the sample, making a total of eleven men and eleven women. (Gladwin and Sarson, 1953:211.)

This Trukese example can be considered a three-part *stratified sample*, with stratification criteria derived from a kind of popularity rating.

The examples illustrate ways in which anthropologists have sought representativeness in their field research materials. They were not, however, truly random samples. Strict random sampling requires that every individual (or other unit of observation) in the population has an equal probability of being selected. Randomness in sampling is highly desirable for any quantified data that are to be analyzed by means of inferential statistics.

Defining the universe

No matter what sampling procedures are used, the first task is the delimiting of a population (of people, events, or other units) from which the sample is to be drawn. The favorite population unit of anthropologists has tended to be "the community," but that is often difficult to delimit. Among many East African peoples, for example, homesteads and neighborhood clusters are spread across the land in such fashion that it is difficult to say where one community ends and another begins. On the other hand, in some societies (e.g., Eskimo local groups and urban neighborhoods) membership is often quite variable depending on economic opportunities, seasonal residence changes, and so on.

In northern Minnesota we found that people identified with different communities depending on whether reference was made to postal address, trade areas, school districts, township lines, or other political/geographical subdivisions. We finally concluded on the basis of informants' statements and other data that "school district" provided the most useful and unambiguous way of defining our research populations. Quite often single communities are highly inadequate as representations of the variability within their regions. Ties of kinship and marriage, occupational specializations, and many other social facts cut across community boundaries and suggest that certain kinds of numerical data should be gathered from a multicommunity universe.

Sometimes effective universes for sampling can be defined in terms of natural ecological features, such as "along the river," "in the valley," or "in the coastal zone." Such definitions of sampling populations depend, of course, on whether they fit with the specific purposes of the research.

In urban settings it is often very difficult to identify the boundaries of a particular ethnic subgroup as even ethnic enclaves always include some people who are not members of that ethnic group, while others of that same ethnic identity live elsewhere in the city. One solution is to restrict research to certain census tracts that are known to contain large numbers of the particular groups. In research in Accra, Roger Sanjek took as his community, "the 423 people living in eleven adjacent apartment buildings in one corner of Adabraka [section]" (Sanjek, 1972).

Different sampling strategies in urban research reflect differences in researchers' theoretical intentions as well as variations in size and complexity of the research settings. Thompson (1974) was able to select one individual (randomly) from each discrete city block in Tieul, a Maya-Hispanic center of 13,000 in the western Yucatán. The strategy resulted in a sample of 123 persons, "designed to be representative of the entire population, including all of the barrios and El Centro." This method of sampling would be impractical (and perhaps misleading) in most larger cities.

Robbins, Thompson, and associates used a complex multistage cluster sampling technique in Kampala, Uganda, "in an attempt to tap the full range of socioeconomic diversity within the urban area . . ." (Thompson, 1975:197). Simié, on the other hand, found such precision of sampling impractical in Belgrade.

In selecting subjects for formal interviews, I initially turned to my personal network of friends and neighbors, who became the first families to be studied in depth. They, in turn, placed me in contact with other households and individuals. For example, an informant who coached an amateur basketball team was able to help me establish rapport with the families of several members of the club. . . . A large Belgrade construction company provided me with a list of workers who had been informed that they would be interviewed by an "American ethnologist." There was a conscious effort to control the sample in such a way that it would represent a wide range of experience in the city. (Simié, 1973:25.)

Even in relatively small communities it is sometimes difficult to obtain a total enumeration of families or households from which to draw a random sample. Robert Mitchell solved this problem in his Nigerian research by using aerial photographs:

(1) With a sharp pencil I numbered every house in the area on the photograph. The total number of houses in Aremo was 741. (2) I selected 100 numbers between 1 and 741 from a table of random numbers. (3) I located each of these numbers on the photograph and circled the house. (4) Using the photograph as a map, my staff and I located the 100 houses. . . . (Mitchell, 1973:104).

Other types of universes

In a study of "time allocation in a Machiguenga community," Allen and Orna Johnson defined a universe of *time units* from which to draw their random samples. During several months of field work in the Upper Amazon of Southeastern Peru, the Johnsons adopted a system of random "spot checks" in order to estimate amounts of time that each Machiguenga individual in their sample spent in various activities. "The population sampled included all households within reasonable walking distance (up to 45 minutes) from our house, so that they could be visited regularly. . . ." The sample of thirteen households was divided into two groups: "upstream and downstream, which were visited alternately at random hours."

"Hours were selected in advance with a table of random numbers, and households were visited during the hour specified. . . . Tabulations show that visits were evenly apportioned by hours of the day and by season. Visits were made on 134 different days, resulting in 3,495 cases (observations of individuals)" (Johnson, 1975).

This method of random spot checks is extremely useful in ensuring that field workers do not introduce biases through nonrandom observations. For example, if we visit household A regularly at 10:00 A.M., and household B at 4:00 P.M. (and household C only rarely), our generalizations about their "habitual patterns of work" will be distorted to the extent that activities in the morning are different from those in the late afternoon.

To an increasing extent, archeologists are using sampling techniques in both surveying and digging of sites. Thomas reports the following strategy in his study of a 300-square-mile area in the Great Basin region (approximately the size of a single Shoshoni family's "territory"):

For purposely practical reasons, I chose to conduct my survey in 500-meter squares. The survey areas, roughly one-third of a mile on a side, became the elements of the survey. There are a total of 1400 of these survey tracts in the Reese River Valley. I soon realized that the total length of time required to survey all 1400 elements was prohibitive – something like 20 field seasons with a crew of 30 people! . . . Figuring that I could probably muster field crews for two summers of fieldwork, I would have sufficient time to survey about 140 or so of the 500-meter square tracts. Thus, I needed a 140/1400 . . . or a 10 percent sample. (Thomas, 1976:130.)

There are many other kinds of sampling universes besides human populations and communities. The universe of "all marriages" (for a given population) is a particularly difficult aggregate to isolate; yet estimates of divorce rates, endogamy, preferred marriage partners, and many other analyses depend on effective delimiting of this domain. Barnes (1967) has discussed this problem in detail, pointing out that one effective definition of the "population" of all marriages is obtained if one includes all the marriages ever experienced by the living members of the (designated) community. In societies with adequate written records it may be possible to select a research universe consisting of "all marriages recorded in (a particular church or civil register)." Naturally, the usefulness of such a universe depends on preliminary ethnographic research on whether all or most marriages in the area are in fact recorded in the register.

Similarly, other written registers, censuses, police records, or archives may or may not be useful as research universes, depending on their correspondence (or lack of it) to the real events they purport to list. Whether populations for sampling are to be based on written records, or on natural, observable aggregates in the research area, field work in the form of participant observation and interviewing is usually necessary in order to select the best possible ways of defining such universes.

Types of sampling

The statistical operations used for making inferences about populations (of persons, events, or other units) require that samples must be drawn randomly from known populations. This is because statistical procedures are based on complex calculations concerning the patterns of equiprobable events. Textbooks in statistics and probability often begin their explanations with an examination of the probabilities of various patterns, such as those associated with flipping coins or throwing dice, assuming that the dice are not loaded and that the coins flipped are fair.

The term "random sampling" thus has a very specific meaning, even though the word "random" is sometimes wrongly equated with haphazardness. Even today there are many research operations undertaken by anthropologists and others in which samples have been gathered by some kind of casual process to which the investigator then attaches (wrongly) the label "random." If, for example, the investigator enters a room in which there are about a hundred persons and haphazardly interviews ten of these persons, he may be tempted to claim that he has taken a 10 percent random sample. But is it really true that each of the persons in the room had an equal chance of being selected for interview? Perhaps a number of persons were sitting in the corners of the room, and the interviewer did not go to these corners, so those persons did not have any chance of being selected. Or perhaps the interviewer has an unconscious bias against persons with red hair; consequently, he did not interview any red-haired persons. We can easily imagine a number of other reasons why the casual interviewer unintentionally selects a biased sample. In anthropological field work, researchers may in fact encounter situations in which strict procedures for ensuring randomness cannot be achieved. The haphazard sample may be the best that can be obtained, given the situation at hand. The researcher should be aware, however, that such a sample does *not* correspond to the strict definition of random sample and should be treated with appropriate caution.

Often the best way to obtain a true random sample is by means of a table of random numbers. In this procedure, a given research population is delineated, and each individual in that population is assigned a number. The researcher then selects a table of random numbers (these are provided in most standard textbooks on statistics) and begins reading these numbers in consecutive order, starting at any point left or right, top or bottom, in the number table. Each time one encounters a number corresponding to one of the numbers in the population, the person with that number is selected for the sample. The investigator continues scanning the table of random numbers until the requisite-size sample has been selected. This method of choosing a sample requires that the researcher be able to designate each individual (or other unit) in his population uniquely. For a research community, this requires a census of the local population.

Frequently, researchers define populations that cannot be enumerated individually in advance, but which can be identified as individual units during the process of the survey. This is often the situation in fairly large populations, in which 100 percent census enumeration is impractical (thus eliminating the possibility of using a table of random numbers). In the Copper Belt towns studied by Hortense Powdermaker, for example, a random sample was obtained by designating every *n*th (household) unit for interviewing. In such cases, the sampled units may be designated as every third, every fifth, every tenth, every twentieth (or other *n*th), depending on the ratio to total population desired in the sample.

A similar method of sampling by designating every *n*th unit is often necessary when one is sampling events. For example, a sample of business transactions in a market might require that the observer sample every fifth or every tenth transaction (depending on the frequency of such transactions), because one would ordinarily have no way of assigning random numbers to such events in advance. An alternative sampling technique in market transactions might be a system of random spot checks, following the Johnsons' example.

Stratified samples

Frequently a research population contains important subgroups such as castes, social classes, or ethnic groups. In such cases, the investigator may want to ensure that each subgroup is adequately represented in the sample. The Tri-Ethnic Research Project, carried out by Richard Jessor, Theodore Graves, and their associates, is an example of this kind of situation. They studied alcohol use, antisocial behavior, and other patterns related to acculturation in a small southwestern town whose population is about one-half Anglo-American, one-third Spanish-American, and one-sixth Indian. Because comparisons among the three ethnic groups was a main aspect of the research design, random samples were drawn separately from the three subgroups. The population was also stratified by sex.

Names were drawn from an alphabetized complete census list of the adult members of the communities; the sampling ratio was 1 in 6 for the Anglos and Spanish, and because of their smaller proportion in the community, 1 in 3 for the Indians. Cooperation was excellent: 96% of the designated respondents who were still living in or near the community were interviewed. The final sample size was 221, comprised of 93 Anglos, 60 Spanish, and 68 Indians. (Graves, 1967:306–21, and Jessor et al., 1968.)

Subdivision, or stratification, of a research population is often necessary, even if the specific intentions of research do not focus on differences among these subpopulations. In many studies, for example, it is important to stratify samples between males and females. Often it is a good idea to stratify a sample in terms of age categories to ensure adequate representation of all generations. In each case the research operation involves the division of the target population into subgroups, after which random sampling is carried out separately in the subpopulations. Stratification by sex, age groups, and other social criteria ensures that these variables can be controlled in later analysis.

For some research purposes, once the designation of strata or subpopulations has been accomplished, samples are drawn from these subpopulations in accordance with their percentages in the overall population. Thus if one-ninth of the population is of ethnic group X, then one-ninth of the respondents should be selected from among them. In many cases, however, this is not necessary or feasible.

When researchers sample disproportionately from subpopulations, they depart from strict randomness for the population taken as a whole. Consequently, statistical adjustments must be made in generalizing about that total population.

Cluster probability samples

Cluster sampling, or *area-probability sampling,* is a technique used to simplify problems of enumerating the total population by first breaking up the research unit into equivalent geographical subunits such as counties, neighborhoods, blocks, and so on. This method of sampling is intended to preserve the criteria of randomness without the necessity for enumerating every individual in the population in advance. In Mexican rural *municipios,* for example, it is often possible to divide the population into a series of named subcommunities and to select a certain proportion of these subunits randomly for inclusion in the survey. Within each unit selected there can be a further subdivision into blocks or subareas of some kind, again selected randomly. Once these smallest territorial units have been selected, individual households or persons can be enumerated and random samples of respondents obtained. Such a procedure eliminates the necessity for a complete enumeration of all dwellings, persons, families, or other primary units within the entire community. It should be noted, however, that this method of sampling can lead to omission of some significant, however small, segment of the population. Thus in our hypothetical Mexican community, random selection of small subcommunities might result in the elimination of all the wealthy people (or some other small but important subgroup) who happen to be concentrated in a single barrio. This point illustrates the need for a preliminary ethnographic survey of geographically defined subunits before any cluster sampling is attempted.

As in the case of our other sampling patterns described earlier, it should be clear that cluster or area-probability sampling can be carried out for other kinds of units besides people or households. That is, it is possible to conceive of clustering events in time sequences, by types of transactions in a commercial scene, by categories of vendors in a large complicated market, and so on.

Nonprobability samples

As already mentioned, the statistical operations frequently used with quantified social data are based on the assumption that sampling has been random from a designated universe or population. The realities of field research, however, frequently present us with situations in which deviations must be made from the ideals of randomness. While haphazard selection of informants, test families, or other units of observation is too naïve for most research purposes, the fieldworker must often make compromises in order to produce data without undue expenditures of time, effort, and money. Where such compromises are necessary, they should be made with full knowledge of the logical weaknesses they entail, and should be acknowledged in research reports.

Quota sampling

Even fairly sophisticated survey research in the United States is often based on sampling procedures that are not strictly random. For example, most public-opinion polls are based not on strict probability samples but rather on so-called *quota sampling*.

In quota sampling the first step is to ascertain some of the important characteristics of the general research population – age, occupations, ethnic groups, income levels, number of years of education, and so on. The sample from the population is then selected to match the general population in all these characteristics. Interviewers collecting individual responses are given considerable latitude in their selection of respondents as long as they keep their designated quotas in mind. After a large portion of the sample has been collected, the researchers can tell by inspection whether the proper proportion of each age category (and other elements of the quota) has been obtained. If the sample is short of respondents in a particular category, interviewers are sent out to get more respondents who fulfill those particular requirements. For example, it may be found that not enough blue-collar workers have been included in the sample. Interviewers then return to the field to correct this shortcoming.

Quota sampling is used in public-opinion polls and other kinds of surveys because it is cheaper and easier than fully random sampling. The researcher who uses this technique should note that, however carefully a quota sample has been constructed to correspond with the total population (in terms of age distribution, occupations, and numbers of other characteristics), this does not ensure that it is representative in other significant social characteristics. Such samples are approximations that may be quite useful for certain rough-and-ready purposes. When the anthropologist (or other social scientist) makes compromises in his sampling procedure, he does so most frequently to save time and money. Short-cuts are sometimes justified, particularly in exploratory studies, in which the anthropologist is testing new research methods and instruments. Also, in some applied situations speedy feedback of information to a client may be more important than exactness of sampling.

The attitudes of the people to be surveyed also affect sampling strategies. The research strategy of Ronald Cohen and associates in Nigeria reflects this aspect of field methodology. They commented that:

> . . . sampling procedures in a non-Western area are a complex result of ideal standards, the exigencies of the field work situation, and the specific goals of the research design. . . . [Our local] research assistants insisted that any random method of selection public or private would create great suspicion. . . . It was finally decided therefore to use local leaders, who promised cooperation, to choose twenty-five respondents of each sex from each research site. The men chosen were to be of three categories; eight of them would be "wealthy," eight "poor," and nine "not-rich-not-poor." (Cohen, 1971:20.)

Although somewhat unusual in form, their procedure could be regarded as a quota sample.

In some cases the anthropologist may feel that the contrast between two research populations is so clear that slight deviations of procedure will not damage the usefulness of the research. For example, in studying mixed Indian-white communities, anthropologists have frequently observed that there are marked differences between the two groups in their patronage of particular stores, entertainment places, and other business establishments. It would be useful to provide some kind of quantified documentation of these observations. If the fieldworker makes several preliminary counts of Indians and whites at, for example, the two different stores in the community, and finds the hunches strongly supported, he may be justified in assuming that the energies and time required for more adequate sampling procedures would not add much additional credibility to the generalizations. However, sampling procedures in connection with structured interviews, psychological tests, and other specialized research instruments should always be as thorough as time and resources permit, because the data from such instruments are usually employed for several different descriptive and correlational analyses.

Honigmann and Honigmann have demonstrated that distortions are likely to be present when fieldworkers use nonprobability sampling techniques. The demonstration involved comparison of nonprobability and probability (random) sampling in a single research site in Pakistan.

The combined random sample shows 9, 60, and 31 percent of the respondents coming from the upper, middle, and lower socioeconomic strata, respectively. In comparison, the opportunistic samples drew 17, 46, and 37 percent of the respondents from those strata. Apparently, by querying men who came to our attention, spoke English, and proved to be willing informants we had especially shown a bias for the uppermost stratum. Why lower-status men were also over-sampled is not clear. (Honigmann, 1973: 278–9.)

The comparisons of the two samples demonstrated that *different results* were obtained from the two samples in assessing awareness of and attendance at films.

Problems of sample size

It has been pointed out that effective random sampling makes possible some reasonable estimates of the characteristics of very large populations, using information gathered from relatively small numbers of persons. For example, a statistically adequate random sample from a population of 1 million needs to include only about two-tenths of 1 percent (ca. 2,000) of the people (Phillips, 1966:265). Enlarging the sample size beyond that point accomplishes very little compared with the cost involved. On the other hand, with small populations of, say, 300 to 500 persons, samples must comprise a considerably larger percentage of the population.

It is commonly accepted that the larger the sample, the greater the accuracy in predicting from this sample to the universe it represents. From this argument it would follow that our samples should always be as large as possible, which gives small comfort to the lonely fieldworker who has plenty of other problems on his or her hands besides trying to get very large samples from all research populations.

There is another element to be considered in this problem of sampling, however. Paul Meehl (1967) has pointed out that the larger our samples, the greater the probability that we will pick up small differences between *any* populations being compared. If we hypothesize that there are differences in IQ between rural and urban populations, we are likely to get *some* result, provided we collect samples of several thousand individuals in the two populations. Large samples can, therefore, provide us with materials in which differences do become apparent as predicted, even though the differences between the sample populations may be very small in magnitude (and theoretical relevance).

Meehl's argument can be used to support research that is designed in terms of relatively small samples. In small samples relationships among variables must be relatively large in order to reach statistically significant levels. Thus any correlations that reach statistical significance are likely to be large enough to be *socially significant* as well. While this argument should not be overextended to justify small samples in every piece of research, it gives some comfort to anthropologists whose haunts are often rather small communities (Benfer, 1968; Rohner and Pelto, 1970).

The fact that anthropologists frequently study rather small samples of individuals should lead them to be all the more careful about sample selection. While it may seem that a sample of fifty men from a total population of eighty-five adult males is such a large percentage that there should be no problems about representativeness, *neither* a large total number nor a large percentage of respondents ensures that a sample is unbiased. Sometimes larger samples are more biased than small samples. This was glaringly evident in the famous case of the *Literary Digest* election polls of 1936. The method of collecting the sample involved bias toward the more affluent in the society (those with telephones); thus the larger the sample, the greater the resulting bias. Similarly, an anthropologist in a small community may collect a large number of responses to an interview, but if he is not systematically guarding against unconscious biases, he may have a sample that is distorted in favor of those persons who like him, those who are more available at certain times of the day or week, those in a particular kin network, or those with other unnoticed tendencies that introduce serious bias.

Small sample sizes (forty to fifty respondents) are not uniformly and universally ideal for the many different purposes for which anthropologists may wish to employ them, but it is useful to point out that small sample sizes are not in themselves automatic barriers to the use of statistical procedures. We occasionally hear researchers claim that their sample was so small that statistical analysis would have been inappropriate. As samples as small as ten or fifteen (persons, items, observations) permit statistical analysis under given conditions, the small size in itself is not sufficient grounds for neglecting statistical analysis. The more likely problem in such cases is that the sample was not collected with statistical procedures in mind and hence could not meet the assumptions of representativeness.

Patterning and sampling

Our commonsense experience in field work and elsewhere tells us that certain kinds of cultural data are so publicly available, homogeneous in patterning, or otherwise apparent that random samples of informants or other kinds of observations are quite unnecessary for establishing their veracity. In most cases, it is perfectly clear that a community has or does not have a school building, that men hunt with bows and arrows, or that it is against the law to burn down public buildings without permission. Also, we do not require a large sample of linguistic informants to produce a working description of standard grammatical forms in English (or any other language). (On the other hand, reliance on single, highly specialized key informants reduces the credibility even of linguistic data.)

No guidelines have been worked out by anthropologists for selecting adequate panels of key informants. However, as attention is focused more and more on the great amount of intracultural variation in beliefs, attitudes, and practices among most human groups, it becomes obvious that some kind of sampling procedure is necessary if ethnographers are to be sure that their sources of information fairly represent intracommunity variations in cultural and social opinions and patterns. Schwab has commented on this problem of selecting informants in connection with his research·in a West African urban community: "The selection of reliable and representative informants became crucial as well as difficult. It was not only a question of whether an individual or group was typical or atypical, but also one of selecting informants who were representative of the diverse social components of the community" (Schwab, 1960:408–21).

Robbins and associates (1969) have suggested that factor-analytic techniques be used to isolate main dimensions of variation within local populations (based on survey or census data) in order that key informants be selected in terms of their representativeness along these main lines of intrapopulation diversity. On the other hand, if fieldworkers feel that the kinds of data they are collecting are most clearly related to a single dimension of variation, say, acculturation or socioeconomic status, it may be sufficient to devise an index or a scale for this one sociocultural dimension and to select informants to be representative, for example, of the high, middle, and low points of this scale.

In addition to the problem of representativeness of key informants, the fieldworker is often confronted with the question of how many informants are enough to establish reliable information about different kinds of cultural patterns. Sometimes the careful selection of four or five persons who are representative of significant intracommunity variations produces such high levels of interinformant reliability that it is unnecessary to add more individuals to the panel.

It may be that there is a marginal zone of data collection, which requires at the outset careful quantitative procedures that include several (independent) informants, but within which the presence of highly patterned responses from a small number of persons can be taken as strong evidence that no further sampling is needed. The general rule might be: "When addition of informants has little effect on the general structure of a complex pattern of data, then the present sample is satisfactory." Unfortunately, no statistical procedures have been worked out for assessing this situation in data collection. This is only one of a series of problems in data analysis for which anthropologists and their numerically inclined friends will need to work out new guidelines and new procedures.

Summary and conclusions

One of the important elements in the operationalizing of research is counting things in order to provide numerical statements of frequencies of different behaviors, ownership of goods and prerogatives, indices of change from one time period to another, and so on. Counting procedures provide clear specifications of the kinds of probability inferences that anthropologists have always worked with in the field (and elsewhere). Also, formalizing one's counting procedures forces the researcher to develop clear definitions of what it is that one claims to be observing. When the anthropologist is asked to be more specific about what he means when he says, "Most of the people visited the city at least once during the year," he may have to redefine the population, saying, "That is, most of the adult males. . . ."

Misplaced quantification is often worse than none at all. Quantification without clear conceptualization of the relevant population, careful selection of a representative sample from the population, and other operational precautions lead to error and mystification. Also, it is clear that many of these methodological precautions require extensive supporting field work – participant observation, interviewing, and other qualitative backup research – to give reality and meaning to the numbers and percentages.

Our initial planning of research projects should, whenever possible, include consultation with statisticians, in order to design sampling procedures and quantitative strategies fitted to effective statistical analysis. Statisticians are of many kinds, though, ranging from "strict constructionists" to more flexible and tolerant numerologists, perhaps more attuned to field research realities in a less than perfect world. Practically all our quantitative research in human communities requires some stretching of basic statistical assumptions. It would, however, be a serious mistake to use that as an excuse to eschew counting and sampling altogether.

8 Measurement, scales, and statistics

Anthropological observations and probability inferences vary from the completely unsystematic quasi counting of some of the old-style ethnographic work to computerized multivariable data processing in many recent works. It is important for us to realize, however, that in most cases the underlying *logic-in-use* of the different studies is much the same, though they look very different in their presentations. As an example, let us briefly examine the logic of Benjamin Colby's computerized analysis of folktales, mentioned in Chapter 6. At first glance his analysis seems complex and strange because (1) the entire process was carried out by computer and (2) the patterns of data are illustrated in a manner that is different from usual renditions of folktale analysis. But we need only look for a moment at these materials to see the simplicity of the entire research plan. It can be conceptualized as follows:

1. (Idea) Perhaps folktales of different peoples can be distinguished in terms of variations in thematic patterning.
2. One way to analyze thematic patterns in folktales is to look at different uses (different frequencies, etc.) of particular words and clusters of words. (Hundreds of folktale analyses have depended on some variation of this essentially simple process.)
3. Counting the frequencies of a great number of different words in a collection of folktales is an incredibly time-consuming process; a computer (when properly programmed) can do the same task much more quickly and accurately.
4. Setting up the folktale materials for the computer requires a more precise format and set of instructions than those generally used by researchers who produce such counting of thematic materials "by hand."
5. Some of the formal trappings of Colby's presentation are derived from the computerization format. However, it would be possible for him to report simply the thematic counts such as those presented in Table 6.2 and make systematic comparisons between Eskimo and Japanese folktales, *without his statistical tests* – the essential logic of the study involves a simple comparison of thematic (word) frequencies in patterned arrays.

Even the most complicated statistical research operations are often quite simple in their logic. Understanding the underlying structure of these procedures is an essential first step in deciphering statistical analyses in the anthropological literature, as well as in developing some elementary numerical operations in one's own work. In the following sections, we will review examples of common statistical usages in anthropological literature. Further information about the mathematical formulas and other features of these procedures can be found in standard textbooks.

Some excellent books in statistics have been written in such straightforward and informative style that anyone with a little background in simple mathematics can follow and make use of at least the more elementary computations. *Nonparametric Statistics for the Behavioral Sciences* by Sidney Siegel (1956) is one such book. Each procedure is illustrated in terms of a simple well-defined problem case. A more recent text, entitled *Elementary Applied Statistics: For Students in Behavioral Science*, by Linton C. Freeman (1965), is also very helpful as a guide to simple statistical procedures. David H. Thomas's recently published book, *Figuring Anthropology* (1976), is the first statistics text designed especially for anthropologists. The book is especially useful in that it includes descriptions of the *coefficient of predictability* (lambda) as well as more complex parametric procedures.

Variables, measurements, and scales

The concepts and categories we use in discussing human behavior are the *variables* used in statistical analysis. If we casually comment that "hunters are self-reliant," we have stated a proposition involving two elements – two variables. For more careful scientific use of those concepts we must define them, find ways to observe (hence measure) them, and relate them to each other. But how is the concept *hunters* a variable? The term "hunters" in that statement takes on meaning only when it is contrasted with some category of nonhunters. The comment that "hunters are self-reliant" really means that "compared with nonhunters, hunting people may be characterized as having a higher degree of self-reliance." The contrast set, hunters/nonhunters, is the *independent* variable in this statement. It is considered the independent variable because it is, in some logical sense, prior to "self-reliance, the *dependent* variable. *Variable* may thus be defined as any of the elements, concepts, or categories in theoretical propositions that are thought to vary in degree or in kind, so as to affect the logic of the propositional statements.

Now that we have identified the variables, the scientific examination of the proposition that "hunters are self-reliant" requires the following steps:

1 Identify a population of cases (cultures, societies, or individuals) that can be sorted into representative samples of hunters and nonhunters.
2 Define "hunters" in such a manner that individual cases can be placed in either the hunter or nonhunter category. Sometimes this step is complicated by the presence of

ambiguous or intermediate cases, so that we may wind up also using an intermediate category in our analysis.

3 Define "self-reliant" in such a manner that observations of the degree of this quality can be made for both hunters and nonhunters. The operationalized definition may be based on judgmental ratings of ethnographic works, psychological tests, interviews with individuals, or other methods of data gathering.

4 Compare the degree of self-reliance to see whether there are differences between hunters and nonhunters.

In this research paradigm the systematic observation of the relevant variables constitutes *measurement*. Thus even the simple assignment of cases into categories – hunter/nonhunter, male/female, or Catholic/Jewish/Protestant – is considered measurement. All measurement consists of assigning scale values – including the judgmental assignment of the values hunter/nonhunter.

Nominal scales

In our research example the independent variable hunter/nonhunter constitutes a *nominal scale*. By definition, a nominal scale consists of "mutually exclusive and non-ordered categories." The categories, or classifications, are not numerically ordered in relation to each other – that is, they are not "more than" or "less than" each other. There are no gradations.

Although nominal scales consist of categories, or classifications, they are *variables* because they constitute different "values" or alternative possibilities of some, more general, concept or class. All of our examples thus far are nominal scales of types of humans. Similarly, the nominal categories matrilineal, patrilineal, or bilateral are different values (types) of kinship systems. The literature of the social sciences involves many variables that are measured as nominal scales – sex, political affiliation, herders versus pastoralists, monolingual and bilingual, ethnic-group membership, disease categories, types of healers, and so on.

The lack of gradation or other quantitative character in nominal categories means that they cannot be manipulated arithmetically in the same manner as, for example, measures of weight or temperature. In general, the only appropriate measure of central tendency, or average, with a nominal scale is the *mode*, the category with the most cases. As a consequence of this lack of quantitative meaning, nominal data can be used for only certain kinds of statistical analysis, as we will discuss shortly.

Ordinal scales

Types of measurement are not absolute, and our data language about human behavior is full of variables that appear as nominal categories in one context and as an ordered series, or ordinal scale, in another. The hunter/nonhunter variable, for example, may make better sense as a "degree of commitment to hunting," rather than an all-or-nothing classification. Societies and/or individuals might be rank-ordered from 100 percent to 0 percent reliance on hunting.

Many of the research tools discussed in the preceding chapters produce data that can be effectively handled as ordinal variables. W. L. Warner's well-known description of class structure in American communities illustrates the way in which nominal categories may be treated as an ordinal scale. The "upper upper class" can be thought of as a discrete category, and, at the same time, it is considered to be the "highest" class in an ordered series. The highest class is thought of as having more of something (e.g., prestige, material wealth) than any of the other classes farther down the scale.

It is important to note in connection with ordinal scales that the measurements do not specify *how much* difference exists between any two categories. We do not know, for example, whether the distance from "lower middle class" to "upper middle" is the same as the distance from "upper middle" to "lower upper class." If we were to use numbers as labels for these social classes, we might designate them classes 1, 2, 3, 4, 5, and 6 to preserve their rank ordering. However, we could just as well label them 1, 4, 7, 11, 17, and 25 – for we can make no assumptions about the magnitudes of the differences among the series.

Any series of observations in an ordinal scale can be simplified into a nominal scale. Warner's six classes can be treated statistically as discrete nominal categories if their ordering is ignored; or the top three categories could be lumped together as the "privileged class," contrasted with the rest, "the common people."

There are a great many kinds of observations in the social sciences that are best treated as ordinal scales. Redfield's folk-urban continuum is based on the assumption that societies can be ranked in terms of degrees of "urbanness" or "folkness." Acculturation is commonly seen as a matter of degree, as, for example, in the Spindlers' research on the Menominee, mentioned in Chapter 5. The series from "Native-Oriented" to "Elite Acculturated" can be treated as an ordinal series measuring the degree of acculturation.

Many personality characteristics are also best expressed in terms of rank ordering. When we say that an individual is "achievement oriented," we generally mean that she or he has more of that personality element than many other people. Many psychological tests and personality inventories are expressed in terms of numerical scores that appear to be precise. IQ test scores, for example, are frequently treated as though the distances between the scores are absolutely equivalent. If this were true, we could be assured that the distance from an IQ of 100 to one at 110 is in some mathematical sense the same as the distance between IQs of 140 and 150. However, at this stage of development in the social sciences it would appear that such test scores are so loose and indeterminate that no such claim of equivalence should be made. In fact, it could be argued that all data regarding human behavior (in the social sciences) are sufficiently inexact that measurements and scores should be regarded as ordinal scales only.

Because the distances between steps (values) in an ordinal scale are not all the same, it is risky to treat them as though they were ordinary numbers. They should not be added, subtracted, divided, or multiplied – at least not without due caution. To express the central tendency of a rank order, for example, we should use the *median* – the midpoint of the rank order – rather than the numerical *mean*. In the following (hypothetical) series in Table 8.1 the computed mean would be 11.8 (177 ÷ 15); the median is 14, and is the more meaningful statistic.

Some observers of the scientific enterprise have argued that most ordinal scales are simply imperfect representations of underlying interval or ratio scales. If more precise measures could be devised, ordinal scales could be eliminated. Even in the "exact sciences" there is an apparent exception, however. The Mohs scale of hardness is based on which minerals can scratch or be scratched by other minerals. Diamonds are clearly higher than glass on this scale, but the "distance" between minerals on this measure cannot readily be expressed in terms of equal units. While most ordinal scales of behavior (e.g., socioeconomic status, religiosity, compassion) are perhaps imperfect interval scales, it is more difficult to imagine precisely equal units to express, for example, the Trukese scale of "putting oneself above another," described by Goodenough (see Appendix B).

Table 8.1. *Scores on a rating of student excellence*

John	17
Jill	17
Ron	15
Bill	15
Jan	15
Nan	15
Dan	15
Tim	(14)
Al	12
Jane	10
Tom	9
Joel	8
Sam	7
Pat	5
Paul	3

What is the underlying (interval scale) dimension in the following rank order of occupational prestige?

> doctor
> college professor
> pharmacist
> policeman
> carpenter
> bricklayer
> waiter

The interval scale

Unlike the uneven or unknown distances between values on an ordinal scale, the "spaces" between numbers on an interval scale (1–2–3–4–5–6 etc.) are numerically equivalent. The distance from 8 to 18 is exactly equivalent to the distance from 18 to 28, and so on. The fact that the distances between any two points on the scale can be precisely defined means that many kinds of mathematical processes can be used in the data analysis. Thus the interval scale is a more powerful tool of measurement than the ordinal scale.

Our measurement of temperature (in terms of Celsius and Fahrenheit scales) presents a good example of interval scales. Temperature scales can, of course, be treated as ordinal scales. That is, we are always sure that 60 degrees is warmer than 50 degrees and that 50 degrees is warmer than 30 degrees. In addition to this ordinal information, however, the measuring capabilities of high-grade thermometers assure us that we can treat the difference between 100 degrees and 99 degrees as equivalent to the difference between 30 degrees and 31 degrees. These properties of interval scales make it possible for us to use arithmetic manipulations to convert Celsius temperature information to Fahrenheit and vice versa. Moreover, the computed *mean* for a series of interval values is a useful and appropriate measure of central tendency.

The ratio scale

The ratio scale has all the qualities of an interval scale, plus one additional feature. It has a true zero point as its origin. Measurement of weight or mass is possible in terms of a ratio scale because the condition of weightlessness (no longer only an imagined theoretical possibility since the advent of space flights) is acceptable as the zero point of the measurements. Thus the numbers associated with a ratio scale are "true" numbers, and only the unit of measure is arbitrary. Further, the ratios between any pairs of numbers are preserved when the numbers are multiplied by a positive constant, and many other mathematical transformations can be applied to ratio scales without fear of distortion.

The level of measurement, or type of scale, involved in a particular set of observations depends on two factors – the things measured and the techniques employed by the researcher. As already pointed out, nominal observations often can be converted into ordinal measurements by improved research techniques. As ordinal measures are refined, they increasingly approximate interval scales. On the other hand, some measurements that have the appearance of interval scales may be so imprecise that they are best regarded as ordinal scales. Thus the types of scales should not be regarded as absolute categories, but rather as central tendencies in observational procedures. In fact, measurements in the sciences are best regarded as a continuum, ranging from rough-and-ready nominal observations at one end of the spectrum to highly refined interval and ratio measurements at the other extreme. Even though it is desirable to refine measurement techniques wherever possible, statistical techniques have been developed to maximize the usefulness of observations in each of the general categories outlined here.

It follows from our examination of different types of measurements (scales) that we must be quite clear about what kinds of data we have in hand before we can select appropriate statistical procedures. Often anthropological fieldworkers have data in the form of ranking (ordinal scale) for two different cultural groups (nominal categories). They should therefore use statistical procedures that are optimally designed for ordinal-nominal combinations of variables. Examples of some of the more usually encountered statistical tests will help to illustrate these points.

Murdock, social structure, and the chi-square test

G. P. Murdock's classic *Social Structure* (1949) contains an awesome array of numerical data that strikes fear into the hearts of some anthropology students. The propositions that Murdock set out to examine statistically consisted of a series of probability inferences deduced from a general theoretical model. His theoretical system focused attention on the relationships between features of kinship terminology and the systems of social behavior within which the kinship terms are used. In terms of our methodological paradigm in Chapter 1, this aspect of Murdock's study can be depicted as follows:

General theory: Principles of learning theory and habit formation (psychology), functional factors (social structural and cultural), and historical events all contribute to the patterning of kinship terminological systems, and the relationships of these to the social structural systems of human groups.

The basic postulate: "The relatives of any two kin-types tend to be called by the same kinship terms, rather than by different terms in inverse proportion to the number and relative efficacy of (a) the inherent distinctions between them and (b) the *social differentials* affecting them, and in direct proportion to the number and relative efficacy of the *social equalizers* affecting them" (Murdock, p. 138, italics added).

A *basic assumption:* Systems of social structure may be regarded (among other things) as systems of "social differentials" and "social equalizers," with reference to the basic postulate to be tested.

Specific hypothesis: "In the presence of exogamous matrilineal or patrilineal lineages, sibs, phratries, or moieties, terms for lineal relatives tend to be extended, within the same sex and generation, to collateral kinsmen who would be affiliated with them under either unilinear rule of descent" (Murdock, p. 162).

Explanation: Thus the unilinear descent groupings (or the principles of social structure underlying them) are believed to operate as "social differentials" (with regard to people in different kin groups) and "social equalizers" (with regard to people within the same kin groups).

Methods of observation: Presence or absence of unilinear kin groups and presence or absence of the relevant features of kinship terminology were adjudged from available ethnographic descriptions for a worldwide sample of 250 societies.

Test of the hypothesis: Supporting evidence for the hypothesis should consist of clusters of observations in the pattern shown in Figure 8.1.

Thus Murdock suggests that where unilinear kin groups are present, the kinsmen presumed to be grouped ("equalized") should be lumped under the same kin terms; in societies lacking unilinear descent groups, the corresponding kin pairs should not be lumped. Because other differentiating and equalizing factors besides unilinear kin groups are presumed to be operating, the observed relationships are not expected to approach a perfect correlation. Rather, the test of the hypothesis requires only that the data show a *nonrandom skewing* in favor of the "hits" (cells a and d in Figure 8.1). Thus Murdock, in using this research model, scanned the available information from a whole series of societies and looked for a clustering as predicted by his theoretical hypothesis. Generalizations made by other anthropologists about relationships between social systems and kinship terminology have often involved the same kind of scanning but without

Exogamous unilinear kin groups

	Present	Absent
Terms for "equalized" kin types are the *same* (e.g. Mother, Mother's sister).	a X (hits)	b (misses)
Terms for "equalized" kin types are *different*.	c (misses)	d X (hits)

Figure 8.1. Relationships between kin groups and kin terms (hypothesized by G. P. Murdock).

either specification of the list of cases scanned or statistical analysis of the resulting data.

From the examination of his population of 250 societies, Murdock found the data as given in Table 8.2. Murdock's table of data looks somewhat different from our Figure 8.1, because he included a number of tests of his hypothesis in a single block of numbers. *Each kin pair* in the table constitutes a separate set of observations. Therefore, we can take the first group (mother–mother's sister) and recast the information in the same form as given in Figure 8.1.

When we reorganize Murdock's first group of observations in the form of a two-by-two contingency table, we have results as shown in Table 8.3. We note that there is, in fact, a tendency for the societies to be clustered in the "hits" (cells a and d), as compared with the "misses" (cells c and b). By inspection we can see that the clustering *does* seem to support Murdock's hypothesis; however, it is important to ask whether such a skewing of the numerical distribution could have occurred quite easily because of *chance sampling factors*.

Murdock's analysis of his numerical data included both the computation of a measure of association (Yule's Q) and a statistical test of significance, or test of independence, referred to as the chi-square test. This statistical calculation is especially useful for the type of data involved in Murdock's hypotheses, for the chi square is an appropriate calculation when *all variables are in the form of nominal scales*. The basic idea of the chi-square calculation involves a computation of the differences between the observed frequencies in each of the four cells in Table 8.2 compared with the frequencies that would be expected in each of the four cells *if the distribution of cases occurred simply by chance*.

Using a standard formula (available in Siegel [1956], Thomas [1976] and most other statistics texts), Murdock found that a pattern of skewing (overloading in cells a and d) as extreme as that found in Table 8.2 would occur *by chance* less

Table 8.2. *Relationships among exogamous unilinear kin groups and features of kin terminology*

	Exogamous unilinear kin groups present		Exogamous unilinear kin groups absent		Statistical indices	
	Same term	Different terms	Same term	Different terms		
Pairs of relatives	(a)	(c)	(b)	(d)	Q	χ^2
Mother–Mo Sis	106	53	31	51	+.51	1,000
Sister–Fa Bro Da	125	29	64	22	+.19	2
Sister–Mo Sis Da	114	31	62	23	+.15	2
Daughter–Bro Da	107	37	34	43	+.57	1,000
Daughter–Wi Si Da	38	25	15	15	+.21	2

Source: Murdock, p. 163.

Table 8.3. *Exogamous kin groups and extension of kin terms*

Pair of relatives	Exogamous unilinear kin groups			
Mo-Mo's Sis		Present		Absent
Same term used	a	106	b	31
Different terms used	c	53	d	51

N = 241 societies
Source: Derived from Murdock, Table 35, p. 163.

than once in a thousand times. This information, which is usually expressed as $p < .001$, suggests to the investigator that *some kind* of nonrandom relationship exists between the two variables. (This is the meaning of the figure 1,000 given at the right-hand margin of Murdock's table of data, Table 8.1.) Applying the same computation to his *second row* of observations, the chi-square probability estimate tells us that these results could occur *by chance* 50 percent of the time. Clearly, it is not wise in this case to discard the alternative hypothesis that this pattern of data occurred because of the vagaries of sampling rather than because of some kind of causal link between the variables.

According to strict statistical practice, researchers should establish their levels of acceptable statistical significance (p values) before making the computation. That is, it is important to decide in advance how much risk the researcher is willing to run of accepting apparently significant results that are caused merely by chance. It is common in anthropology, as in some of the other social sciences, to regard a significance level of $p < .05$ as sufficient to reject the null hypothesis. If there is less than one chance in twenty that the observed pattern of frequencies could have occurred by chance alone, the investigator feels justified in assuming that the observed variables are related. In the case of Murdock's data, the chi-square analysis lends support to the general theoretical proposition only in the first and fourth rows of observations. The other three computations are statistically nonsignificant.

Although the chi-square test is most frequently used in situations in which the data can be arranged in a two-by-two contingency table, it should be noted that the calculation can be made with data arranged in any number of columns and rows. For example, in Cohen's research on divorce among the Kanuri we find a statistical table (Table 8.4) that examines the patterning of divorce frequency in relation to urban-rural differences.

Although the data on divorces per person can be treated as an ordinal scale,

Table 8.4. *Comparison of numbers of divorces of rural and urban persons among Kanuri*

Persons	Divorces per person		
	Low (0–1)	Medium (2–5)	High (6+)
Urban	25 (52)	55 (37)	20 (11)
Rural	86 (59)	25 (43)	4 (13)

(N) = expected frequencies if the variables are unrelated.
$p < .01$.
Source: Adapted from Cohen, 1971:137.

the chi-square computations treat each of the six cells as discrete conjunctions of nominal variables. The computation tells us that the overloading of rural/low divorce and urban/medium divorce, along with the lack of rural/high-divorce cases, represents a distinctly nonrandom (hence meaningful) pattern. The circled numbers show the frequencies that would be expected if the cases were randomly distributed.

Some cautions in the use of the chi-square test

It should be noted that all inferential statistical tests such as the chi-square test are based on an assumption that the data to which computations are applied were randomly selected from a definable universe. One of the criticisms that has been made of Murdock's statistical analysis is that his samples were not, in fact, random samples from a universe of human societies. His data were drawn as a special kind of quota sample based on criteria such as the availability of kinship information on particular societies, representation of societies from all of the major culture areas of the world, and avoidance of overrepresentation of any particular culture area. The justification for using a statistical test on this imperfect sample (and in many other similar situations) is that although it is frequently impossible to achieve the ideal in sampling, it is useful to do the best that one can with available resources. If Murdock's hypothesis testing had depended on only a few chi-square calculations, the deficiencies in the sample would create serious doubts about the usefulness of his work. The fact is, however, that *Social Structure* is based on over a hundred chi-square computations. Because these computations tended overwhelmingly to support his major hypotheses (or theorems), the massed pattern of data is a partial compensation for the weakness in sampling. Just as "one swallow does not make a summer," one or a few statistical tests may not prove much, but a large number of computations in support of a *network* of hypotheses has considerable credibility.

According to some statisticians, the chi-square test calculations are not reliable if the expected frequencies in some of the cells are too small. In the two-by-two contingency table the expected frequencies of each of the cells should be at least five. When the number of rows or columns is larger than two, the chi-square test may be used if no more than 20 percent of the cells have an expected frequency of less than five. (Also, no cell should have an expected frequency of less than one in this case.) Frequently, researchers encounter situations in which a number of cells in a large contingency table may have small expected frequencies, so that it is necessary to group or combine cells in order to prepare the data for a chi-square calculation. In cases in which the expected frequencies of cells fall below the requirements for chi-square computations, the researcher may turn to the Fisher Exact Probability Test, which is particularly useful when dealing with small numbers of cases. On the other hand, there is recent evidence that chi-square tests with small numbers of cases do not lead to serious error.

The chi-square test, as mentioned, is a particularly widely used statistical computation because it can be applied to data that are assigned simple, categorical values. That is, the chi-square test requires the theoretical minimum of sophisticated measurement. This statistical operation also has the virtues of being self-apparent in its logic and is easy to compute.

Tests of independence and measures of association

Returning to Murdock's statistical procedures, we note that the numerical analysis was aimed at two main goals. First, with the chi-square calculation Murdock tested the hypothesis that two different "populations" (those with unilinear kin groups and those without) are different in terms of a given dependent variable (kin-term patterns). The result of the chi-square test, as we have seen, allowed him to state with a high degree of probability that the two populations are indeed different (in their kin terminological features). This type of statistical test, which is a most familiar hypothesis-testing device in social sciences research, is called a *test of independence*. Such a test tells us about the probability that two populations, defined in terms of some variable, X, are different from each other with respect to another variable, Y. If they are different, then the variables X and Y (e.g., types of societies and systems of kinship terminology) *are related to each other in some way*.

Measures of association, on the other hand, are designed to provide a statement about the *amount of relationship* between two variables, X and Y. In Table 8.1 Murdock used a measure of association called Q and gave these measures for the five separate relationships examined. It should be noted that, with large samples, relatively small amounts of association (or correlation) between two variables can sometimes be statistically significant (high probability that variables X and Y are not independent); on the other hand, with small samples, an association that looks impressive may be statistically nonsignificant.

In addition to the widely used chi-square test, there are several other tests of independence that are frequently encountered in anthropological works. Also, for each of the measures of association commonly used by behavioral scientists there is a (usually simple) method of computing the probability that a given level of association is a chance result of sampling. Thus, although the two kinds of statistical tests should be clearly differentiated conceptually, they are often used together.

The Fisher Exact Probability Test (nominal variables)

This statistical tool is particularly useful in cases of very small samples, for which chi-square computation is considered by some people to be inapplicable. Like the chi-square, the Fisher Exact Probability Test is a calculation for discrete data in nominal form. Interval or ratio-scale data can also be used in these statistical calculations, as the more powerful kinds of measurements can always be treated as if they are weaker in form – i.e., as nominal or ordinal data.

Aronoff's comparisons of fishermen and cane cutters in the West Indies include several Fisher Exact Probability computations (see Table 8.5). In this case it would have been technically possible for Aronoff to use the chi-square computation, but the small sample makes the Fisher test more applicable. In a case of this kind the Fisher test is a more powerful tool than the chi-square test, because the latter provides only an approximation rather than a calculation of exact probabilities. The computation of the Fisher test is a tedious procedure, but Siegel's text provides shortcut tables for finding the probability values of small

Table 8.5. *Response to projective question: "What happens when the man over you doesn't treat you right?"*

	Active response	Passive response
Fishermen	10	4
Cane cutters	4	11

p < .025 (Fisher Exact Probability Test).
Source: Adapted from Aronoff, 1967:137.

samples (up to thirty cases) without any computations. With larger samples it is best to turn to calculators or electronic computers.

The Mann-Whitney U Test (one ordinal and one nominal variable)

In the examples thus far the data have been arranged in the form of contingency tables, in which all of the information was treated in the form of nominal categories. When one of the variables is in the form of ranked or ordinal data, the use of chi-square or Fisher tests results in throwing away information about rank differences. The Mann-Whitney U Test is a more appropriate test where ordinal measurements are available. This is a powerful test that can be used to determine whether two groups have been drawn from the same population. Like the Fisher test, the Mann-Whitney U Test is applicable to very small samples.

Another of Aronoff's statistical analyses from the West Indies can serve as an illustration of this analytic technique. As described in Chapter 5; Aronoff used the sentence-completion technique to compare fishermen and cane cutters. He suggested that the fishermen of the community are higher in self-esteem than the cane cutters. The data in Table 8.6 compare the two groups in numbers of "esteem responses."

If we consider these data to represent a ranking in terms of the number of "esteem responses," we note that the man with 20 responses is rank one, 18 responses is rank two, and so on. The top four ranks are all fishermen. At the bottom end of the ranking there is a group of nine cane cutters having fewer esteem responses than any of the fishermen. The Mann-Whitney U Test is an excellent technique for assessing the probability of "no difference" in the rank ordering of the two groups. As indicated in the statement $p < .001$, it is highly unlikely that

Table 8.6. *Frequency distribution of the cane cutters' and fishermen's responses on the esteem level*

		C																		
		C		C																
		C		F																
		C	C	C	F	F														
		C	F	C	F	F														
C		C	C	F	F	F	F	C			C			F		F			F		F
0	1	2	3	4	5	6	7	8	9	10	11	12	13	14	15		18		20
(Number of esteem responses)																				

F = Fishermen
C = Cane cutters
$p < .001$ (Mann-Whitney U Test).
Source: Aronoff, 1967:76.

this pattern of observations occurred by mere chance. (The closely similar Wilcoxen two-sample test is described in Thomas [1976] with applications for anthropologists.)

Measures of association

The measure of association known as Yule's Q was one of the earliest statistical computations of covariation and is called Q in honor of Quételet, the nineteenth-century statistician. Q is a very easy statistic to compute, but Driver (1961:321) and others have argued that the arithmetic derivation of Q is arbitrary, hence the meaning of this measure of association is difficult to interpret. Also, the value of Q will be 1.00 (spuriously indicating a perfect covariance) if one of the cells in a two-by-two matrix happens to be zero. Nonetheless, the simplicity of the computation is an argument in its favor.

The formula for Q is simply:

$$\frac{ad-bc}{ad+bc}$$

Filling in the equation from Murdock's first chi-square test (cf. Table 8.2), we get

$$\frac{106 \times 51 - 31 \times 53}{106 \times 51 + 31 \times 53} = \frac{3763}{7049} = .53$$

Phi correlation coefficient (nominal variables)

The computation of a phi correlation (ϕ) is slightly more complicated than that for Q, but this statistical operation has some distinct advantages. The value of phi as a statement of covariation does not automatically go to 1.00 if one of the cells in the matrix happens to be zero. Also, unlike the Q computation, phi can be directly related to the computation for chi-square. That is (in two-by-two tables), $X^2 = \phi^2 N$.

If we apply this formula to the chi-square value in the first of Murdock's kin terminology hypotheses, we find that $\phi^2 = .276$. We notice immediately that phi is smaller than the .51 Q value that Murdock presented in his data tables. This is generally true of phi as compared with Q, except in certain extreme cases. Driver (1961) has presented a useful discussion about chi-square, phi, and related statistical computations.

Because the value of phi and Q approaches 1.00 as any two variables are more and more closely related, we can see that the relationship between Murdock's kin group type and kin terminology is not particularly close, even though, as previously noted, the relationships are statistically significant. We may make the assumption that, although there may be some kind of causal relationship between the two variables, many other (unknown) factors must be affecting the occurrence of the two variables.

When the data are such that only nominal measures have been obtained and when the data can be organized in the form of a two-by-two contingency table, the phi coefficient of correlation would appear to be an appropriate computation. In cases in which the extent of the relationship between the two variables in such a table is not immediately obvious, the researcher makes more information available when he presents the phi computation as well as the test of significance. This is all the more useful when a whole series of computations is presented; we may wish to compare the magnitudes of relationships in the series, regardless of the computed levels of significance. Examination of phi coefficients may enable us to make some judgment concerning the theoretical and practical significance (as opposed to the statistical significance) of particular sets of relationships.

Guttman's coefficient of predictability: lambda (nominal variables)

Compared with Q and phi, the coefficient of predictability (lambda) is a more recently developed statistical technique that has considerable logical appeal. We can look upon measures of association as aids in guessing or estimating the value of variable X from our knowledge of Y (e.g., the likelihood of correctly guessing the kinship terminological system of a given people if we know their type of descent system). Increased values of phi or Q (or some other measures of association) all imply improved possibilities of prediction. Lambda, unlike our other correlational computations, is a direct arithmetic statement of the *improvement of prediction* of a variable, X, provided by knowledge of Y. (See Freeman, 1965:71–8, for simple instructions.)

Poggie (1968) examined the relationship between occupational categories and aspirations for sons' education among people in the vicinity of a new industrial city in Mexico. Table 8.7 presents his data on the two variables.

Table 8.7. *Relationships between occupation and aspirations for sons' education*

Desired education for sons	Workers	Young farmers	Old farmers
Primary	15	71	42
Secondary	13	9	8
Professional	59	21	7
Other	8	10	6

Lambda: Workers vs. young farmers .37; Workers vs. old farmers .38
Source: Adapted from Poggie, 1968:166.

His computation of lambda (which is relatively simple shows that 37 percent of the errors in guessing the level of education desired for a son can be eliminated by knowing whether the respondent is a worker or a young farmer. Slightly higher predictive success is obtained in the comparison of workers and older farmers. In this kind of calculation the variable to be guessed is considered the dependent variable. A combined coefficient of predictability can be calculated, involving the estimates in both directions of dependence.

The Kendall rank correlation coefficient: tau (ordinal data)

Sometimes a researcher is fortunate enough to have ranked, or ordinal, measurements of two variables whose relationship is to be examined. Such ranked data can always be broken down, or collapsed, into two-by-two tables for computing simple measures of association. However, this means throwing away some of the information. When two variables are both in the form of ordinal data, Kendall's tau is a very useful statistical computation.

An example will make clear the simplicity and usefulness of the Kendall tau coefficient of correlation in research on differences between "tight" and "loose" societies (Pelto, 1968). We developed a Guttman scalogram of societies ranked in terms of twelve elements of social structure that we felt registered the relative "tightness" of the social system. In examining possible causal factors associated with relative tightness of societies, we examined the relationship between tight societies and density of population. Table 8.8 shows the rank order of societies in relative tightness and the estimated densities of the populations.

The Kendall tau computation is an estimation of how well the rank ordering of a second variable (in this case, population density) compares with the rank ordering of the other variable (relative tightness of society). If the rank order of population densities were in exactly the same order as the rank ordering of social systems, we would say that there is a perfect correlation. However, examination of Table 8.7 points out that the correlation in this case is far from perfect.

Using the Kendall tau formula (see Thomas, 1976:406–12) we learned that tau is .276. As even relatively small values of tau are statistically significant, it would appear that there is some kind of direct or indirect causal link between population density and the relative tightness of social systems. The actual probability of a given tau value can be computed by converting to a z score. In our example, the z score turns out to be 5.5, which has an associated level of significance so extreme that many tables of z do not go that high. Therefore, we feel justified in rejecting the null hypothesis in favor of the alternative statement that there is a significant relationship between population density and tightness of societies.

Siegel has also described a procedure that Kendall developed for a *partial* rank correlation coefficient. This statistical computation is useful for comparing

Table 8.8. *Relationship between population density and relative tightness of society*

Society (in descending order of tightness)	Estimated population per square mile	Rank order of population densities
"tight" Hutterites (North America)	50.0	12
Hano (Arizona)	1.3	18
Lugbara (Uganda)	150.0	5
Pahari (Northern India)	100.0	8
Kibbutz (Israel)	110.0	7
Hidatsa (Northern Plains)	70.0	9
Samburu (East Africa)	2.7	16
Taira (Okinawa)	1,440.0	1
Ting Hsien (China)	850.0	2
Mixtecans (Mexico)	120.0	6
Serbians (Eastern Europe)	160.0	4
Orchard Town (New England)	52.0	11
Napaskiak (Eskimo)	0.5	19.5
Aritama (Colombia)	66.0	10
Tarong (Philippines)	2.0	17
Gusii (East Africa)	450.0	3
Basseri (Iran)	8.0	15
Kapauku (New Guinea)	9.0	13.5
Skolt Lapps (Finland)	9.0	13.5
Cubeo (Brazil)	0.5	19.5
"loose" !Kung (South Africa)	0.1	21

Tau = .276
$p < .001$

ranked data on three variables. In such a case, we may wish to determine the relationship between variables X and Y when variable Z is held constant, or partialed out. Also of interest is Kendall's coefficient of concordance: w. This coefficient is computed to determine the agreement among a whole series of variables. The calculation is particularly appropriate when a researcher has a set of data that has been ranked or rated by several different judges.

The Spearman rank correlation coefficient: rho (ordinal data)

The Spearman rank correlation coefficient was the first of the correlation coefficients to be developed for ranked data and is perhaps the best known today. This statistic is often referred to simply as rho. Whereas Kendall's tau computations involve the concept of "the natural order of rankings in the second variable," Spearman's rho is based on the computation of the "aggregated differences between the two rankings."

Table 8.9. *Correlations between self-rating and community consensus in an Indian caste structure*

Castes	Correlation coefficient of "rating of own caste" and rankings by other members of the village
Brahman	.97
Baniya	.96
Jat	.98
Bairagi	.94
Mali	.97
Jhinvar	.95
Gola Kumhar	.86
Nai	.85
Chamar	.95
Churha	.98

Source: Adapted from Freed, 1963.

An interesting use of the Spearman rho correlation of rank is presented by Stanley Freed in "An Objective Method for Determining the Collective Caste Hierarchy of an Indian Village" (Freed, 1963:879–91). Freed examined the hypothesis that individuals in Indian villages will consider their own caste to be of higher rank than do the rest of the people in the village. He first obtained a set of average rankings of the castes in the village and then compared these village averages with the rankings of the people in particular castes. That is, he compared the Brahman self-ranking with the village average, the self-ranking of the Jats with the average of the village as a whole, and so on. The results of these comparisons are given in Table 8.9. Freed concluded that most members of caste groups in this Indian village assign ranks to themselves in approximately the same way as do other members of the village; however, the two castes whose members' correlations with the rest of the village fall below .90 show a tendency to rank themselves higher than do other members of the community.

Goodman and Kruskal's coefficient of ordinal association (gamma)

Linton Freeman considers gamma to be "the most generally useful ordinal measure of association" (Freeman, 1965:79). Its attractiveness lies in the fact that, like lambda, gamma is a measure of the improvement in guessing about X, given information about Y. Hence it is a coefficient of predictability. Gamma is useful with ordinal data, with or without "tied ranks." We can illustrate the computation of gamma with tied ranks by referring to Cohen's divorce rates among the Kanuri, presented here in slightly rearranged form. In Table 8.10 we can

Table 8.10. *Numbers of divorces as predicted from "degree of urbanness"*

Degree of urbanness	Divorces per person		
	High (6+)	Medium (2–5)	Low (0–1)
High	a 20	b 55	c 25
Low (rural)	d 4	e 25	f 86

n = 215

Computation:

Step 1 Reading from left to right, count the number of cases (individuals) that fall *below and to the right of each cell*; multiply that number of cases (below and right) by the the number within the cell itself; then add the totals.

For cell a: 25 plus 86 multiplied by 20 equals 2,220
For cell b: 86 multiplied by 55 equals 4,730
For cells c, d, e, f: no cases 0,000
Total equals ("agreements" or "hits") 6,950

Step 2 Reading from right to left, count the number of cases that fall *below and to the left of each cell*; multiply by the number within the cell; then add all these.

For cell c: 4 plus 25 multiplied by 25 equals 725
For cell b: 4 multiplied by 55 equals 220
For cells a, f, e, d: no cases 000
Total equals ("inversions") 945

Step 3 Compute: $\dfrac{\text{agreements} - \text{inversions}}{\text{agreements} + \text{inversions}}$

$$\frac{6,950 - 945}{6,950 + 945} = \frac{6,005}{7,895} = .76$$

Source: Adapted from Cohen, 1971:137.

consider the urban-rural variable to be a collapsed ordinal scale of "degree of urbanness." "Divorces per person" is similarly a collapsed or simplified ordinal measure. Because both variables have been collapsed, we have a large number of tied cases in each cell. The results show that there are 76 percent more agreements (correct predictions) than inversions (misses) when we predict higher divorce rates for urban dwellers, contrasted with lower divorce rates for people of rural status (see also Thomas, 1976:414–18, for useful examples).

Parametric and nonparametric statistics

Until recently it has been common for statisticians to insist that only nonparametric statistics should be used in the analysis of nominal and ordinal data, particularly in cases in which a normal distribution of values or frequencies cannot be assumed. In fact, all of the statistics for which we have given examples thus far *are* nonparametric procedures. As stated by Siegel,

A nonparametric statistical test is a test whose model does not specify the conditions about the parameters of the population from which the sample is drawn. Certain assumptions are associated with most non-parametric statistical tests, i.e., that the observations are independent and that the variable under study has an underlying continuity, but these assumptions are fewer and much weaker than those associated with parametric tests. Moreover, non-parametric tests do not require measurements so strong as that required for the parametric tests; most non-parametric tests apply to data in an ordinal scale, and some apply also to data in a nominal scale. (Siegel, 1956:31.)

Parametric tests, on the other hand, are generally acknowledged to be more powerful statistical operations when the assumptions underlying their use can be met. The *t* and *F* tests are among the commonly used forms of inferential parametric statistics. In recent years there has been increasing evidence that use of parametric statistical procedures does not lead to invalid results even though some of the assumptions and conditions of such tests have been violated. Occasionally, it is useful for researchers to check statistical results, using both parametric and nonparametric procedures. Many of the more complex statistical procedures that are increasingly being used by anthropologists involve parametric analysis. Researchers should not shy away from these research tools simply because of fear that all the statistical assumptions cannot be rigorously met. On the other hand, use of these statistics challenges the anthropologist to improve basic measurement procedures.

We have presented basic nonparametric statistics because these procedures provide certain advantages for anthropologists, particularly at the precomputer stage of data analysis. These advantages include the following:

1 For very small samples there is sometimes no alternative to using nonparametric statistics, unless the population distribution can be described exactly.

2 Because nonparametric statistics make no assumptions about the equivalence of distances between scores in a series of ranks, we do not need to worry about the exactness of our measurements, as long as we are sure that, for example, X is greater than Y and Y is greater than Z. In some cases nonparametric statistics are employed on materials that can be categorized only as plus or minus (more or less; better or worse).

3 Nonparametric methods can be used on data that are simply classified in terms of a nominal scale. Parametric tests often cannot be applied to information of that type.

4 It is especially interesting to note that nonparametric statistics are typically simpler than their parametric counterparts; hence they are easier to learn and often may be carried out without recourse to calculators or other "hardware." Frequently, provisional statistical analyses should be carried out *during* field work. The ease of computations of nonparametric statistics is a distinct advantage under field conditions.

5 Some of the nonparametric procedures involve logical manipulations that are quite clear and intuitively pleasing – as, for example, the Mann-Whitney U Test described earlier.

It is only fair to list here some of the disadvantages of nonparametric tests.

1   Nonparametric tests are wasteful of the data. Because nonparametric statistical operations treat rank order and/or nominal categories, the additional measurement power
inherent in interval or ratio scales is simply discarded in nonparametric analysis. Such
wastefulness means that the power-efficiency of nonparametric tests is lower than that
of equivalent parametric tests.
2   Nonparametric techniques have not been worked out for some of the more complicated, multivariable types of analysis.

Statistical tests do not prove causation

The notion is widespread (especially among lay people) that it is possible to
"prove" theoretical propositions by means of statistical operations. This is defi-
nitely not the case, and we must be very clear about the logic involved in the use
of statistical tests of independence and other computations. When our calculations lead us to reject the null hypothesis in a particular instance, we are able to
say (in terms of given degrees of probability) that the variables we have been examining are linked in some way. The distributions of the independent and
dependent variables are not random with respect to one another. If by this operation we have demonstrated the probability that a variable, X, is in some way
linked to another variable, Y, we do not know whether X causes Y or whether Y
is an antecedent to X. And we must also assume the possibility that the variables
are related to each other through the action of other, unknown factors. Our particular theoretical explanation of the observed relationships must compete with
all possible alternative explanations.

In general, it is now widely agreed that statistical tests of independence have
been overdone in the literature of the social sciences. Frequently, the data to
which such tests have been applied cannot meet the requirements of random
sampling. Because these tests tell nothing about the magnitude of the observed
relationships, it is usually more informative to provide some form of correlation
coefficient or other measure of association.

The literature of the social sciences is full of cases in which the concept of *significance level* is misused. Often it is apparent that the individual researcher has
not established any particular level of significance for accepting or rejecting the
null hypothesis, but rather has made his statistical computations and decided
about his level of significance afterward. Thus we find instances in which the
researcher has found that his chi-square or Fisher Exact Probability Test computation results in a p value of .065. He then declares that the relationship is "almost significant." In discussing this "almost significant" finding, he may make
statements such as, "The data show a strong tendency in support of the
hypothesis."

Strict application of the logic of these statistical tests leaves no room for this kind of post hoc interpretation of data. If the researcher is operating with a .05 level of significance, his finding of a p value of .065 requires that he accept the null hypothesis. If he intends to consider a p value of .065 as representing "strong tendencies in support of his hypotheses," then he should establish a significance level of .10 before proceeding to statistical analysis.

We should note that there is no absolute rule about what level of significance should be used. Some social scientists appear to consider anything that does not reach the .01 level of probability to be unworthy of further consideration. (There is a widespread understanding that certain journals of psychology are extremely reluctant to accept any research results that do not operate with a .01 significance level.) We have mentioned that the .05 level of significance is quite commonly applied in anthropological work.

The central point to understand is that levels of significance are a simple technical device for assisting the researcher in making decisions to accept or reject particular hypotheses. It would seem likely that the researcher is most interested in making the correct decisions from his statistical analysis. If he insists that his results must be at the .01 level of statistical significance, he can be relatively confident that he is making no mistakes involving rejection of the null hypothesis when it should not be rejected. On the other hand, when such stringent requirements are invoked, the researcher greatly increases the chances of *accepting* the null hypothesis, when it in fact is not true. Statisticians refer to these two different mistakes as Type I and Type II errors. Rejecting the null hypothesis when the null hypothesis is correct is a Type I error. Failure to reject the null hypothesis when one should do so is a Type II error. From the previous discussion we can easily see that the probabilities of these two types of error vary inversely. Thus the overly strict researcher does not maximize correct decision making. Rather, he is maximizing a particular kind of decision for which he is paying a cost – in the form of a higher probability of making a Type II error.

Different statistical tests have different efficacies in promoting correct decision making. The efficiency of a statistical test in furthering correct decisions is referred to as the *power* of the test. Comparisons of the relative powers of different tests are often given in statistics texts. Statistical computations are also available to determine the respective probabilities of Type I and Type II errors, given a particular statistic.

Statistical significance does not mean the same thing as theoretical or practical significance. As already noted, with a very large sample of subjects one can always find *some* statistically significant differences between populations. Yet the true differences between the populations may be relatively trivial. Triviality, of course, is itself a relative matter, depending on the nature of the subject. If the question is the relative numbers of Republican and Democrat voters in a given population, a true difference of 1 percent in either direction can be highly signif-icant practically (that is, politically), even though the amount of difference is not particularly large. On the other hand, if we are interested in examining, say, the differences in "intelligence" between population A and population B, a dif-ference of 1 or 2 percent between the two populations may be significant statis-tically, yet the information is not particularly useful theoretically or practically, for it would not enable one to predict anything about the performances or activi-ties of the two populations.

Statistical computations cannot, therefore, tell us all we wish to know about our data. The calculations assist us in making certain decisions and statements about these data, but beyond the point of accepting or rejecting null hypotheses and making some other descriptive statements, including the degree of associa-tion, we should step back from statistics and exercise common sense. Indepen-dently of statistics, we must make our decisions about the magnitude of contribu-tion, or the usefulness as information, of particular research findings. Usefulness must be assessed in terms of how well the particular data help to fill gaps in the networks of propositions in social sciences theory, and at the same time individ-ual research findings can be evaluated in terms of the possibilities of making cor-rect, practical predictions of human behavior related to social problems.

More complicated statistical operations

The anthropological literature includes many studies that have more compli-cated statistical operations than any we have so far examined. There is, of course, no limit to the complexity of statistical operations that may prove useful in the study of human behavior. Naturally, complexity (whether of statistics or any-thing else) is not valuable in and of itself. As a matter of fact a cardinal rule of science is frequently given as: Other things being equal, the simplest explanation (or operation, or statistical computation) is the preferred one.

Multiple regression analysis

In the simple statistical techniques we have just reviewed, only two variables can be examined simultaneously. Thus from a complex, multifaceted world of in-terrelated events and things, the investigator must pick out just two or three im-portant concepts for analysis in a computation, trying to "hold everything else constant." This is a difficult and frequently unrewarding assignment, because in natural events many variables affect the outcome of observations.

Sometimes the anthropologist would rather devise some way to examine a whole series of variables, X_1, X_2, X_3, X_4, X_5, and so on, to see what *combination of these variables best predicts the values of a particular dependent variable, Y.* Multiple regression analysis offers one means of accomplishing this complicated assessment of interrelated data.

Schensul (1969) used multiple regression analysis in a study of cognitive responses to modernization in Uganda (see Chapter 5). He used a structured interview schedule to collect a mass of information about his Banyankole informants, including the size of household, income, number of coffee trees owned, number of cows, measures of "modern information," a scale of material style of life, and so forth. Also, as described earlier, he obtained informants' responses to a modified semantic differential task.

Schensul's statistical adviser suggested that he experiment with a multiple linear regression analysis in order to identify predictors of the semantic differential responses. From the computerized analysis, it appeared that among the sample of Banyankole people the ten most important predictors of responses in the overall semantic differential task were as follows:

1 Number of brothers and sisters who have left the area.
2 Income (cash).
3 Percent of income received from wages.
4 Number of moves the household has made.
5 Number of coffee trees (major cash crop) owned.
6 Age.
7 Number of cows (important factor of wealth) owned.
8 Possession of traditional goods (Guttman scale).
9 Religiosity (Guttman scale).
10 Articulation (Guttman scale).

As an example of the information produced by the multiple regression analysis we can look at the relationships between the independent variables and responses concerning "inhospitable–hospitable" as applied to the informants ratings of themselves. In Table 8.11 we see that the independent variable with the strongest predictive power (highest correlation with the dependent variable) is income, with a correlation of .32. The next predictor variable is number of cows, which adds .08 of predictive power to that provided by the first variable. The third variable, siblings who have migrated, adds only .04 more predictive power, and so on down to the tenth variable, number of changes of residence, which makes very little further contribution to the linear regression equation. The total cumulative multiple R of .56 indicates that the combined force of the ten most significant independent variables leaves a considerable portion of the variance unaccounted for.

Table 8.11. *Multiple regression analysis to predict informant's ratings of self on dimension of hospitable–inhospitable*

Variable	Multiple *R* (cumulative)	Increase in *R* (rounded)	Direction of relationship
Income	.32	—	high income = inhospitable
Number of cows owned	.40	.08	more cows = hospitable
Siblings who have migrated	.44	.04	more siblings migrated = inhospitable
Age	.46	.02	high age = hospitable
Possession of tra- ditional goods	.49	.03	more traditional goods = inhospitable
Number of coffee trees owned	.51	.02	more trees = hospitable
Knowledge of na- tional system	.54	.03	high knowledge = hospitable
Number of people in household	.55	.01	more in household = hospitable
Religiosity	.56	.01	more religiosity = hospitable
Number of changes in resi- dence	.56	.007	more moves = hospitable

Source: From Schensul, 1969, Appendix.

This statistical analysis allowed Schensul to make the following inferences:

1 Banyankole perceptions of their social world (defined in the semantic differential task) vary intraculturally in relation to economic position (income, number of cows, coffee trees, etc.), and a number of other factors.
2 Although economic factors were important in the list of predictor variables, noneconomic factors such as religiosity and knowledge were also significant.
3 The independent variables that were importantly related to particular conceptual definitions (decisions in the semantic differential) differed in ways that made sense in terms of the contemporary ethnographic picture of the Banyankole. For example, hospitality behavior involves significantly increased expenses for wealthier people. Hence the higher-income people are ambivalent about hospitality.

Although this example of multiple regression analysis represents a tentative exploration, and requires the support of qualitative documentation, it would appear to have much intuitive appeal for the holistically inclined anthropologist, because it permits examination of the simultaneous effects of a large cluster of variables.

Factor analysis

One of the more commonly encountered complex statistical techniques is that of *factor analysis*, which is, basically, a technique whereby a large number of categories of data and their intercorrelations can be reduced to a small number of basic "factors," to simplify data analysis.

Sawyer and Levine (1966) used factor analysis in an examination of Murdock's World Ethnographic Sample, which consists of a table of thirty basic economic, ecological, social, and political characteristics for a sample of 565 societies. They first computed correlations between each pair of variables. The intercorrelations between all pairs of variables formed a matrix of data from which the factor-analysis procedure (computerized) was used to select clusters of interrelated variables. (A number of different factor-analysis procedures are possible, and they produce somewhat different results.) Each succeeding cluster of variables (these clusters are called *factors*) selected in this process is statistically independent of other such clusters.

Sawyer and Levine found that ten factors, or clusters of variables, accounted for 74 percent of the variance in Murdock's World Ethnographic Sample. Tables 8.12 and 8.13 show their results. Some of the inferences one can draw from inspection of these data are surprising.

1 The "patrilineality complex" (factor 6) is surprisingly independent of matriliny (factor 7), cross-cousin marriage (factor 8), animal husbandry (factor 2), and even father-uncle differentiation (factor 10). One might well have expected, instead, a high negative relationship between patrilineality and matrilineality.

Table 8.12. *Thirty cultural variables on ten factors*

	1A	Agriculture	6A	Patrilineality
I	1B	Male involvement in agriculture	6B	Patrilineal exogamy
	1C	Cereal agriculture	6C	Patrilocality
	1D	Permanence and clustering	VI 6D	Bilaterial descent of kindreds
	2A	Animal husbandry	6E	Community exogamy
II	2B	Male involvement in animal husbandry	6F	Bride price
	2C	Domestication of animals	7A	Matrilineality
III	3A	Fishing, etc.	VII 7B	Matrilineal exogamy
	3B	Male involvement in fishing, etc.	8A	Cross-cousin marriage
IV	4A	Hunting and gathering	VIII 8B	Cousin-sibling differentiation
	4B	Male involvement in hunting and gathering	9A	Social stratification
	5A	Nuclear-family household	9B	Political integration
V	5B	Extended-family structure	IX 9C	Slavery
	5C	Household size	9D	Hereditary political succession
	5D	Polygyny	X 10A	Father-uncle differentiation

Source: Adapted from Sawyer and Levine, 1966:715.

2   A high positive correlation between patrilineality and animal husbandry has often been claimed and partially demonstrated; and a number of theoretical statements suggesting correlations between patrilineality and several other variables fail to find support in Sawyer and Levine's data.

3   It is also quite surprising that family composition (factor 5) generally is unrelated to either subsistence systems (factors 1, 2, 3) or kinship systems (factors 6 and 7).

4   One can argue from these data that, at least for Murdock's particular sample of societies, the subsistence factors are the most powerful in predicting variation in other cultural traits, although the patrilineality factor is also important.

5   Conversely, cross-cousin marriage (factor 8) and father-uncle differentiation (factor 10) seem relatively insignificant as predictors of cultural variation according to this set of data. Devotees of theories concerning marriage alliances could do well to ponder the implication of these findings.

Naturally one should take Sawyer and Levine's factor analysis results with a large grain of salt, for there are a great many criticisms that can be made concerning the basic quality of the World Ethnographic Sample data. The results suggest directions for further exploration rather than finished theoretical propositions. Nonetheless, the careful researcher can examine these data with profit – telling himself that "something is going on" that requires much further study with other techniques of analysis. This impression is strengthened by Sawyer and Levine's demonstration that broadly similar results are obtained when one considers the intercorrelations and clusters of variables separately for the six major cultural regions of the world.

Driver and Schuessler (1967) have also factor-analyzed Murdock's World Ethnographic Sample. Their methods differed somewhat from those of Sawyer and Levine in that they derived phi coefficients of correlation rather than Pearson product-moment correlations for their matrix of thirty cultural variables. The factors that they extracted bear a considerable resemblance to those produced by Sawyer and Levine.

Factor analysis: inductive search for patterns

Factor analysis is most commonly used by anthropologists and other researchers for identifying patterns or statistically meaningful clusters in masses of data. Typically, factor analysis is used when the researcher has a large number of cases (households, sites, individuals, artifacts) and data on a considerable number of variables for each case. There are generally correlations among the variables, and perhaps a great deal of redundancy in that two or three variables may be measuring approximately the same underlying dimension.

In most cases factor analysis is only an intermediate step in research. The grouping of variables into a manageable number of factors makes it possible for a

Table 8.13. *Loadings of thirty cultural variables on ten factors*

Variable	1	2	3	4	5	6	7	8	9	10	Commu-nality
1A	.88	.16	-.03	.00	-.05	.05	.06	.00	.01	-.20	.85
1B	.72	.08	-.14	-.10	.01	-.13	-.09	.04	.09	.03	.60
1C	.63	.30	-.30	.20	.04	-.01	-.01	-.01	.19	.16	.68
1D	.78	-.02	.25	-.09	-.11	.05	.03	.02	.09	-.08	.71
2A	.12	.84	-.23	-.16	.02	.15	-.06	.09	.16	.06	.87
2B	.07	.86	-.18	-.07	.02	.09	-.09	.03	.14	-.07	.83
2C	.27	.84	-.09	-.16	.05	.14	.00	.02	.09	-.05	.85
3A	-.12	-.31	.85	-.03	-.03	-.09	.05	.01	.00	-.06	.85
3B	.03	-.13	.90	.05	.00	-.10	-.01	.06	-.01	.10	.86
4A	-.50	-.37	-.01	.64	-.02	-.02	.04	-.06	-.14	.05	.83
4B	.04	-.13	.02	.88	.04	.07	.02	-.02	.00	.01	.80
5A	.11	-.16	.01	-.16	.81	-.19	-.08	-.06	-.04	.11	.78
5B	.20	-.11	.01	-.12	-.70	.03	-.01	-.06	.17	.00	.59
5C	.05	-.39	.05	-.14	-.61	-.17	-.06	.08	-.21	.30	.71
5D	-.34	.20	.08	.33	-.37	.24	-.01	.01	.17	-.43	.68
6A	.11	.19	-.11	-.02	-.02	.86	-.20	.17	.05	-.05	.87
6B	.04	.01	.01	.10	-.05	.82	.15	-.32	-.10	.01	.82
6C	-.07	.10	-.09	-.08	-.02	.70	-.40	.03	.15	.03	.69
6D	-.15	-.13	.11	04	.04	-.68	-.35	-.34	-.08	.08	.78
6E	-.30	.11	.02	.07	-.09	.59	.15	-.10	.02	-.06	.50
6F	-.06	.50	-.10	.14	-.04	.35	-.15	.08	.25	-.14	.51
7A	-.01	-.07	.01	-.01	.00	-.10	.89	.18	.02	-.14	.86
7B	-.03	-.15	.04	.03	-.04	.11	.88	-.28	.07	-.11	.91
8A	.07	.05	.11	-.07	-.04	-.08	-.10	.89	.05	-.03	.84
8B	-.08	.14	-.10	.08	.04	.39	.37	.52	-.08	.18	.64
9A	.23	.29	.05	-.24	-.06	-.04	-.03	.01	.71	.18	.74
9B	.28	.39	-.04	-.19	.04	-.06	-.06	.03	.59	.19	.65
9C	.06	.19	.02	.19	-.08	.08	-.06	.01	.68	-.13	.57
9D	-.11	-.28	-.14	-.03	-.11	.21	.12	.04	.52	-.41	.62
10A	-.21	-.09	.03	.05	-.05	.02	-.20	.02	.06	.80	.74
Percent of total variance	10.6	11.7	6.3	5.5	5.7	10.9	7.4	4.9	6.4	4.6	74.0

Source: Adapted from Sawyer and Levine, 1966:715.

researcher to use these statistically produced variables for testing relationships with other data. For example, it is often useful to employ factor analysis to reduce a large number of variables, which are then statistically independent of each other (uncorrelated) and can be used as independent variables in a multiple regression analysis to find the degree to which they collectively provide predictive information in relation to an independent variable (e.g., the multiple regression by Schensul, mentioned earlier).

The logical workings of factor analysis, and something of its possible uses, can be made more apparent by means of a "plasmode" – a specially prepared and well-understood data set. Robert Benfer (1972) has factor-analyzed a set of books from his personal library in order to test and illustrate aspects of this statistical process. Figure 8.2 shows the variables in his analysis. He used thirty-three books (evenly divided in subject matter between statistics and human evolution) and included a mixture of nominal, ordinal, and interval measurements in the list of twenty-nine variables.

Table 8.14 shows the results of Benfer's factor analysis, based on an orthogonal "varimax rotation," a type of factor analysis commonly used by anthropologists and other social and behavioral scientists. Factor II clearly represents a series of "thickness" measurements, along with type of binding and the hardcover-versus-paperbound dimension. Factor III turned out to be a use-and-contents cluster, including the interesting finding that Benfer apparently consults his human evolution books more than he does the works on statistics. About the analysis Benfer commented that "the first factor was puzzling to me. . . . Factor I seems to be that of an area rather than height or width . . ." (p. 538). He noted that there tends to be a high correlation between length and width of books; hence these two dimensions do not emerge separately in the factor analysis.

To demonstrate the effects of using different kinds of factor analyses Benfer ran his plasmode variables using several other computerized routines. The resultant factors, or variable clusters, were not drastically changed, though some rearrang-

OBSERVATIONS
1. Rectangularity: 1 = more, 0 = less rectangular
2. Binding: 2 = perfect, 1 = perfect-sewn, 0 = sewn
3. Mullness: 1 = hardback, 0 = paperback
4. Author(s): 1 = multiple, 0 = single
5. Contents: 1 = statistics, 0 = human evolution
6. Use: 2 = much, 1 = average, 0 = little

MEASUREMENTS

7. BF	15. IK	22. BC
8. MO	16. FH	23. Circumference IJKL
9. DH	17. BH	24. Circumference MNOP
10. AB	18. AD	25. Date of publication
11. NM	19. AF	26. Twice BF
12. CD	20. BO	27. 1/2 MO
13. EF	21. BK	28. (MO/IK) × 100
14. BD		29. Random number

Figure 8.2. Book plasmode measurements and observations (adapted from Benfer, 1972:537).

Table 8.14. *Factor analysis of book plasmode measurements*

Variables		Varimax			
		I	II	III	h²
1	Rectang.	.5			.3
2	Binding	−.5	−.6		.6
3	Hard-Paper	.5	.7		.7
4	Author(s)	.4			.2
5	Stat-Hu. Evol.			.6	.5
6	Use			−.5	.4
7	BF	1.0			1.0
8	MO	1.0			1.0
9	DH	1.0			1.0
10	AB		1.0		1.0
11	NM		1.0		.9
12	CD		1.0		.9
13	EF		1.0		.9
14	BD	.7	.4		.7
15	IK	1.0			1.0
16	FH	1.0			1.0
17	BH	.9			.9
18	AD	1.0			1.0
19	AF	1.0			1.0
20	BO	.9			.8
21	BK	1.0			1.0
22	BC	.9			1.0
23	IJKL	.8	.6		1.0
24	MNOP	.4		.4	.3
25	Date		−.4	.4	.3
26	Twice BP	1.0			1.0
27	½MO	1.0			1.0
28	MO/IK × 100	.7			.6
29	Random			−.4	.2
Cumulative % of Variance		56	72	76	

Source: Benfer, 1972:540.

ing of variables emerged. Some of these "solutions" were more clear-cut and made better sense than others, but the results of the different variants would not have led Benfer to totally different conclusions about the patterned relationships in his personal library plasmode.

The most important conclusions emerging from Benfer's factor-analysis experiment include:

1 ". . . measurements which *intuitively* might have seemed independent were found to be *almost totally redundant* within the sample."

2 ". . . measurements which *intuitively* might have appeared *redundant* were sometimes found to possess . . . independence to some degree" (p. 549; italics in original).

3   Where possible, the patterns of variables that emerge from factor analysis should be treated as hypotheses to be verified by other means.

The examples from Benfer's research, and the many other uses of factor analysis in anthropology, illustrate some basic principles of data analysis:

1   All research, in anthropology as in other sciences, is a search for meaningful patterns among the "pieces," the units, items, or variables we select for study.
2   The patterns or relationships that we "find" in our data depend very much on *which* items or pieces or units we choose to include in the first place. Consider what Benfer's plasmode analysis might have looked like had he included items such as "excellence," "readability," "color," "publisher," "size of type," and so on.
3   No matter what items or variables we include or exclude, and no matter what statistical mode we choose for analyzing them, some surprises are likely to emerge. The numerical analysis will generally produce results that differ in interesting ways from our *qualitative* hunches and impressions. Furthermore, the product of numerical analysis (factor analysis, etc.) takes different shapes depending on which rules of analysis (e.g., the type of factor analysis) are invoked. The different outcomes are not necessarily correct or incorrect; but they are more or less useful, more or less sensible, and more or less interpretable.

The Meehl paradox: some problems in hypothesis testing

In psychology, sociology, and other sectors of the social sciences it has become usual to find research structured in the following general form:

1   Statement of a problem involving two or more variables and their interrelationships.
2   Presentation of research hypotheses.
3   Statement of methods of research.
4   Statistical tests of significance concerning the hypotheses.
5   Acceptance (on the basis of statistical tests) of the hypotheses.
6   Explanation concerning one or two relationships that "did not turn out" in the predicted manner.
7   Statement concerning the theoretical advances achieved.

It is important to note in connection with this research paradigm that the main efforts of the researcher are directed toward finding some kind of statistically significant differences between two populations, or two sets of observations. This general model of theory testing has been subjected to a damaging critique by Paul E. Meehl (1967).

Meehl points out first that there is a basic contrast in the way measurements are used in physics (and the other hard sciences) and in the social sciences. Measurements in physics are intended to present *point values* of variables, whereas the research designs of the social sciences are concerned not with point values but with predicting *probable differences*.

For example, temperature as a dependent variable in a physics experiment is usually predicted exactly from a mathematical equation; in a social science situation a comparable dependent variable is most likely to be predicted in a general form, such as: "It will be greater," "It will vary inversely with (another variable)," or simply, "It will be correlated with. . . ." The exact *value* of the variable is not predicted. Meehl points out that, given this fundamental difference in measurement strategy, increased precision in physics (and related sciences) logically should lead to more and more rigorous testing of theoretical propositions, whereas increased precision of measurement in the social sciences *logically leads to the increasing probability of finding some differences, hence a weaker corroboration of the hypotheses tested.* Meehl shows that "in most psychological research, improved power of a statistical design leads to a prior probability approaching one half of finding a significant difference in the theoretically predicted direction" (Meehl, 1967:103). This same argument would of course apply to similar hypothesis testing in other social sciences, including anthropology.

One of the ways in which researchers in the social sciences regularly "improve" their research designs is to increase the size of the sample. Increasing the size of the sample, as already pointed out in earlier discussions, can lead to a situation in which there will be a high likelihood of finding statistically significant differences between populations. To demonstrate this proposition empirically Meehl and his associates, using a sample of over 55,000 Minnesota high school seniors, tested the interrelationships among variables such as sex, birth order, religious preference, number of siblings, vocational choice, club membership, college choice, mother's education, interest in dancing, interest in woodworking, liking for school, and so on. They found statistically significant relationships in 91 percent of the pair-wise associations tested. The logic of limited possibilities assures us that, because differences in populations (generally) can have only two directions, the researcher's hypothesis is bound to be right *one-half of the time* in randomly appearing *but statistically significant differences* in the populations.

Meehl points out that two populations will "quasi always" differ, because there is an infinite number of external factors, problems of reliability, and other elements that will differentially affect the two populations. Improvement of measuring devices (or other social sciences operations) is likely to *increase* the probability of such differences becoming statistically significant.

Meehl also points out that researchers typically find that some of their predicted associations do not turn out the way they had expected, and in such cases investigators usually present post hoc explanations of the results, pointing to contaminating variables that had not been considered in an earlier analysis of the research design. Such post hoc analysis of statistical results cannot be regarded as successful tests of a hypothesis; they have no status in theory building other than serving as suggestions for future research.

If social scientists take Meehl's argument seriously (as they should), the entire structure of theory building by means of statistically manipulated hypothesis tests is called into question. Particularly questionable are any results of hypothesis tests based on extremely large samples of cases, however paradoxical this statement may appear at first glance. Also open to suspicion are all propositions about relationships that have been tested *only once*. However, there are some roads that may lead past the apparent impasse.

Clearly, any theoretical investigation that involves the testing of whole networks of hypotheses, on several different samples of data, with each theorum examined in terms of a *series* of hypotheses, is a much stronger research design than is the one in which only one hypothesis is tested with one statistical operation. For example, Murdock (1949) presented a fairly strong statistical case in his cross-cultural research on social structure because he tested his general ideas with a battery of over a hundred statistical operations. Similarly, Aronoff's theoretical structure concerning psychological differences between fishermen and cane cutters in the British West Indies is supported by a network of thirty or forty tests of hypotheses.

Anthropological research usually includes a feature of methodology that is often lacking in psychological and sociological research. Anthropologists, however much significance they attach to statistical tests in parts of their data, generally prefer to have a large amount of contextual information – including personal observations, anecdotal evidence, descriptions of logical interrelationships, demonstration of linguistic behavior, and other nonquantified explanation – built up in support of the propositions tested. Thus the "credibility" of the statistical material is enhanced.

Some of the main ways in which social scientists can minimize the effects of Meehl's methodological paradox are as follows.

1 Any given general proposition should be tested in the form of a large network of hypotheses. Support for the general proposition or theorem should involve confirmation in the overwhelming proportion of individual statistical tests.
2 Propositions should be tested on a number of different populations.
3 The propositions should be subjected to test by a series of different research instruments.
4 Propositions should be subjected to a reexamination by other investigators using the first investigator's specified operations.
5 Random samples should be carefully selected and should not be particularly large.
6 If statistically significant results are found in an examination of relatively large sample populations, these differences should not be accorded much theoretical importance unless the demonstrated associations are fairly large in absolute magnitude.

Specialized competence in statistics

From even a casual review of recent anthropological literature, it seems clear that an increasing number of anthropologists have developed competence in the use of statistical procedures. This trend will continue in the future. But statistics represents only one of a number of different new areas of competence that anthropologists may feel a need to acquire. Boundaries between disciplines become blurred, and some anthropologists have invested considerable effort in learning the tools and theoretical procedures of sociologists, for example. Others, interested in economic patterns among various peoples, have felt the need to learn new research techniques from the economists. Ecologically oriented studies frequently appear naïve if the anthropologists have not familiarized themselves with the expertise of geographers, agricultural economists, biologists, and so on. Mastery of statistics, then, presents but a further indignity to the already thinly spread efforts of the anthropologist. It is even more discouraging when the anthropologist who has made a considerable attempt to learn the rudiments of statistics finds that the new research tools only increase his or her vulnerability to criticism from people with (supposedly) more statistical sophistication.

In many cases anthropologists (and other social scientists) would be well advised to seek the counsel and friendship of competent statisticians. It often requires some searching to find statisticians who are interested in the problems of the social sciences and who are willing to be somewhat flexible in the face of the harsh realities of anthropological field work – in which samples are, strictly speaking, never absolutely random and many supposedly crucial assumptions of statistical procedure must be violated. Our experience has been that, for every statistician who throws up his hands in horror at the looseness of statistical usage in anthropology, another can be found who finds no difficulty in making a few methodological compromises because of the realities of field data. The anthropologist who needs statistical help should, therefore, keep searching until he or she finds a flexible statistician – one who has some knowledge of the problems of the social sciences.

Any anthropologist undertaking a project that involves quantification, population sampling, and statistical testing of hypotheses should seek the advice of a professional statistician. Larger projects should, if possible, employ statisticians as part of their multidisciplinary staffs. But the anthropologist should be aware of differences among statisticians, for not all statisticians will fit in satisfactorily with a social scientist research team.

All this does not excuse anthropologists from learning the rudiments of statistics for themselves. There are three main reasons why every anthropologist should develop competence in statistical analysis.

1   In many areas of research anthropologists will encounter situations in which at least elementary statistics are needed. A certain minimum level of statistical orientation is necessary in order to recognize these situations and either apply statistical procedures or seek competent advice.

2   On those occasions when anthropologists clearly need statistical advice of a more sophisticated nature, they must be able to communicate with the statistician – to describe research intentions in ways that make sense to the latter and, in turn, to understand the advice that is offered.

3   Finally, anthropologists nowadays must be able to read and understand a wide variety of literature that involves statistical operations. While the producers of statistically analyzed research usually make attempts to present their data in such form that it is easily understood by nonstatistical readers, an increasing number of complicated discussions concerning interpretation of statistical material are appearing. It is no longer possible for the general anthropologist to ignore the statistical debates current in the literature; and it is not easy to make an honest assessment of those materials without at least an elementary background in statistics.

9 Art and science in field work

Strategies in the art of field work

Anthropologists have awakened to the need for a thorough examination of the processes of data collection in the field. Research in human communities is inevitably complex and personalized, but many parts of it can become more systematic than they have been in the past. Open discussion of ethnographers' experiences and methods is removing some of the mystique of field work and is helping to identify those aspects that can be made more explicitly operational and quantified. Some of the important literature on field work includes edited collections of papers such as Freilich's *Marginal Natives* (1969), Epstein's *The Craft of Social Anthropology* (1967), *Anthropologists in the Field* (Jongmans and Gutkind, 1967), and Spindler's *Being an Anthropologist* (1970). Powdermaker's autobiographic recollections in *Stranger and Friend* (1966), Bowen's *Return to Laughter* (1954), Beattie's *Understanding an African Kingdom* (1965), and Berreman's *Behind Many Masks* (1962) are good examples of the growing collection of illuminating personal documents on field work.

Anthropological research has most often been carried out through intensive study in one or a few relatively small communities. Thus the anthropologist who engages in field work in a society (e.g., Navajo, Zulu, Tiv, Mexican peasants) does not generally take that entire society as the unit of study. Instead, some community within that society is selected as the primary base of operations. Intensive study is carried out in the chosen community, and observations about other villages, localities, or groups in the general population usually assume a secondary role.

If there are important differences among the communities of a particular society (e.g., coastal versus upland peoples), the anthropologist may limit generalizations to one group or the other. Often, however, community studies are presented as typical of a given culture or subculture, without regard for the possible subcultural variations among the towns, villages, or other local units of the society.

Community study has persisted as a principal mode of anthropological field work because of some very important advantages. First, it generally provides a clear definition of the research area; boundaries can be drawn, and the population to be studied can (usually) be clearly delimited. Second, transportation requirements are minimized if much of the researcher's time is to be spent in a single village, hamlet, or town. Many of the informants or research subjects will be within walking distance.

Anthropologists have made certain assumptions about the naturalness of communities as social units. It is generally felt that villages or towns are "complete" social systems, in which most of the significant variables or factors affecting individual behavior are to be found within the local system. Influences from the outside world must certainly be noted and described, but these are frequently thought to be less important than the local cultural patterns and, particularly, the primary, face-to-face social relationships that occur within the bounds of the community.

One important reason for anthropological concentration on community studies is often overlooked. Because field-work projects, whatever their structure, usually involve months and sometimes years of residence in cultural milieus that are much removed from the anthropologist's home base, it is likely that the fieldworker has strong psychological needs to develop a network of local social ties, at least to organize the means of obtaining the basic necessities of life. Housing is needed; clothing must be laundered; food must be traded for, purchased, or produced by the fieldworker; and dozens of other everyday details of living require attention. These requirements of living imbed the fieldworker in the community of residence. However much he tries to gather data to an equal extent from a number of different areas, he always turns out to have far more information about, and involvement with, his primary base of operations. (Generally, anthropologists have found it unsatisfactory to commute to their research sites, though exceptions can be noted.)

In addition to fulfilling standard physical needs, the community comes to satisfy more diffuse psychological needs as well. Usually, anthropologists establish special friendly relationships with one or two best informants. They may confide in them about problems of adjustment; they often spend nonworking hours engaged in idle conversation or other recreational activities with these friends, and may need to rely on them for special help, such as a loan of money and supplies. The lone anthropologist is, of course, especially in need of companionship, but married couples too are not immune to these psychological needs. However amiable the relationships between spouses in the field, both husband and wife will often feel the need for solid friendships outside the tight confines of the research team. These psychological needs do not force field work to be structured in the form of community study, but maximum congruence between the fieldworker's personal needs and research goals is often best attained in the community-study research structure.

Choosing a site

John Beattie has described in some detail how he chose a research community among the geographically dispersed Bunyoro:

First, the community I settled in had to be, so far as I could judge, a reasonably representative one; as typical as possible of rural Bunyoro. Of course I could not at that time know with certainty exactly what *was* typical, but at least I could exclude from consideration areas that were obviously not so; those which were close to and therefore affected by either of Bunyoro's two towns, for example, or which neighbored one of the country's few nonnative estates . . .

Secondly, my chosen area had to be reasonably remote not only from Hoima, but also from the local county or subcounty chief's headquarters. These were generally on or near main roads, and to have lived too close to one, with its office and court and, sometimes, its English-speaking clerks, would have made direct contact with the rural community itself more difficult. . . .

. . . thirdly (and not perhaps wholly consistently with the foregoing), my base had to be accessible, if not too easily so, by motor vehicle, so that I could move my equipment there, obtain supplies and mail, and maintain some contact with the outside world without undue difficulty and expense.

And lastly, and most importantly of all, I wanted to find an area where not only did the local subcounty chief and his headmen seem to be reasonably cooperative and to have some understanding of what I was aiming to do, but also where the people themselves . . . seemed willing to put up with an intrusive European and even to help him in his task. (Beattie, 1965:13–14.)

Beattie's statement about his criteria for selecting a research site illustrates some common tendencies in anthropological practice. The typical village (or hamlet or district) is sought among those that are relatively removed from towns and villages, for they are thought to be "more pure." On the other hand, the community selected for research must be socially tolerable. Other things being equal (and even if they are not), the anthropologist will tend to study those communities in which the people seem cooperative and friendly.

Anthropologists have not always stressed the search for a typical community. Some research sites appear to have been selected because they were *atypical*. The most isolated and traditional community is often chosen; sometimes the most impressively beautiful town is selected; in other cases anthropologists choose a community because they happened to establish social contact with some of its members before they actually arrived on the local scene. In a significant number of cases anthropologists have selected particular research communities because the same community had been studied earlier by another anthropologist, thus providing a base line for comparisons (Gallagher, 1961; Phillips, 1966; Oscar Lewis, 1963; Charles Leslie, 1960; and many others).

Selection of field habitation

Usually the fieldworker's first concern after selecting a research community is to find a suitable headquarters – a combination household-research center. Locating such a base of operations often depends on obtaining "official" permission to carry out research in the community. The researcher's quarters should be relatively central to "where the action is," but ideally they should be neutral with regard to significant social cleavages in the community. That is, the fieldworker nearly always assumes that the choice of living quarters will be a significant item of information in terms of which the local people judge his or her social role and affiliations. To accept housing in, for example, the governmental office building, the rectory, or the police station requires careful consideration of the local people's attitudes toward these authorities.

In some relatively tight communities, with well-developed boundary-maintenance mechanisms, fieldworkers may find that they must accept the dictates of local authorities with regard to the selection of residence, if they have been successful in obtaining permission for the research activity. For example, those anthropologists who have studied total institutions, such as prisons and mental hospitals, often must accept the quarters assigned to them by the administrators.

Fieldworkers frequently have a choice between living with a family in the community or setting up a separate household. Their decision in the matter involves a number of factors – willingness of local families to accept strangers, extent of personal equipment, information about the social characteristics of potential "landlords," type of research intended (study of family interaction and socialization practices may be greatly facilitated by living with a local family), and relative centrality of the available alternatives. Thomas Rhys Williams maximized centrality in his choice of living arrangements among the Dusum: "In Sensuron we rented the village headman's house for about five dollars a month. The house was already a focal point of daily village routines and centrally located. The headman moved next door into another house" (Williams, 1967:14).

In many communities there are no "vacancies," and new houses must be built for newcomers. Powdermaker has described some features of her house in Lesu:

Both men had supervised the finishing of my house (begun before my arrival for visiting government patrols), the building of the privy, the making of a primitive shower, adding a room to the cook-house for a servant's bedroom, and all the other details of settling in.

Compared to the one-room village huts whose floor was the ground, my house seemed luxurious. It was raised from the ground and had two windowless rooms with a wide veranda between them and a narrow one around the sides of the house. One room was for sleeping and the other for keeping supplies. I worked, received company, and ate on the wide section of the veranda. The thatched roof was an advantage in the tropics. (Powdermaker, 1966:51–2.)

Berreman (1962, 1963) was able to find rather less than comfortable quarters for his research in a Pahari village in northern India. He comments: "My village house consisted of three small connecting rooms, one of which was occupied continuously by two to four water buffalo, and all of which were inferior to those inhabited by most villagers."

Joel Halpern, in his study of a Serbian village, lived at the home of the secretary of the local village council. In this case the decision about residence was made by the local officials:

Upon our arrival in Orašac, a conference as to where we would be lodged was immediately held among the leading officials: the Director of the school, the President and Secretary of the Village Council, and the President of the Village Cooperative. The house of the Secretary of the Village Council was unanimously agreed upon, and there we remained for our year's stay.

His house had the disadvantage of being located some distance from the center of the village. This was more than compensated for by the fact there were six members – three generations – in the household: his parents, his wife, and his young son and daughter, all of whom were very friendly and later proved themselves to be eager and dependable informants. (Halpern, 1958:xii.)

There are, of course, many field research situations in which housing as such is not a problem, because the people – particularly in nomadic herding and hunting-and-gathering groups – rely on relatively simple and portable dwellings. In such cases anthropologists can erect their tents in whatever location the local group suggests; they are rather more concerned with establishing social ties than in finding a place of residence. In extreme cases the would-be researcher may have major difficulties even in finding the group chosen for study. Allan Holmberg described his initial (and successful) contact with the nomadic Siriono as follows:

We followed the rude trails which had been made by the Indians about 3 months earlier, and after passing many abandoned huts, each one newer than the last, we finally arrived at midday on the eleventh day of March just outside of a village. On the advice of our Indian companions, Silva and I removed most of our clothes, so as not to be too conspicuous in the otherwise naked party – I at least had quite a tan – and leaving behind our guns and all supplies except a couple of baskets of roast peccary meat, which we were saving as a peace gesture, we sandwiched ourselves in between our Indian gudes and made a hasty entrance into the communal hut. The occupants, who were enjoying a midday siesta, were so taken by surprise that we were able to start talking with them in their own language before they could grasp their weapons and flee. Moreover, as their interest almost

Table 9.1. *Habitation during field work (fifty-one fieldworkers)*

Rented house or apartment in local community	29
Lived with local family	16
Commuted from nearby town or city	11
Lived in tent or trailer	1
Natives built me a house	7
Lived in school or other special building	3
Lived in outbuilding of local family (barn, storeroom)	3
Total	$\overline{70^a}$

[a]Total is more than fifty-one because several had more than one dwelling in the course of field work.

immediately settled on the baskets of peccary meat, we felt secure within a few moments' time and sent back for the rest of our supplies. (Holmberg, 1969:xxi.)

In a survey of fifty-one anthropologists (Pelto and Pelto, 1973), we found that the most usual habitation during field work was a rented house (or apartment) in the research community. We also found that the fieldworker is typically accompanied by his or her spouse (usually no children), and the cuisine usually consists of locally available foods; the fieldworkers usually cook for themselves instead of taking their meals with local people (see Table 9.1).

Impression management

In obtaining permission for research, selecting living quarters, announcing one's self to the populace, contacting prospective informants, and making other opening moves of field work, the fieldworker is highly conscious of the importance of what Berreman and others have referred to as *impression management*. Success in the art of field work depends, to a considerable extent, on establishing a very special social role that legitimatizes a kind of information-getting behavior that was not previously part of social expectations within the community. Thus it is not true that anthropologists try to become "just like" the people they study. They may identify with local inhabitants, vis-à-vis certain kinds of outsiders, eat the same foods and subject themselves to the same diseases and hardships, learn some of the special skills and crafts, and learn to dance and sing like a native, but the role of gatherer of information, persistent questioner, and stranger from another culture is always part of one's social identity. The local people do not forget that the anthropologists will ultimately leave them, carrying their notebooks, films, and other information-storing apparatus back to that other world from whence they came.

Normal human communities do not include within them social roles that permit individuals to ask relatively personal questions of all families, factions, and social types. In the first place, much of the information gathering is unnecessary for persons *within* the system, for they already know the answers. Also, even in the most benign human groups there are sharp limits to the amount and kind of social information that is allowed to pass from one family or group to another.

The situation in a Ladino community of Chiapas, Mexico, described by John C. Hotchkiss (1967) illustrates a fairly extreme expression of these common human tendencies. The walls of their houses, the shawls that women pull tightly around their faces (and over their market baskets), and the conversational habits of both men and women sharply restrict the flow of social knowledge within the community. For the Teopiscanecos, as Hotchkiss notes,

Information about oneself that becomes a topic of general gossip has escaped one's control. It might be used in ways that are damaging to one's reputation. A Teopiscaneco is concerned about his reputation because he knows that in his face-to-face encounters with others, the image of self that he presents must be congruent with his reputation, which nearly everyone in town has knowledge of or holds opinions about. (Hotchkiss, 1967:713.)

Because of the severe restrictions on the flow of information, children of the community are trained to gather gossip as they go about their errands of shopping, vending, carrying water, and delivering messages. "When a child returns from an errand, he is extensively interrogated by an adult of his household to find out what the child has learned" (ibid., 715).

Not all human communities restrict the flow of social information as much as do these Ladinos of Chiapas, but the work of an ethnographer requires that one be permitted to elicit much more of such gossip than would be customary. Since members of every human society seek to suppress knowledge of their personal failures, family secrets, economic and social strategies, and many other topics, the anthropologist must, in seeking access to such information, establish a radically new kind of role in the community – that of neutral observer. In some respects he or she must be like the children of the Teopiscanecos – defined as outside the adult social-prestige system. On the other hand, children are known to carry tales back to their parents; the anthropologists must make it known that they do not betray confidences.

Some people have written that ethnographers gain access to local private information to the degree that they become identified as locals, or *insiders*. This is, of course, very important – up to a point. Beyond that point fieldworkers are privy to significant social information because they are *outsiders – different* from every other member of the community. They are different because their core prestige ultimately rests on membership in another, socially distant society; they are neutral in the local competitive scene; they do not generally judge people's conduct in moral terms; and they offer social rewards in exchange for information. Occasionally they pay in cash or goods. Often they can be relied on for medicines and transportation. But, perhaps most important of all, they provide the possibility for social interaction in which the rules are suspended to a certain extent. Friendship and social affiliation can be obtained from them with relatively little social risk, because they are not competing for prestige in the same social arena. In some respects their role is not unlike that of the psychotherapist, as described by William Schofield in his *Psychotherapy: the Purchase of Friendship* (1964). The difference is that ethnographers receive information rather than money in the exchange.

Hazards and punishments of field work

Maintaining an effective researcher role appears to be relatively easy in some types of societies, particularly those lacking well-defined boundary-maintenance mechanisms or serious intracommunity social cleavages (Pelto, 1969). Even in unusually benign instances the field researcher must be very sensitive in the presentation of self and the management of social interactions. In most cases, though, the fieldworker encounters social complexities and problems at every turn, and successful role maintenance demands great presence of mind, flexibility, and luck. (Serendipity in scientific research always looms large, as Beveridge and others have demonstrated [see Chapter 2]; field work is no exception.)

Even the fieldworker's good luck often has ambiguous consequences. In the opening moves of field work he may be overjoyed when certain individuals begin to overwhelm him with information and attention. But every firm social relationship with a particular individual or group carries with it the possibility of closed doors and social rebuffs from competing segments of the community. This social-competition effect may be particularly operative in early phases of field work, when the anthropologist is highly vulnerable psychologically and before he has had a chance to teach his audience the dimensions of the special participant-observer role.

Berreman's (1962) play-by-play description of social management and field work in a Himalayan village is a striking illustration of how complex the fieldworker's problems can become, frequently without one's awareness. Having selected his research site with considerable care, Berreman entered the village accompanied by his high-caste interpreter-assistant and bearing a letter of introduction from a merchant who had had contacts with the village. Unknown to Berreman (1962:6), the merchant had engaged in sharp practices in his dealings with the villagers, so that, "As might have been expected, our benefactor was not beloved in the village and it was more in spite of his intercession than on account of it that we ultimately managed to do a year's research in the village." (Furthermore, the note was addressed to a high-caste man who was one of the most suspicious people in the village.)

After weeks and months of initial difficulties and frustrations the social identification of Berreman's assistant enabled the research team to develop relatively good rapport with some of the high-caste families of the community, so they were able to gain entrée to some "backstage" aspects of community life. On the other hand, social contacts among low-caste groups were correspondingly distant and frustrating. Thus Berreman found:

> Our informants were primarily high-caste villagers intent on impressing us with their near conformity to the standards of behavior and belief of high-caste plainsmen. Low-caste people were respectful and reticent before us, primarily, as it turned out, because one of us was a Brahmin and we were closely identified with the high-caste villagers. (Ibid., 9.)

At that point serendipity, disguised as catastrophe, entered the picture. Berreman's highly capable and loyal assistant became ill and had to leave the field. Morale dipped to a new low as the researcher cast about for a substitute to fill this delicate role. His new assistant was a Muslim, who was immediately defined by the community as low in general status, though his age engendered a measure of respect. As field work progressed under these new social conditions (which inevitably had strong effects on Berreman's role in the eyes of the village), a new and different side of the community began to emerge. The researcher soon developed rapport with low-caste people, who proved to be much more open and informative than the Brahmins and Rajputs. Gradually, a coherent picture of the intricacies of local social organization began to emerge. Had he entered the village initially with this assistant, however, the whole research effort might have failed, Berreman felt. "I might well have been unable to establish rapport . . . if my initial contact had been in the company of a Muslim interpreter" (ibid., 21).

Sources of tension in field work

While the problems of gaining acceptance in the local community (and a host of other frustrations and dangers) may have been exceptionally difficult in Berreman's Himalayan village, it is likely that most field ethnographers work under severe psychological tension much of the time. Köbben (1967) noted about his field work among Bush blacks of Surinam that

> since an ethnographer studies people and not insects, his field work also causes emotions in himself. Personally, I lived under great psychological stress and felt little of the proverbial peacefulness of "country life." Few books touch on this subject, but I know that the same is true of quite a number of other field workers. Perhaps it is even a *sina qua non* for field work. (Kröbben, 1967:46.)

Another important source of these psychological tensions is the moral conflict that arises whenever the human values of fieldworkers conflict with events in the community (and with scientific attitudes). Anthropologists, who are generally assumed to be more than usually sensitive as human observers, are, in the course of field work, frequently introduced to human misery that could be prevented if they were permitted to use their social power and economic resources to intervene in local affairs. In some cultures anthropologists may encounter food practices that systematically deprive children of an adequately balanced diet (Gerlach, 1964); yet, as outsiders and guests of the community, they cannot easily interfere. On occasion they may have information that might permit subservient or disadvantaged peoples to protect themselves from the actions of the dominant elite of a community, but interference by fieldworkers in local affairs would seriously jeopardize field work, without necessarily producing any significant changes in local power relations.

Scientific purists might insist that the anthropologist in no way interfere with the course of local cultural behavior. However, most fieldworkers have felt no qualms (scientific or otherwise) in providing medicines, drugs, and other special aid to people who would normally have no access to these facilities. Fieldworkers have also been generous in providing transportation (the research jeep, Land Rover, or station wagon often becomes the village bus), as well as other resources that would not have been available had the fieldworker not entered the village.

The dilemma of the fieldworker, then, is not *whether* to interfere in the local cultural scene but *how much* to interfere. Beattie has commented on the moral dilemmas of field work:

Anthropologists have sometimes written as though all that need be considered is the effect of field work on the fieldworker himself; much less attention has been given to its effects on the people studied (Barnes 1963 is a notable exception). But, consciously or unconsciously, the anthropologist is affecting the people he is working with all the time. Obviously no responsible anthropologist will betray to the authorities the fact, say, that a neighbor has been distilling illicit liquor, or has successfully evaded a tax obligation. But it is very much a matter of degree. When I learned, for example, that a respected neighbor, employed in the local hospital, was stealing styringes and giving injections with an unsterilized needle to local people for a fee, I felt justified in suggesting to the medical authorities that increased vigilance might be desirable (and in attempting to persuade the amateur physician of the importance of asepsis). But I did not feel justified in reporting the matter to the police. The anthropologist who learns a good deal about his neighbors in confidence must respect that confidence, except for overwhelming reasons, though it is of course conceivable that there might be occasions when he should not. No hard and fast rules can be laid down; these are matters of conscience rather than of science. (Beattie, 1965:55.)

Some anthropologists have found themselves in serious difficulties because of complex political machinations touching on, and affected by, their research activities (e.g., Diamond, 1964); it is therefore generally taken for granted that the fieldworker should avoid getting involved in politics. Lisa Peattie (1968) has, on the other hand, described her intentional involvement in political action in the course of work in the Venezuelan new city of Ciudad Guayana. Valentine (1968) goes even further. He argues that the fieldworker *should* become a political activist on behalf of the people he is studying if they are (as is frequently the case) relative have-nots in the developing world.

This view of participation also makes it possible for the ethnographer, within the limits of his own value system, to act from the ethical position that he has major obligations to the people he is studying. . . . It is in these ways that some ethnographers have become advocates or spokesmen for groups among whom they have worked, on occasion acting as vigorous partisans. (Valetine, 1968:188–9.)

This position stems in part from the fact that it is presented in the context of research on the urban poor – particularly the poor of the black ghettos. Frequently, the anthropologist who engages in this kind of research is already committed to partisanship before entering the field. But these political (and ethical) issues are becoming more and more directly relevant in every field-work setting. Making choices about these issues adds to the psychological pressures on fieldworkers.

Thus to the complexities of assuming and managing the ambiguous role of resident researcher is added a series of problems in self-management – of maintaining emotional balance and effectiveness under severe pressures. (We have not discussed here the serious problems of physical health often faced by ethnographers. Berreman describes the importance of this factor, and Allan Holmberg's accounts [1969] of struggles with disease, fatigue, and plagues of insects are a vivid illustration of the physical side of the field-work experience.) Unless the anthropologist can maintain balance in these social and psychological aspects of research, his or her good intentions about operationalizing variables, sampling procedures, and other elements of methodological rigor are useless.

Rosalie Wax has written a vivid account of the anxieties she experienced during research in a Japanese relocation center. In the early stages of field work – that period nearly every researcher experiences when nothing is going well, when informants are hostile and evasive, and when the entire effort seems meaningless and farcical – she "succumbed to an urge to eat enormously and in three months gained thirty pounds" (Wax, 1960b:175).

Although solid data on this subject are scarce, widespread anecdotal evidence suggests that most fieldworkers experience periods of anxiety, despression, and helplessness, often accompanied by a strong tendency to withdraw from all data-gathering activity. One fieldworker tells privately of a considerable span of field time during which he spent most of his days perusing *The Reader's Digest* and eating peanut-butter sandwiches. It is perhaps not surprising that we find numbers of instances in which fieldworkers mention eating as an anxiety-relieving mechanism. Jean Briggs reported from her field work among the Eskimo: "My tent had become a refuge, into which I withdrew every evening . . . to repair ravages to my spirits with the help of bannock and peanut butter. So reviving were those hours of self-indulgence that I dreaded their loss" (Briggs, 1968:333). Psychiatrist Ronald Wintrob has also examined the various ways in which anthropologists react to the stresses of field work (Wintrob, 1969).

Our sample of fifty-one anthropologists reported considerable psychological tensions in field work, though the *modal* category of researchers is the group reporting "general excitement, relaxation, enjoyment." It is not too surprising that field work in some distant region generates more psychological tensions, apparently because of greater cultural differences, as well as because of the separation from usual social relationships (see Table 9.2).

A number of fieldworkers have noted that brief vacations away from the research community can be excellent tension relievers – with beneficial results for both informants and researchers. After all, at least in small communities the ubiquitous presence of "the man with the notebook and a thousand questions" can be very taxing for the local inhabitants. They must surely wish that for once they could enact a small bit of local custom without having to explain it all to the anthropologist. A few days – or even longer – spent in the city, at the beach, hiking in the mountains, or visiting a nearby game reservation can give the fieldworker time to dissipate anxieties and hostilities, get some needed physical rest, and perhaps restock some supplies. At the same time, the research community itself gets a rest. Often the return of the fieldworker after a brief vacation is an occasion for a warm welcome, a reaffirmation of friendships. One may be treated like a returning relative, and a few slightly reluctant informants may show a new willingness to give information.

Table 9.2. *Ethnographers' reports of psychological and physical experiences*[a]

Culture shock		8
Some psychological tensions		19
General excitement, relaxation, enjoyment		30
Much physical illness		1
Some illness		27
No illness		10
Frequent tiredness		1
Psychological tensions reported during		
research in:	*None*	*Some*
North America	9	0
Europe	2	5
Other parts of the world	12	20

[a]Individuals were allowed to check off more than one response.

The social-psychological hazards of field work, which make every successful research project an elaborate combination of scientific techniques and social artistry, may account for some of the mystique that has grown up around the subject. At this stage of our discipline we know distressingly little about the personalities of anthropologists and the effects on personality of the field-work "rite of passage." Dennison Nash, in his essay "The Ethnologist as Stranger," has reviewed psychological data (Rorschach tests, etc.) on twenty-five anthropologists that indicate that "these anthropologists would be able to tolerate the ambiguity, inconsistency and predictable flux of the stranger's experience without resort to the perceptual distortions that more authoritarian types would find necessary" (Nash, 1963:161).

Any extensive discussion of the art of field work should include (among other things) sections on the selection of informants, on gifts and payments, on when to take notes, or tactics with photographic equipment, on interactions with outsiders, on the giving of parties, on when to break taboos, and on many other subjects related to the central issue of impression management. In the course of successful field work the anthropologist builds up and maintains a complicated role of "inside-outsider," "privileged stranger," or some variant on this theme, but the specific content and dynamics of this presentation of self vary a great deal from one community to another, and from one anthropologist to another. Because human communities differ so much in their cultural context, and because the personalities of anthropologists exhibit great variation, fixed rules and procedures for the artistic social-management side of field work cannot be prescribed.

Sex and field work

The fieldworker's sexual relationships with members of the research community can be quite complex and difficult, but very little information has been published concerning sexual behavior in the research setting. As the typical field ethnographer is a lone male, local people (especially males) are usually concerned about his intentions regarding their women. At John Beattie's "housewarming party" (during his first days in a Bunyoro community), an important man of the settlement admonished him "not to make friends with the local women" (Beattie, 1965:16). Robert Maxwell (1969) has commented on sexual involvement in the course of his field work in Samoa.

Female anthropologists, on the other hand, generally have the difficult task of making clear to local males that they are sexually unavailable. Among those many peoples of the world who are unaccustomed to seeing women of marriageable age going about with no evidence of a husband and family, the female anthropologist has some difficult explanations to make to both sexes in the research community. Powdermaker told her Lesu friends that she had been married and was divorced, adding that her ex-husband "had not worked well, one of the reasons for native divorce" (Powdermaker, 1966:63). Apparently this explanation was accepted. Establishing a successful role definition with regard to sex requires subtlety in nonverbal communication as well as verbal statements. Young anthropologists who have persistent trouble in warding off sexual advances, or who are accused of making sexual advances, are often causing difficulties by inadvertent behavior patterns that are sexually provocative by local standards.

The matter of sexual relationships with the research community can become a problem in another way in later phases of field work. Sexual relations are an important aspect of amicable ties within communities, and it is not uncommon in male-dominated societies for the male anthropologist to be offered access to females as a gesture of friendship. Such a situation presents the fieldworker with a complex dilemma: Sexual involvement with local women can lead to serious difficulties; on the other hand, to refuse can be interpreted as an unfriendly act. Adding to the problem are the insistent psychophysiological pressures of unrelieved sexual needs.

More than a simple expression of ingroup solidarity was at stake in an incident described by Colin Turnbull (1962), in which he found himself suddenly presented with a beautiful sleeping partner from one of the Bantu villages of the northeastern Congo region. Apparently one of the subchiefs, in seeking to cement relationships with the elusive Pygmies, hit upon the idea of creating an alliance by giving his daughter to the anthropologist. "No doubt the chief had in mind the considerable bride-wealth he could demand should, by any chance, his daughter bear a mulatto child. Still, it was good of him to send his prettiest daughter" (Turnbull, 1962:143). Turnbull reports that he extricated himself from this delicate situation by a complex agreement with Amina (the chief's daughter). "She was to stay with me and cook my food – and mend leaks in the roof every night. This way she would preserve her reputation and I mine, and there would be no complications. And so it was" (Turnbull, 1962:144). This arrangement lasted for some while, until the Pygmies moved camp, at which time Amina took the opportunity to return to her village.

Clothing, personal habits, and impression management

Very little is known about the effects of anthropologists' clothing styles on their research. When we consider that in every human society styles of clothing are important signals of social status and role, it follows that fieldworkers can *always* influence local attitudes by adopting particular habits of costume. At first thought we would be tempted to conclude that the anthropologist should dress like everyone else in the village. But there are many reasons why this is not always the solution to be adopted.

1   In some cases fieldworkers have been admonished by their informants that they should *not* dress like the ordinary villagers, because that would be a form of condescension. "If you dress up in a suit to go to see government officials, why do you not dress that way when you visit other people?" Naturally, the attitudes of people vary greatly with regard to such interpretations.

2   Where the local populace has a distinctive local costume, early adoption of that mode of dress by fieldworkers may be regarded as presumptuous, because it implies an insider status that they have not yet attained. On the other hand, at a later stage of field residence, it may be expected, or even required, that anthropologists adopt local garb as they come to be defined as members of the local community.

3   Many peoples in the world of anthropological experience seem to be willing to accept the suggestion that the fieldworker comes from a cultural background where people have different customs, which legitimates somewhat unusual tastes and habits. Laura Nader apparently had a bit of difficulty in convincing her Zapotec friends in Talea and Juquila that she was culturally different from them, but when she did, she gained some important advantages. Nader writes, "The women constantly badgered me to grow my hair, to change my clothes. By experimenting I finally discovered that the best reply was to tell them that were they to visit my home country dressed as they were with such long pigtails they would be ridiculed. Much laughter would result from such conversations. I capitalized on their indecision as to how to categorize me and gained the greatest freedom of movement among both men and women." (Nader, 1964:vi.)

4   Many male anthropologists return from the field with luxuriant beards. In many cases the decision to grow a beard arises in part from the difficulties and discomforts of regular shaving (e.g., procurement of hot water may involve complex procedures), but beard growing has certain psychological accompaniments as well. Sometimes the extended field-work situation offers a man his first opportunity to try growing a beard. On the other hand, Michael Robbins and Philip Kilbride report that they were discouraged from growing beards by their Baganda informants. Having a beard was associated with certain disliked people from another region. In some areas wearing of beards is associated with missionaries, which invokes status imagery that anthropologists usually try to avoid. Again, male fieldworkers in Mexico frequently grow mustaches after a time – possibly as a response to one signaling element in the general *machismo* complex of male prestige.

5   With regard to clothing, anthropologists should try to avoid elements of dress that symbolize locally disliked types of persons, such as administrators, missionaries, rich merchants, and the like. If the "people from the government" wear shiny leather boots, the anthropologist finds other types of footgear; if the police wear heavy leather belts, it is perhaps best to find some other type of trouser support; and so on. The same principles apply with female fieldworkers, though they usually have a broader variety of symbols to work with. Sometimes the simple practice of wearing lipstick is enough to disassociate one's self from suspicion-arousing roles, such as that of missionary.

6   While the status-signaling aspect of clothing and personal adornment is extremely important, practical considerations should not be lost sight of. Fieldworkers must protect themselves from cold, heat, and other physical hazards; at the same time they must be able to carry certain minimal equipment – at least a notebook and a pencil – at all

times; and fussing with the complexities of clothing must not interfere with field work. Because the anthropologist does *not* generally become defined as a complete insider, some defiance of dress style, whether dictated by practical needs or other motives, is usually feasible.

7   Research in urban environments presents a new set of problems about clothing strategies. Frequently, the anthropologist does well to adopt the rule of dressing inconspicuously. In some situations (e.g., door-to-door interview work) it is important to signal a certain measure of prestige and status by wearing appropriate clothing. At other times, in working with low-status groups in an informal setting, much more casual costume is called for. The fieldworker who attends parties among urban hippies probably should not wear a suit and tie.

All of the comments here are intended only as general suggestions about dress habits in field work; few anthropologists report on these things, leaving beginning fieldworkers to explore the problems for themselves.

At this point some observers of the anthropological enterprise would suggest that the nature of ethnographic work, because of the kinds of problems just reviewed, makes "scientific" field studies impossible. But examination of the stuff of anthropological research demonstrates to us that fieldworkers have, despite these hazards and problems, been able to carry out a truly amazing variety of specialized data gathering. In their complicated insider–outsider roles, anthropologists have collected meticulous census and genealogical data; they have gathered information about private family activities and possessions; their notebooks have been filled with details of juridical cases and other special events that would astound the most intellectual and knowledgeable of local leaders; and they have obtained psychological tests, blood samples, urine specimens, accounts of dreams, life histories, and myriad other data, which, had these been gathered by any native insider in the community, would probably have resulted in his being lynched or at least removed from social respectability.

Because descriptions of ethnographic field work provide extensive documentation of *both* the artistic and the scientific sides of research, we should now turn our attention to the empirical aspect of field data gathering. In spite of the large role of intuition (and artistry) in field work, we have no reason to shrink from the possibility that a considerable portion of our field materials can be operationalized and quantified.

Elements of community study

All of the research issues to be discussed here involve the use of the basic instruments of field research outlined in Chapters 5 and 6. In this section, however, we deal with sectors of information and tactics of community study that usually require a mixture of observational tools. We are concerned here with the types of data to be gathered, and where to find them, regardless of which specific means of observation (interviews, direct observation, etc.) one chooses to employ. Therefore, the following discussion represents the next level of abstraction above tools of research. Several important works in the anthropological literature set out details of *what* the fieldworker should study in the community, though these sources often give few details of *how* the tasks should be carried out. *Notes and Queries* (1951) has long been an important field guide for anthropologists, and Murdock's *Outline of Cultural Materials* (1950) is also a standard item in field research. There are also a number of more specialized guides to field operations, such as the *Field Guide for the Study of Socialization* by Whiting and associates (1968). If we examine the kinds of data that are present in most good ethnographic studies, it appears that certain field-work operations can be regarded as fundamental to general community description, however specialized the theoretical orientation of the anthropologist.

Census taking and mapping

The fieldworker should try to make an enumeration of family units and their membership (or a random sample of such units) near the beginning of field work. This is often an ideal first task for one's local field assistants; the accuracy of their work can be checked systematically by spot inspection. In many research contexts today, some kind of enumeration of household units is available from the records of municipal authorities, the school system, church records, the post office, or other authorities. These records may also provide additional information, such as occupations and birthplaces of householders. Where written records are available, fieldworkers will need to spend a considerable number of hours and days in transferring these basic census data to their own records – preferably onto large file cards to which they can add much more information as field work progresses.

Besides enumerating social units within the research area, fieldworkers should map out the spatial relationships of significant social groups, constructed physical features, and other elements of the sociophysical landscape. (It is a source of constant surprise that many ethnographic reports do not contain maps of the physical setting within which social behavior takes place.) Such maps should locate major action settings (e.g., ball fields, religious places, marketplaces), major social divisions of the community, agricultural areas, directions and distances of neighboring communities, and major natural features such as rivers, mountains, and swamps.

Mapping and preliminary census taking often do not require language facility or a great deal of rapport with informants, so these activities can be carried out before the fieldworker is fully assimilated into the community. Problems can easily arise, of course, and the fieldworker must be aware of the possibility that this data collection will be misinterpreted by the local people. A most common fear, increasingly encountered in modern times, is that census taking is part of a governmental attempt to increase tax collection in the community. A related concern is that mapping may be preliminary to some new land confiscation. Fieldworkers should, therefore, develop effective explanations for this behavior. If they are able to establish this data collection as legitimate and harmless, they will usually find that the activities are very effective as an introduction to the majority of local inhabitants. In fact, introducing one's self to everyone in the community can be a rationale for carrying out a preliminary census operation. Powdermaker's comments about her census taking in Lesu are useful in this connection (1966:60–2).

A constant feature in field work is the rechecking of data collected in earlier phases of the study. Thus a census taken at the beginning of field work should be frequently spot-checked, corrected, and updated. Fieldworkers have from time to time commented on local mobility (intra- and intercommunity) of particular peoples. Such movements, if carefully studied, may be extremely important for understanding the dynamics of household and familial structure, but the data can be obtained only if the fieldworker periodically rechecks basic census materials (or some selected sample thereof).

Köbben (1967) has described the joys and sorrows of collecting extensive census data among the Djuka of Surinam. It required a great sacrifice of time, during a year of field work, to collect these quantified data on a mere 176 persons (all adults in the village of Langa Uku).

People at first objected: "Where are you going to take those figures? Perhaps you'll take them to other villages! They'll be jealous when they find out how many children we have here." It was only after I had been there some months and after I had made the necessary libations (like everywhere else the living here help their ancestors drink) that I was permitted to take my census. (Köbben, 1967:49.)

There were all kinds of problems – refusals to talk about dead children, lack of exactness in people's numerical concepts, male mobility as an obstacle to assigning residence in particular households, and so on. In the end, Köbben felt rather unsure of the validity of some of his data, but his extensive field work made it possible to assess the usefulness of different portions of the materials. Adoption patterns and genealogical relationships among the people in the community were illuminated by his numerical data, as were comparisons concerning religious experience.

In my village 20% of the adult population were mediums of some deity, on the Tapanahony river 37%. Even before my co-fieldworkers and I had collected these data it was already our impression that the Tapanahony people experienced their religion more intensely than the people of my region, but this was no more than an impression. We took the percentage of mediums as an operational definition of "intensity of religious experience." The difference indicated above we regard as a confirmation of our hypothesis. (Ibid., 52.)

Many writers have commented that serious misinterpretations of survey and census data can result if the interview procedures are not carried out in close articulation with intensive ethnographic field study. Leach has presented one such example in "an anthropologist's reflections on a social survey" (1967), dealing with a survey of fifty-eight villages in Ceylon (Sarkar and Tambiah, 1957). He pointed out that the sampling unit in the survey was the household, defined as "persons who cook their rice from the same pot." In his ethnographic work, however, he found that every young married couple has a separate cooking pot even when they live in an extended family household (a very common pattern). Thus, in the case of a man with three married sons, four separate households are recorded in the social survey. Therefore, "my anthropological appreciation of the total situation has led me to suspect that a proportion of the 335 landless households were landless simply because the householders were young, recently married adults who were heirs to still living parents" (Leach, 1967:80). He introduces similar technical problems concerning the identification of sharecroppers and owners and the calculation of the degree of bias toward males in inheritance patterns.

Some of the problems Leach described could be corrected, it would seem, through a careful analysis of the survey protocols in the light of detailed ethnographic information. For example, spot checks in a few of the research communities might make possible a correction factor in terms of which the problem of multiple separate rice-cooking pots in extended households could be adjusted. But some of the survey data were inaccurate because the questions – the mode of operationalizing key variables – were not shaped realistically.

Clearly, the quantified data of survey research or other standardized interviewing require close support from participant observation and general informal interviewing. But the converse is equally true. The lesson in all this, as Köbben made clear, is that field research entails a great amount of tedious, time-consuming work – both qualitative and numerical.

Genealogical inquiry

In addition to a complete enumeration of a population in terms of household of residence and major kinship affiliation, the fieldworker usually needs much more detailed data concerning the consanguineous and affinal linkages that knit the community into a complex fabric of kinship. This body of information may be of crucial importance for making sense of many social events and transactions; hence the researcher is often well advised to begin this work as soon as possible.

In a classic paper published in 1910, W. H. R. Rivers set out the procedures for collecting individual informants' "pedigrees" with such clarity and order that his description can still be regarded as a primary field-work guide. Referring to his sample genealogy from Guadalcanal, Rivers tells us:

I began the inquiry by asking my informant, Kurka or Arthur, the name of his father and mother, making it clear that I wanted the names of his real parents and not of any other people whom he would call such by virtue of the classificatory system of relationship. After ascertaining that Kulini had had only one wife and Kusua only one husband, I obtained the names of their children in order of age and inquired into the marriages and offspring of each. . . . I obtained the names of (his mother's) parents, ascertaining as before that each had only been once married, and then asked the names of their children and obtained the marriages and descendants of each. . . . In collecting the pedigrees the descendants in both the male and female lines are obtained, but in writing them out in order to use them for the purposes to be considered in this paper, it is well to record on one sheet only the descendants in one line with cross-references to other sheets for the descendants in the other line. (Rivers, 1910:1–2.)

It is important to note that in this initial phase of the method the only relationship terms normally required are those of father, mother, child, husband, and wife. Rivers commented:

A most important feature of the method is to record as far as possible the social condition of each person included in the pedigrees. In order that the pedigrees may be used in the ways I propose to describe it is necessary to be satisfied that they are trustworthy. In collecting the pedigrees of a whole community, there will be much overlapping; people who belong to the paternal stock of one informant will come in the maternal stock of another, and in the wife's ancestry of a third, and there will thus be ample opportunity of testing the agreement of the accounts of different informants. In nearly every community in which I have worked I have found that there are people with especial genealogical knowledge, and it is well to make use of these as much as possible. In my experience it is very dangerous to trust to the young men, who nearly everywhere are no longer taking the trouble to learn the pedigrees from their elders. (Ibid., 3.)

Turning to the use of the genealogical data for eliciting kinship terminological systems, Rivers said:

. . . my procedure is to ask my informant the terms which he would apply to the different members of his pedigree, and reciprocally the terms which they would apply to him. . . . I am in the habit of supplementing the genealogical method by asking for a list of all the people to whom a given man applies a term of relationship. (Ibid., 3–5.)

The network of relationships obtained in this fashion can be used as a frame of reference against which to elicit information about property rights, succession to special offices, residence rules, prescribed and prohibited marital or sex partners, and many other topics. In earlier decades ethnographers sometimes used genealogical data simply to establish the presence of supposedly unitary cultural traits, such as lineality of descent, matrilocal or patrilocal residence, and marriage rules, but recent treatments of kinship structure concern themselves rather more with behavioral systems.

Reviewing Rivers's genealogical inquiry, J. A. Barnes commented that:

> . . . his method can scarcely be improved, except for one alteration. I suggest that it is often useful, before beginning on a sequence of inquiries structured by the ethnographer, to record first whatever information about his kinfolk the informant thinks important, in the form in which he presents it . . . it provides the best indication of how the informant perceives his kinfolk and what version of their names, status, numbers, and relationships he wishes to present to the ethnographer. (Barnes, 1967:106.)

Barnes's paper on the genealogical method is an important addition to Rivers's work.

Ethnographers going into the field have sometimes been advised that the collecting of genealogies is an excellent opening gambit, because these data are usually considered to be very interesting and nonthreatening. Perhaps there is some general change taking place in the world with regard to the meaning of kinship; at any rate, there are increasing reports of peoples who feel quite threatened by inquiries about genealogies. Gerlach reports, for example, that the Digo of East Africa are extremely wary of giving genealogical information, because these data are central to numerous disputes over property rights in a situation where matrilineal, patrilineal, and bilateral principles of reckoning are all invoked and debated in the course of litigation. Also, it appears that in a world full of new kinds of social striving, the rubrics of pedigree have taken on added significance in connection with racial, aristocratic, or other standards of presumed social excellence. One of our informants proudly informed us that his biological father was an Englishman who occasionally visited Lapland on fishing excursions.

Inventory of occupations and material goods

Without necessarily espousing economic determinism in one's social and cultural theory, it is reasonable to assume that the subsistence basis of a community is primary for any descriptive or theoretical study. The fieldworker will usually find it quite easy to learn a great deal about the agricultural practices and other income-producing behavior of the people, though in most cases systems of distribution and exchange of goods and services constitute a much more complicated area of study. Communities in which everyone has the same basic economic pursuit are becoming increasingly rare, and inventorying the basic occupational subdivisions of a community is an important step in the early phases of field work. These data can, of course, be included in a general census-taking operation.

In every human community there are differences among individuals and families in their access to, or control of, the local good things in life. In all societies, too, some of these scarce resources are material goods, whether primarily food, clothing, housing, or other things. Although many ethnographic descriptions of earlier times have stressed the egalitarianism and homogeneity of local groups, such facile characterizations have in recent years been subjected to much criticism. (Social historians some day will be concerned to explain why anthropologists during much of the twentieth century showed rather little interest in local social stratification, except in obvious situations such as the caste system of India.)

An important point of concentration, then, in the study of local culture patterns is the *differences* between the materially more successful and those who are less wealthy (by local standards). The assumption should not be made that all aspects of social differences follow the lines of material differences, but the variations in material style of life are often easiest to discern in early phases of field inquiry.

Differences in house style will usually be noticeable to the fieldworker from the first day of research. In some cases the differences may simply reflect differences in optional use of local materials; or they may reflect subcultural differences that have no connotations of social stratification. In most instances, though, the variations in construction and materials of roofs, windows, walls, and so on, indicate differential economic success among the members of the community.

House furnishing and equipment generally follow this same pattern. Some households have kerosene lamps; others do not. Factory-made beds, tables, or other furniture may be in evidence in some households. In many parts of the world the presence of radios (or even television sets) distinguishes the economically more successful households. Often these marks of relative wealth are at the same time evidence of the intrusions of generalized Western technology; therefore, the fieldworker must begin early to sort out (where possible) the conceptually separate dimensions of affluence and acculturation.

Inventories of material objects are useful in examining many social distinctions and relationships. Also, examination of material things is, in many communities, a relatively nonthreatening procedure. People often enjoy talking about their possessions, even to outsiders, and in any case establishing the presence or absence of these materials is usually easier than with nonmaterial cultural elements.

Any community, of course, contains hundreds of thousands of material objects. The fieldworker should list some representative items that appear to be significant as both functionally useful equipment and social differentiators.

Land tenure

Perhaps the most ubiquitous mark of social position in rural communities is differential access to useful land. Land is, of course, physical and identifiable, but people are not always willing to give specifics about ownership patterns. Agriculturalists are often quite secretive about landholdings, and the rules of land tenure are usually so complex that the anthropologist must work for weeks, or even months, before the system (or systems) of landholding becomes clear. In some societies, local records or other sources offer quick and easy data on individual landholdings. Again, there are societies in which people make no secret of the size and productivity of their plots.

Careful description of the rules of landholding (and transactions in land) as well as the differential holdings of the social units (individuals, families, or other social units) is crucial for understanding the basic social processes in most food-growing communities. Where land is of great importance, the researcher should expect to begin studying this aspect of field work early and to continue working on it throughout most of the research period.

Animal husbandry

Among some peoples – in East Africa, Southwest and Central Asia, and elsewhere – ownership of valuable animals is of much greater concern and significance than are matters of landholdings. Here again the fact that animals are physical and observable makes the beginnings of field work seem relatively simple, and pastoralists generally are more than willing to talk about their animals at great length. But the complex social relationships and obligations involving the animals can be at least as intricate as matters of land tenure. To add to this, keeping large numbers of animals requires land, so that economic processes in pastoralist communities may involve complicated interrelationships among people, land, and animals. Robert Pehrson has described some of these kinds of relationships in a Lappish reindeer-herding community (Pehrson, 1957); and the work of Vayda and others (Leeds and Vayda, 1965; Rappaport, 1967) illustrates the interrelations of populations, pigs, and territory in New Guinea.

Where herds of animals are of paramount importance in local affairs, the fieldworker can begin with rough estimates of herd sizes (often available nowadays from official tax sources, though very inaccurate). At the same time, a most important task is to learn the taxonomic system for identifying and describing the animals. For the most part usually this involves at least the dimensions of sex, age, and major physical (usually color) characteristics. Most pastoralists are eager to impart this kind of information to anthropologists, and even young boys of the village are often excellent informants, because the lore of animal management is central to the male role they are most interested in.

Event analysis

So far our discussion of field work has concentrated on the physical things in the research setting – the people, habitations, material goods, geographical features, land, and animals. Although there are exceptions to this idea, the opening moves of field work can often begin most fruitfully in this sphere of concrete, observable things. Social relationships will often be manifest in these physical things, and discussions of social relationships in the abstract, without reference to physical spacing, ownership of resources, and differential control of scarce goods, is an empty, unrealistic exercise.

Much essential information about those physical objects and relationships is imbedded in nonmaterial social action. To study more directly these social actions and relationships the anthropologist must shift attention to the analysis of significant private and public events that take place in the research community. Such events come in all sizes, and eventually fieldworkers seek to study as many as they can, though it is useful to turn first to an examination of major public events, for these often mirror (however distortedly) important social relationships. Moreover, they have frequently been a focus of anthropological concern, and usually the major events (fiestas, religious ceremonials, annual fairs, market days, etc.) are publicly open to fieldworkers even before they have established strong social ties in the local community.

As an example of a major public action we will describe some aspects of a Saame[1] reindeer roundup. Like many public events, it has significant practical purposes; yet it is considered to be a festive celebration as well. Simply the fact that considerable numbers of people from many different communities assemble in one place (with an air of excitement and suspense) gives a clue to the relevance of the scene. Our analysis of reindeer roundups is not intended as a full theoretical treatment, for only certain main highlights will be examined here as a guide to field-work procedure. The location for the following observations is the Muddusjärvi Association roundup site in northeastern Finnish Lapland.

In Finnish Lapland, reindeer roundups or "separations" occur several times a year in each of the fifty-eight reindeer districts. Many of the separations are

[1] The Saame are the reindeer-herding people of northern Europe previously referred to as Lapps.

carried out at permanent locations that are equipped with a complex of inner and outer corrals for capturing and holding fairly large numbers of animals. Some of these corrals are located in distant backlands, but others are situated near main roads, making them more accessible to meat buyers, peddlers, and (nowadays) tourists.

The principal activity in these roundups is the capture of individual reindeer by lassoing. The herds that are brought to the roundup sites are usually very mixed in ownership, so that individual owners must recognize and sort out their own animals one by one from the milling throng of reindeer and people. Captured individual animals may then be sold, given over as debt payments, marked and turned loose, or taken home for winter herding (Pelto, 1962). Recognition and proof of ownership of reindeer throughout Lapland is achieved through a complex system of notches, slits, holes, and other marks in the ears of the animals.

Observing the reindeer roundup for the first time, the fieldworker can set out a number of key questions that should be answered if he is to understand the overall events, for example:

1 Who are the different kinds of people involved in this action?
2 How are these people grouped in alliances, oppositions, partnerships?
3 What are the sequences of action in which these people express these relationships?
4 Are the social relationships among these people visible in terms of geographical spacing in the roundup corral and adjacent areas?
5 Are there symbols of status – for example, clothing, emblems, equipment – that differentiate among some of these groups?
6 Which groups have the most power or decision-making capacity in this action?
7 Are there police, judges, referees, or other agents of social control?

Earlier it was suggested that mapping and census taking are important beginnings for community study; the same applies to the study of an event. We found, in our first exposure to a reindeer roundup, that mapping the physical structure of the corral and nearby dwelling units provided a nearly complete outline of the structure of the social interaction taking place (Pelto, 1962:124–40). Figure 9.1 shows the geography of the corral and the cubicles immediately adjacent to the arena into which reindeer are brought for separation, or sorting. The first observation to be made about these cubicles is that the Skolt Saame positions tend to be bunched together on one side of the corral, although this segregation of Skolts from other groups is not complete. Second, the cubicles of any one reindeer association tend to be together, and the relative positions of the associations are visible in the organization of the cubicles. That is, the Muddusjärvi Association owns the corral, and the other associations present (Utsjoki, Paatsjoki, Paistunturi) are neighboring associations whose animals often stray into the herds of the Muddusjärvi people.

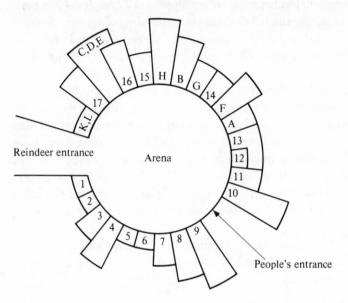

Figure 9.1. Reindeer roundup site in northeastern Lapland.
Key: 1–17 Cubicles of non-Skolts (Finns,   5, 6, 7 Utsjoki Association
              Inari, Lapps, etc.)   14   Muddusjärvi Association
      A–L   Cubicles of Skolt herders and   K, L   Paatsjoki Association (including
              their associates   Skolts)
       1   Paistunturi Association   9   Meat buyers

The placement of the Paatsjoki "visitors" indicates that they are socially closer to their fellow Skolts of the Muddusjärvi Association than to other groups in the area. The positions of the cubicles in this case correspond to both the social and territorial placement of these people. (Of course, the verification of the social observations comes from intensive field work in other contexts.)

Also evident in the geography of the corral scene is the fact that the cubicles of the reindeer herders tend to sort out into those of Skolt Saame, Inari Saame, Tundra Saame, and Finns. The cultural groupings are not conterminous with the reindeer districts, however, and the separation into the four cultural groups is not complete.

But what are the relationships within the groups that "own" each cubicle? This is a relatively easy piece of information to obtain, and it is of great importance. Generally speaking, a cubicle is "owned" by men who herd their reindeer together throughout the winter. They are the basic winter herding groups. But there are exceptions. Some of the cubicles are "owned" by confederations of two or three winter herding groups.

During the action of sorting reindeer in the corral, it is possible to observe that each individual herder generally brings reindeer to only one cubicle, the one with which he is associated. Here, together with some of his neighbors and kinsmen (usually four to ten owners), he collects his own herd for transfer back to home pasturage. But there are some exceptions. When one of these exceptions occurred, it was important to ask (that person or some other handy informant) why this person brought a reindeer to someone else's cubicle. The answer was usually clear: He was helping someone. In some cases, though, he was paying a debt.

There were two cubicles, however, to which many people brought animals as they caught them. Before long it was possible to observe that one of these was a reindeer meat buyer. The meat buyer and his assistants kept careful tally of their purchases, and later, at the coffeehouses, the cash settlement of these transactions could be observed. The other cubicle that received some reindeer from a number of different persons turned out to be owned by the Muddusjärvi Association itself. Animals brought to that cubicle were mainly unmarked or unidentifiable animals that were auctioned off, proceeds going to the association.

The other important physical features in the Muddusjärvi reindeer separation site are a number of cabins, ranging from tiny two-man huts to the four large centrally located "coffeehouses." Inquiry into the ownership and use of the cabins showed that living accommodations at the roundup site tend toward congruence with arrangements in the corral itself, but again exceptions appear. Table 9.3 presents the winter herding-group affiliations of a number of persons who domiciled in the cabins with which the Skolt Saame were most closely associated. The list is incomplete, and the patterns changed somewhat from one occasion to the next, but certain important generalizations can be made from this mapping. A principal observation that begins to emerge from the mapping and census of cabins and their occupants is that social relationships, as expressed through sleeping and eating patterns, are very flexible and individualized.

Mapping the reindeer roundup site and making a census of the categories of persons at the roundup produced a great amount of information about important social relationships. Many of these observations were made, however, in the course of watching the principal *actions* in this complex event. From the outset it was clear that most, but far from all, significant action occurred in and near the corral itself. After the second day it was clear that the general sequence of events would be the same, day after day, until the end of the roundup.

Each morning at dawn the association herders brought a herd of reindeer into position for driving into the corral. Volunteers were then called out to guard the "wings" of the "trap," as the animals were lured into the enclosure. When this capturing operation was completed, the animals were allowed to remain undisturbed in the outer enclosure for an hour or so, during which time the men walked quietly through the herds, identifying animals and noting which calves followed particular cows. (During the milling around in the inner corral calves become separated from their mothers and cannot be identified as to ownership unless they have been "recognized" during this earlier inspection period.)

After the preliminary inspection had been completed, part of the herd was driven into the inner enclosure, and roping began. As the number of uncaught reindeer diminished, more and more herders drifted off to the coffeehouses to rest, drink coffee, eat, and talk, until another portion of the herd was brought into the inner corral. When all the identifiable animals in the inner corral had been caught, the remaining, unidentified reindeer were driven into the association cubicle for auctioning. The (usually brief) auction was the final phase before a fresh herd was brought into the inner corral and the entire sequence was repeated. When all the animals in the outer enclosure had been processed, the day's work was over and the people retired to the coffeehouses and cabins to eat, drink, play cards, or otherwise pass the time.

The sequence of events that make up a separation is an ideal target for the anthropologist at an early stage of field work because patterns of action are repeated many times in approximately the same format, so the fieldworker can depend on the next day's repetition to fill in details that were missed earlier. There are few crucial moments, and no serious losses of data occur if the fieldworker takes a break for coffee or gets into a long conversation with one of the participants.

The roundup corral was not the only scene of important social action, however. At the coffeehouses there was music and other entertainment; a huckster of clothing and miscellany held forth for several hours a day outside one of the larger cabins; and occasionally one or another of the groups held a meeting to discuss some issue that had arisen.

When the roundup was completed, and we returned to the village, it was possible to put together the "big picture" of the event. As we filled out our description, we found that the questions raised by the first field work in a roundup pointed in two directions. First, it was important to see the gaps in the data about the roundup itself – these gaps would have to be filled in when we had a chance to observe another roundup. Second, we needed to find out whether social relationships in other big events and in day-to-day social transactions corresponded with the inferences that we had made from this first Muddusjärvi reindeer roundup.

We have gone into some detail about preliminary field analysis of the reindeer roundup because it is a clear case of an important social event that offers the fieldworker an opportunity to observe a considerable amount of social information as it is dramatized in spatial and interactional terms. The repetition of this kind of large-scale social event provides an important part of the anthropologist's data concerning social processes. The following generalizations can be made concerning analysis of events:

Table 9.3. *Some residence patterns at the Muddusjärvi reindeer roundup (demonstrating mixing of Skolt Saame sleeping arrangements)*

Camp owners	"Guests" (persons who sleep there)	Herding-group affiliation[a]
1 Jankkilan Jussi (a Finn) (coffeehouse)	Most of the Skolt Saame from Sevetti village	Group H
2 Karpis Pekka (a Finn) (coffeehouse)	Most of the Skolt Saame and others from Paatsjoki district	I, K, L
3 Oskari and Erkki Fofanoff	Oskari's son Vasko	A
	A. Feodoroff	E
	P. Semenoja	K
	Two Sarre boys	A
4 Olli Gauriloff	Jakkima Feodoroff and son	G
Evvan Semenoff	Aapo Aikio	F
	Saveli Fofanoff	E
		G
		G
5 Piera Porsanger	J. Högman	G
Jaakko Gauriloff	Eero Aikio	G
	Veikko Paltto	H
	Illep and Elias Fofanoff	G
		Paatsjoki
		C
6 Nikolai Killanen	Nikolai's four sons	F
Aleksi Fofanoff	Evvan Kiprianoff	B
	Matti Sverloff	F
		H
		H
7 Evvan, Erkki, Mikko,	Jussi Gauriloff	D
and Aleksi Sverloff		D
8 Seurujärvi (a Finn) (coffeehouse)	Paavo, Vasko, and Kiurel Fofanoff	B
	Vasko R. Fofanoff	C
9 Valle Niiles (Inari Saame) (coffeehouse)		
	Jeffim Feodoroff	F
	Timo Gauriloff	G

[a] In 1959 there were twelve different winter herding groups among the Skolt Saame reindeer herders; each consisted of from four to fifteen families.
Source: Pelto, 1962.

1   All social events occur in some kind of physical setting, and the use of the physical setting, especially the spacing and movements among the participants, provides the first important clues to social relationships and processes. The fieldworker's first task, therefore, should be to identify the kinds of persons present in an event and to map out their spacing in relation to the physical stage on which they act out this particular drama.

2   Key informants are very important as an information source but are best used in connection with the concrete events observed by the fieldworker. The important kinds of questions to ask are often in the following forms: What is that (building, enclosure, object) used for? Who is that man who is carrying the platter of food? Why is he going first to those people in the corner? Why is the man in the center dressed differently from the others?

   During a pause in the event it is possible to ask questions about previous events of the same type, such as the following inquiries: Is the action that we just witnessed very much the same as, or very different from, the previous enactment of this same event? How is it different? Which parts seem to you to be exactly the same? (Key informants often show much better recall of a past event when they are immersed in the memory-jogging setting pertinent to that event.)

3   Any social events that are repeated a number of times during the field period should be treated as a series of intracultural comparisons. That is, variations in the size and structure of a social event may be related to important social patterns. The size of weddings and fiestas may be indicators of relative wealth and/or social centrality; the sequence of actions in a ceremonial may be different depending on the ritual excellence and status of the central actors; law cases may result in different kinds of resolutions, depending on differentials in social status and political power. It follows, then, that any social events that occur a number of times should be observed systematically in ways that permit numerical analysis.

4   Certain standard elements of any action can, and should, be quantified. The number of persons in particular categories should be counted. Counts of persons should be made at several different times during the course of the event, if possible. Counting makes it possible to give substance to statements such as: "This fiesta is bigger than the one last year," or "There are fewer costumed dancers now than there were in the winter ceremonial." In general, the fieldworker should make an attempt to predict the kinds of quantified statements one will need in describing the event. He can imagine himself writing portions of the analysis and note the points at which he uses expressions such as "many," "few," "more than," "shorter than," "constantly increasing." These are clues to significant points to be counted. In addition to counting types or categories of persons, the researcher may quantify the following:

   a   Amounts of significant material things, such as platters of food, jugs of beverage, roast pigs, candles, musical instruments, cars and other vehicles, placards, bolts of cloth, gifts (of all types).
   b   Repetitions of important acts, such as prayers, ceremonial drinks or bites of foods, speeches, dances, bows, gestures.
   c   Distances – from one group to another, of races run, of processions, and so on.
   d   Amounts of elapsed time of important activities, time of beginning events, time at termination of events.
   e   Cash amounts of transactions, usual cost of particular items, total expenditures for special events, and so on.

5   It should be clear that quantification of aspects of an event is not the primary objective. Many other aspects of events are more important than counting persons or items or costs, but quantification should be seen as an *essential* secondary feature in the analysis of events.

Microevents

In practically all significant social events there are features that are repeated a number of times or there are sequences that involve a large number of different combinations of persons in identifiable *microevents*. Some examples of such repeated actions or combinations include "helping" in the reindeer roundup, transactions in the market, ceremonial drink exchanges, choosing dance partners, speaking in a meeting, presentations of gifts, racing or taking part in other contests, renditions by performers, and acts of harassing initiates.

For each type of microevent the fieldworker may want to amass certain standard information. Of what kin group were the persons? How much did the initiate cry out or show fear? What was the price of the item? What were the social identities of the persons who cooperated? How much did the buyer and seller haggle over price? And so on. Decisions about *which aspects* of microevents require systematic recording depend on the fieldworker's theoretical orientation and the social nature of the persons involved in the events.

These items, and many more than the reader will be able to think of, represent observational problems for fieldworkers because they will need to generalize about the patterning of these actions, but in most cases they will not be able to observe all of that class of transactions. Usually fieldworkers resort to stating the "typical" example of an event or transaction, but a much more satisfactory procedure is to observe a *sample*, especially a random sample, of such actions.

Most microevents can be handled in an approximation of a random sample if the fieldworker plans carefully. In observing a busy market, for example, the fieldworker can use a preliminary map of the scene to select a number of segments or subtypes for sampling. He may then select particular vendors by rough-and-ready means such as "every third one in the row," or "three each (at random) from each of the five rows of fruit-vegetable stands." Where the number of actions is very great (e.g., roping of reindeer in the roundup), timed samples, such as "every instance of roping in this section during the first ten minutes of every hour," or "all instances of roping in the section during alternating one-hour periods (10–11, 12–1, 2–3, etc.)" may be effective. Inventive fieldworkers will be able to devise many other ways of field sampling, especially if they use mapping and census data as aids.

Rare events

Significant social events differ a great deal in their periodicity. Fieldworkers usually have several opportunities to observe the weekly market, monthly dances, semiformal family parties, and certain kinds of sports events. On the other hand, they may have only a single opportunity to witness a wedding, a funeral, or an initiation ceremony. Accordingly, researchers should if possible prepare a list of the major events likely to occur in the research area. For those events that will occur only once or twice during the fieldwork period, researchers should, through questioning, form a tentative framework, or plan of action, in terms of which they will organize those precious moments of field observation. It may be wise to arrange a short period of rest before the event, for many important occasions turn out to be endurance contests for the fieldworkers, especially if interminable drinking, eating, and celebrating makes up an important part of the action.

As part of their preparation the fieldworkers can write up an outline of main pieces of data to be obtained. Each expected event requires its own specialized "notes and queries," as a generalized framework of expected information.

The case method

The term *case method* has usually been applied to the study of some delimited class of social events of which the fieldworker can observe a large number of instances. The study of law cases is the most common example. The method could also be profitably applied to the study of curing, witchcraft, aspects of religion, economic transactions, and many other facets of culture.

The fieldworker who adopts the case method must be careful to identify all the times and places in which the given social event regularly occurs. Curing, for example, may take place at the home of the sick person, at the "doctor's office," or at another specially designated area, such as a shrine or religious center. The researcher must devise means to gather cases from each of the relevant settings. Usually the fieldworker cannot observe all instances of the given social event, so he or she should develop some means of sampling systematically from the total population of cases.

A. L. Epstein recently reviewed the methodological problems and issues in "The Case Method in the Field of Law" (Epstein, 1967a). As he pointed out, the case method has been long and usefully employed in anthropological studies of law, for careful analysis of a body of legal cases has distinct advantages over the research method that relies on the interviewing of juridically important persons about their legal rules. He suggests that legal processes may operate very effectively even though the jurists in the system are not willing or able to formulate clear abstract principles or rules on which their legal decisions are supposed to be based.

Through the detailed examination of a series of cases the researcher seeks to define the regularities in recognized rules of conduct (e.g., rights and duties of particular social persons) as they are applied by judicial bodies, as well as the formal procedures and reasoning used for arriving at legal decisions. Epstein discusses a case from one of the Urban Courts of the Copper Belt to illustrate the concept of "the reasonable man" as a measuring rod by means of which members of the court judged a divorce case.

In handling the case, the Urban Court took into consideration the total nature of the marital relationship, which involved behavioral expectations between the spouses, but also includes codes of conduct regarding consanguineous and affinal kinsmen.

After establishing that the marriage had been properly contracted, the court inquired about previous misunderstandings between the couple. The wife said that there had been trouble in the past, and once before her father had wanted to see the marriage dissolved. She then embarked upon a lengthy account of how her husband had not come to offer his sympathy when her father was ill; he did not greet his father-in-law with the customary salutation when the latter returned home from work; on another occasion he had refused to go into the bush to seek medicine for a sick child; and so on. Let us see how the court took up these points.

Court: Is it true that you refused to fetch medicines for a sick child?
Husband: No, I did not refuse to fetch it.
Court: But did you go and get it?
Husband: No.
Court: Do you think the relatives of your wife would have been pleased about that?
Husband: No, they were not very pleased.
Court: Yes, you see. That is where you were very foolish. And don't you know that whenever your father-in-law comes back from work in the evening you should clap before him in accordance with our Bemba custom?

Another member of the court who was of the Kaonde tribe intervened:

Member: According to the customs of the Kaonde, if I were to come to you and seek to marry your daughter, what would you say?
Husband: I would be pleased.
Member: Would you not say this son-in-law of ours will help us in all our difficulties?
Husband: Yes, I would.
Member: Well, that is exactly the point here. You should know that you made a mistake by refusing to go where your father-in-law directed you. Listen now, if your chief came and married my daughter I would be entitled to make him climb trees. (This was a reference to the Bemba custom of performing service for one's in-laws by cutting trees and making gardens for them.) There is a proverb in Bemba that a chief does not marry the daughter of a fellow chief unless he is anxious to cut trees. Now what have you to say about your wife? (Epstein, 1967a: 220–1.)

This instance of the court's reasoning about the expected marital conduct of a reasonable man is doubly revealing because it involves cross-cultural regularities in the sense that the court made reference to both Bemba and Kaonde behavioral codes in reaching a verdict. As Epstein points out, the Urban Court had no intention of enforcing a specific rule – that the husband must climb trees for his wife's people – but they were concerned with the general matter of whether the husband had shown "reasonable care and respect" for the wife and her kinsmen.

A study of the principles and procedures of particular judicial bodies requires the scrutinizing of a number of cases in order to sort out the relatively invariant from the more variable and idiosyncratic patterns of decision making. In this kind of research the anthropologist must know a great deal about the cultural patterns of the society studied and must spend as much time observing behaviors of everyday life as in collecting and analyzing cases. One does not need to study everything in the culture in detail, but it is important to consider the *possibility* that seemingly esoteric aspects of culture may be relevant for understanding the nuances of individual cases.

Concerning observation in the court scene itself, Epstein states that

. . . we must note where the hearing takes place, whether in a court-house or yard or in an open space; what persons are involved and the capacities in which they are present or serve; when and under what circumstances the body is convened; what powers it has and how far these are limited by jurisdiction, by the right of appeal, or otherwise. But the central problem here is the nature of the adjudicatory process itself: the aims which the process is designed to serve, and the means by which they are achieved. (Ibid., 219.)

He goes on to say:

All this requires much more than a summary of the facts and arguments of a case. It demands careful and detailed recording of all that passes at the hearing, including where possible the murmured *obiter dicta* of the judges, as well as the reactions of the audience. This is at the best of times a laborious and time-consuming task, and even when the field worker has a fair degree of fluency in the vernacular the use of idiom and metaphor and elliptic references to persons, events, or topography make it all too easy to miss vital points in the cut and thrust of argument. (Ibid., 222.)

Whether the research topic is law or economic exchanges or some other specialized cultural feature, the scene that the anthropologist must try to record and understand is often a veritable three-ring circus, with many different events and conversations taking place simultaneously. How is the fieldworker to do this job effectively? Epstein's own solution to the problem is to train an assistant to record the proceedings as carefully as possible, and "at the same time I myself took notes of the hearing, recording passages or phrases verbatim in the vernacular. The two records were then checked against each other, discussed and clarified, and combined in a final typed record of the case" (ibid., 223).

Delineation of groups and networks

Because of the powerful impact of the British school of social anthropology (supported by influences emanating from sociology) much ethnographic field work has been devoted to the exploration of social groups, their corporate natures, and their interrelationships. Although some emphases have changed, this aspect of field analysis is still very important. The significant social groupings vary from one community or culture to another, but many recurrent types, such as unilineal kin groups, bilaterally reckoned groups like the Saame herding bands described by Pehrson (1957), voluntary associations of the kind described by Kenneth Little (1965) for West Africa, as well as territorial groupings of varying degrees of complexity have all received deservedly intensive study concerning their significance in the organization of social action.

In communities that are relatively "nondocumentary," socially significant groups are often most easily identified, and their roles most easily blocked out, through intensive analysis of major events, as illustrated in the case of the reindeer roundup. In large annual celebrations major social groups make their presence known through joint participation, symbolic enactments, and many other communications. Newman has described how he identified significant kin groups among the Gururumba of the New Guinea highlands by watching and recording their ritual enactments (Newman, 1965).

Legal cases in local dispute settlements also can be a rich source of data about the nature and properties of social groups. The following are some of the main points about social groups that aid fieldworkers in their identification:

1　Social groups often have names.
2　Often they have distinctive clothing or insignia.
3　They may have special rites for admission to membership.
4　They carry out activities, including ritual performances, as a visible collectivity.
5　They defend property and other rights, vis-à-vis other groups and individuals.
6　They may have special words and slogans that help to make them (and their ideologies) distinct from other social bodies.
7　They have special rules of behavior that help to make them distinct from other groups (e.g., special ways of eating, special norms of honesty in commercial transactions).
8　They have modes of communicating, as a group, with other significant social bodies (e.g., some kinship groups exchange spouses in marriage as part of their general structuring of alliances).
9　They often have internal differentiation or structure in terms of which communication and decision making are carried out (e.g, there may be a leader and possibly other officers, as well as internal segments).

No communities are without some kind of important social groups, even though their presence and operations may in certain cases be difficult to delineate. Sometimes, however, fieldworkers have been so imbued with the idea that social action is shaped by social groups that they have sought group corporacy where there was none, at the same time failing to observe other patterns of social interaction in which groupness and corporacy were not paramount features (see, e.g., Pelto, 1970).

Network analysis

In many complex scenes and events observed by the ethnographer, the patterning of action involves interconnecting links of reciprocities (or other contacts) among chains of individuals who do not sort out into bounded groups. These situations may be effectively studied in terms of the personal networks that individuals utilize in trying to realize personal goals. Aspects of behavior in complex societies may be particularly amenable to this kind of descriptive analysis.

Adrian Mayer (1966) has studied an election in Madhya Pradesh (India) by means of a network analysis. He found it useful to trace out the chains of individual relationships of a political candidate in order to understand the basis of his political power. The actual field procedure involves observing and interviewing numbers of individuals, in each instance exploring for further links and connections through which some element of social action (in this case voting) is mobilized on behalf of a particular protagonist. Social groups may, of course, play an important part in defining some paths of personal networks, but socially corporate aggregates are far from defining the total structure of the election. (See Figure 9.2.) Mayer tells us:

It is clear that a candidate cannot be elected on the support of a single caste, or of a single occupational interest. Hence, pressure has to be brought on various sections of the electorate. This may be in terms of policy, or it may be through linkages stretching from each candidate directly or through intermediaries to the voter. The pattern of the Congress candidate's linkages, as they were described to me and as I observed them, is given in the diagram. (Mayer, 1966:106.)

In his discussion of the election Mayer pointed out that

. . . these are not the only contacts made by the candidate with the public; nor do they show all the reasons why people supported him. Some, for instance, may have done so because of his party's official policy; others may have voted for him because of the auspiciousness of his party's electoral symbol – the best example in the election of purely ideological support, which in other cases might underlie other reasons (e.g., support of a caste-mate is partly ideological and partly self-interested.) (Mayer, 1966:107–8.)

The research strategy of exploring networks, of the kind just described, was first set out in detail by Barnes (1954) in his study "Class and Committee in a Norwegian Island Parish."

During the 1970s there has been a rapid burgeoning of interest in network

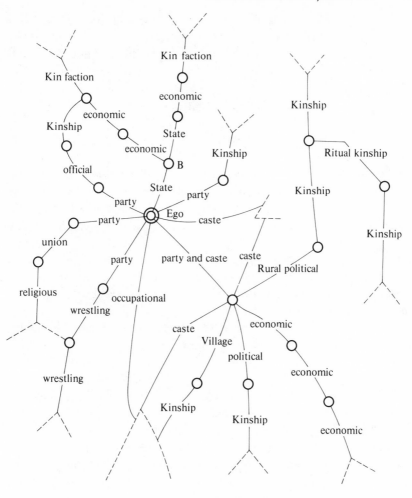

Figure 9.2. Congress candidates' linkages in the election campaign (adapted from Mayer, 1966:107).

studies, somewhat parallel to the earlier "discovery" of corporate kin groups as a central research topic. Roger Sanjek (1972) demonstrated the usefulness of network analysis in the study of interethnic relations in a West African city; Boissevain (1969) made extensive use of network analysis in the study of modernization in Malta; and Whitten (1965) has shown the importance of personal networks in the social organization of blacks in a coastal Ecuadorian town. Several review articles on network analysis are now available, and a collection edited by Boissevain and Mitchell, *Network Analysis: Studies in Human Interaction* (1973), includes some useful examples of field-work strategies.

Network analysis, case studies, event analysis and the other field-work tactics discussed in this section generally require combinations of interviewing, direct observation, and other research techniques. Reliance on a single structured interview procedure is likely to produce inadequate and distorted information; observation alone is often impractical because the researcher cannot be everywhere at once; but in field work extended over several months the anthropologist has ample opportunity to devise effective combinations of research activities.

Description and hypothesis testing

Regardless of his or her area of topical interest or theoretical framework, the fieldworker is, in effect, continually forming hypotheses and testing them. Frequently, the hypotheses are simply descriptive, such as, "most of the people in the village own land" or "the rate of divorce and separation seems high in this community." The evidence used to test such hypotheses is often of a qualitative, anecdotal nature in most monographs, but fieldworkers can devise means by which such statements are given the additional credibility of quantified analysis.

Robert Paine's two volumes on *Coast Lapp Society* (1957, 1965) are good examples of quantification imbedded in the context of descriptive community study. Generalizations about numbers of bachelors, outmigration of females, family incomes, age at marriage, and a great many other social facts are supported with numerical data. Paine moves back and forth between his tabulated data and the more interesting, flesh-and-blood descriptions of individual events and social processes. With data of this type the use of complex inferential statistics is often unnecessary (Paine uses none), because the aim of the ethnographer at that point is description rather than theory building.

Anthropologists enter the field with research plans that range from highly specific hypothesis-testing designs to general commitments to "study the ecological adaptation of these people." The more specific the research plan, the more likely it is that the researcher finds the realities of the field situation incompatible with the stated research aims. Generally, the first weeks and months of field work produce detailed data about local conditions that force significant modifications in the research plan. Research procedures that worked well in some other society may turn out to be ineffectual because the local people either refuse to cooperate or do not understand what the researcher expects of them. Also, the significant social divisions within the community may be quite different from those that advance information has suggested.

In any case, from the first days in the field the researcher is concerned with adjusting research plans to the realities of the study site and, at the same time, with looking for the significant questions in the aspect of culture or social structure that constitutes the main research focus. It is often an excellent idea to make lists of significant questions pertaining to several different aspects of culture and social structure. These questions can be phrased in quite general terms at first, but later they must be refined and operationalized. The following section illustrates this deductive–inductive process of field problem solving as it developed in the course of research in a marginal rural area.

A major assumption underlying our research plan in northern Minnesota (Schensul, Paredes, and Pelto, 1968) was that the region is "economically depressed." The national war on poverty had been declared during the early phases of the project, and we soon realized that an important research task revolved around the question, "What is poverty?" This very general question could be broken up into a series of smaller, but still quite vague, queries.

1 What do the people of the area *lack* compared with supposed ideal standards and compared with people of other areas?
2 What do the people of the area *have* that other populations lack?
3 How much effort must they expend to maintain this balance of advantages and disadvantages?
4 What information and attitudes do the people have concerning the "affluent society"?
5 How do the people conceptualize "the good life," "our town," "the city," and so on?

To answer the first question we needed information about incomes, household furnishings, and other material goods, as well as data about patterns of behavior such as recreation and visiting. Therefore, an interview schedule was administered to random samples of persons in five communities of the area. Formal and informal questioning about life in the area gave us at least the idealized information about the advantages the people felt they had over city people and other populations. Through interviews and participant observation we learned about working hours, jobholding, and other aspects of the people's effort levels.

Special research methods seemed to be necessary in order to examine the ways in which people conceptualized aspects of their life style in relation to supposedly more affluent sectors of our society. If possible we wanted to make quantified, systematic comparisons between the northern Minnesotans and some other population. Also, it was important to compare different groups *within* our northern Minnesota communities. The research instrument that seemed best suited to this task was a modified version of Osgood's "Semantic Differential" technique (which was described in Chapter 5 in connection with Schensul's comparison of northern Minnesotans and East Africans).

The people's responses to this instrument provided quantified confirmation of our impression that northern Minnesotans regarded their rural communities as being close to "the good life" except in matters of economic opportunity. The city was seen as offering more possibilities of earning satisfactory incomes. It was interesting to note that the people did not see the city as markedly less religious than their own communities.

When we had put together some preliminary answers to the questions raised previously, we noted the ways in which the socioeconomic conditions in northern Minnesota differed from situations of poverty in urban slums and in the rural poverty pockets of Appalachia and the Deep South. From these data we put together our description of "the twilight zone of poverty." In this situation people have adequate food supplies and housing, as well as most other basic necessities, but they see themselves as deprived to the extent that they make unfavorable comparisons between their lives and the "affluent society" that they observe on television and read about in magazines and newspapers.

One paradigm of problem solving during field work can be summarized as follows:

1 Delineate an important question to be examined, based on information particular to the research site. Often the significant question is derived from some particular body of social science theory, related to special features of the research region.

2 Through observation and interviewing, locate the persons and the settings that will provide the most information about the research question.

3 From the inventory of research tools and techniques that have been used by anthropologists and other social scientists select procedures that appear most likely to produce the desired information.

4 Modify the chosen research instruments to accord with local conditions.

5 Select a representative sample from the (theoretical) population of all possible observations. The sample may be cases, persons, time periods, or other units.

6 Collect the data.

7 Examine the data to see if the questions raised have in fact been answered. If they have not, some other method of data recollection will be necessary.

8 The data obtained by these research operations will frequently leave many facets of the question unanswered. Through participant observation and informal interviewing, additional information can be accumulated that will throw further light on the problem and will also strengthen the credibility of the information derived from the more formalized research operations. (As a general rule, *every* research finding should be supported by more than one kind of data.)

9 The several different pieces of data that have been obtained must be logically interrelated, and they must also fit with other aspects of the local culture. This process of conceptualization should also relate the specific local data to some body of general theory.

Every field project can be seen as a series of key questions and answers imbedded in the ongoing routines of standard data collection. Much of the fieldworker's time is taken up with the routines of collecting census materials, maps, and a large assortment of other general descriptive material, but the researcher should never lose sight of isolating and answering key questions in this sea of routine.

Multicommunity research projects

When a multicommunity project is inaugurated, it is important to select the communities in terms of very clear criteria. In some instances it may be useful to draw a random sample of communities from a region, but this is seldom done. More usually, communities are selected in terms of some main dimensions of variation that are relevant to the dominant hypotheses of the research project. Thus in the instance of Redfield's study of folk communities in the Yucatán, the selection of research sites was guided by his interest in the "folk-urban continuum." The range of variation from "most contact with outside world" to "most isolated" appears to have been involved in the selection of research communities in a number of projects.

Some measure of control over extraneous variables can be made possible by careful selection of communities. Thus size of community and "distance from urban contact" may vary together; yet communities can be selected in which size is held constant while the major independent variable changes systematically. Another research design could involve the selection of one community from each subgroup in the area, where major differences (and similarities) among them are to be described. Then a central concern might well be to select the most typical community from each of the subgroups of the region. Such a selection necessitates systematic pilot research, such as a preliminary interview of officials (or other key informants) in each community. A preliminary survey of a region may help to spot possible natural experiment situations.

We should note that project research in which a number of different communities and/or cultures are studied by different members of a research team is not a new phenomenon in anthropology but goes back at least to the Torres Strait and Jesup expeditions late in the past century and the beginning of this century (cf. Lowie, 1937).

Multicommunity projects and survey research

A basic requirement in multicommunity research is that comparability among the several sites be established through the use of survey research. For example, in the Saskatchewan project of John W. Bennett and associates,

. . . a single basic survey instrument – a detailed open-ended interview schedule – was administered to a large sample of persons and families from each of the several ethnic, religious, and occupational groups in the region. . . . A basic regional foundation was thus laid for the interpretation of the very different slices of data obtained by many other methods from the separate cultural groups. (Bennett and Thaiss, 1967:300.)

It needs to be repeated that in projects of this kind the use of a basic survey instrument with a wide sample of respondents is *not* a substitute for the standard anthropological methods of participant observation and detailed interviewing. The use of a standardized interview process is *a necessary addition* to other methods of data collection.

Frequently the anthropologist's use of survey techniques will be carried out in situations and with intentions that are different from the survey research designs commonly used by sociologists. Most often anthropologists carry out their research in cultures quite different from their own, and this requires meticulous care in translating questions into the local language, to mention just one obvious problem.

In the Sahagun project in Mexico, we found it useful to engage the services of the Mexican Institute of Social Studies to carry out the survey portion of field research (Pelto, 1972; Poggie, 1968; Miller, 1973). This arrangement permitted the collection of over a thousand interviews in a relatively short period of time, with fairly effective standardization of training for the field interviewers. Such contracting for a basic survey should be carried out only when the anthropologists in the field have close contact with the organization carrying out the interviewing. Frequent conferences should be held with the field team, and the anthropologist must devote much time to spot checking the interviewing procedures. Also, organizations hired to carry out survey research ideally should be experienced in the type of social milieu in which interviewing is required. Interviewers who are highly trained for urban surveys may not be suited for rural agricultural communities. (Contracting with local research organizations has also been successful in parts of Africa and elsewhere.)

As mentioned, survey research methods often uncover significant areas for investigation that require more intensive informal interviewing and observation. In some cases it may even be useful to plan on a follow-up interview schedule, after intensive field work has ironed out the main issues involved in certain complex areas of questioning. In matters of land tenure, for example, finding out the relevant questions may require months of field work. Once such field work has made clear how the system operates, a specialized interview schedule can be extremely useful in obtaining the quantified data relevant to aspects of landholding.

When an interview survey has been carried out in a research region, the fieldworkers (regardless of special area of interest) have available to them the standardized basic information about the particular communities chosen to study. Knowledge of the range of variation in the communities (in material style of life, kinship behavior, landholdings, etc.) gives them a standard against which to measure contacts with informants. They may find that for one reason or another they tend to encounter persons at the top of the local hierarchy of wealth and prestige. (This is often the case, though the problem is not always recognized by fieldworkers.) Data from the survey tell them *what kinds of persons* they have thus far failed to reach through informal contacts in the communities.

Assistants

It is more and more usual nowadays for anthropologists to take to the field several assistants (usually graduate students) who can aid in a variety of tasks as an early phase of their training in the discipline. Often the fieldworker also finds it convenient to hire local persons to assist in administering interview schedules. Sometimes assistants can be recruited from regional universities or they may be local bilinguals, such as teachers or social workers. In some areas the best local assistants may be students in secondary schools (cf. Schensul, 1969; Beattie, 1965; Powdermaker, 1966).

Writers have occasionally expressed doubts about the dependability of native research assistants. As in most other aspects of field work, the situation varies greatly from one cultural setting to another. A brief excerpt from A. J. Köbben's field notes is useful as an anodyne:

19th Jan. Today went to Pikin Santi to count the huts. The *kutu* took a long time and the gods proved to be very thirsty indeed. As we were going back Fanaili (my informant) said: "It is really a waste of time . . . couldn't we count the huts clandestinely from now on?"

15th April. To Agitiondro for the great mortuary feast. Took advantage of the occasion to count the huts, which wasn't easy since they are planted pell-mell with no sort of order while moreover we were continually interrupted by other visitors to the feast who greeted us. To have some means of checking our results Fanaili and I each counted separately. He came to a total of 219 huts, I had 215. I resignedly wrote down the average, 217 in my notebook, but Fanaili was not so easily satisfied: "No, we must do it well if we do it at all, let's start again." (Köbben, 1967:54.)

The use of local persons as researchers has been of great importance to the work of anthropological field research. Boas, for example, many times emphasized the magnitude of the contribution that his informant and field assistant, George Hunt, made to his research on the Kwakiutl. Boas trained Hunt in phonological transcription and set him to collecting texts on every conceivable aspect of Kwakiutl culture. White (1963) and Rohner (1966) have estimated that more than two-thirds of the Kwakiutl materials were contributed by this indefatigable field "assistant."

Beattie has described the crucial role that his Bunyoro assistants played in his second tour of field work in Uganda:

They acted as permanent informants, even though, as I remarked above, they often knew less to begin with about such aspects of Nyoro culture as sorcery, divination, and spirit mediumship than I did, from other informants and from the study of native court records.

But they very quickly learned. On such topics as kinship, marriage, and family life they provided clear and direct information from the start. They helped me in making sense of difficult texts, and in interviewing and "softening up" reluctant or suspicious informants. They recorded statements (texts) dictated by illiterate informants, and they wrote long accounts (case histories) of incidents in their own lives or that they had been told about. They assisted in house-to-house surveys, and they made use of their own ties of kinship and neighborhood to follow up promising clues and lines of inquiry. The best of my few assistants were not just clerks or interpreters but apprentice social anthropologists, and without them my work would have been very much poorer and more superficial than it was. (Beattie, 1965:27.)

Anthropologists have often discovered in the course of field work that their local assistants can be excellent tactical advisers, boon companions, and tireless collectors of information. Frequently, these assistants become fascinated with finding out about their own patterns of culture through the systematic procedures of the anthropologist. (The lore of field work includes many tales, some of them probably apocryphal, about the native assistants' joy in discovering phonological and syntactical regularities in their native speech, or fascinating nuances of their kinship system.)

Powdermaker (1966) found an exceptionally able assistant named Phiri during her field research in the Copper Belt. "He became a kind of alter ego, and I can not imagine how the study would have been made without his help." She continues:

During the survey I knew he was the best interviewer, but his many other abilities became apparent when he began working more intensively with me. Equally important, he became truly *engaged*, identified with the project and with me [emphasis in the original].

Night and day, seven days a week he worked. Sometimes I suggested he take a day off, but he rarely did. (Powdermaker, 1966:261.)

In larger projects, involving field teams, the use of local assistants becomes, if possible, even more important to the success of the research. Multiperson projects are generally more visible in the local scene, and often have serious public-relations problems. Local assistants can smooth over the occasional rough edges of research encounters and keep project personnel informed of adverse local reactions and attitudes. More important, the local assistants can play a large role in keeping research discussions reality oriented. The field team, in concentrating on elements of the research design and in its weekly or twice monthly research seminar discussions, can have a tendency to become abstruse and theoretical. Such flights of theory and speculation will be useful if they can be related to the empirical realities of the local scene. Here the down-to-earth pragmatism of local assistants is a healthy corrective in asking questions such as: What does family solidarity really mean? What kinds of things make you say that these people are inner-directed? What does social stratification mean?

Thus local assistants are of great importance in bridging the gap between the abstracted, theoretical realm of social sciences discourse and the everyday empirical realm of life in the research communities. Naturally, they cannot fulfill this function unless they are trained to do so; and it helps a great deal if they are treated in every way as apprentice social anthropologists (as Beattie suggests) rather than as simply employees or assistants.

Researchers need to be alert to possible personality conflicts between assistants and the people of the research communities, and they should also be highly aware of the particular social ties that assistants might have with segments of the local population. Some otherwise useful assistants might, for example, be unreliable in amassing information about their own kin groups, because they may be under pressure to cover up blemishes in the record.

When pretests of the interview schedule are being made (preferably in separate, pretest communities), anthropologists should accompany their field assistants in order to watch their styles of self-presentation and interaction with respondents. Also, where possible, anthropologists should administer some of the interview schedules in order to get first-hand experience with the kinds of situations and data involved in the structured-interview process. The anthropologist who has conducted no interviews himself is in a poor position to discuss or argue with assistants over the deletion, revision, or addition of particular items in the schedule.

Whether one's field assistants are recruited from universities in the host country or directly from the local population, anthropologists should keep in mind their obligation to train local persons for competence in the social sciences by interrelating field research with formal university programs. Some of the fieldworkers discovered by anthropological teams have gone on to become highly competent, fully professional members of the scientific community. This same obligation to help field assistants toward professional training applies to research in our industrialized, urban centers – for example, in projects dealing with city ghettos.

Communication among fieldworkers

The lone field researcher generally becomes more and more distant and alienated from the academic world of anthropology. This has some advantages, for the researcher is then forced to immerse himself or herself in the life of the research community. Under these circumstances the novice must cope with all variety of field problems alone, relying on the (semimythological) lore of field work as imparted by instructors. Anthropologists place a high value on this individualistic mode of field work, and certainly some excellent and important research has resulted. On the other hand, we have no way of counting the casualties of the field, and many anthropologists who hardly count as casualties report periods of reduced efficacy in the field, due partly to isolation from the stimulation of fellow researchers.

In multicommunity research there are often a number of fieldworkers in the region at one time. Each may be carrying on a special project in his own chosen community, but communication in the field is quite feasible. Fieldworkers can, and should, get together to compare notes about methods of research, special insights, new research hypotheses, and so on. It is desirable that fieldworkers visit one another's research communities, in order to bring to light similarities and previously unnoticed differences among the local subpopulations.

Where several fieldworkers and a field director are in the field at the same time, frequent (usually weekly) meetings can provide a framework for the exchange of theoretical ideas and concrete information. In this situation each fieldworker need not go through the entire process of trial-and-error learning on his own. Each can profit from the experiences of others in the project. No careful research has been done to test the efficacies of different styles of research organization, but it seems likely that sustained hard effort in field projects can be maintained at least as effectively by frequent interaction and exchange of information among the field team as it can by the pattern of prolonged isolation characteristic of one-person research.

Almost all fieldworkers have periods when they lose perspective and feel that they are not getting anywhere. A typical complaint is, "I've been here for three months, and I still don't know a thing about the community." To these reactions the presence of a substantial body of data in a survey interview provides some consolation, but a more important source of morale boosting is the frequent comparison of personal progress with the state of data collection of workers in other, not very distant, communities. The field director of the research team should, of course, play an important part in morale maintenance, through individual conferences with the members of the field team, as well as through careful management of the weekly conferences or seminars.

Frequent research seminars in the field serve other useful functions as well. When field work is somewhat advanced, individual members of the field team can present working papers on particular topics that are the foci of their research. The seminar presentation forces the fieldworker to make an inventory of his or her present state of data collection, and feedback from other members of the field team helps the individual to sharpen conceptualizations of theoretical problems. In the absence of a team project, such sharpening of field materials through seminars usually occurs after a fieldworker returns to home base, when it is too late to correct mistakes or to fill in data gaps.

Part of the rationale for multicommunity team projects in anthropological field work is that field training and research should be thoroughly integrated with the other side of anthropological study and work, which consists of conferences, seminars, and other modes of collaboration and communication. The structure of team projects can build some of these feedback mechanisms into the research situation itself. At the same time, team projects make possible data collection on a large enough scale so that quantified comparisons and other more complex data manipulation can be carried out.

In our random sample of (North American) anthropologists, we found the following breakdown of field situations:

lone fieldworker	6
fieldworker and nonprofessional spouse	9
fieldworker and assistants	18
husband-wife professional team	7
team of professionals (other than husband-wife)	11

It is significant that the most usual category of field assistants, in nineteen of fifty-three reported cases, was "local community," followed by an additional eleven cases from "local university." The role of field assistant appears to be an important educational stepping stone for some of the people anthropologists meet and interact with in their research communities.

Team research at special events

In any field project, there will be numerous special events – fiestas, weddings, markets, county fairs, or other special occasions – in which more effective coverage would be achieved if several researchers worked together. If one community of the region has a fiesta, for example, all or most of the fieldworkers can converge on the occasion, working under the leadership of the person who is most familiar with that community. This leader's task, before the fiesta, is to develop some kind of "scenario," or program of events, which will make it possible to allocate specialized tasks of observation to different members of the team. One person may have responsibility for covering the parade, another the religious ceremonies, a third and a fourth member the nearby market, and so on. Communications among the members of such a team should be carefully worked out, so that researchers do not become too obvious a foreign element in the local scene. Tactics of team research, once worked out, can be shifted from one community to another as occasions arise. The presence of several researchers in one community during complex events makes possible fuller overall coverage, provides means of validity checking of important generalizations, and facilitates important quantified observations, such as counting the number of dancers in the powwow, the number of out-of-town cars, the number of special costumes among the visiting delegations, and so on. Fieldworkers are notorious for their differences in focus of observation. It would seem likely that any *one* fieldworker necessarily produces a one-sided, personalized view of a complex event. Such biases may be quite useful if balanced by the presence of other fieldworkers in the same scene. Of course, the one fieldworker in a community can build up a special team of local assistants to cover special events. Frequently, a mix of field researchers plus local assistants makes an excellent combination for study of complex festivals or other large-scale social action.

Interdisciplinary research

In the past anthropologists generally tried to cover all aspects of social and cultural patterns in their ethnographic reporting. The well-rounded monograph contained linguistic, historical, and geographical data, as well as information on the local economic system, psychological characteristics, social organization, and intercommunity relations. Often the ethnographer was expected to give some consideration to data pertaining to soil science, botany, and zoology as well. The old-style anthropologist was truly a jack-of-all-trades.

But the problems posed and the types of information used in different disciplines have become more complex and sophisticated, and the all-around anthropologist can no longer claim in good conscience that he can do the entire job himself. Bringing in collaborators from other fields greatly increases the research competence of the team and ensures that essential data are gathered from the point of view of advanced methodologies appropriate to the area of inquiry. Thus informant narratives about prices and costs are generally not sufficient for any serious economic analysis in a region, but economists collaborating with anthropologists can specify the kinds of data that would provide a sound basis for certain types of theoretical work. The Culture and Ecology project of Goldschmidt and associates in East Africa is an excellent example of a situation in which the contributions of a geographer (in the analysis of land use, rainfall, and soils) added a great deal to the research results (Goldschmidt et al., 1965).

Agricultural economists and agronomists have carried out a great deal of research in so-called developing nations, and their analyses of technological procedures, as well as input–output analyses of local agricultural economics, can be important additions to the anthropologists' work. Because many anthropological analyses now deal with peoples and places on the margins of cash-crop economies, the agricultural economist's analysis can be an important adjunct to the study of adaptive strategies of individual farmers with reference to the "marketized" sector of local economies.

Statisticians provide a different kind of expertise to anthropological research projects. They deal not in a specific area of data, but rather provide the criteria and rationale for determining the kinds and amounts of data that are needed for particular forms of numerical analysis. Thus any well-organized research project needs to engage the services of a statistician before full details of research design are worked out. A most common complaint among statisticians is that social scientists ask for advice *after the data are collected*, when weaknesses in meeting the requirements of statistical procedures cannot be corrected.

Collaboration between social/cultural and physical anthropology

In recent years there have been increased instances of genuine research collaboration among the different subdisciplines of anthropology, especially between sociocultural and biological researchers. Chagnon and associates' field work among the Yanamamo of South America, for example, has included a population study, an examination of medical problems, genetic relationships, as well as a thorough study of sociocultural dimensions of lifeways (Chagnon, 1974). Medical anthropology, it appears, is becoming a strong integrating force promoting biocultural and biosocial research ventures. Studies involving nutrition and health, for example, generally require the expertise of both sociocultural and biomedical researchers if reasonable and credible data are to be marshaled on particular problems.

There are good reasons for both "sides" of anthropology (sociocultural and biological) to seek new ways of collaboration. While the older lines of physical anthropology were frequently concentrated on fossil remains, plus other data concerning earlier human evolution, newer interests include studying physiological adaptations to difficult environments, diseases and other pathologies, diet, motor patterns, and other data that involve close interaction of cultural and physical processes. Modern studies of ecological adaptation are greatly strengthened if both physiological and cultural data are included in the research design. Certainly, the cultural anthropologist cannot afford to ignore data about illness and levels of physiological functioning in considering the patterning of food allocation, work habits, and other aspects of social organization.

At the same time, the studies that physical anthropologists pursue with respect to genetic (biologically inherited) patterns in human groups depend, to a considerable degree, on sociocultural data such as actual marriage patterns, estimated rates of extramarital liaisons, and other demographic data that the social anthropologist should be able to provide. Several of the hotly debated issues concerning acclimatization to heat, cold, and high altitude require sophisticated handling of interactions between sociocultural and physiological data. All of these studies argue for closer integration of the subdisciplines of anthropology.

Most research projects involving cooperation between physical anthropologists and sociocultural researchers have been methodologically weak because *the two kinds of data (physical and sociocultural) were not collected from the same individual members of the research populations.* Cultural descriptions of communities, no matter how thoroughly documented, cannot be fully integrated with genetic and physiological studies unless covariations of sociocultural and physical characteristics can be examined in terms of particular *individual* members of the communities studied.

Problems of interdisciplinary research

It has been noted that interdisciplinary collaborative efforts have frequently involved serious problems of communication, with much frustration experienced by well-meaning (and puzzled) would-be collaborators. Team members from the different research fields have sometimes had very different theoretical conceptions of human behavior, so that interdisciplinary discussions became battles over whose theory is "right," instead of how the theoretical fields interrelate and support one another.

Interdisciplinary difficulties have been aggravated further by situations in which no methodological agreement existed concerning the assessment of evidence. This problem was particularly characteristic of teamwork between psychoanalytic and anthropological investigators during the 1930s and 1940s. Each side held to an all-embracing theoretical paradigm concerning human behavior, which was generally supported by ad hoc logical argument plus *ex cathedra* recitation of theoretical dogma. No method of data gathering and analysis could be agreed on as suitable for critical testing of rival theories.

More recently, however, the various social sciences appear to have grown more tolerant of each other's points of view, and at the same time investigators have become more knowledgeable about the methodological requirements for analysis and presentation of evidence. In a time when anecdotal illustrations could pass for evidence, rival theoreticians argued ad infinitum without the possibility of reaching a decision. When, on the other hand, a theoretical statement is tested by predicting a pattern of responses, or by systematically counting the cases for and against a proposition in a sample population, it becomes feasible to select the more probable and apparently more useful among alternative paradigms of explanation.

Increased methodological rigor in field-work investigations has often resulted in data that are much more complex than had been predicted by earlier theoretical positions. Perhaps this mounting evidence concerning the complexity of human behavior has made all of us more humble concerning all-or-nothing theoretical positions.

Interdisciplinary projects can often continue fairly effectively in the face of serious theoretical difference among members of the team if there are understandings in the form of "agreements to disagree." Such working agreements can help to ensure that field work will not be disrupted by the interminable debate, and separate data analysis and separate publication can honestly reflect the alternatives of interpretation current in the research team.

One important aid to effective interdisciplinary collaboration is the preparation of a clear and methodologically rigorous research proposal. If the types of data to be collected are clearly set forth in the proposal, and the several responsibilities for their collection are unambiguous, the basic research proposal becomes a kind of "contract" that can be referred to by the team members in settling disputes. Once the data are collected and field work is complete, theoretical arguments can be productive in generating new ideas concerning data analysis.

Summary

Anthropological field work is much too complicated to be covered in a single chapter as we have attempted to do here. This is not said in order to perpetuate any kind of mystique about field work but simply to indicate that we have touched on a number of subjects very lightly and have omitted entirely some important aspects of field research. Our intent has been to suggest a number of problem areas for discussion and to mention some of the literature and points of view on these subjects.

Some of the needless mystery surrounding the field-work process will be dispelled as anthropologists add to the presently growing body of recollections and autobiographical statements about their individual field expeditions. Guidelines for the pursuit of the artistic, intuitive, social-interactional side of field research must be gained by each new recruit through reading this collected lore of the profession, to which must be added the accumulation of personal experience through field-training sessions and apprenticeships in team projects.

On the operational, systematic data-collection side of field research there is much more in the way of standardized use of instruments, modes of sampling, and logical structuring and interrelating of data that can be built into the working repertoire of anthropologists. There is, after all, a definable "kit of tools" by means of which anthropologists have usually collected their data. Each new cultural context may call for some modification of these basic tools, but these accommodations to the realities of field work can be made nicely if the researcher has a good grasp of the main prototypes.

Also, new research techniques are needed – particularly for those situations in which fieldworkers find themselves studying large populations in which cultural heterogeneity, rapid change, and multiplex communications with other social systems are the order of the day. In urban anthropology we find the fullest expression of these research problems.

Anthropological study of small, supposedly homogeneous societies has usually been justified in part by the assumption that the gleanings from these efforts can be usefully transferred to more complex social scenes. Thus our anthropological literature abounds with theoretical propositions and concepts that originated in studies of bands and villages, but which now should be tested in towns, regions, and cities. But these theoretical materials often require more complicated methodological structuring if they are to be used in culturally and socially heterogeneous contexts.

We have suggested that team research involving multicommunity research designs is an increasingly important and productive part of the anthropological enterprise. The advantages of this kind of field work include, among other things, simply the amassing of very much more data than single individuals can accomplish and, related to that, the possibility of careful collection of much more numerical data than has been usual in anthropological research. But these advantages are gained at a price. Valentine (1968) has argued, in essence, for one-person research even in the complex scene of urban problems, because of the very real advantages of rapport and personalization of the research process. The loss of these qualities must be balanced by the maximizing of gains that are only achievable in team research. If the possible methodological advantages of large-scale research are not maximized, then nothing is gained. The team members are simply getting in each other's way.

There is an advantage to the larger research projects that we have not yet mentioned. They provide the time and other resources to experiment with new research techniques. If our analysis is correct that new research techniques and tools must be developed, then a situation that maximizes experimentation earns a large plus on the balance sheet of advantage and disadvantage. Lone individual anthropologists often experiment with new techniques of data collection in the field, to be sure. But time is usually so short that the experimenter must often be content with a less than thorough weighing and matching of alternatives. The fieldworker experiments but does not have time or resources for the necessary control cases.

Nothing in this discussion should be read to mean that all field research by single individuals is inferior – far from it. The best, the most strikingly original research, will continue to be done by special individuals who bring the right combinations of abilities into the propitious research moment. The accumulation of more and more useful theoretical paradigms in the human sciences depends in part on these (few) highly innovative lone wolves of field work *and* also on the patient amassing of data and testing of theory on a scale matched to the enormity of problems in modern society – made possible through cooperative research on a larger scale than has been the mode heretofore. The logic of the situation in anthropology appears to call for a mix not only in the qualitative and quantitative techniques of field work but also in the scale of research enterprises as well.

10 Research methods, relevance, and applied anthropology

An important part of my creed as a social scientist is that on the grounds of absolute objectivity or on a posture of scientific detachment and indifference, a truly relevant and serious social science cannot ask to be taken seriously by a society desperately in need of moral and empirical guidance in human affairs. Nor can it support its claims to scientific purity or relevance by a preoccupation with methodology as an end and by innumerable articles in scientific journals devoted to escapist, even though quantifiable, trivia. I believe that to be taken seriously, to be viable, and to be relevant social science must dare to study the real problems of men and society, must use the real community, the market place, the arena of politics and power as its laboratories, and must confront and seek to understand the dynamics of social action and social change. The appropriate technology of serious and relevant social science should have as its prime goal helping society move toward humanity and justice with minimum irrationality, instability, and cruelty. If social science and social technology cannot help achieve these goals then they will be ignored or relegated to the level of irrelevance, while more serious men seek these goals through trial and error or through the crass exercise of power. (Kenneth B. Clark, *Dark Ghetto*, 1965: Introduction.)

The issue of relevance

In recent years social scientists have been the target of severe criticism of the kind that Clark alludes to: that abstract theoretical concerns and preoccupation with methodological niceties have diverted social scientists from the "prime goal [of] helping society move toward humanity and justice. . . ." The evidence in support of this criticism is not hard to find. It has frequently been difficult for anthropologists to demonstrate that obtaining a new kinship terminology from still another culture adds significantly to the problem-solving capacity of the discipline; for psychologists the addition of one more variation on the maze-learning performance of rats or college sophomores is difficult to articulate with pressing contemporary social issues; and in sociology, abstract theoretical materials on "the integration of stable systems of social interaction" are often unconvincing as to their practical application, from the point of view of nonscientists.

On the other hand, anthropologists (and other scientists) usually offer two main counterarguments:

1   The freedom of the scientist to inquire into whatever most excites his or her interest and curiosity must be preserved, in order to maintain the broad freedoms of research and expression that have historically produced highly useful new knowledge.

2   Events in the physical sciences have demonstrated repeatedly that seemingly inconsequential discoveries are often essential ingredients of later technical developments of the utmost practicality and "relevance." This argument is usually expressed in the statement: "No one can predict in advance the potential future usefulness of a particular scientific discovery." (Examples supporting the argument usually include the apparent impracticality or irrelevance of early developments in atomic theory, Ben Franklin's experiments with electricity, James Watt's toying with steam engines, and so on.)

The "freedom-of-investigation" argument is a rather convincing one, but it would be more convincing if social science research reports reflected a higher degree of truly exploratory and innovative research. Unfortunately, social science journals and other publications reflect a distressingly large amount of conforming and unimaginative research. T. S. Kuhn (1962), who has examined the conservative and noninnovative side of established scientific activity, noted that most scientists, social, physical, and biological, are not latter-year Franklins, Newtons, Darwins, and Pasteurs. They are, rather, the patient and plodding followers of one or another established school of theory, concerned less with blazing new and hitherto unexplored scientific pathways than with converting established theoretical positions into yet another publishable paper.

In general, we feel that social scientists, like workers in other research disciplines, can demonstrate the potential practical relevance of a very wide range of seemingly obscure information. The whole past and never-to-be-relived history of human culture is an area of study from which able investigators can produce practical evidence concerning basic patterns of human behavior. Cross-cultural comparative studies have demonstrated the theoretical importance of descriptive data from the more exotic societies of humankind, and the resulting theoretical findings can have powerful application to the problems of our modern day.

But the arguments concerning the ultimate usefulness of any and all theoretical investigations cannot be entirely convincing to those many people – including legislators – who are insisting that social sciences research money should be spent directly in the areas where the problems are. The fact is that none of the proponents of the more obscure and theoretically abstract areas of research claims that concentration directly on relevant and pressing social issues is *less* likely to produce useful information for our publics and policy makers. None of the arguments for a disinterested social science can show that Clark is on the wrong trail when he suggests that we "must dare to study the real problems of men and society, must use the real community, the market place, the arena of politics and power as [our] laboratories." At some of our more awkward moments of defensiveness we tend to take our role models from the "hard sciences" of physics and chemistry, but in this instance we might be better off to look at the example of the medical sciences; there a high level of concentration on relevant and immediate problems (such as seeking the eradication of various poxes, plagues, and pestilences) has demonstrated a very considerable balance sheet of scientific successes. Looking to the medical sciences for a general research strategy, we might come to the conclusion that definition of research goals in terms of socially relevant problems has great potential productivity.

Clark's statement is a plea against the posture of detachment and indifference. And, when it comes down to the question of which research projects will be – or should be – funded, he has a great deal of right in the matter. The claim to relevance of the social scientist who wants to study an abstract theoretical issue, unrelated to contemporary social problems, is sometimes an alibi to mask indifference to social issues.

There are in the world uncountable numbers of theoretical problems to be solved, and only some of these are anywhere near the heart of the matter when it comes to the "urban crisis," the "crisis in our schools," "the American dilemma" of race relations, the "population explosion," and dozens of other problems that trouble us on the contemporary scene. There are millions of potential theoretical problems, but there are only some thousands of social scientists, and only some hundreds of these will have the wit and opportunity to make important inroads on the scientific questions they select for research. Where should the emphasis be?

Not all anthropologists (and other social scientists) need to rush headlong into the study of our American urban problems, however. First of all, no one has argued that *all* the relevant and pressing social issues are found in continental North America; scientific concerns should not be based on any nationalistic or provincialistic biases. The social problems of people everywhere – people adjusting to the bewildering pace and patterns of modernization and "technologizing" of the world – are all fit subjects of our social science.

There would appear to be two main ways in which relevant research could be programmed. Examples of both types may be found in current anthropological work. The first type of project is one in which a particular problem (or whole set of problems) *in a particular locale* is selected for study. Some contemporary examples include a number of ongoing projects in urban ghettos; studies of mental health and community organization, such as the Leighton Stirling County project (and several others designed along similar lines); and studies of the effects of particular socieotechnological developments, such as Elizabeth Colson's and Theyer Scudder's study of the effects of the Kariba Dam in Southeast Africa. A second, and equally relevant, kind of research is that which aims at some crucial social issue – for example, human overpopulation or human aggression – which is studied through a series of investigations that may be carried out in a number of different locations.

The first alternative typically involves examination of the systematic interrelationships of a great number of variables, perhaps sorted out into several subsystems at various stages of the investigation; the second type of study tends on the whole to deal with a somewhat narrower slice of human behavior but in a more "nomothetic" cross-cultural perspective.

In addition to the investigation of relevant social issues from an essentially theoretical perspective, there is one branch of anthropology that is explicitly devoted to practical, problem-solving research. After a decline of interest in applied anthropology during the late 1950s and early 1960s there is now a resurgence of research and other involvement in medicine and mental health, education, as well as what is called "minority group advocacy." These applied activities are sometimes directly linked with long-term theoretical research; in other instances, however, the contexts of community action and involvement are sufficiently different from ordinary research that we have to consider a special set of methodological techniques and strategies. Applied anthropology or action anthropology does not always involve the same methodological issues as the rest of the anthropological enterprise.

The following set of research activities are examples of applied anthropology, some of which may present special methodological problems:

1   An anthropologist is attached (as researcher-consultant) to an experimental education project in an inner-city school.
2   Anthropologists are invited to evaluate a program designed to give blacks on-the-job training in a previously all-white industrial plant.
3   An ethnographer is asked by an Indian community to help with community public relations, a legal case, and other problems.
4   Anthropologists are asked to monitor and advise in connection with a hydroelectric dam project in an economically marginal rural region.
5   Anthropological linguists are asked to advise and assist in seeking solutions to a new nation's decision about the choice of official language(s).
6   Government officials with anthropological training have the responsibility for design and implementation of sweeping land reform in a Latin American country.
7   Anthropologists have once again been asked to "explain" why some rural peasants appear to resist adopting new agricultural techniques, including new "miracle" varieties of seeds.
8   Medical anthropologists are asked to give "cultural consultation" and advice in a hospital serving a large Spanish-speaking population.
9   Anthropologists become involved in a community mental health program, serving as cultural brokers between the people of an ethnic enclave and the medical (especially psychiatric) establishment.
10 Anthropologists are asked to help in planning the architectural (and other) design of new facilities for senior citizens.

11   Anthropologists are hired by an Indian community to help develop their bilingual, bicultural education system.
12   Anthropologists are asked by an ethnic subcommunity to assist in developing a small handicrafts enterprise.
13   A newly formed urban Indian organization asks for ethnographic books and other information in order to revive certain of their traditional dances and ceremonial activities.
14   Anthropologists participate in a rent strike movement in an eastern urban area.
15   Archeologists are asked to excavate a local historical site and to help the local community use the site for promoting its Bicentennial observances.
16   A physical anthropologist is asked to identify some skeletal materials to determine whether the remains are possibly the result of recent homicide (rather than an Indian burial from earlier centuries).
17   Physical anthropologists are asked to consult in a genetic counseling program in connection with sickle-cell anemia.
18   Archeologists and ethnologists are asked by an Indian organization to assist in establishing their tribal claims to aboriginal territories.
19   An anthropologist predicts the likely and possible consequences of a new road under construction in a previously isolated tropical rain forest.
20   Physical anthropologists and ethnologists are asked to participate with other social scientists and planners in considering the population policies of an (apparently) over-populated island.
21   Anthropologists participate with other activists in developing a consumer advocacy system aimed at improved medical services.
22   An anthropologist is asked to study the noncomputerized registration system of a large university to examine the feasibility of converting to computerized procedures.

Examining this list, we see that in many situations the major contribution provided by the anthropologist is *descriptive information*. "Getting the facts" or developing a body of descriptive data is an essential part of almost all applied anthropology.

Frequently, as in examples 3, 13, 15, 16, and 18, the anthropologist is asked to provide a reconstruction of past events from available evidence; this is practically never "mere description," however. Even the seemingly unchallenging task of describing a bygone traditional ceremonial procedure (example 13) requires a holistic integration of ethnographic data. Adequate communication of a traditional ceremonial enactment should include information about *who* (performers, spectators, etc.), when (appropriate times, sequences, pacing, intermissions, etc.), where (adjustment to indoors, size of arena, special ceremonial locations, etc.), and why (significance of individual ritual items and elements).

In court cases anthropologists have had to learn legal (operationalized) definitions of landownership in order to testify effectively about Indian territorial claims. (Curiously, one of the most sweeping land claims ever won by a North American aboriginal group is that of the Alaskan natives (Eskimos and Aleuts), about whom we have been accustomed to reading that "Eskimos do not have concepts of landownership as such.")

The most common type of applied research is that which requires an anthropologically sophisticated answer to the question: "What's happening in this situation?" This often boils down to a kind of troubleshooting, as described by Homer Barnett some years ago (Barnett, 1956).

Example 7 in the preceding list calls for the kind of field work anthropologists love best – mingling and talking with people to find out *their* view of the proposed technical innovations – of the new "miracle seeds" or whatever – along with some assessment of the state of communications between the local people and the "outside agents." Often the essential descriptive information most valuable to all parties is a careful, objective assessment of the ways in which a set of technological and behavioral innovations has different potential usefulness for different types of households or groups in a community or region.

The best way to see the special problems of research method in applied anthropology is to take up specific cases.

Case study I: Chicanos and anthropologists in Chicago

Beginning in 1969, Stephen Schensul and his associates (1973, 1975) were involved in anthropological research in a West Side Chicago mental health program. The area served by the program has a large and growing Chicano population, as well as an adjoining neighborhood that is still considered "Middle European." The program was not just another set of storefront mental health outposts. Attuned to the mood of the late 1960s, the directors of the program took the view that an effective mental health effort should work to promote community organization and community development as a major aspect of preventive medical services.

During the first year or so, the anthropologists sought to generate basic descriptive information about the "catchment area" communities, definitions and perceptions of the mental health needs of their inhabitants, as well as their styles of interacting with the "mainline" medical establishment. In this phase the research methods of the anthropologists were essentially participant observation and key-informant interviewing, with the addition of two or three small-scale pilot surveys. Even in a complex, urban situation, there is no more effective way for fieldworkers to "get the lay of the land" than by "hanging around," seeking out key informants and effective contacts within local community groups.

As the anthropologists were gaining increasing rapport with some of the people in the Chicano neighborhoods, Chicano activists were beginning to develop new community organizations. Most anthropologists become strongly identified with the people among whom they do research; no wonder then, that in this case Schensul and his researchers came to define their anthropological mission as *serving the action organizations* within the community. As Schensul and Bymel put it:

We are attempting to construct an action research model in which . . . the community is both the object of study and the most important recipient of the results . . . and research-ers, service providers and community activists collaborate with one another in basic re-search . . . such as problem formulation, data collection, data analysis, and dis-semination. (Schensul and Bymel 1975:441.)

In the later phases of the project (1972–4) most of the anthropological research was initiated in discussions with the Chicano leaders. Some of the main research and communication activities included:

1 Writing grant proposals for Chicano community programs
2 Helping to plan a bicultural-bilingual mental health training program, administered by Chicano community people
3 Surveying needs and community attitudes in connection with proposed new programs
4 Research on *curanderos*, spiritualists, and other folk healers and their relationships to various Chicano styles and patterns of health-seeking behavior
5 Assisting in establishing a health clinic with the support of a group of physicians

One research operation in this Chicago example illustrates a special problem of applied research. The Chicano activists and the anthropologists agreed that data were needed to assess specific needs and directions for a new youth program. During the 1960s and early 1970s these West Side ethnic communities were in-creasingly threatened by escalation of violence among the street gangs. (Lincoln Keiser's *Vicelords: Warriors of the Streets* deals with this part of Chicago, and Thrasher's classic study of gangs (1927) gives many examples of earlier gang ac-tivity in these same neighborhoods.)

A comprehensive schedule was designed for interviewing members of youth gangs as well as nongang teenagers in the areas served by the Chicano commu-nity programs. Somehow the interview instrument just grew and grew. Pretesting was slower than originally planned, and the recruiting of volunteer interviewers was not an easy task. The project languished; gang leaders and other youths be-came restive. By the time the project was well under way (quite rapidly by usual research standards), the pressures for launching the youth programs were in-tense. The program simply could not wait for the study. While the researchers were still wrestling with problems of fouled-up computer programs, and the other predictable delays in data processing, the community leaders had been forced into a series of program commitments that rendered the survey quite obsolete.

On the other hand, some of the anthropological data in this project proved useful over much longer time spans. Basic ethnographic data, for example, were useful both as base-line information and as general description in later program planning. Thus the methodological requirements in this example ranged from the need for relatively "quick and dirty" data gathering to a variety of longer-term, carefully planned research projects. With experience, the research team learned how to generate data quickly, while at the same time sustaining longer-term research.

Case study II: a local program and non-local politics

In 1973 T. Marchione (an anthropologist acting as a technical assistant to the Caribbean Nutrition Institute) was asked to design a project to evaluate a new auxiliary health aide program in a Caribbean community. The program was ambitious and many sided. In project communities the local health auxiliaries were hired and trained to carry out health education, nutritional consultation, demonstrations, and other preventive medical activities among the impoverished population. The directors of the program wanted data on the effectiveness of the project in improving people's dietary habits, child care, and health levels. Marchione and his associates were also interested in another question: How does the program articulate to the larger political picture of the community and the nation?

The researchers developed a comprehensive household survey, which was administered by the health aides, who were given special training in the management of the interview. A random sample from the total population was carefully chosen, and base-line data were collected (Marchione, in press). In addition to the interview information, children under one year of age were weighed and measured in order to establish direct measures of nutritional status, based on weight/age and height/age ratios.

The follow-up evaluation research was scheduled for 1975, but meanwhile a serious economic recession had occurred. The program directors were very uneasy about the follow-up research, believing that the results would show deterioration in health standards as a consequence of worldwide economic events beyond their control. In order to control for the economic decline and still compare health practices and child health in target families with those of households not directly affected by the program, Marchione's evaluation research design took the form shown in Table 10.1.

The project is a striking illustration of the fact that a before-and-after (test-retest) research design is extremely vulnerable to extraneous factors (such as economic fluctuations) *unless* a control group comparison is included in the design. As a model of evaluation research, this project has a number of important features:

Table 10.1. *Health practices and infant health*

	1973	1975	Change (%)
Program households			
Nonprogram households			
			Comparison of changes

1 Target population clearly specified
2 Clear statement of goals of project
3 Test-retest design *with control group*
4 Interviewing carried out by *local,* trained individuals
5 Random sample of households
6 Interview data plus *direct observation* (measurement of infants)
7 Qualitative data available from participant observation and informal interviewing
8 All variables clearly operationalized for statistical analysis
9 Good cooperation from the program directors and other personnel

As the second stage (1975) of the research began, it became evident that the health aide program involved higher-level politics. There had been a change of administration during the intervening years. Furthermore, the health auxiliaries were unevenly distributed in the target communities – apparently reflecting significant political pressures. Evaluation of those aspects of the program could not be carried out systematically within the narrow framework of the original research design.

Evaluation research of planned programs, whether in health, agriculture, or other fields, involves several different levels. Often the directors of action programs want answers to very specific, low-level questions – for example, is the program having the predicted effects *in the target households?* (In some cases the directors of programs are not particularly interested in "the truth" at that level, for what they need is *favorable* information that supports and justifies a program to which they have already committed their energies and reputations.)

A second level of evaluation, which anthropologists are seldom equipped for, is concerned with the cost-effectiveness of particular programs. Even if Marchione were to find that the health auxiliary program was having the intended effects, *it would still not be clear whether the observed effects were worth the cost of the program.*

Whenever researchers set out into the thickets of full-scale cost-benefit analysis (a type of evaluation in which our government agencies are increasingly interested), it is essential to weigh *all* the latent and manifest benefits of a program –

not just the narrowly defined outcome goals. For example, the health aide program Marchione evaluated was not just a health and nutrition program. It obviously served also as a source of employment for a significant number of people, some of whom would have had to obtain other kinds of governmental support in the absence of this project. Sometimes these seemingly secondary effects of programs are the primary goals from the point of view of the political leaders who promote them.

At another level of analysis, Marchione felt it was important to ask whether such health auxiliaries programs can have any significant effects on a nationwide basis, given a particular economic and political establishment. Another way to phrase this is: "What are the political, economic and cultural constraints at regional and national levels that make this project either trivial (tokenism) or, on the contrary, an important model for a nationwide effort?"

Asking that larger question required qualitative information about the ways in which this particular program articulated to the food economy and public health system of the region and the nation. Marchione discovered that the health aide program posed a serious threat to some segments of the health care delivery system, all of the people who had vested interests that were threatened by the paramedical, lay-participation aspects of these kinds of programs. Marchione concluded that some improvement in nutrition levels had occurred in part of the population, but the changes appeared to stem from economic factors at the national and international levels, rather than to stem from the work of health aides.

Marchione's project illustrates the major dilemma of most applied research, (especially evaluation research): The more rigorous the methodology, the more removed are the results from the "big questions." Yet it *is* important for anthropologists to be able to research and evaluate the small questions as well as the bigger ones. In the first place, applied anthropologists are often employed for just those tasks, and we must develop skills for carrying them out. Often the effective resolution of the small questions gives leverage for understanding and *redefining* the larger social issues. Of course, this process works in both directions.

Fortunately, this example of applied research included sufficient flexibility for the anthropologist that he could address himself to both the "little end" and the "big end" of the policy dilemma. This kind of research flexibility practically always implies a thorough mixing of quantitative and qualitative data.

Case study III: "Stay Where You Were" –
anthropological study of an employment project

Padfield and Williams's study of a job program for the hard-core unemployed in San Diego is an illustration of another type of applied anthropology, in which the researchers came on the scene with outside financial support and were not expected to develop information for directly modifying the job program.

The National Association of Businessmen sponsored a number of minority-group job programs during the late 1960s, as a reaction to the ghetto riots and the political force generated by the black power movement and related processes. Padfield and Williams originally intended to focus on one group of hard-core unemployed in their new factory job situation, believing that the most theoretically interesting developments would be in the on-the-job interactions. However, "modification [of the research design] evolved rather quickly when it became obvious that the forces impinging upon the trainees *outside* the plant were more significant than factors in the plant . . ." (Padfield and Williams, 1973:277, italics in original). "The theoretical framework and the objectives of the study were elaborated to observe the trainees systematically in two social settings – the plant and the ghetto community" (Padfield and Williams, 1973).

Padfield and Williams collected quantitative data on absenteeism and lateness on the job, arrest records, family composition, types of role conflicts, "index of male marginality," and other information. These materials, while providing significant supporting evidence, were not as central to the project as was the mass of nonquantified data from informal interviewing and observation of the trainees in a variety of on-the-job and nonjob settings.

The researcher's intentions were to develop theoretical perspectives in a thoroughly inductive fashion, utilizing an experimental setting that had come into being because of the social-political events of the 1960s. Carefully predesigned hypothesis-testing research was not particularly feasible, in their view, but hypotheses and research design evolved into a coherent form in the process of research. Thus their strategy resembled that advocated by Glaser and Strauss in *The Discovery of Grounded Theory* (1967).

Although it is clear that Padfield and Williams *could* have formulated precise hypotheses before they began the research, it is equally evident from their detailed description that the most useful sectors of data arose in quite unpredicted areas. One of the methodological strengths of anthropology is that researchers are generally flexible enough to *discover* new areas of information not foreseen in their original research plans. This is part of the constructive holism of the discipline.

As research on the hard-core trainees progressed, the researcher discovered that "full employment" created strains on family role structure, friendship patterns, and other aspects of behavior. In some instances these strains were intolerable; the conflicts were too great; and individual trainees dropped out of the job program. Predictably, there were strains in the factory as well, as union employees with seniority saw their own jobs threatened. Most of the trainees who stayed in the program throughout the year were able to effect some major changes in role relationships in their households. The theoretical implications of these data, from the Padfield and Williams point of view, relate particularly to the psychosocial dynamics of "male marginality" in economically marginal sectors of our modern society.

One practical application of this study is the suggestion that job programs for hard core unemployed people are likely to fail unless special measures (counseling, legal aid, and other services) are provided to help resolve the inevitable wide range of role conflicts generated by regular employment. In fact it appears from some of their discussion that the researchers engaged in counseling and a variety of forms of direct intervention in the program. ("This morning I spoke to Bobby alone and laid it on the line. I told him I didn't want any playing around, because we were taking a 'hands off' attitude from now on regarding him and the courts" [from notes by Williams, p. 136, in Padfield and Williams].)

"Stay Where You Were" is like Marchione's St. James research in one important finding: that a focus exclusively at the local, intraprogram level can easily oversimplify, or seriously distort, the interpretation of the data. It is important that Padfield and Williams demonstrated the ways in which "It's not enough to give people jobs. . . ." On the other hand, their focus on the family, friendship network, and neighborhood factors affecting the economic strategies and adjustments of the hard-core trainees can easily be misinterpreted (e.g., by administrators and legislators) in a manner that places primary causality on the people themselves in accounting for poverty and its attendant ills.

The authors did not fall into this theoretical-methodological trap, but in an assessment of their work Delmos Jones (1974) points out that:

Padfield and Williams are acutely aware of the conditions under which the ghetto poor must live. Yet they appear to view that problem in terms of personal adjustment instead of in terms of the social context in which it originated. "Is a job alone enough?" they ask at the end of the book. . . . The real issue is the political and economic forces blocking the creation of enough jobs to make a difference – not to a few hard-core individuals but to the poor as a whole. (Jones, 1974:311–12.)

In addition to their interpretation of the data, Padfield and Williams's verbatim selections from interviews and notes, plus summary statistical data about the hard-core trainees, are important raw materials for others to work with. Although their data are concerned with only twenty-eight trainees in one aircraft plant, the credibility and versatility of these materials can be rated very highly because of the in-depth, multitechnique field methods they used.

This fascinating study points out the ethical and practical problems applied anthropologists face in their uses and interpretations of data, precisely because their research is directed to social problems for which people seek solutions. The Padfield and Williams data might possibly be interpreted to fit a conservative frame of reference; they can also be used to fuel revolutionary change. Each applied anthropologist must make value judgments and philosophical decisions in communicating the import of research data. So far our profession has not completely faced up to the dilemmas involved in this translation process.

Case study IV: videotape and applied research:
an educational example

The field of education, like health care, is rich in opportunities for applied anthropology. And, as in medicine, the focus of applied research is often directed to problems of communication between ethnic minority people and the professional people who operate and control these major social institutions. Fred Erickson's research in the Chicago school system involved the use of videotape documentation of encounters between "gatekeepers" (school counselors and job interviewers) and minority-group members. He collected approximately 30,000 feet of film in documenting 82 interaction cases (600 minutes of face-to-face interaction) (Erickson, 1976:121).

Erickson reported that "It was through fieldwork that I gradually came to identify the gatekeeping encounter as theoretically salient and appropriate for detailed study. I did not begin by looking for gatekeeping encounters" (Erickson, 1976:113). Thus his progression of research resembles that of Padfield and Williams in that appropriate targets for intensive observation, and the design for observing them, developed in the course of field-work experience.

This project required meticulous coding of the videotape materials, in an attempt to isolate significant elements of interaction in the gatekeeping encounters. Verbal and nonverbal behavior in the videotape scenes were coded, supplemented by commentaries by the participants, as they watched reruns of the interviews.

Erickson's analysis of the gatekeeping encounters included a variety of elements, including "uncomfortable moments," "asymmetrical segments," and other constructs. He found that the most significant social dimension explaining variations in interviews was that of "pan-ethnicity": white versus Third World. Detailed analysis of the tapes demonstrated a number of ways in which pan-ethnicity affected the likelihood of unfavorable outcomes of interviews for individuals from Third World ethnic membership.

Although Erickson employed statistical analysis throughout his data processing, he noted that his samples were rather small and the statistical results therefore vulnerable to criticism. However,

Do policy makers want certainty from policy research? If so, then no amount of empirical evidence is sufficient. . . . The controversy over the Equality of Educational Opportunity Survey (EEOS) conducted by James Coleman and associates (1966) is a case in point. Here a study . . . with a nationwide sample of 600,000 students, is characterized by different researchers as statistically ambiguous, methodologically wrong-headed, or valid and embarrassing in its conclusions. (Ibid., 142–3.)

Erickson goes on to note that the kinds of patterns he found in his videotape data, because of their richness "and because of the high redundancy in the systematic organization of the phenomena studied, produce results that are less problematic than survey research . . ˙. and more amenable to illustration by simple statistical procedures" (ibid., 143).

Some methodological issues in applied research

The need for speed

In the academic scene we are a bit surprised if data are published within a year or two after the research is completed. We are only mildly surprised, and not shocked, when data are published ten to fifteen years after they are collected. But in applied research the data must often be available within days or weeks. After a few months the information may well be obsolete.

It is a trifle embarrassing to talk about "quick n' dirty" research. Yet applied researchers are constantly faced with requests for information that must be made available quickly. For example, faced with the question of mounting an all-out effort to get the medical clinic going in the 26th Street area, Schensul's Chicago research team felt that a survey of opinion and potential support for such a project was essential. But door-to-door canvassing in a population of 20,000 people was out of the question. The "quick n' dirty" solution was to draw up a list of approximately 35 known leaders and activists in the area and to interview them using a ranking and rating procedure. Each of the opinion leaders was asked to give a rank order to a series of possible projects, in terms of: (1) the *need* for such projects; (2) their *willingness to support* such a project, and (3) the feasibility.

From the survey the researchers learned that a new medical clinic was *not* the highest priority, but it had relatively strong support, as well as a high feasibility ranking. Assessment of the meaning of these data, and their relation to the proposed action, depended in turn on the anthropologists' accumulated knowledge and sophistication about the relationships of the opinion leaders to the political alignments and factional complexities of the target community.

The importance of ethnographic background

Almost any collection of quantitative data from an interview, census, or other source requires a strong supporting mass of contextual, descriptive information.

Action researchers with ongoing relationships in particular communities will usually have the opportunity to develop this information through long-term research. In such contexts the speed of data gathering and interpretation in individual projects is greatly facilitated by the available ethnographic information.

In the Chicago work the success of the anthropologists in working with Chicano activists depended in part on the masses of basic descriptive data from several different household surveys. These data provided quantified generalizations about the extent of Spanish language use in the community, levels of employment, variations in orientation to Mexican cultural traditions, recency of migration to Chicago, and other characteristics. Marchione's Caribbean research demonstrates the same point. His assessment of the health aide program required a large amount of *contextual* data. Some of this data could be collected in quantified form, but a great deal of it was of a qualitative nature, about economic and political alignments and philosophies.

Focus on individuals and households

Frequently, the information most useful to action programs is based on behaviors, qualities, and situations of individuals and households – especially the differences among them – rather than broad-gauge generalizations that seek to characterize an entire community or "culture."

In the Padfield-Williams research there were important variations among the hard-core unemployed – and these *differences* had significance for the outcomes. Some individuals stayed with the program and were considered successes; others dropped out. A focus on intragroup differences of situation can help to account for the varieties of outcomes. Similarly, in Marchione's Caribbean research one primary goal of evaluation was to identify *intra*community variations affecting the outcomes of the health aide program in different households.

The importance of intracultural differences was particularly clear in the Chicano community where Schensul and his associates were working. Governmental agencies and other external groups (including some anthropologists) have tended to treat Mexican-Americans as if they all adhered to an identifiable "Mexican-American culture pattern" (with an associated "modal personality"). A major contribution of the Chicago anthropologists included the delineation of *diversities* in the Spanish-speaking population. Schensul and his researchers found that the "Mexicans" (recently immigrated from Mexico) and "Tejanos" (from Texas and other areas in the Southwest), differed in significant respects from the considerable group of Spanish-surname people who were born and raised in Chicago and other parts of the Midwest, many of whom did not speak Spanish, and who identified only very selectively with Mexican culture.

The need for emic and etic perspectives

Both emic and etic perspectives provide significant information for planners and activists and other users of anthropological data. During the past decade, health authorities, for example, have become very sensitive to the importance of folk definitions of physical and mental illness. In Spanish-speaking communities, including those in Chicago, concepts of *susto, mal de ojo*, the hot–cold model of illness and curing, and related ideas have now become salient for many medical people. Qualitative descriptions of the behavior and practice of *curanderos* and *espiritistas* also convey more information from an emic perspective.

But how many people in these ethnic communities (Chicano, Puerto Rican, others) believe in and practice these ideas or seek out the services of folk practitioners? What is the patterning of *intracommunity diversity* with regard to these general cultural ideas? Often it is most useful to ask such questions in terms of etic categories, such as material style of life, degree of ethnic identity (an etic measure constructed from emic information), geographic location, situational factors (both emic and etic), and other variables derived from participant observation and informal interviewing.

Erickson's research on gatekeeping encounters involved cross-checking between emic and etic categorizations. His coders produced painstaking etic analyses of verbal output, body movements, and other details in the videotapes. On the other hand, they played back the tapes for the individual conferees in order to get their emically sensitive definitions of important scenes and stressful episodes. The resulting data analysis was focused on those segments of behavior in which emic and etic categorizations coincided.

Often the role of the applied anthropologist is that of a "cultural broker" (Weidman, 1973). Sometimes this role may be an explicit focal concern of the project; at other times it may develop as a quite tangential aspect of some other activity. For example, in research among Alabama Creek people J. Anthony Paredes extended his role as ethnographer to include such cultural-brokerage activities as preparing a public relations brochure for the community (Paredes, 1976). Probably most field researchers have taken on the role of brokers in at least minor ways, particularly in mediating practical matters like getting medical care and dealing with governmental red tape.

The near-ubiquity of the culture broker role among anthropologists, whether in applied projects or in supposedly nonapplied research, arises from a core methodological feature of anthropology. Almost all anthropologists operate with a basically emic perspective in certain aspects of field work. However etic the final product is intended to be, most fieldworkers look at peoples' lifeways from an insider's point of view and come to identify with the local people in a variety of ways. This hallmark of the ethnographic enterprise (it also applies to much of the research in other subdisciplines of anthropology) is so taken for granted by many nonanthropologists that it is sometimes thought to be the major raison d'être of anthropology.

What is it that is applied in applied anthropology?

Most social scientists, anthropologists among them, assume that what is applied is theory. We take the general body of our theory and apply it to particular situations or programs, just as the building of a nuclear-powered electrical plant is an application of theory from physics.

The question that arises from that analogy is: What theory does anthropology have that can be applied? There seems to be rather little systematic theory in anthropology that is directly applicable to the concrete situation in which applied anthropologists work. Moreover, people who seek anthropologists' help and advice often appear to have their own general theories about the situations they seek to control or the results they desire to achieve. Moreover, the culture broker often played by anthropologists suggests that applied anthropology involves transactions of cultural information. The information is often of a quite specific nature, practically always with reference to a particular community or social context at a particular time.

We suggest that the word "applied" refers above all to methodology. George Foster (1969) and others have made much the same point. The combined emic-etic, qualitative-quantitative mix of field research method in anthropology produces an especially useful kind of descriptive information. The agencies and programs that employ anthropologists often do so because (supposedly) "anthropologists know how to find out about the local culture." Local community groups (including North American tribal organizations) hire anthropologists: "They know about our culture and how to represent us to the government (and other agencies)." The information to be transacted is usually highly particularistic, such as "the facts" relevant to a particular land claims case or other court action.

But many will object that there is no such thing as a nontheoretical description. Every descriptive presentation, every communication, must be organized in terms of some conceptual frame of reference. Pure inductive description is impossible. Agreed.

There is a metatheory of anthropology, we feel, that gives the shape and rationale to our data-gathering methods. We outlined this general point in Chapter 1. Furthermore, each applied anthropologist injects his or her own personal theory consciously or unconsciously into the work of application. In fact, some applied anthropologists are Republicans, others Democrats, still other Marxists. Those various aspects of theoretical position affect our research methods and strategies and research outcomes. They do not, however, constitute clear and explicitly stated propositions and hypotheses consciously tested in the research process. Aye, there's the rub, so many different animals travel under the rubric of "theory" that it's hard to know for sure what constitutes a theory and what does not. Yes, there is no theory-less research, but some research is more theoretical than others.

Relevance and methodological rigor

It is an accepted tenet of science that, to be useful, scientific statements should have high truth value. Here we approach one of the sore points in the debate between social scientists and their critics. The partisans of relevance have often mistaken emotional commitment and persuasive philosophy for the stuff of scientific veracity. Their favorite social scientists are more often applauded for their polemics than for diligent testing of hypotheses. And some anthropologists have joined this argument, insisting that productive research depends on emotional involvement with the people whose problems are a focus of study.

Emotional commitment – even fanaticism – on the side of humanity and justice does not ensure either scientific excellence or its opposite. Some highly productive scientists have carried out their research with serene detachment from the daily affairs of the world, but there are many examples of highly emotional, politically motivated (some would even say bigoted) researchers who have contributed much to the growth of knowledge.

It is probable that much of the criticism that has been leveled at "irrelevant" social science is aroused by the fact that second-rate (or even worse) research materials abound in our journals. Some of the materials that are attacked as irrelevant or intellectually sterile are vulnerable because their theoretical underpinnings are confused or tautological; the supporting evidence is incomplete, unrepresentative, or conjectural, and the concluding generalizations unwarranted. Some social scientists whose work can thus be criticized are, in fact, devoting their attentions to relevant problems – only their methodologies betray them.

Most of us justify our science with the assumption that true information is a most powerful force for effective social adaptation. In fact, our version of human cultural history is generally made up of a chronicle of the successful accumulation of knowledge. Clearly, at this time we are woefully lacking in social knowledge about many aspects of our technosocial scene. To obtain that knowledge is not easy, but there are ways of enhancing our knowledge-building performance. The ways that have been suggested here are, for the most part, fairly uncomplicated, time-tested ideas that are current in the culture of general science. Application of these cultural patterns to the data-gathering process in anthropology (and the other social sciences) lags in part because of problems in translating principles of naturalistic observation into the domain of human activity; but the culture lag is also due to inhibiting factors in the social organization of our disciplines.

We are suggesting that relevant research in the social sciences should exhibit a blending of concern about current public issues with methodologically sound information gathering.

One important aspect of anthropological research operations that is often misunderstood by both critics and some theory builders is the significance of basic descriptive information. Many crucial research areas are characterized by an overwhelming dearth of factual information concerning what is really happening. The data on urban ghettos, for example, are thick with references to crime, delinquency, broken homes, and other pathological elements, but materials on many other significant aspects of day-to-day living are inadequate. Relevant research often requires that at the outset a high priority be placed on basic descriptive data – not just any description, but careful delineation of representative arrays of facts concerning people's physical and psychological adaptations.

Social scientists frequently repeat a cliché to the effect that "mere description by itself is worthless; only when descriptive statements are relatable to theoretical propositions do they become useful knowledge." This kind of statement is frequently accompanied by another "axiom": that to provide useful knowledge social scientists must be able to predict outcomes or consequences of actions.

These statements are particularly in error when it comes to practical applications of social information, for very often the predictions of consequences, or other forecasts, are made by administrators, planners, or other agencies (including reformers and revolutionaries), not by social scientists. Their policy decisions, we may assume, are most effective when they are based on accurate descriptive data. Existential statements – such as "Twenty-three percent of these people are malnourished [by some stated standard]" or "At any given time about one-third of the men are away from home, working at the plantations" – are frequently of direct practical usefulness, provided such information is available at the time and place "where the action is."

It must be emphasized that research that is oriented toward the solution of particular social problems often involves a strategy different from the usual paradigms of theory building. The difference is clear when we examine the sequence of research projects of individual investigators. When a social scientist successfully completes a particular research venture, he often shifts his area of investigation (both conceptually and geographically) to some *theoretically* related domain. For example, successful conclusion of a study of role behavior in a hospital setting may lead the investigator to seek an expansion of his theoretical system through the application of the new-found theory to a different setting, perhaps to behavior in an industrial plant.

Problem-oriented research, on the other hand, involves the assumption that the successful piece of research concerning role behavior in hospitals brings to light *related research questions in the hospital setting*. This is because it is highly unlikely that a single research effort really solves any problems. More likely, it aids in the understanding of some one problem, concerning which a number of other, as yet unstudied, factors are also of importance.

To put the matter in somewhat homelier terms, if initial investigation tells us that one of the correlates of poor performance in the family automobile is the fact that it burns a lot of oil, a problem-solving research approach calls for further investigation into the excessive oil consumption in *this* automobile. On the other hand, a theory-building approach, particularly as seen in the social sciences, would likely result in a comparative study of other automobiles, and perhaps other types of internal-combustion engines, with regard to oil-consumption characteristics. Seen in this light, certain of the paradigms of theory building that have become widespread in the social sciences have a fairly low probability of *directly* contributing to the practical issues about which our critics (and some of our financial backers) are deeply concerned. This is not to say that a comparative study of internal-combustion engines would be of no practical value; but we must be aware of the fact that our "clients" are often more concerned about this particular automobile, right now.

One of the most telling criticisms of social science research calls attention to our modes of reporting the results of our studies. How can we claim that our social science research is relevant to the interested public when so much of it is buried away (in terms of language and place of publication) in materials that are of interest and usefulness only to fellow social scientists? Our reporting styles graphically reveal the nature of our reference groups. Our language of research expression has grown up as an ingroup argot, in terms of which fellow members of our particular subsociety understand and appreciate our contributions to the ingroup-oriented body of knowledge. To be relevant, newly discovered information must be communicated. We need to develop new kinds of research-reporting channels (and language styles) that will maximize the flow of useful knowledge to the people and agencies of social action.

In anthropology the language of research reporting has very seldom taken into account the matter of communicating directly with the populations studied. Until recent times most of the people studied by anthropologists could neither read nor write, nor were they particularly concerned with knowing many details of the information the fieldworker collected. After all, the local "native" already knew all about his or her local culture. Now things are a bit different. The anthropologist is very likely to be studying some aspects of adaptation to recent sociocultural change (rather than trying to recapture details of the people's golden past), and the local people are increasingly aware that the data are of practical importance. Indian groups in the United States have been particularly vociferous in insisting that the anthropologist should report *back to them* with useful information – or what was he doing there anyway?

Therefore, one of the central ethical and practical problems that anthropologists must solve is that of feeding back relevant social information to the population they have studied. To do this will require:

1   A research orientation that does, in fact, product socially useful information.
2   Development of modes of communication, or styles of retranslation, that can convey our scientific information to interested publics in a form that articulates with their local modes of talking about their social experience.
3   Direct involvement of the local community people in the research process, so that they become linked to the basic information-gathering.

We have not intended to suggest that all anthropologists must now redirect their research interests toward social issues that are currently at the top of the public's list of critical problems. But we do think that Kenneth Clark's statement, and many others like it, must be taken seriously by our profession; and that our departments and other organizations should carefully consider the matter of research priorities, as well as other aspects of our responsibilities and relationships to the social world of which we are all a part. The questions raised by the whole matter of relevance are directly related to problems of research methodology because research must be methodologically sound before it can be relevant for anything.

11 Building anthropological theory: methods and models

Most of our methodological discussion has concentrated on "the little end" – operationalizing the units or elements (variables) observed in the course of direct field research. We have focused on the more concrete observational aspects of the anthropological enterprise because these are, in our opinion, fundamental to everything that goes on in the more abstracted realms of theory building. Referring again to the diagram, the "Domain of Methodology" from Chapter 1 (Figure 11.1), we can see that most of the cases and examples in previous chapters reach up, at best, to "low-order propositions."

Where does *real* theory building come in? And where are the models? How do we develop a general theory of human behavior? A general theory of cultural evolution? A model of an ecological system? Indeed, what "is" a theory beyond the bare-bones definition in Chapter 1?

Full exploration of these questions would require another book, a book with a focus somewhat different from this one. On the other hand, every piece of research has some relationship to theory, and everyone develops some explicit or implicit strategy (or set of strategies) that link day-to-day research activities to broad theoretical frameworks.

The theoretical frame of reference: general paradigms

All researchers and writers in all scholarly fields – in fact all human beings (we believe) observe the world in terms of an overall world view – a paradigm, or the-

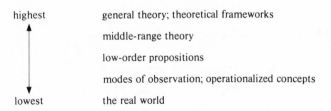

Levels of abstraction

highest	general theory; theoretical frameworks
↑	middle-range theory
│	low-order propositions
↓	modes of observation; operationalized concepts
lowest	the real world

Figure 11.1. The domain of methodology, or theory building in anthropology.

oretical system that suggests main features, principles of causality, and favored modes of observation. As we suggested in Chapter 1, an anthropologist's theoretical framework generally includes two major components: (1) the explicitly anthropological theory (structuralism, biocultural ecology, and so on) and (2) a series of unstated and perhaps unrecognized *assumptions* derived from personal experience ("humans are innately good"; "the world is falling apart"; "rural life is superior to city life"; "human behavior is practically infinitely malleable"; "everyone has a price"; "the squeaky wheel gets the grease"; "humans are political animals"; and so on).

Here is an example of a hypothetical anthropologist's theoretical frame of reference:

general theory	biocultural evolutionism and ecology
additional features	probabilistic view of causal relationships in all living things (many other features could be added)
preferred locus of research	nonmodern, small-scale communities (especially tropical, subtropical)
preferred topics of research	food-production systems
preferred mode of comparisons	two to three cases in localized region
assumptions about cultural data	prefer mixture of emic and etic sources and categories
quantitative/statistical style	prefer mix of quantified and qualitative research
field-work style	informal; "hang around" with key informants, supported by structured interviewing and other quantitative data gathering; small field team of self, professionally trained spouse, and two to three local assistants
preferred supporting fields and data	geography, botany, agricultural economics

Although our hypothetical anthropologist has a seemingly coherent and organized frame of reference, many of the individual items could be changed without altering her or his identification with the general theory of biocultural evolutionism. She might, for example, just as easily prefer a focus on health and illness, with supporting fields in biomedical and nutritional sciences.

Deductive, inductive, and abductive research strategies

Given this general theoretical frame of reference, our hypothetical anthropologist *could* use a clear, deductive research strategy. This would involve the following steps:

1 *Codification* of a system of general propositions concerning biocultural evolution and ecological systems.
2 *Selection* of a particular subsystem of propositions, with more specific content, applicable to a specific context.
3 Development of general hypotheses to be tested.
4 Concretizing of the general hypotheses in relation to the known conditions in a particular geographical locality.
5 *Operationalizing* the variables in the hypotheses by specifying the field observations that will produce empirical data for testing the hypotheses.
6 Collect data; test hypotheses and relate back to the higher-order theory (see Figure 11.2).

There have been many arguments about the place of deductive operations in scientific research, and most anthropologists have taken the compromise position that *both* deductive and inductive processes are fruitful in the social and behavioral sciences. Brim and Spain, for example, have commented that:

Whether one works from "theory downward to reality," or from "reality upward to theory" (in other words, whether one takes a deductive or an inductive approach) one is doing science. . . . . out of all [the philosophical debate] . . . has come widespread recognition of the great value of both, and indeed, of the difficulty in distinguishing the two in many contexts. (Brim and Spain, 1974:3).

Inductive research purportedly reverses the logical order shown in Figure 11.2. The process *begins* with the empirical observations, developing and testing concrete hypotheses about them, and then linking those supportable hypotheses with other similar constructions or propositions, in higher-order, more ab-

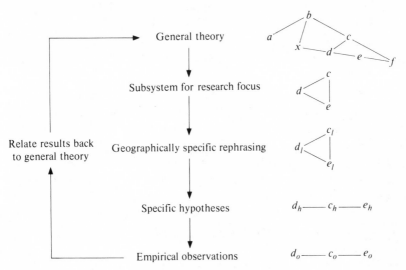

Figure 11.2. The deductive method.

stracted systems. Inductive methodology is common in anthropological field work, because much of the joy of the field-work enterprise lies in the discoveries made in the field context.

Abduction refers to yet another sequence – actually a mixture of inductive and deductive research. Pollnac and Hickman have outlined it as follows:

1   Surprising phenomena – p_1, p_2, p_3 – are encountered.
2   These would not be surprising if a (new) hypothesis were true. They would follow as a matter of course from that hypothesis.
3   Therefore, there is good reason for elaborating and proposing it as a possible hypothesis.

"In the . . . research process the next step would be one of deductive hypothesis, then inductive theory building, followed by another round of abductive hypothesis generation . . ." (Pollnac and Hickman, 1975:29).

The role of models

Perhaps one of the major confusions in anthropological work, as in other sciences, results from the fact that most current published research results give the *appearance* of a structured, deductive process. Thus researchers usually begin with a set of assertions from a general theoretical perspective, then move to specific hypotheses, and follow with the data tests of the hypotheses. The *actual* processes and steps of research are seldom given in print, and description of the mistakes and blind alleys of research are especially scarce in published accounts. Much more research must be done, in fact, on the day-to-day routines of scientific workers, in order to lay a firmer base for a realistic, *empirical* description of science, as opposed to the idealized philosophical writings on "how science works."

Fortunately, there are a few biographical accounts of the scientist at work, some of them revealing a backstage reality widely divergent from the stuff in tightly constructed books on scientific method. One of the most exciting of these autobiographical accounts is James Watson's description of the discovery of the structure of DNA in the somewhat controversial book *The Double Helix* (1968). In the preface he sets the tone with the comment that "As I hope this book will show, science seldom proceeds in the straightforward logical manner imagined by outsiders. Instead, its steps forward (and sometimes backward) are often very human events in which personalities and cultural traditions play major roles" (Watson, 1968:ix).

From Watson's account it appears that he and his colleagues had very little in the way of a "master theory" about the DNA molecule when they began the research. Also, it should be noted, it is rather difficult to identify a clear starting point in their research process. Perhaps it is appropriate, symbolically, that he opens with "In the summer of 1955, I arranged to join some friends who were going into the Alps. . . ."

There was a growing realization in biochemical circles during the mid-fifties that the DNA molecule is of great importance in connection with genetic processes and that identification of its structural principles would contribute greatly to our understanding of many significant biological questions. Watson, Crick, and other researchers (in several competing schools) worked at assembling an eclectic patchwork of theoretical bits and empirical observations. Of course the structure of the DNA molecule had to fit with certain widely known laws of chemistry. That is, the structure had to make sense of the possible arrangements and combinations of a sugar-and-phosphate framework plus some kind of chain(s) of four types of nucleotides. There was, however, no way to *deduce* systematically the structure of DNA from a concatenation of physical and chemical laws.

The *empirical* observations that proved crucial to the solution of the problem were in the form of X-ray crystallography, the interpretation of which suggested some sort of helical structure (though there were disagreements among scientists over what it was, precisely, that the X-rays showed). There were several other bits and pieces of theory and observation making up the jigsaw puzzle.

Reading *The Double Helix*, we are struck by one central feature in the Watson-Crick research strategy: Midway in the research they constructed a *physical model* of what they guessed the DNA molecule might look like. Using this physical model as a frame of reference, solution of the DNA puzzle involved three kinds of data manipulation ("research"):

1 *Deductive.* Checking features of the model against requirements of established chemical and physical theory (e.g., well-established laws of physical chemistry govern the ways in which the phosphorus, sugars, hydrogen ions, and nucleotides can be linked up).
2 *Inductive.* Checking features of the model against new empirical observations (e.g., the DNA crystallography).
3 Internal checking (mathematical computations) of structural coherence within the model itself.

The research method is exemplified in Watson's statement that "Soon, when several atoms had been pushed in or out, the three-chain model began to look quite reasonable. The next obvious step would be to check it with Rosy's quantitative measurements. The model would certainly fit with the general locations of the X-ray reflections . . ." (Watson, p. 64). Later in the book we learn that the three-strand model simply didn't fit together effectively – they rebuilt the whole thing in two chains, and soon were closing in on their Nobel Prize–winning discovery.

It is now widely believed, by practicing scientific researchers and theoreticians as well, that much successful theory-building research involves the use of models – not usually physical structures like the double helix — but any representation that provides a simplified "rough draft" around which to organize inquiry. The rough draft may be a set of equations, diagrams, or even a poetic verbal description that calls up appropriate mental images.

Here are some examples of models commonly encountered in anthropology and related disciplines:

1   The age-area hypothesis, concerning cultural diffusion (often likened to the concentric spread of ripples when a rock is thrown into a pond).
2   A provisional map of an archeological site, drawn by researchers as a model from which to estimate likely locations for further excavation.
3   Freud's hydraulic model of libidinal energy, with imagery (mainly verbal) about "flow," "blockage," "release," "damming up," etc.
4   A computer simulation of a process, for example, Zubrow's description of a population simulation model: "The system consists of four components: a population growth function, a population resource check, a settlement locator, and a longevity function" (Zubrow, 1976:248).
5   Figure 11.2, showing deductive theory building.
6   Any game as a model of some aspect of human realities; chess, for example, as a model of political-military relations among heads of state in bygone times; "Monopoly" as a 1930s model of "getting ahead in business. . . ."
7   Kinship diagrams as models of social behavior and kinship terminology.
8   E. Goffman's *Presentation of Self in Everyday Life* (1959) as a model of everyday life as dramatic performance, with actors, downstage, upstage, etc.

Models come into use at various levels of analysis and abstraction. All of us, consciously or unconsciously, create models (hypothetical estimates or projections) in our daily encounters, in and out of research.

Returning to the double-helix model, we see that a model may incorporate elements from *several different theoretical realms.* Models thus are not simply representations of individual theories, as some people have insisted. Anthropologists, we suggest, always develop working models of the social system of whatever communities they happen to be studying. Berreman's *Behind Many Masks* describes the way in which a very biased model of a community was sharply modified by new and different information (see Chapter 9).

To be useful, models – whether they are drawn on paper, constructed of Tinkertoy sticks, or programmed in a computer – must permit us to test the goodness of fit with existing general theory, devise hypotheses for empirical testing, and should also suggest directions of fruitful research. Models appear to arise in the course of research through intuitive processes, generally through both deductive and inductive processes, if these terms are even applicable. At the simplest level, any hypothesis can be regarded as a tentative model to be checked out against observable things and events in the real world.

Models of research design

In addition to the theoretical models of human behavior, communities, cultural systems, and other pattern systems of which we can draw verbal or pictorial diagrams, anthropologists also carry mental images, or models, of research procedures. These models specify modes of data collection, the forms in which variables are presented, as well as the statistical or qualitative analysis with which we operate on the data. Some of the more usual models (some people prefer to call them "paradigms") in anthropological research include:

1 Community studies.
2 Two-case comparisons.
3 Worldwide, cross-cultural (statistical) method.
4 Regional-variation models.
5 Selected cases as in the Six Cultures project (see later discussion).
6 Intensive, intracultural analysis.

Most anthropologists carry out research in more than one of these research modes; some researchers, on the other hand, are well known as advocates or role models associated with one particular research strategy. The list of research models here is far from complete, but is intended to suggest the range of variation, around which many other combinations and variants occur.

Model I: two-case comparisons

Although two-case cross-cultural comparisons have most often been used simply to illustrate *differences* between cultures, this research model has occasionally served to test and develop propositions about the uniform effects of definable causes. This is the methodological structure employed by S. F. Nadel in his well-known paper "Witchcraft in Four African Societies" (Nadel, 1952).

Nadel examined two paired comparisons involving the presence of particular patterns of witchcraft beliefs. In one paired comparison he presented evidence to show that the Nupe and the Gwari of Nigeria have similar social structure and culture in practically all respects except one. The significant difference is that, among the Nupe women are important traders who often hold economic and social power over their husbands. This crucial difference in social organization, Nadel felt, accounts for the observation that the Nupe associate witchcraft with females and generally expect the attacks of witches to be directed at males.

The Gwari, on the other hand, have no such sexually biased beliefs about witches, because females in their social system do not have the economic and social power of the Nupe women. From this evidence Nadel argued that the patterning of witchcraft fears *is caused by* the tensions aroused by the special features of the female role found in the Nupe social system. The research model can be conceptualized in terms of Figure 11.3.

While Nadel's argument is well presented, closer examination reveals serious problems. As diagramed, the argument hinges on the claim that elements A and B (and *all other cultural traits*) are truly the same in the two cases and that *there are no other causal elements in the two societies that remain uncontrolled*. Careful reading of the descriptive statements given by Nadel makes it clear that he has only quite general and incomplete information about the child-training practices, economic structures, and social organization of the Nupe and Gwari. His claim that other factors are held constant is not supported by extensive demonstration of equivalence in the two groups.

As a matter of fact, demonstration of the equivalence of any two societies would be an enormously time-consuming task, considering the great complexity of human culture. Many anthropologists would insist, moreover, that the functional interrelationships among the elements of cultural and social systems make it impossible for two communities (or societies) to be the same except for one crucial difference. We would expect, on the contrary, that a significant difference in, for example, female role *must* be accompanied by many differences in variables such as socialization practices, male-female interactions, and a wide variety of other elements.

The propositions advanced by Nadel have strong face validity; they make theoretical sense; and they are supported by individual illustrative cases from other areas. But his claim that the theoretical propositions have been put to a rigorous scientific test cannot be accepted. Two-case comparisons thus appear to be a very weak basis for the demonstration of proposed causal relationships, particularly when the explanation is post hoc, as is true in the Nupe/Gwari case. Later, we

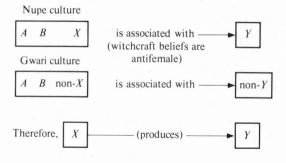

Figure 11.3. A logical model of Nadel's two-culture comparison.

shall examine a special kind of situation in which a two-case comparison can be more methodologically effective.

Model II: statistical cross-cultural comparisons

Because of the methodological problems inherent in studies involving only one or two societies, some researchers have moved to a method of cross-cultural comparison utilizing large numbers of societies as cases. This is the logical position, for example, of Murdock's *Social Structure*, mentioned in Chapter 8. The cross-cultural anthropologist reasons as follows:

1   In terms of some theoretical system, a causal relationship has been suggested between cultural elements X and Y.
2   If such a causal relationship exists, cultural elements X and Y should be found to covary in their occurrence among the world's cultures.
3   A first question to be resolved, therefore, is the empirical matter of the correlation between X and Y.
4   Answering the empirical question requires finding information about X and Y in some representative sample of the world's cultures.
5   If a sample of societies is selected, the covariation of X and Y can be examined statistically, in order to permit an inference concerning the relationships of X and Y in the total universe of human societies.
6   If X and Y are found to covary in human societies, this empirical information permits the theoretician to continue his belief in the usefulness of the explanatory system from which the relationship between X and Y was postulated.

As we noted earlier, Murdock decided, on the basis of over a hundred tests of covariation among elements of kinship terminology and social structure, that his general theory of social structure is a useful predictive paradigm for explaining one aspect of human sociocultural patterns.

Because the method of cross-cultural statistical comparison is, to some extent, a substitute for the two-case controlled comparison, we must immediately ask whether other factors are controlled more effectively in this paradigm than they were in the two-case analysis. Since only variables X and Y are examined, what happened to the other variables? The cross-culturalist's assumption is that extraneous variables have been controlled by the fact that they are "randomized out." While the presence of variables X and Y has been carefully identified, extraneous variables have supposedly been free to vary at random; hence their effects have influenced the relationships of X and Y only insofar as they have introduced random errors into the cross-cultural observations. If random errors have occurred (and they always have), the strength of the relationship between X and Y has in all probability been *reduced* somewhat, so that the researcher may assume that the real relationship between X and Y is *stronger* than the cross-cultural statistics demonstrate.

Of course, another theoretician can always claim that some other crucial variable is *not random* with regard to X and Y and that the other variable, Z, accounts for the observed covariation of X and Y. Such a rival hypothesis can be tested empirically by the same statistical procedure as that used to examine X and Y.

Cross-cultural statistical research differs from most other models of anthropological inquiry in the dependence on already existing ethnographic data. Another feature of the cross-cultural method is that it is the most clearly *nomothetic* of all the research strategies in anthropology. All other research styles focus on more locally specific and time-bound generalizations.

Carol Ember's study of "residential variation in hunter-gatherers" (1975) will serve to illustrate the paradigm and to raise some questions about its strengths and weaknesses. The theoretical question she addressed arose from the incompatibility between two different models of hunter-gatherer social organization: "Radcliffe-Brown, Service, and Williams assume that patrilocality is the normal hunter-gatherer pattern of residence, while Eggan and Lee postulate nonunilocality as the more general form" (Ember, 1975:199). These competing models actually represent the *deduced* products of differing general theories.

Ember's research concentrated on testing the importance of division of labor, warfare, and group size in predicting patrilocal, matrilocal, and bilocal residence tendencies. The theoretical model can be diagramed as in Figure 11.4.

The sample. In most cross-cultural studies the units of analysis are individual cultures, each assumed to be internally undifferentiated in terms of the relevant variables. Ember's first task was, therefore, to select a worldwide sample of cultures identified as hunter-gatherers. This task has been made easy by the fact that Murdock and associates have developed the *Ethnographic Atlas*, which provides a list of cultures around the world, along with a series of coded variables for each of these societies. The user (Ember) adopts a criterion for the selection of cases: "I considered societies to be 'hunter-gatherers' if they had less than 15 percent dependence on agriculture and/or herding according to the *Atlas*" (Ember, 1975: 200). Fifty cultures were found to fit the selection criteria, including the question of having data available for examination of the several interrelated hypotheses.

As we noted earlier, the selection of a sample should conform to random-sampling principles; but this ideal is virtually impossible in cross-cultural studies.

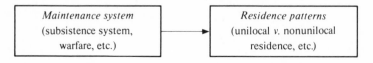

Figure 11.4. Model of the relationship of maintenance system and residence patterns.

One reason for this problem is that investigators are limited to those cases or societies for which data are available. Thus the most that a researcher can claim in the random-sampling process is that the selection is representative of "those cultures for which anthropologists have amassed sufficient data."

Operationalizing the variables. In cross-cultural research using the *Ethnographic Atlas* some of the variables can be operationalized in terms of specific codes (ratings or "measurements") listed in this published source. This is not technically different from many other operationalized variables, which are defined as "the list of XX in such and such archival source . . ." (e.g., the size of urban areas, crime rates, the number of institutions of higher education, infant mortality rates, etc.)

Many standard social and economic variables have been coded in Murdock's *Ethnographic Atlas*, so researchers are spared the hard work of operationalizing these variables for themselves. However, the general structure of worldwide cross-cultural comparisons often depends on *new* variables from ethnographic descriptions. How do you code an ethnographic account in terms of "resource variability," for example? Most general ethnographies are unlikely to include systematic data on this concept, and even if they did, it would be difficult to interpret, because comments about resource variability would be conceptualized differently by different researchers, depending on their prior experience. Ember took a different approach. She noted that ethnographers, discussing the seasonal variability of resources, often refer to rainfall as a major factor predicting vegetation, locations of animals, and related food sources. Therefore, she adopted *variability of rainfall* as her indirect measure of variability of resources. Such data are, in fact, available for most areas of the world nowadays. Very often, cross-cultural statistical researchers must turn to such indirect indicators for the expression of particular variables to be tested.

Often the variables to be included are available in descriptive form in ethnographic accounts. In those cases, the task of the researcher is to define the *content rules* by which research assistants (preferably kept ignorant of specific hypotheses to be tested) rate or "measure" the particular variable for each society in the ethnographic accounts. Anyone planning cross-cultural statistical research these days would be well advised to consult the now large number of studies in which excellent, sometimes ingenious, procedures have been devised for operationalizing variables.

The cross-cultural method adopted by Ember implies a particular model of statistical analysis. The statistical treatment is in the form of a two-variable matrix, as illustrated in Table 11.1.

Although the data table does not give the precise rank orderings of male-versus-female contribution to food production, we can see from the table that: (1)

Table 11.1. *Male-female relationship between division of labor and residence patterns*

Residence pattern	Male contribution in work–low		Male contribution in work–high	
Patrilocal	④	Murngin Sanpoil White Knife Yahgan	⑬	Aleut Coeur d'Alene Crow Dorobo Klallam Micmac Montaignais Sekani Semang S. Ute Squamish Tehuelcheix Yokuts
Patrilocal with matrilocal alternative	⑥	Ainu Maidu Nootka Tiwi Tubatulabal Yurok	⑤	Angmagsalik Bella Coola Gros Ventre Kutenai Pekangekum
Bilocal	⑧	Andamanese E. Pomo Hukandika Kung Mbuti Shivwits Wappo Yavapai	⑤	Aweikoma Chimariko Comanche Kidutokado Nunamiut
Matrilocal with patrilocal alternative Matrilocal	⑤	Chiricahua Mataco Beaver Bororo Choroti	③	Yukaghir Siriono Warrau

p < .014, by Mann-Whitney U Test.
Source: Ember, 1975.

when residence patterns are clearly patrilocal, the male contribution to food getting is high (13 to 4); (2) when we find bilocal residence patterns, the contribution of males to food getting tends to the low side (8 to 5); and (3) the same tendency applies to the groups with matrilocal residence patterns (5 to 3). Statistical analysis of these data could easily be handled with a chi-square statistical test. On the other hand, the researcher had available somewhat more refined, ordinal data that permitted the use of the Mann-Whitney U Test.

Using this same two-variable matrix, Ember produced statistical support for the generalizations that: (1) depopulated groups tend toward bilocal (instead of unilocal) residence; (2) larger local groups (more than fifty persons) tend toward patrilocality of residence patterns. The data matrix for this last generalization in simplified form looks like Table 11.2.

We have selected this particular example of the cross-cultural research model as, in many respects, typical of this particular research strategy. The evidence seems fairly credible; care was taken in definition of the variables; and the statistical analysis is straightforward. However, a series of questions has been raised about this worldwide cross-cultural method, and the answers to these questions are useful to us as they reflect on other paradigms of anthropological research. For some people the fact that the cross-cultural method goes directly to the matter of cultural universals, of nomothetic principles, is a compelling reason for a greatly expanded research effort in this mode. On the other hand, there are critics whose caveats would suggest that cross-cultural statistical research is not worth the effort. Here are some of the major questions:

What about various alternative explanations of the observed relationships?

The observed relationship that Ember and others relate to a particular ecological theory can be interpreted as support for more than one alternative theoretical model. Thus statistical relationships practically never "speak for themselves." An effective, credible theoretical structure is built of solid and substantial statistical analysis, plus a variety of qualitative data, logical argument, and other materials. When competing theoretical explanations are proposed, the social scientists concerned with the debate should devise a research situation in which the competing theoretical systems would predict *different* empirical results. Such a critical test would permit rejection of one or the other theoretical system. If no situation or set of data can be devised for which the competing theories would predict different results, one must conclude that the two theoretical systems are not in fact different – they are different labels for (or they focus on somewhat different

Table 11.2. *Typical group size related to the unilocal versus bilocal variable*

Residence pattern	Small groups (50 or fewer persons)	Larger local group (usually more than 50 persons)
Unilocal (matrilocal or patrilocal)	4	12
Intermediate (variable)	3	5
Bilocal	5	2

p < .027, Mann-Whitney U Test.
Source: Ember, 1975.

aspects of) a single system. (In some cases theoretical systems are discussed at such a high level of abstraction that no operationally useful tests of the theory can be devised.)

Why are there so many "exceptions" to the statistical trends if there really is a relationship between variables?

Many of the apparent exceptions in the statistical analysis may be errors. Errors may arise during the process of field work (ethnographer error), during the content analysis (coder or rater error), or somewhere in the data processing (typographical error). Almost everyone who has examined cross-cultural statistical tables closely has noted instances in which it seemed clear that the rating for particular societies seemed to be in error (usually in the case of a society in which one has done firsthand field work).

Another important reason for exceptions is that single-factor explanations of behavior patterns cannot by themselves account for all of the great complexity of human culture. Usually, therefore, exceptions in the statistical tables reflect the influence of other kinds of causal factors in operation. Sometimes these other factors will be so powerful as to obliterate completely the covariation one has predicted. More careful research design, controlling for some of the major "other variables," can correct for this problem. Thus the logic of cross-cultural statistical analysis is based on the idea that, "other things being equal, controlled, or operating at random with regard to these observations," a particular relationship among variables is predicted.

If there are errors in the production of the data and the analysis from which cross-cultural statistics are compiled, how can we be sure that the errors did not cause spurious correlations?

As already noted, the cross-cultural researcher assumes that most errors (especially typographical and coding errors) will be random. Random errors would have a tendency to *obscure* relationships rather than to produce them; hence the researcher assumes that the relationships found among cultural items are probably more powerful than the data reflect, as random errors (which are "quasi always" present) work *against* demonstration of correlations.

But to leave it at that is begging the question. A more thoughtful approach to this important problem is provided by Naroll (1962) in his *Data Quality Control*. This is an important book and is essential reading for cross-cultural researchers as well as their critics. Naroll points out that in the type of correlational study we have examined, a systematic bias on the part of either ethnographers or content analysts that affects *only one of the variables in question* will not lead to spurious correlations.

Naroll states the strategy of data quality control as follows:

Field reports are classified by conditions of observation. Circumstances are selected that seem likely to affect the reliability of field reports and to produce either random error or systematic bias. Those reports gathered under supposedly more favorable conditions are (compared with) the "unfavorable reports."

Statistical tests are made to see if there is a statistically significant difference between favorable and unfavorable reports. Thus, for example, the investigator tests to see if favorable reports are more likely to report high rates of suicide than unfavorable reports. (Naroll, 1962:14.)

Naroll suggested that "unfavorable conditions of field reporting" might include the facts that the ethnographer did not live among the people he studied, the field research was too brief, the ethnographer was not fluent in the native language, the investigator was not a professionally trained ethnographer, and several other factors. In systematic statistical testing for the effects of these factors, Naroll uncovered a startling fact: Reporting of the prevalence of witchcraft accusations and fears is correlated with the length of stay of the fieldworker. Evidently, those anthropologists who stay longest in the field are the most likely to find out about the local attitudes on witchcraft, because this is an emotionally charged subject and belief in it is often denied or suppressed by informants. This finding should be taken as a very serious warning by all cross-cultural researchers.

Are not all cross-cultural statistics invalid because the samples are not strictly random?

It is clear that truly random samples of societies are very difficult to attain in cross-cultural research. In the first place, it is not possible to define exactly the nature of the universe from which the samples are drawn. Furthermore, the availability of the data is very uneven, and cross-cultural researchers must often construct "opportunistic samples" focusing on the societies for which the requisite data are known to be available. Estimates of the total number of human societies range from about 3,000 upward, depending on how particular researchers define a society. And the small percentage of societies that have been adequately covered ethnographically cannot be considered a random sample of the total human universe, however defined.

How can the cross-cultural researcher justify using these impure samples? A statistical purist would, of course, insist that inferential statistics cannot be used in these works. But the cross-cultural researcher is hardly the only one who has problems in attaining "purity" in random sampling. It was noted earlier that the majority of public-opinion pollsters do not use strictly random samples. Practically all social surveys are subject to the unknown and nonrandom effects of the not-at-homes, refusals, wrong addresses, and numerous other problems. All mail-in questionnaires are subject to the very serious effects of differential cooperation among the respondents. Nowhere in the social sciences, except perhaps in certain laboratory situations, can one find truly blameless random samples.

Given the harsh realities of sampling in the real world of people, the social scientist must often adopt the position that *some* statistical analysis is better than none at all. Often it may be useful to present correlation coefficients, without placing inordinate faith in the strict application of tests involving set levels of significance. On the other hand, it is always useful to know something about the probability that a particular array of statistics occurred simply by chance.

There is another argument that should be included. Frequently, cross-cultural investigation is best regarded as exploratory. The results of any one statistical test should not be regarded as definitive but should be supported by other studies with other samples. In exploratory research, it can be argued, considerable adventurousness and risk taking are necessary. In most cases the relationships suggested by cross-cultural research can be tested by other kinds of research designs; strong support of particular theoretical positions should involve systematic interrelating of cross-cultural covariations with other kinds of supporting materials.

What about "Galton's problem"?

When E. B. Tylor presented his famous statistical analysis of in-law avoidances and marital residence before the Royal Anthropological Institute in London (in the late nineteenth century), Sir Francis Galton raised a question that has continued to be one of the most important problems concerning cross-cultural statistical comparisons. According to the minutes of that discussion, Galton noted:

It (would be) extremely desirable for the sake of those who may wish to study the evidence for Dr. Tylor's conclusions, that full information should be given as to the degree in which the customs of the tribes and races which are paired together are independent. It might be, that some of the tribes have derived them from a common source, so that they were duplicate copies of the same original. Certainly in such an investigation as this, each of the observations ought, in the language of statisticians, to be carefully "weighted." It would give a useful idea of the distribution of the several customs and of their relative prevalence in the world, if a map were so marked by shadings and color as to present a picture of the geographical ranges. (Tylor, 1889, reprinted in 1961:23.)

Although it is probable that this so-called Galton's problem has been exaggerated, it is an important point for consideration. The various tribes and groups of Australian aborigines provide an excellent illustration of the problem. In many elements of social structure and other cultural traits the Australian groups resemble one another a great deal – in, for example, complex rules of prescribed marriages, initiation patterns, beliefs about supernaturals, subsistence techniques, and the structuring of authority. Galton's question is whether these Australian groups can be considered separate tests of any hypothesis concerning covariation of traits or whether all of them should be considered a single "case" in a cross-cultural sample.

A strategy for handling this problem that has frequently been adopted is one suggested by Murdock. In his World Ethnographic Sample, Murdock divided the geographical regions of the world into an exhaustive series of culture areas and subareas. He then constructed his ethnographic sample in such a way as to include societies from each of the culture areas and subareas of the world. The particular societies included for any one subarea are, of course, those for which sufficient ethnographic data is available to warrant their listing.

With the World Ethnographic Sample as a basic listing of societies (or, more recently, the *Ethnographic Atlas,* also prepared by Murdock, 1967), relative independence of cases can be assured by selecting only one or two societies from each of the geographical regions. If more than one society is chosen for each subarea, they may be chosen from different linguistic groups or from noncontiguous localities. A number of other refinements in sampling procedures have also been suggested for handling this same problem.

The logic of cross-cultural research requires that any valid relationship between variables should hold up under statistical analysis *within* culture areas as well as worldwide. If the correlations between cultural elements or items is found to hold for only certain portions of the world, the purported associations may be accidental or historical rather than arising from "true" causal factors. Many cross-cultural researchers do, in fact, test their hypotheses separately in the major cultural areas.

Driver and Schuessler (1967), for example, examined regional variations in their factor analysis of Murdock's World Ethnographic Sample. Examining the internal consistencies in their trait clusters, these authors found, for example, that *independent family, nuclear or polygynous,* and *patrilocal residence* correlate $-.11$ for the world, $-.01$ in North America, and $-.51$ around the Mediterranean. Here important historical differences appear to contribute to explaining these relationships. Also, they found that bride price and patrilineal descent yield a worldwide correlation at .41, but in North America it is only .03, while around the Mediterranean it is .60. Driver and Schuessler felt that the relationships between bride price and patrilineal descent involve functional and structural "causes," but they were puzzled by the lack of correlation in North America. They suggested that "we must assume that in the New World patrilineal descent lagged behind changes in residence, which were more closely related to bride price. In the Old World no such lag took place, or patricentered social organization had more time to become stable" (Driver and Schuessler, 1967:343).

This case illustrates a second important point about a geographical examination of cross-cultural statistical correlations. Region-by-region comparisons of such interrelationships bring to light differences that can lead to significant refinements of functional, ecological (and other) theoretical constructs. They can also lead to improvement of definitions of categories themselves. As we suggested previously, categorizations such as "patrilineal descent" and "bride price" may be more realistically considered as *"degrees* of patrilineality," *"salience* of bride price," and so on.

Model III: intraregional comparisons

Driver's thorough statistical examination (1966) of kin avoidances in North America is a further refinement of geographically controlled cross-cultural studies. Driver assembled data on the varieties of avoidance patterns as related to marital residence patterns and other kinship variables in a large number of North American Indian tribes (Driver, 1966:131–82). He felt that this exhaustive, geographically controlled study permitted sorting out the effects of geographical-historical factors as against psychofunctional factors of the kin avoidances. He summed up his findings as follows:

Probably all the psycho-functional "causes" of kin avoidances advocated by Tylor, Fraser, Freud, Lowie, Murdock, and Stephens and D'Andrade have had some influence on the origin, maintenance, and dispersal of these behaviors. Even the most geographical-historical enthusiast needs a package of psycho-functional "causes" to get the avoidance behavior started. Once such behavior has become firmly established, however, it seems to diffuse by intertribal marriage to peoples who lack some or even most of the "causes" discovered so far. It also fails to occur among some peoples who possess most of the "causes."

This study shows that essay-style descriptions collected even in great bulk cannot produce valid generalizations about so complex a phenomenon. Tabulated or mapped data are also comparatively ineffective alone and do not produce a general explanation. Cross-cultural correlations based on fewer than 100 ethnic units may shed some light on psycho-functional "causes," but reveal little of geographical-historical relationships. These methods combined, as I hope to have shown, yield a more complete explanation. In addition, historical interpretation is considerably sharpened by treating language families and culture areas as variables. (Driver, 1966:147.)

In the past, comparisons of cultural, social, and other characteristics within regions usually took the form of relatively unsystematic collections of independent cases from which some ad hoc generalizations about patterns were developed. The study of the variations in the Plains Indian Dance is a classic instance of intraregional comparison, as the analysis progressed from the earlier historical and diffusionist interests to more functionalist theoretical frameworks (Bennett, 1944).

Regions that have been intensively studied over decades by a variety of researchers provide contexts for the development of "regional theory" – sometimes particularistic, historical theory (theories about the "Mayan collapse," the spread of the Sun Dance, the peopling of Oceania, the origins of the *cargo* cults in Melanesia, etc.) or as constructs intended as stepping stones toward more universal, nomothetic principles (e.g., the rise of cultural complexity, the nature and functions of revitalization movements).

Redfield's (1942) well-known folk-urban continuum was a regional comparison of four communities in the Yucatán Peninsula. These communities were chosen as a range of variation from "most isolated and homogeneous" to "least isolated and heterogeneous." A series of other variables – including family structure, religious behavior, commercialism, and others – was studied as they varied through the continuum. Although the setting was Mesoamerica, Redfield presented the folk-urban continuum as a universal, nomothetic model. The particular details of family structure, commercial systems, religious practices, and other aspects of culture might differ in other parts of the world, but the overall trends (e.g., secularization) he felt to be cross-cultural.

In the 1950s and 1960s the regional-research paradigm took on a somewhat different form. Expanded funding from federal and foundation sources made possible relatively large-scale projects that were often designed as systematic multicommunity comparisons. The regional-research model in some instances has appeared to serve particularistic, localized purposes. Much of the output from the long-term Harvard project in Chiapas, Mexico, for example, is descriptive in research style.

Whatever the degree of nomothetic versus ideographic intent, the model of intensive intraregional study has been widely adopted because of several distinct advantages:

1 The study of a *range of variation*, compared with a two-case comparison, provides stronger, more credible evidence of the covariations between cultural and other variables.
2 Compared with worldwide samples, on the other hand, the regional comparison permits inspection of a larger number of variables in a *system* and in the *context* of a particular environmental and historical setting.
3 At the practical level the regional-comparisons research strategy permits a research team to carry out coordinated field work, usually (but not always) with a single field language. The logistics of supply, maintenance of relations with host nations, and other practical matters also contribute to the popularity of this kind of research.

The Stirling County project in Maritime Canada (Alexander Leighton and associates), begun in the early 1950s, involved systematic comparisons of a number of communities, representing a range of variation in the "organization–disorganization" in social systems. Thus a community variable (degree of disorganization) was examined for its effects on the dependent variable of individual psychiatric disorder. The nature of the project was strongly interdisciplinary. Anthropologists, sociologists, psychiatrists, and others were involved in various phases of the work.

Related to the social organization–disorganization variable, the communities also included contrasts between Acadian-French and English-speaking (Protestant) groups. The interdisciplinary team and the long-term duration of the project (nearly twenty years) resulted in a large body of statistical and nonstatistical data related to the sociopsychiatric theoretical system (A. Leighton, 1959; Hughes et al., 1960; D. Leighton et al., 1963). As in the case of the folk-urban continuum, the theoretical models of the Leighton project were intended as nomothetic constructs rather than regional, particularistic generalizations.

Frank Miller (1973) and colleagues used a regional-comparison model in the study of the effects of a new industrial city, "Ciudad Industrial," in Central Mexico. Communities in the area had been studied in 1957–8 by Frank and Ruth Young (1960, 1966), so that Miller's research group had the important additional advantage of a base line of earlier data for studying rates and patterns of change. The Youngs had developed a rank ordering of "institutional complexity" of communities in the region, using the Guttman scaling technique (see Appendix B). When Miller and co-workers began their research in the area, they were able to examine changes in "institutional complexity" by using the Youngs' original questions and returning to the same communities. Table 11.3 shows the patterning of institutional complexity in 1966.

The Youngs presented the hypothesis that modernization in the form of institutional complexity had developed most rapidly in the *newer communities* of the region, because of presumed greater social solidarity. Poggie and Miller, examining the patterns from 1958 to 1966, found that the *smaller*, less complex communities had the greatest amounts of change during that period and that the strongest predictor of changes in these simpler communities (scale steps I–V in Table 11.3) was "degree of contact with the industrial center" rather than "newness" or "solidarity."

An unusual and a highly successful variation on the regional-research model is that of Goldschmidt and associates in the Culture and Ecology project, carried out in East Africa (Goldschmidt et al., 1965; Edgerton, 1971). Their strategy was to locate a geographical area in which tribal groups were ecologically divided into pastoral and farming subgroups. To examine and to control for the effects of general cultural variables they selected two cases of southern Nilotes and two cases of Bantu-speaking people. Table 11.4 presents the logical structure of this research.

Using this research design, Goldschmidt and associates were able to examine differences between pastoralists and farmers – I versus II in the table – compared with differences across the four tribes – versus b_x versus c_x versus d_x – as well as the differences between the two linguistic groups – ab versus cd. As a result of these two-way comparisons, the researchers felt they had excellent evidence for the importance of ecological factors in accounting for differences among the subgroups. That is, in many characteristics, the farmers resembled each other *across* tribal boundaries and differed systematically from their "tribal brethren," the pastoralists. Farmers in all the groups tended to be more hostile and suspicious, as well as "more indirect, abstract, given to fantasy, more anxious, less

Table 11.3. *Scalogram of institutional complexity, 1966, in the region of Ciudad Industrial*

Community		Scale items													Scale steps
	1	2	3	4	5	6	7	8	9	10	11	12	13	14	
1. Los Llanos	X	X	X	X	X	X	X	X	X	X	X	X	X	X	10
2.	X	X	X	X	X	X	X	X	X	X	X	X	X		
3. Benito Juárez	X	X	X	X	X	X	X	X	X	X	X	X	X		9
4. Malapan	X	X	X	X	X	X	X	X	X	X	X	X	X		
5. Cerro Grande	X	X	X	X	X	X	X	X	O	X	X	X	X		
6.		X	X	X	X	X	X	X	X	X	O	X			8
7.		X	X	X	X	X	X	X	X	X	O	X			
8.		X	X	X	X	X	X	X	X	X	X				7
9. Adonde		X	X	X	X	X	X	X	X	O	X				
10. Cristóbal	X	X	X	X	X	X	X	X	X						6
11.	X	X	X	X	X	X	X	X	X						
12. Rocavista	X	X	X	X	X	X	X	X							5
13.	X	X	X	X	X	X	X	X							
14. Santa Cecilia	X	X	X	X	X	X	X								4
15.	X	X	X	X	X	X	X								
16. San Manuel	X	X	X	X	X	X									3
17.	X	X	X	X	X	X									
18.	X	X	X	X	X	X									
19.	X	X	X	X	X	X									
20.	X	X	X	X											2
21.	X	X	X	X											
22.	X														1

Coefficient of reproducibility = .99
Coefficient of scalability = .93
Scale items:
1. Named, autonomous community
2. Church
3. One or more organizations
4. One or more officials
5. School building
6. Functioning school
7. Access to railroad
8. Electricity
9. Railroad station
10. Six grades in school
11. Public square
12. One or more telephones
13. Doctor
14. Secondary school
Source: Miller, 1973:50.

Table 11.4.   *Comparison groups in culture and ecology project (East Africa)*

		I Pastoralists	II Farmers
Kalenjian (Nilotes)	Sebei	a_1	a_2
	Pokot	b_1	b_2
Bantu	Kamba	c_1	c_2
	Hehe	d_1	d_2

Source: Adapted from Goldschmidt et al., 1965:400–447.

able to deal with their emotions, and less able to control their impulses. The herders, on the contrary, are direct, open, bound to reality, and their emotions, though constricted, are under control" (Edgerton, 1965:446).

This research project included within its logic a series of parallel tests of main propositions. Each intratribal comparison between herders and farmers is logically independent of the others.

Model IV: natural experiments

So-called natural experiments are usually systematic comparisons within specific geographical contexts. Morris Freilich (1963) has described the natural experiment as one in which "the researcher selects a situation for study where *change of a clear and dramatic nature* has occurred." He has suggested that this type of situation permits the investigator to make a strong case for assuming that the particular dramatic change can be regarded as the independent variable in a standard experimental design. It should be quickly pointed out, however, that standard experimental research structure is not achieved unless the investigator is able to find a second, comparable society or community in which the clear and dramatic change *has not occurred.* This control case is essential if the investigator is to show that the hypothesized effects are logically relatable to the dramatic change (independent variable). In the great majority of cases the control case is to be found in geographically adjacent communities, immediately outside the zone of dramatic change.

The logical structure of the natural experiment should in most cases assume the same diagramatic appearance as that employed by Nadel in comparing the Nupe and Gwari (Figure 11.3). (Also, a moment's reflection concerning this research model suggests to us that Goldschmidt and associates' Culture and Ecology project corresponds in many respects to the requirements of a natural experiment. The ecological differences between the pastoralists and the farmers may be regarded as substituting for a "clear and dramatic change." However, a significant degree of additional control is provided whenever the time and nature of a clear and dramatic change can be specified.)

Field experiment.   Because the natural experiment would be a fairly powerful research tool if anthropologists could find appropriate dramatic cultural changes to match the needs of their theoretical systems, a logical step would be for researchers purposefully to bring about the experimental conditions themselves. This is what is done in the "field experiment."

Allan Holmberg (1954) described field experiments in which he markedly increased Siriono technological effectiveness by presenting the people with some steel axes and machetes. This experiment produced, he felt, a noticeable rise in ingroup hostility.

One of the first effects of the increased production of wild honey, for example, was an increase in the supply of native beer and in the number and duration of drinking bouts. This in turn led to a more frequent expression of aggression, since drinking feasts are the principal occasions when both verbal and physical aggression are expressed among the men. . . . On one such occasion, in fact – and this was a direct result of the increased production of native beer – the aggressions expressed at a drinking bout of considerable intensity resulted in such a strong hostility among the members of two extended families that the unity of the band itself was threatened. Needless to say, this was an effect which I had not anticipated at the time the tools were introduced. (Holmberg, 1954:108.)

This example provides a very clear illustration of why anthropologists have been wary of carrying out field experiments. Any introduced changes that are large enough to be theoretically interesting are also likely to have relatively wide-reaching consequences beyond the prediction of the experimenter. Some of the consequences may be socially undesirable. For that reason many anthropologists have taken the position that field experimentation can practically never be justified on moral grounds.

But in a world in which extensive cultural changes are ubiquitous, it is surely near-sighted of anthropologists to avoid any and all cultural innovation. By their very presence in their research communities all fieldworkers have introduced changes among their informants and hosts. Few anthropologists have had sufficient moral strictness to refuse aspirin and other medical aid to the people of their research sites, even though such involvement in local activities almost certainly had consequences beyond the immediate expectations of the parties involved.

One solution to this problem about field experimentation is to introduce cultural items or situations that are already intermittently present in the community. Thus an experimenter might examine the effects on intrafamily behavior of the introduction of bicycles by giving a few two-wheelers to families lacking these vehicles, these families being in a community where some of the people already have bicycles. In fact, practically every human society exhibits considerable differentials in ownership of resources (and information). Thus, at least on an individual and household basis, there are possibilities for the introduction of experimental variables that are not totally new and untried in the population as a whole. Similar intracultural experimental possibilities are, of course, offered by the fact that individual villages and hamlets may vary a great deal in their rates of acquisition of new items from the wider world.

French (1953) has reviewed the possibilities of field experiments from the point of view of social psychologists carrying out research within the American cultural scene. The experimental manipulations he discussed include, for example, increasing the levels of social interactions in a housing project to test for changes in morale, and changes in the structure of factory organization to test for effects on efficiency. Anthropologists are now deeply involved in the study of various aspects of American culture, particularly in urban research, where it would appear that controlled experiments could be of great potential usefulness. Special education programs, neighborhood health clinics, and many other changes provide natural experiments for possible research.

Whether experiments are introduced by the anthropologist or provided by natural happenings, their usefulness is strongly affected by the following considerations:

1   The testing of specific hypotheses derived *in advance* from a theoretical framework is a much stronger methodological model than one in which only post hoc explanations are provided of the experimental events.
2   Presence of a control group or case is essential in order to have a standard against which to measure the effects of the experimental variable.
3   The outcome of hypothesis testing remains in doubt if variables are not clearly defined in operational terms.
4   Where possible, researchers should use more than one type of instrument or method for observing the relevant variables.
5   In most cases some kind of quantification is very useful for measuring the strength of the experimental effects and for examining the statistical significance of the observed results.

Researchers in psychology, sociology, and related fields have learned about a number of pitfalls in experimental research design through long and sometimes painful experience. Any would-be experimenter is well advised to examine some of their methodological statements carefully before choosing a particular research structure. Campbell (1957), for example, has published a useful statement on "Factors Relevant to the Validity of Experiments in Social Settings."

Model V: intracultural analysis

The favorite mode of anthropological research has always been the detailed analysis of a single case – a community or a "culture." This is also the most criticized mode of research, because it appears to be intensely particularistic and non-theoretical. At first blush it would appear that any kind of research focused on just one community of Trobrianders, Sirionó, or Mexican rural farmers cannot possibly be a step toward nomothetic inquiry. It is localized, ideographic inquiry. But what about all those studies of, for example, college sophomores, that allegedly contribute to the nomothetic discipline of human psychological study? Or how is a highly theoretical study of the psychosocial stress factors in illness among Detroit low-income groups *more* nomothetic, or universalistic, or hologeistic than the *same* research model invoked in careful study of the Yoruba, Inuit (Eskimo), or the Zulu of southeastern Africa?

Research that is focused on a single community – however small or distant from modern urbanized lifeways – is not intrinsically less scientific or less universalistic than research carried out in Euro-American cultural contexts. It is the design and intent of data gathering that make the difference. When the principal goal of research among a relatively isolated Amazonian community is to *describe* the people's unique and different lifeways, then the research, however worthy, can be considered ideographic. When, on the other hand, a researcher among these same people seeks to test general theoretical ideas, or develop some new model of human behavior using general cross-cultural constructs, then the work is in principle nomothetic and universalistic. (We noted earlier that research does not have to be nomothetic to be "scientific.")

The single-case model has continued to be the primary focus of research in anthropology for several important reasons:

1   The focus on a community permits the maximum combination of quantitative and qualitative data-gathering techniques, hence enhanced overall credibility, or face validity, for the results.
2   The greater need for strictly comparable, hard data, the more likely it is that much initial preparation must go into developing rapport, as well as *locally appropriate*, valid structured-interviewing procedures through firsthand field work.
3   The growth of ecological theory has required greater attention to specific environmental data, thus further reinforcing localization of research strategies.
4   Disillusionment with the almost insurmountable task of working up truly comparable two-case comparisons, and the relative paucity of clear-cut, multicommunity natural experiments have also contributed.
5   Many applied anthropology questions involve specific locations, within which particular medical, social, or other problems are the focus of theoretical and practical attention.

6　Increased recognition of intracultural diversity of cognitive patterns, socioeconomic situations, and practically everything else (cf. *American Ethnologist*, 1975) has led to recognition of untapped research potentials inherent in intracultural, intracommunity variations of behavior.

Many of the research projects mentioned in previous chapters have been based on the intracultural diversity model. The general idea takes the following form:

1　The researcher is interested in constructing an explanatory-predictive model of X (an illness; innovative behavior; or other variables that can be identified in *individuals* or other small-scale units).

2　She or he finds that variable X does indeed vary in occurrence in community C (or a set of communities).

3　A series of explanatory variables, Y, Z, W, L, . . . N, is selected for study of their systematic covariations with X.

4　Quantified systematic data in community C are collected to include all the previously mentioned variables (and usually many more).

5　Participant observation and other qualitative data-collecting methods are used to gather a framework of "thick description" to set the context for testing statistical relationships.

Intracultural diversity in medical modernization: a case example

Clyde Woods carried out extensive data gathering concerning medical modernization in the Guatemalan community of San Lucas Tolimán. At the time of the research in 1965–6, thirteen shamans still practiced medicine in San Lucas, but changes toward increased use of "modern" medical resources were everywhere evident as "alternative solutions to medical problems [were offered] by Ladino pharmacists, spiritualists, practical nurses, lay curers, and university-trained doctors" (Woods and Graves, 1973:12).

Woods selected a basic sample of forty Indian households and fifteen lower-income Ladino households, and over a six-month period he kept a running account of the medical practices of these people by recording (at least once a week) reported illnesses and what the people did about them. He also recorded costs of medication and a host of other supporting data about these behaviors.

Data on a large number of other variables were gathered *from the same households*, using structured survey techniques. Some of the major explanatory variables in this study included cash income, traditional beliefs (based on forty-eight items), innovativeness, exposure to modern ideas (education, travel, contacts with mass media, etc.). Each of these variables was constructed or derived from a constellation of individual questions and observations.

The statistical analysis, described in the monograph, *The Process of Medical Change in a Highland Guatemalan Town* (Woods and Graves, 1973), involved a complex testing of the *patterns* of intercorrelations, along the lines suggested by Blalock for developing causal inferences from correlational data (p. 401). Figure 11.5 shows the theoretical model for explaining medical change (and similar behaviors) developed by Woods and Graves.

These researchers felt that the best fit of the intercorrelated data from San Lucas is achieved when the "traditional beliefs" variable is considered to be a *resultant* of the changed behavior rather than the other way around. The authors suggest that the major causal factor inducing people toward change is their cash index, which affects their likelihood of exposure to new ideas, leading to tendencies to innovations – of which medical innovation is one variety. Thus the intercorrelational model is intended to contribute to *general* models of modernization and cultural change. This research example also has the following features:

1 The data from 1966 can serve as a base line for statistical comparisons with later years. Any restudy of these processes can include statistical comparisons with a time-depth feature.
2 The variables in the theoretical model are in principle cross-cultural, even though the specific ethnographic context of San Lucas, including the specific beliefs and practices of (Mayan-speaking) Indian peoples, makes up the primary data base. (This feature is not in principle different from a theoretical study of college sophomores – for general theoretical variables are *always* based on some specific, local, culturally shaped behaviors, beliefs, and materials.)
3 The specific findings as given in Figure 11.5 may be doubted, reinterpreted, or reshaped by critics; and in any case the results are tentative, suggestive, like all research. The credibility, however, is enhanced by the contextual data Woods and associates are able to command to support the statistical analysis.

The Six Cultures study: a case example

The Six Cultures study, to which we referred earlier (Chapter 6), was basically designed on the intracultural variation model, combined with an important ad-

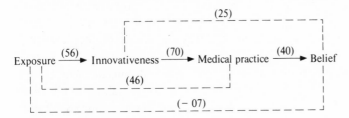

Figure 11.5. Hypothetical model of the change process in San Lucas Tolimán (from Woods and Graves, 1973:36).
Key: Solid arrows represent hypothetical causal links. Dotted lines represent relationships assumed to be artifacts of these causal links. The figures in parentheses represent obtained correlations between the key measure of each concept in this model.

ditional feature; the modes of intracultural research were carried out in six widely separated locations. The researchers (B. and J. Whiting, W. W. Lambert, and others) developed cross-culturally applicable data-gathering procedures, instruction manuals and other guides for fieldworkers. Fieldworkers were carefully instructed in painstaking details of ethnographic field work before going out to field sites. The male-female teams left for Okinawa, the Philippines, India, East Africa and Mexico, with a sixth team remaining in the United States to pursue research in a New England town. In each of the six locations comparable samples of children of specific ages were selected; their mothers were interviewed with comparable questions; and other parallel data-gathering steps were carried out.

In addition to the quantified data, each field team was instructed to collect general ethnographic data, especially concentrating on patterns affecting child training. (The ethnographic case studies from the six different communities were published separately from the statistical, theory-building analyses.)

The data from the interviews with mothers were analyzed in a design involving factor analysis. The information from a total of 133 mothers was grouped (in a computerized process) into ten factors including "warmth of mother," "mother's emotional stability," "responsibility training," and "aggression training." Having isolated these elements of mother behavior in the six cultures, the researchers then investigated the antecedents of socialization practices in residence patterns, household size and structure, extended kin groups, and patterning of sex roles. They found that a number of the patterns of child training were significantly related to *ecological variables* involving family and household structuring. For example, as shown in Table 11.5, they found that mothers tend to show more warmth and stability in socializing their children when there are a number of male adults in the household (e.g., in extended families).

The design of this project had another important methodological advantage. Both intracultural and cross-cultural relationships could be examined within a single statistical analysis. The researchers found that in a number of dimensions within the data *intra*cultural variations were more important than cross-cultural contrasts in accounting for the totality of differences among the 133 mothers in their maternal behaviors.

Note that the relationships in Table 11.5 constitute independent, parallel demonstrations of the hypothesized patterns. Thus the overall credibility of the evidence is greater than it would have been had only one case, one community, been involved in the analysis. These data are also stronger than the typical cross-cultural statistical analyses, because those studies do not have the intensity of contextual supporting information and are constructed from uneven and highly variable primary ethnographic sources.

The logic of the Six Cultures study did not place heavy emphasis on the repre-

Table 11.5. *Maternal instability related to number of male adults in household*

Society[a]	Instability rating	Number of male adults in household	
		Low	High
Mexico	High	9	3
	Low	7	3
Philippines	High	10	2
	Low	7	4
Okinawa	High	10	1
	Low	7	6
India	High	6	5
	Low	4	9

Source: Adapted from Minturn and Lambert, 1965:263.
[a]U.S. and East African samples were not tested because they have no significant variations in the number of male adults in households.
Cumulative z score for the four cases = 3.28. (Chi square) $p < .01$ (two tailed).

sentativeness of the six cases as a sample from societies around the world. Rather, a main criterion for selection appears to have been the geographical separation, hence historical and cultural independence, of the communities.

Statistical correlations and causal models

In the research models discussed previously, data analysis often takes the form of statistical statements, usually correlations between two or more variables. The statistical correlations give a numerical framework or structure to the verbally presented theory. For example, the statistical manipulations of Woods and Graves's data analysis were intended to provide support for a very general, potentially nomothetic theoretical system about processes of modernization. This theory includes the core proposition that "involvement in the case economy [is] a prime mover in promoting a more modern way of life. This results in some forms of increased exposure to people and ideas outside the local community, which in turn fosters a predisposition to innovativeness" (Woods and Graves, 1973:40). Their theoretical model also includes the idea that belief systems change in response to behavioral changes rather than the converse.

At this point someone may recall the familiar slogan: "Correlations do not prove causation." If they do not, then what does? And why are Woods and Graves and many other researchers so intent on examining correlations if they cannot "prove causation"?

The answer to these questions requires considering a strikingly important general point: *Nothing proves causation*. Theories and theoretical systems *cannot be proved*. They can only be rendered more or less plausible, more or less useful in prediction and explanation. Theories in all branches of science are supported to varying degrees by accumulated evidence, *especially evidence that has eliminated plausible alternative theories*. The Woods and Graves model, the statistical tests in Murdock's *Social Structure*, Ember's correlations of residence patterns with male-female division of labor, and similar numerical analyses are intended to show some plausibility – that is, some empirically demonstrable relationships – that fit with the broader theoretical constructs.

The statistics present us with *patterns* – relationships that make some of the other, competing theoretical propositions less plausible and *less useful* in predicting outcomes and events. The Woods and Graves model, for example, predicts that a sharp increase in cash resources will produce more direct effects on people's medical practices than will educational programs aimed at affecting their health-and-illness beliefs. (Note that the question of the *desirability* of any changes is a separate question, not handled by this theoretical structure.)

Actually, Woods and Graves do not claim that their theoretical model applies exactly to communities or situations beyond the confines of San Lucas Tolimán. However, their nomothetic intent is clear when they say that one purpose of their research was to "see if this empirical evidence might help clarify some of the theoretical controversy . . . concerning culture change." Thus the patterns of culture change in San Lucas support the *credibility* of a general theoretical model of culture change, as against some alternative theories. One swallow does not make a summer; and we would not accept the theoretical model in Figure 11.5 as "highly probable" unless we found that data from other studies, in other kinds of communities, provided patterns of culture change that fit with the information from San Lucas. The nomothetic value of any one research project is expanded if the theoretical model can be shown to fit in more than one case. The East African research by Goldschmidt and associates and the Six Cultures study are two large projects that were intended to contribute to nomothetic theory building through parallel comparisons in different cultural groups.

Causal inferences and correlation patterns

The statistical steps that Woods and Graves used in arriving at the model in Figure 11.4 are too complex for brief treatment here, but the logic of their work is based on ideas developed by the sociologist, Hubert M. Blalock, Jr. (1964). The basis for this causal analysis of intercorrelations can be seen in an analysis of some North American ethnographic data. Driver and Massey (1957) had devel-

W ─────────────► X ─────────────► Y ─────────────► Z
(Division of labor)   (Residence patterns)   (Land tenure)   (Descent system)

Figure 11.6. Causal sequence of culture traits (postulated by Driver and Massey; adapted from Blalock, 1964).

oped a theoretical model involving the interrelationships of sexual division of labor, residence patterns, land tenure, and descent systems. Figure 11.6 shows their proposed causal model.

Blalock compared the Driver-Massey model of causation with one proposed by David F. Aberle, who suggested that, in addition to the causal chain as given in Figure 11.6, division of labor (W) should be expected to have a direct relationship to the system of land tenure (Y). Thus Aberle's causal model can be diagramed as in Figure 11.7.

Figure 11.7. Alternative causal model (Aberle, adapted from Blalock, 1964).

The logical basis for Blalock's tests of causal inference is quite simple. Because many other factors are presumably affecting the intercorrelations (e.g., differential time lag of culture change, effects of different ceremonial and belief systems, different soil fertilities and crops grown), he reasons that the correlations between any two *adjacent* variables in the "causal chain" should be higher than the correlations between variables that are more distant in the postulated sequence. The correlation between W and X should be higher than the correlation between, for example, W and Z. Applying the alternative causal models just given, we note that Aberle's model (Figure 11.7) predicts a higher correlation between W and Y than does the Driver-Massey model (Figure 11.6). Table 11.6 shows the intercorrelations for the relevant matricentered traits among North American Indians as compiled by Driver and Massey.

Table 11.6. *Intercorrelations for matricentered traits of North American Indians*

	W	X	Y	Z
Matridominant division of labor	—	.49	.53	.39
Matrilocal residence	.49	—	.61	.51
Matricentered land tenure	.53	.61	—	.80
Matrilineal descent	.39	.51	.80	—

Source: From Blalock, 1961:75.

Blalock's logical assumptions provide that the relationships between two distant variables (e.g., W and Y) should be equal to the product of the intervening correlations, hence: Correlation WY = Correlation WX × Correlation XY. Computation of the expected correlations for each of the relationships indicates that the observed relationships between WY and WZ are both higher than the Driver and Massey model predicts. (WZ should be .24, as a product of .49 times .61 times .80.) The WZ correlation actually found (.39) fits better with the Aberle model, which predicts a correlation of .42 (.53 times .80).

Blalock noted explicitly that

. . . we have *not* established the validity of Model II [Aberle's model]. We have merely eliminated Model I. As pointed out previously, there will ordinarily be several models that yield identical predictions. In particular, we cannot distinguish between Model I and the situation in which all arrows have been reversed, i.e., $Z \leftarrow Y \leftarrow X \leftarrow W$. (Blalock, 1964:76.)

Most frequently the anthropologist who wishes to test causal inferences in this manner is likely to find that he lacks sufficient data. Also, many of the causal models provided by anthropological theory are so diffuse and complex that the logical structuring necessary for predicting particular correlations cannot be determined. However, Blalock's work provides us with two excellent suggestions:

1   We need to examine cross-cultural covariations in terms of more complex patterns than the usual piecemeal two-variable style provides.
2   We need to refine our theoretical constructs to the point where parts of them can be examined in logical terms analogous to the example given previously. That is, we must transform our verbal models into statistical models.

Multiple hypotheses: the strategic elimination of alternative explanations

There are many ways in which provisional evidence can be amassed in support of a theoretical proposition. A statistical cross-cultural comparison, a regionally controlled comparison, a specialized field experiment, or an intracultural comparison can each in its separate way provide support for a theoretical statement. An effective theory-building strategy should combine all of these research modes. As suggested in Chapters 2 and 3, theoretical work is most effective when the goals of particular pieces of research are clearly spelled out and when the steps of research are defined in a manner that permits replication. These are guidelines for the structuring of individual investigations, but what can be suggested concerning the most effective planning of *sequences* of investigations? How can the individual bits of theory construction be made solid and enduring – providing an increasingly elaborated frame of explanation for sectors of human behavior?

We have already suggested elements of a successful general research strategy in connection with several points taken up earlier. The investigatory attitude that seems to us the most promising is that particular style of theoretical eclecticism that was long ago labeled "the method of multiple working hypotheses" by the geographer T. C. Chamberlin (1890). Chamberlin contracted his methodological suggestion with that style most commonly encountered in many sciences – namely, that of deductive verification from a general theoretical framework. This latter research strategy usually involves an unstinting collection of *evidence in support of one's ruling theoretical position.* Anthropology is full of examples: of those who labored to pile up the evidence in favor of a theory of unilinear evolution; those who have collected instances of diffusion and borrowing to illustrate a nonevolutionist historicism; and all those tireless workers who have gathered up instances in support of the proposition that rituals and other social features reinforce and maintain social integration and solidarity. In psychology there are the workers in the vineyards of "cognitive dissonance theory" who have been ingenious in finding additional instances of situations in which the theoretical formulation can be made to apply; the classic example of this particular research strategy is found in that very large output of Freudian psychoanalytic theory, in which, over the years, nearly every aspect of individual behavior and nearly every element of culture have in one way or another been subsumed within the extension of the Oedipus complex, castration anxiety, and other primal touchstones of the Freudian scenario.

Now the point of all of this is that these "ruling-theory" research paradigms generally involve an increasing ego involvement of the scientist with his personal theory, with increasing reluctance to entertain alternative forms of explanation. Not uncommonly, rules of evidence become lax, and cases that support the theory are accepted uncritically because their fit with the main theory makes them seem almost self-evident; hence there is no need for careful sifting of evidence. As Chamberlin put it:

A thousand applications of the supposed principle of levity to the explanation of ascending bodies brought no increase of evidence that it was the true theory of the phenomena, but it doubtless created the impression in the minds of the ancient physical philosophers that it did, for so many additional facts seemed to harmonize with it. (Chamberlin, 1897:841.)

Concerning the dangers of emotional involvement with one's pet theories (and a way to avoid such dangers), Chamberlin said:

The moment one has offered an original explanation for a phenomenon which seems satisfactory, that moment affection for his intellectual child springs into existence, and as the explanation grows into a definite theory his parental explanations cluster about his offspring and it grows more and more dear to him. While he persuades himself that he holds it still as tentative, it is none the less lovingly tentative and not impartially and indifferently tentative.

To avoid this grave danger, the method of multiple working hypotheses is urged. It differs from the simple working hypothesis in that it distributes the effort and divides the affections. . . . Each hypothesis suggests its own criteria, its own means of proof, its own method of developing the truth, and if a group of hypotheses encompass the subject on all sides, the total outcome of means and of methods is full and rich. (Ibid., 843.)

Francis Bacon, more than three centuries ago, suggested this same research strategy:

The induction which is to be available for the discovery and demonstration of sciences and arts, must analyze nature by proper rejections and exclusions; and then, after a sufficient number of negatives, come to a conclusion on the affirmative instances. . . . [To man] it is granted only to proceed at first by negative, and at last to end in affirmatives after exclusion has been exhausted. (Bacon, reprinted 1960:99, 151.)

John R. Platt has suggested that those sciences that appear to be making rapid progress at this time – for instance, molecular biology and high-energy physics – seem to be doing so because of their extensive employment of the strategy involving step-by-step elimination of alternative hypotheses. He feels that supposed differences in the kind of subject matter and relative tractability of various areas of research have been exaggerated and that the areas of continuing progress are notable mainly for their methodological excellence. As he puts it:

Unfortunately, I think there are other areas of science today that are sick by comparison, because they have forgotten the necessity for alternative hypotheses and disproof. Each man has only one branch – or none – on the logical tree, and it twists at random without coming to the need for a crucial decision at any point. We can see from the external symptoms that there is something scientifically wrong. The Frozen Method. The Eternal Surveyor. The Never Finished. The Great Man with a Single Hypothesis. The Little Club of Dependents. The Vendetta. The All-encompassing Theory Which Can Never Be Falsified. (Platt, 1966:29.)

The step-by-step elimination of competing hypotheses does not proceed in a vacuum, however. As we suggested earlier, the framework for organizing significant research is provided by *models*, which by their nature can suggest ways in which more than one theoretical system can be plugged into a research design. Properly designed models also highlight the locations and potential significance of alternative explanations. In the Woods-Graves model, for example, the plausible claims concerning the causal power of traditional beliefs can be directly examined and compared with countersuggestions. New variables, arising from the research of other investigators in other communities, can similarly be integrated into the model. Finally, adequate provisional models should allow for truly multivariable systems, even though some individual research projects might focus attention on only a portion of the larger system.

There are two important classes of alternative hypotheses that should be routinely examined by every anthropologist in the course of his investigations.

Methodological hypotheses

In any research it is imperative that the null hypothesis be considered – that the results of a particular set of observations (e.g., a co-occurrence of two cultural or social traits) happened because of sampling error.

A related alternative hypothesis is that the observed co-occurrence or pattern derives from nonrepresentativeness in sampling of cases: "He happened to find an exceptional society." A third possibility is that the observed pattern is caused by biases in the quality of the data themselves. A variant of this methodological question involves the possibility that the observed pattern is caused by biases in informants' *response styles* (e.g., on a questionnaire or psychological test) rather than by "true" cultural patterns.

Most of the studies we have looked at in this chapter involve the examination of some of these methodological alternatives, particularly the statistical hypothesis that the results obtained occurred because of chance errors in sampling. The data quality control methods of Naroll, Rohner, and others are concentrated attempts to test for a whole series of alternatives concerning biases of the ethnographer, biased effects of the field-work situation, and other sources of error in field-work observations.

Theoretical alternatives

When all of the procedural hypotheses have been considered, the anthropologist can move on to consider alternative theoretical formulations – the competing explanations variously labeled "psychological explanations," "social structural theory," "functionalism," "evolutionism," and "economic determinism." Here a crucially important point must be emphasized: Consideration of alternative hypotheses must be structured in a manner that permits the rejection of one or the other alternative. Rival theoretical positions, if they truly make a difference, must at some point *predict different results* under some specifiable condition. It is the job of the investigator to locate such critical differences in theoretical formulations and put them to the test. Blalock's statistical testing of two different explanations of the relationships among division of labor, land tenure, residence, and descent is an example of a situation in which the researcher was able to discard one alternative hypothesis in favor of the other. At the same time, he admitted that other alternative formulations could be found that would require further testing and refinement of the data.

The statistical analysis by Driver of relationships between in-law avoidances and marriage among North American Indians is an example of a frequently encountered situation in which rival theories each appear to contribute to the full explanation of the data. Thus, instead of discarding one or the other alternative, Driver suggested that the co-occurrence of the two trait clusters requires an explanation incorporating both psychofunctional and historical elements of theory. A next step in this kind of research situation is to design investigations that permit the measurement of the *relative strengths* of these two causal factors in a variety of circumstances.

Methodology and the culture of anthropology

A principal weakness in much anthropological work is that investigation is not recycled. Most frequently, the social scientist who has finished a neat piece of work publishes the conclusions and then moves on to another somewhat related area of research – to expand on the supposedly successful model of explanation – rather than submitting it to critical retesting. It is not difficult to see that there are important features in the general culture of the social sciences that encourage poor methodology. Pressures to publish – and to produce *new and novel* conceptualizations – encourage premature closure of investigation. And our social-science culture provides too few rewards for patient hesitation, recycling, and replication of research. Instead of hearing applause for a replication of observations, the anthropologist more often hears a scornful "That's already been done by ———, ten years ago."

One of the most pervasive features of anthropological culture is the general commitment to holism. If this ideological commitment is translated always in terms of general depictive integration and other qualitative portrayals of cultural systems, serious obstacles are put in the path of methodological improvement; on the other hand, holism is just as easily translated into a multimethod, multihypothesis research style that fits well with the general strategy of investigation outlined previously.

In some ways the most important area for immediate application of the "method of multiple working hypotheses" is that of anthropological data-gathering techniques. The inventory of anthropological research tools has been subjected to very little in the way of critical analysis. All of the techniques – interviewing key informants, survey techniques, projective tests, analysis of unobtrusive measures, and participant observation – need to be compared with one another in order to eliminate techniques that are weak in reliability and validity, and to develop new tools of observation whose precision can make the testing of alternative hypotheses a more productive enterprise.

Throughout this discussion of anthropological research methods we have been suggesting, in agreement with Platt, that the apparent weaknesses of anthropological work derive much less from the inherent difficulties of our subject matter and much more from persistently nonproductive features of our anthropological subculture. These nonproductive features are perpetuated through direct transmission within our programs of graduate instruction. They are also perpetuated by some very general tendencies in the institutional make-up of the social sciences. We have written this book with the hope of furthering a pattern of culture change that already seems to be gathering momentum. Possibly new methodological developments will arise that can bring about a true revitalization movement.

Appendixes

A Notes on research design

Research design involves combining the essential elements of investigation into an effective problem-solving sequence. Thus the plan of research is a statement that concentrates on the components that *must be present* in order for the objectives of the study to be realized. The trimmings, the tangential matters – all the behind-the-scenes details of "what really happens in research" – are left out in order to present an idealized master plan.

Effective structuring of research designs is essential to productive scientific work, although the ablest scientists are those who are also masters of the unspecifiable interstitial skills that make up the art of scientific investigation. Creative development of new research ideas cannot be planned; effective exploitation of research serendipity often follows no preestablished sequences; and many other important aspects of the research enterprise are not included in our formal statements of research plans. Nonetheless, it is useful to review some main elements of structure that enhance the researcher's chances of achieving his knowledge-building objectives.

Formulation of a research problem

In anthropology we find a wide variety of research intentions, ranging from precisely defined testing of hypotheses (e.g., concerning covariations of a few cultural elements) to general explorations of one or another cultural domain, such as kinship or religious beliefs. Some of the main types of productive research goals in anthropological work are the following:

1 Description of a selected cultural or social domain

As already noted, this type of anthropological research objective has been accorded a rather low status in much recent methodological writing. However, examination of a wide range of research in other sciences indicates that this type of research may be the modal style in some disciplines (though it is sometimes disguised by post hoc references to hypotheses, theoretical models, etc.). Examples of straight descriptive research in other areas of science include reports of newly discovered diseases, genetic anomalies, subspecies of animals, behavior of animals (e.g., microvolt electric signals emitted by fish; signaling behavior of bees), descriptions of new fossil finds of significance for geology, paleontology, and so on; and findings about the general environment such as descriptions of solar-radiation measurements in unusual locations, amounts of strontium-90 in ocean waters, and descriptions of plant assemblages in particular ecological contexts.

In anthropological literature we often find studies that involve research questions such as: How do the ——— (tribe or other cultural group) conceptualize and categorize the plants and animals in their environment? What are main features of organization in the market system of ——— (town or region)? What is the role of animal husbandry among the ——— (tribe or society)? What kinds of mental illness are found among the ——— (tribe or society)? What are main elements in the relationships between males and females among the ——— (tribe, society, or region).

2 *Examination of covariation of an element, X, with a trait, Y, with which it is thought to be linked causally*

This is probably the most common hypothesis-testing paradigm.

Examples: A test of the proposition that the degree of acculturation is related to ——— (various) psychiatric characteristics.

A test of the proposition that keeping large domesticated animals is causally related to patrilineal systems of descent. Other examples are the many hypotheses about relationships of particular kinship terminological systems and types of residence, descent, and marriage systems.

3 *Search for the "causes" of phenomenon X*

This type of research question is particularly prevalent (with good reason) in the medical sciences. Much of the history of medical science is a chronicle of discoveries of the specific factors responsible for yellow fever, cholera, kuru, heart disease, and so on.

Examples in anthropology: What are the causes of mental disorders among the
——— (tribe)? What accounts for the presence of transvestites in a number of
cultural groups? Why do some groups have complex, painful male initiation
rites? What factors account for *cargo* cults?

4 Examination of the consequences or effects of particular events or cultural features

Whereas in research goal number 3 the focus is on a search for the independent
variables, examination of the *effects* of a cultural element specifies a prominent
independent variable and seeks to identify the resulting dependent variables.

Examples: What are the effects of relocating a village? What are the social and
cultural effects of a technological innovation, for example, the development of a
new agricultural practice? What are the effects of a new industrial plant?

5 Complex research designs involving combinations of the preceding four types of goals

Anthropological research activities usually involve complex combinations of
these basic research paradigms. However, it is essential that the investigator sort
out basic analytic units and clarify the research design in terms of each such
question as a quasi-independent research enterprise. Many research activities are
hazy in conceptualization because they involve a combination of several different basic questions and the researcher failed to segment the research work into
manageable subroutines. Often anthropologists focus on a particular social insti-
tution, for instance, initiation rites, and develop a series of research questions
that include a mixture of all the types of paradigms listed previously. They treat
initiation ceremonies at times as a dependent variable, at times as an independent variable (that has certain effects on other cultural and social patterns). No
harm comes of such a mixture if researchers are aware of the logical requirements of the different perspectives adopted at different points in such a research
project.
    Earlier, we discussed Blalock's testing of alternative hypotheses concerning the
relationships among division of labor, postmarital residence, land tenure, and
descent system. Although this research problem can be broken down into an examination of the covariations of each pair of cultural patterns, the logic of the
research problem also included the linking of the correlations among the four

traits into a more complex system. Thus research problems of a simple correlation type are often the precursors of complex systems research.

6   Research in complex systems

When a researcher programs his/her research in such a manner that the interactions of several variables are observed simultaneously, we can refer to it as "systems research." An examination of the covariations among pairs of variables is often a precursor to systems research problems, for it is often useless to set up a complex model of interactions among variables unless the relationships among some of the pairs have been established in at least a preliminary way.

Examples in anthropology: All of the computer simulation studies mentioned in Appendix C are examples of systems research. In these research problems the investigators specified relationships among at least four or more variables, and it was assumed that the "true picture" of the relationships among the several elements (e.g., demographic characteristics, marriage rates, types of preferential marriage performances) could not be approximated unless all these contributing variables were present in the system.

Depending on *how* the researcher phrases the questions, a systems analysis *may* be similar in appearance to the type of research problem in which the investigator asks, "What causes X?" Thus, in the computer simulations by Kunstadter and associates and by Gilbert and Hammel, a particular variable (having to do with a preferred marriage pattern) had the appearance of being the dependent variable. But the structure of the computer simulation (as one type of system) makes it possible for the researchers to shift focus from one variable to another without any modification of the basic research structure.

Elements of a model research plan[1]

The basic elements of a model research plan are the same in any good piece of anthropological investigation. However, in the several different kinds of research goals discussed previously, the pieces are put together somewhat differently. The outline presented next is structured in terms of a research goal number 4 – study of the effects of a particular event or innovation (independent variable).

---

[1] The application forms provided by foundations and government agencies for research grant proposals vary in their make-up; thus the ordering and arrangement of the items in this outline must be adjusted to the requirements of specific funding agencies. In any case, the model set forth here is to be regarded more as a guide for the anthropological researcher than a model for grant application.

Model for study of the effects of the introduction of irrigation
among the ————

- I   Introduction.
    - a   Historical background: brief ethnographic sketch of the ————; situation prior to irrigation; chronology of events.
    - b   Practical and theoretical significance.
    - c   Brief summary of relevant studies and literature.
- II   Statement of specific research goals.
    - a   Aspects of culture and social organization to be the focus of research (e.g., agricultural practices, land use, kin relations, etc.).
    - b   Specific hypotheses (if any) to be tested.
    - c   Definitions of terms.
- III   Specification of research operations.
    - a   Description of intended research tools to be used as the basis for operational definitions of key terms in II.c.
    - b   Mention of general descriptive procedures as well as quantifiable research operations.
    - c   Mention of hypothesis-generating features of initial research phase.
    - d   Description of interfering variables and how they will be controlled.
- IV   Research population and sampling procedure.
    - a   Methods to be used in delimiting communities or other populations to be studied. (If the population is large, the methods of selecting and studying the representative sample should be specified here.)
    - b   Specification of control population – group *not* experiencing the effects of experimental variable (irrigation).
- V   Diagram of research design.
     The researcher should set up a plan in the form of a diagram in order to visualize the logic of data-gathering operations. Such a diagram need not be included in a written grant application, though it is often useful for clarifying points of research strategy (Figure A.1). This diagram calls attention to the fact that the researcher must provide the following information:
    - a   The prior situation in both experimental and control populations.
    - b   Clear evidence that irrigation was introduced into one group and not the other.
    - c   Observations on dependent variables for both populations.
- VI   Analysis of results.
    - a   Types of statistical and/or other analysis to be used.
    - b   Statement of types of results that would lead to *rejection* of the hypotheses listed in II.b.

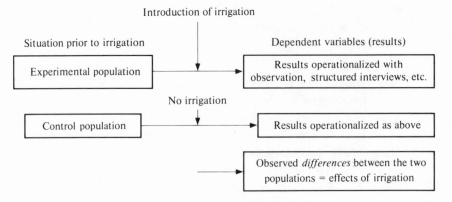

Figure A.1. Hypothetical research diagram.

VII   Significance of the research (sometimes included in the Introduction).
    a   Practical social implications, for development programs, and so on.
    b   Significance for anthropological theory.
    c   Additional advantages, including professional training.

Additional features of a research proposal not part of essential design

VIII   Timetable (chronological sequence with estimated dates).
    a   Travel (and preparations before entering field site).
    b   Initial period – rapport building, and so on.
    c   Construction and development of research instruments.
    d   Pretesting of research tools and techniques.
    e   Selection of populations (samples).
    f   Collection of main data specified in research diagram, V.
    g   Preanalysis of data before leaving the field.
    h   Collection of further supporting data as time allows.
    i   Data analysis and writing.
IX   Personnel.
    a   Principal investigators.
    b   Assistants (including local persons in research area).
    c   Supporting persons in other fields.
X   Facilities available.
    a   In field area.
    b   Supporting informational sources.
    c   Data analysis and other assistance (computer center, statistical consultants, and so on).

XI   Budget.
    a   Personnel – salaries, wages, insurance, and so on.
    b   Equipment – tape recorders, cameras, typewriters, and so on.
    c   Supplies – paper, notebooks, film, tapes, and so on.
    d   Travel – to the research site; internal travel during research.
    e   Computer and other data-processing facilities.
    f   Gifts for informants and other miscellaneous data-collection costs.
    g   Duplicating – maps, records, other archival materials.
    h   Shipping, mailing, and so on.

As already mentioned, each different type of research goal requires its particular ordering of essential design elements. For example, general descriptive study usually includes no hypothesis testing and ordinarily requires no control samples or populations. The operational definitions of terms often arise from the initial phase of research, rather than being delineated in advance. On the other hand, research designs involving advanced mathematical or statistical manipulation should be conceptualized in the form of equations and dummy statistical tables in order to clarify the types and relationships of the variables to be examined.

The creative field researcher will avoid strait-jacketing data-gathering operations in unalterable research designs; at the same time, one should remain fully aware that planless fact gathering usually results in a hodgepodge of incomplete (hence useless) materials.

B The Guttman Scale: a special type of ordinal measure

Social scientists have developed a large number of indices and scales for quantifying important sociocultural traits and variables. For example, the social stratification indices mentioned in Chapter 5 usually provide numerical scores in terms of which individuals in a community can be ranked along a continuum of social prestige and/or socioeconomic success. The Guttman scale is a specialized technique that is intended to produce an ordinal scale with a built-in logical structural feature that demonstrates the unidimensionality and fitness of the items included as indicators (Guttman, 1944).

Goodenough (1963) has discussed some of the logical properties and potential uses of the Guttman scale for anthropological research. An example from his study of social behavior among the people of Truk provides an excellent illustration of this technique of analysis.

From inspection of the patterning in Table B.1 we note that the elements of respect behavior are ranged from left to right in decreasing order of some quality that we can regard as "implied respect value." Performance of a high-respect be-

Table B.1. *Duty scale of "setting one's self above another" in Truk*

Scale type	Relationship concerned	A Must say *faajiro* (respect term)	B Must crawl	C Must avoid	D Must obey	E Must not scold	F Must not fight
1	Nonkinsman	Yes	Yes	Yes	Yes	Yes	Yes
2	Man to female *neji*	No	Yes	Yes	Yes	Yes	Yes
3	Man to older *pwiij*	No	No	Yes	Yes	Yes	Yes
4	Man to male *neji*	No	No	No	Yes	Yes	Yes
5	Man to younger *pwiij*	No	No	No	No	No	Yes
6	Man to wife of younger *pwiij*	No	No	No	No	No	Yes
7	Man to *semej*	No	No	No	No	No	No

Source: Abridged from Goodenough, 1963.

havior (e.g., using the respect term *faajiro*) carries a greater implication of respect than does avoidance behavior.

A second feature of the ordering is that the list of relationships to which these rules apply are of descending significance in terms of this particular dimension of respect behavior. That is, a chief is owed more respect than is a man's older *pwiij* (brother); and a man's older *pwiij* commands more respect than does a man's younger *pwiij* (item 5 on the scale). Now the patterning of these variables demonstrates that the set of six behavioral elements belong together in a single dimension, because knowledge about one part of the pattern allows us to predict other parts. If we know that a particular behavioral element (e.g., avoidance) is required in a relationship, then we can be confident that the relationship also requires the full set of duties *lower* on the scale as well. Presence of rule C (avoidance behavior) implies the presence of rules D, E, and F. Conversely, if we know that rule C does not apply to a particular relationship, we know automatically that the higher rules (A and B) also do not apply. Goodenough points out that the patterning evident in this scale of behavior makes possible a number of further observations, including the assessment of the seriousness in breaches of these rules.

While Goodenough's scale of "setting one's self above another" is concerned with Trukese *ideal* behavior, it is often practical to develop scalograms concerning real behavior (or other attributes) of persons in order to rank them on a significant social dimension. Paul Kay (1964) has described consumer behavior in a sample of Tahitian households by means of a Guttman scale of durable goods. Table B.2 presents an abbreviated version of his scale.

This scale of consumer goods represents the same logical pattern as that of Goodenough's scale presented in Table B.1. The goods are ordered from left to right in terms of increasing frequency. The reverse direction would appear to be an ordering of their relative scarcity value. The households are ranked from high to low in terms of their material possessions. The scale provides a very useful base line of material style of life in terms of which intracommunity comparisons can be made.

Unlike Goodenough's ideal scale of "setting one's self above another," we note that this pattern in Tahiti is not perfect. In terms of the logic of the scale, household 6 should have a two-wheeled motor vehicle; and household 11 should not have a refrigerator, because they do not have the preceding item, a kerosene or gas stove. Such errors in the scale are always to be expected in real human behavior, and it is important to know how many errors a scale can include without destroying its usefulness as a scale. Put in different terms, it can be argued that an array of items is *not really a unidimensional scale* if there are too many errors. Louis Guttman, the originator of this analytic technique, has suggested a way of deciding how many errors is too many to permit acceptance of a Guttman scale.

Table B.2. *Scalogram of ownership of durable consumer goods in Tahiti*

Household	Scale type	Automobile	Refrigerator	Kerosene or gas stove	Two-wheeled motor vehicle	Radio	Bicycle	Primus stove
1	7	X	X	X	X	X	X	X
2		X	X	X	X	X	X	X
3	6		X	X	X	X	X	X
6			X	X	0	X	X	X
8	5			X	X	X	X	X
10				X	0	X	X	X
11	4		⊗		X	X	X	X
13					X	X	X	X
17	3					X	X	X
24	2				⊗		X	X
25							X	X
33							X	0
34	1							X
35								X
40	0		(household has none of the items)					0

Rep. (in original scale of 40 households) = 1 – 8/320 = .98
Source: Abridged from Kay, 1964.

He proposes a "coefficient of reproducibility" which is calculated from the formula:

$$\text{Rep.} = 1 - \frac{\text{number of errors}}{\text{number of entries}}$$

Since Kay's scalogram involves information about 8 items for 40 households, he has a total of 320 pieces of information. The total matrix of data shows 8 errors of the type discussed previously. Hence his coefficient of reproducibility is .98. Guttman suggests that a reproducibility of .90 is sufficient for regarding a particular set of data as "scalable." Other measures of the adequacy of Guttman scales have been developed, notably a "coefficient of scalability," by Menzel (1953).

A number of social scientists have produced Guttman scales involving cross-cultural aggregates of data. Freeman and Winch (1957) developed a cross-cultural scale of social complexity: Carneiro (1962) has examined propositions about general cultural evolution using Guttman scales; White (1967) has demonstrated that matrilineality and patrilineality can be usefully expressed as ranges of variation in scalogram form in place of the usual typological categories; and Frank and Ruth Young have used scalogram analysis in a number of studies concerning cultural change and regional development. Young (1965) has also used this same technique in a cross-cultural study of initiation ceremonies.

Pauline Mahar (1960) has produced a very interesting scale of ritual pollution in terms of which Hindu castes are ranked in a village in Uttar Pradesh. From structured interviews with eighteen respondents (representing eleven different castes) she was able to demonstrate a consistent cultural ranking. Table B.3 gives the pattern of response for one respondent, a forty-year-old female of the Brahman caste. Mahar points out that the final version of the ritual pollution scale

Table B.3. *Scale picture of responses indicating ritual distance (Manbhi, Brahman caste, female, aged 40)[a]*

Castes	Item[b] 13	10	1	2	7	11	4	8	6	9	12	3	5	Score
Rajput	X	X	X	X	X	X	X	X	X	X				10
Merchants	X	X	X	X	X	X	X	X	X	X				10
Water-Carriers	X	X	X	X	X	X	X	X	X	0	X			10–11
Goldsmiths	X	X	X	X	X	X	X	X	X					9
Genealogists	X	X	X	X	X	X	X	X	X					9
Barbers	X	X	X	X	X	X	X	X						8
Goosaaii	X	X	X	X	X	X								6
Shepherds	X	X	X	X	X	X								6
Carpenters	X	X	X	X	X	X								6
Potters	X	X	X	X	0	X								5–6
Washermen	X	X	X	X	X									5
Grainparchers	X	X	X	X	X									5
K. B. Weavers	X	0	X	X										3–4
Joogiis	X	0	X	X										3–4
Mus. Rajputs	X	X	X											3
Oilpressers	X	X												2
Miraassiis	X	0	X											1–2–3
Ch. Weavers														0
Shoemakers														0
Ag. laborers														0
Sweepers														0

[a] Manbhi's own caste is omitted from the analysis here.
Items used in final version of the scale.
[b] Key to numbered items in this table (asterisk indicates items used in the final version of the scale):

*13 Can touch our children
 10 Can accept dry, uncooked food
* 1 Can touch me
  2 Can sit on our cot
* 7 Can smoke bowl of pipe
 11 Can take water from his hand
* 4 Can touch our brass vessels

* 8 Can accept fried food from him
  6 Can smoke our pipe
* 9 Can accept boiled food from his hand
 12 Can touch our water vessel
  3 Can come on our cooking area
  5 Can touch our earthenware vessels

Source: Adapted from Mahar, 1960.

was not isomorphic with the responses of any one person in the community. That is, while the final overall ranking is fairly consistent with all respondents' rankings, it can not be derived from any one individual's ranking.

We should make it clear that the demonstration of a Guttman scalogram in a matrix of data does not provide unequivocal evidence that the scale measures or expresses the particular dimension claimed by the researcher. Any set of items in such a scale is open to interpretation as to the nature of the underlying dimension. The use of Guttman scales to infer chronological sequences (e.g., in the works of Carniero and, occasionally, by the Youngs) is especially open to question. Graves et al. (1969) have demonstrated that the items in a Guttman scale for a series of communities in Mexico (originally studied by Frank Young) did not appear in individual towns in the chronological progression implied by the scale. Apparently, *some* new items spread very rapidly, once they make their appearance. Thus from Kay's scalogram it is not safe to infer that the list of items demonstrates a *chronological ordering of the appearance of those durable goods in Tahiti.*

As with all methodological tools, there has been considerable sharpening and refining of Guttman scale techniques in recent years. Statistical programs in the Statistical Package for the Social Sciences (SPSS) and other "canned programs" include routines for obtaining Guttman scales and judging their scalability. Marshall and Borthwick (1974) have recently suggested (with examples) more stringent criteria for assessing the adequacy of Guttman scales. Their excellent paper is based on perhaps the most ambitious set of raw data ever collected for scaling purposes – 784 responses from each of 109 persons! The paper is well worth studying in detail whenever one intends to make extensive use of scalogram techniques.

Methodological rigor in Guttman scales, as in everything else, should be kept in perspective, however. When the scalogram pattern is intended as a complete data analysis demonstrating a theoretical point (as in most of our preceding examples), then strict statistical criteria should be used, as Marshall and Borthwick demonstrate. When, however, a researcher is trying to operationalize a variable such as "material style of life," "religiosity," or some aspect of social prestige as one part of a multivariable system, a Guttman scale – even a slightly questionable quasi scale – is often better than an impressionistic "high–low" or "present–absent" measurement. Anthropologists are seldom in a position to be statistically fussy about *every* variable in a complex system.

We have presented details about the use of Guttman scales at some length here for several reasons:

1   Scalograms provide the ordering of cultural (or other) items into logically consistent sets whose internal patterning provides a *range of variation* rather than typological (nominal) categorizing of observations (persons, events, etc.).

2   The rank ordering that emerges from this analysis makes possible more powerful (and more convincing) statistical tools, such as rank-order correlations, the Mann-Whitney U Test, and others.

3   The procedures involved in Guttman scaling of data – whether intracultural or cross-cultural – provide anthropologists with new tools for examining logical assumptions about dimensions of cultural systems.

4   Demonstration of Guttman scaling effects can be used as a method for assessing the quality of data. The high levels of *consistency* in the Namoluk islanders' ratings of fellow islanders on political competence (fitness for particular offices) give us a fairly strong indication that the interview questions made sense to the people interviewed. The total pattern of responses can therefore be used with confidence for a variety of hypothesis-testing purposes (Marshall and Borthwick, 1974).

C On using computers

As anthropologists become more and more accustomed to counting things and giving numerical statements concerning frequencies of behaviors, traits, and events, as well as computing expressions of the covariations among these cultural elements, the tasks of recording, storing, and analyzing these data become more and more complicated. Moreover, because we tend to be holistic in general orientation, we prefer to manipulate rather large numbers of different variables simultaneously. That is, none of us is particularly happy with the examination of individual cultural items, or pairs of items, torn out of the context of broad behavioral patterns to which they are related. Anthropological analysis usually involves a multivariable strategy.

Beyond a certain point the tasks of storing and manipulating these data become so enormous that we lose track of our materials, or our inventory and management of the data become overly cumbersome and time consuming. At some point in the growing complexity and perplexity we can save time and energy by turning to electronic computers for assistance.

Many people seem to react emotionally at the mention of computers. With some of our friends, the word "computer" brings an instant flush to the cheeks, a brightening of the eyes, slight dilation of the pupils, and a quickening of the pulse that signals excitement and enthusiasm. Other people we know tend to snort with contempt at suggestions of computerizing and thus "dehumanizing" the delicate art of data manipulation.

With large amounts of data in hand the anthropologist may find that even simple operations such as a tally of frequencies and percentages of traits or items can require hours and days of hand calculations, while the electronic computer can do the same job in a few seconds. The catch is, of course, that it may require hours and days of work to prepare the data in such a way that the computer can be utilized. Organizing, coding, key punching, and verifying the data are themselves long and tedious processes, to which must be added the time-consuming task of preparing the instructions for the computer to carry out the data analysis.

If one is quite certain that a given set of procedures can be specified that will require only one pass through the data, then even fairly large bodies of materials can be hand-processed, once and for all, without serious inefficiency. But in the vast majority of cases we must review our data in many different ways; we are constantly discovering new ways of looking at the data, and most often the nature of later analytic procedures depends on what we find in our preliminary analyses. These repeated processes of looking through the data can often be done most efficiently by computer, even though the preparation of the materials requires a large initial investment of time and effort.

Types of computer operations

In this brief appendix we shall not go into detail about various computer operations, for that would require another book. However, it is useful to list some of the tasks for which anthropologists have found computerization useful.

Data storage

Large amounts of information – in the form of numerical codes or as words, phrases, or other nonnumerical symbols – can be stored on IBM cards or magnetic tapes for quick retrieval by the computer. Linguists, folklorists, and other language specialists store textual materials in forms that make it possible to retrieve (and count) the occurrences and contexts of individual words, types of words (in the form of noun and verb counts, etc.), and other shapes of textual elements. A great variety of content analytic methods can be employed with data stored in this form. Benjamin Colby's analysis of folklore materials, discussed in Chapter 5, is an example of this kind of usage.

Sebeok (1965) has described a complex storage and retrieval system used at Indiana University in connection with an analysis of folklore. To facilitate retrieval of stored folklore data Sebeok and associates have developed several different procedures, including a Co-occurrence Tally Program, Unit Inventory Program, Segmenting and Enumerating Routine, and Alphabetic Sort Routine, and several other automatic routines. For those of us most concerned about the "dehumanization" of the research process that overdependence on computer technology might bring, it is of some interest to note what Sebeok says about browsing:

To affirm that the creative process is a human function is not to deny that a properly conceived mechanical system could enhance the process through simulation of browsing, both in non-directed and in directed fashion. In non-directed browsing the machine is instructed merely to draw units at random from an area circumscribed by an investigator who is guided by a suggestive clue he accidentally discovered in a previous drawing. In directed browsing, on the other hand, a specific area, exhaustively analyzed, must first of all be fed into the machine. A program of controlled associations enables the computer to locate items linked with the original area. Then the machine samples successively, to the extent instructed, from more and more remote areas. Such a method might, for instance, be used to identify significant tropes in poetic discourse. (Sebeok, 1965:271).

Archeologists are often faced with problems of keeping track of artifacts – from a few hundred to (more often) thousands or hundreds of thousands of items. For each item certain key data about material, physical state and characteristics, location, and so on, must be recorded. We once heard an archeologist state that it would be just as easy for him to write, by hand, the information on 70,000 potsherds as it would be to prepare the same materials for computerized processing. This is quite probable, but had he prepared those data for the computer, he would have been able to do a great number of different kinds of analysis of the materials; and storage of the data in this form makes recovery of particular items of information much easier.

Statistical analysis

The computer utilization most familiar to anthropologists is that of statistical analysis. While simple chi-square computations, Mann-Whitney U Tests, and correlation coefficients (see Chapter 8) can easily be computed by hand for small numbers of cases, it is often more economical to computerize these operations when correlation matrices of twenty or more variables are involved. More complicated operations, such as factor analysis and multiple regression analysis, are practically always best carried out by computers.

Going to the computer

In recent years the seemingly formidable job of going to the computer has been made much easier for everyone. In the first place most universities and colleges have special courses designed to introduce the veriest novices to computer utilization. (Remember, it is not necessary to have a knowledge of mathematics to use the computer.) Many such introductory computer courses are based on specially designed "canned programs" of computer routines, of which perhaps the most widely used is the SPSS.

SPSS is a comprehensive set of computer routines organized in such a manner that only modest expertise is needed to use the programs. An extensive handbook of description and guidelines to SPSS is available (Nie et al., 1975), in addition to which there is an "SPSS Primer" that offers the beginner some simple statistical routines, described in nontechnical language (Klecka et al., 1975). Most graduate students (and undergraduates too) can quickly learn the rudiments of computer use from the SPSS manuals, particularly when there is an experienced computer user around to coach the novices. Many students find it useful to take a course in data processing, which usually includes SPSS as well as some of the other specially designed computer-use packages. These other special programs include OSIRIS (Organized Set of Integrated Routines for Investigation with Statistics), DATATEXT, BMD, and others. Each of these programs has its special features, and each its characteristic strengths and weaknesses.

Computerized simulations

Complex social actions such as warfare, marriage-exchange systems, games, and economic transactions can sometimes be broken down into a manageable number of key operations (variables) that can be integrated into a simulation model for experimental purposes. When a sufficiently large set of variables has been identified, and the relationships among them postulated, it is possible to construct physical models of a given system (e.g., a battlefield with troops, commanders, supplies, fortifications, transport and communication systems, etc.) in order to experiment with different strategies and situations. One can see what happens when the attacking army concentrates its main force on the left flank of the defenders, and so on.

When quantified relationships can be postulated among the variables, the matter of building a model can be carried out completely in mathematical terms. Instead of moving armies or supplies in a physical model, the experimenter calculates equations employing series of rules governing the behavior of variables under various conditions. Experimentation with such mathematical models very soon leads to enormously complicated and time-consuming mathematical work, beyond the time and energy available to the average anthropologist. This situation is ideal for computerization. Once the model has been accurately set up, the computer can run through a great number of sequences of experiments with the model, turning out solutions to various possible strategies, changes of operating rules, or modifications of situations.

Kunstadter, Buhler, Stephen, and Westoff (1963) carried out a computer simulation to "determine effects of variation in demographic variables such as population growth, birth rate, death rates, and age-specific marriage rates on the operation of an ideal pattern of preferential marriage." In this, as in all such computerized simulations, the specification of the variables (e.g., birthrates, death rates) and the rules for interaction of the variables depended on empirical data from well-studied populations. The investigator does not construct his model from "just any old" patterns of variables but must find quantified descriptive data from which to build up the details of his model. If he has realistic values for parts of his model, and can state realistic rules of relationship between these known values and another, unquantified variable, he can substitute a number of different values for the unknown variable to find out what range of values works in the model.

Kunstadter and associates found that "the proportion of ideal marriages is directly related to population growth, and to marriage rates, and that variability in proportion of ideal marriages is inversely related to population size" (Kunstadter et al., 1963:518). Gilbert and Hammel (1966) used a computerized simulation in trying to answer the question "How much, and in what ways, is the rate of patrilateral parallel cousin (FBD) marriage influenced by the number of populations involved in the exchange of women, by their size, by their rules of postmarital residence, and by the degree of territorially endogamic preference?" (Gilbert and Hammel, 1966:73).

Unlike the computer applications involved in simple storage and retrieval, counting and listing, and computations using standard statistical techniques, computerized simulation of necessity involves the development of elaborate sets of instructions in terms of which the computer is to carry out the simulation. These detailed instructions, or programs, must be written perfectly. That is, unlike human beings, computers cannot tolerate errors or gaps in their instructions. Thus the most time-consuming element in computer simulations, computerized "games," and other complicated operations is the writing of the program of instructions.

The culture and social organization of computer use

In any discussion about what can or cannot be done with computers, or in debates pro and con concerning the suggestion to "computerize the whole operation," one main element should never be lost from sight. Successes and failures with computerization are best seen as reflections of social organization, cultural patterns, and personality. Of these, the crucial problem, in our experience, is the matter of social relations.

In one of our worst encounters with the computer (and most veterans of these campaigns can top this story) a rather large body of interview materials was coded and ready for key punching (transfer of data to IBM cards) in September. Researchers – some of whom planned to finish term papers by Christmas – waited patiently for the advent of the electronic miracle of data processing. The first problems encountered were, of course, in the coding of the data. All the sheets of coded data had to be rechecked. Somehow the months rolled on as we checked through the coded materials, double-checked the IBM cards, and then instructed our programmer concerning the specific blocks of data we needed to analyze.

More weeks went by as the programmer occasionally checked back to inform us that his program apparently still had a few bugs in it but would soon be running. At one point he informed us that several days had been lost because someone at the computer center apparently had dropped the data deck and mixed up the IBM cards (approximately 20 cards of data per household, for 500 households). The first signs of spring were in the air when we began to get the first useful output from the computer.

In this example, and many others like it, we have found that the maintenance of communications with the various persons in the data-handling process – particularly the programmer – is a major element in successful management of computer utilization. Because we frequently need the services of more experienced programmers, we must be able to communicate with them effectively, and for that we need to understand the rudiments, at least, of how computers "think" and how programmers communicate with their electronic friends.

It is also clear that many, many problems in computerization arise through human errors in the coding and data-listing processes that occur before the data are punched onto IBM cards. In hand analysis these slip-ups are often overlooked and processing goes on; but the computer is less tolerant of error – missing information and information coded in nonexistent categories often bring the machines to a grinding halt.

In spite of the great speed with which computers can process data – when *everything* is done correctly – utilization of these machines requires great patience. A program of data processing practically never makes it through the works on the first attempt. Repetition of the process of resubmitting data decks to the computer center is a humbling and thought-provoking process – which can, however, be turned to advantage as we rethink our data logic and plan for a cleaner, more precise research operation the next time.

In addition to the immensely expanded range of data analysis made possible by the advent of the age of computers, another very large gain registered by anthropologists in the utilization of mechanical data-processing devices is the greatly increased precision with which we now regard our data. When we begin to use these precision tools in handling our data, we are forced to define our units of analysis explicitly and to code our observations carefully.

There are many numerical operations that anthropologists should do by hand – out in the field or in their studies. And, up to a certain point, the well-equipped anthropologist should be ready at all times to do a computation or two, and to scan a block of data by hand, without having to rely on computers. There are now a great variety of battery-operated, pocket-sized calculators available at modest prices. Some of the more expensive models are practically minicomputers. (If you take one of them into the field, remember to provide for a good supply of batteries!)

When the anthropologist has the kinds of data storage and retrieval tasks or series of statistical analyses, or other manipulations that can be economically handled by computers, the following points should be kept in mind:

1   Coding, key punching, and other preparation of data for computer processing must be done with great care and patience. Too often we underestimate the time and expense involved in these preparatory operations, thus reducing our efficiency in computer utilization.

2   Almost all computer centers provide consultants who will assist and advise in selecting the right computer operations in terms of the researcher's particular data needs. It is of great importance to consult the computer advisers and statistical specialists *before data are coded*. (Of course, one should have extensive consultation with statistical advisers before data are collected.) Poorly organized data categories and codes can make computerized analysis very difficult and cumbersome.

3   Although the anthropologist does not usually expect to do his own programming of computer operations, it is extremely useful to develop some familiarity with computer language and to develop a general understanding of the requirements, restrictions, and possibilities inherent in computer use. Communication with programmers and with other persons in the social organization of computer facilities is extremely difficult if we remain ignorant of their informal and formal cultural understandings.

4   The great speed with which statistical operations can be carried out, once the data are fully prepared, makes it possible for the researcher to run numbers of different kinds of analyses and data checks rather than adhering to a few habitual routines. To maximize our data-processing capabilities we should be continually on the lookout for new kinds of computer usages.

5   The convert to computer use should not set his hopes too high at first, nor should he be discouraged about frequent setbacks when programs must be resubmitted a number of times before they operate successfully. (We *once* had a program that went through the first time it was submitted – a truly remarkable event.)

6   If anthropology departments had adequate financing for all the facilities and services needed for optimum effectiveness of research, each department would have a staff computer adviser. Most departments cannot afford to employ such computer specialists, however, so that the next best thing is to seek out a computer consultant who has an interest in the social sciences. Sometimes social scientists in other departments have developed special skills in computer utilization, which they are willing to share with anthropologists. These are the kinds of people with whom we need to develop interdisciplinary research projects. Another solution to the problem of developing special information about computer utilization is to attract mathematically oriented students into anthropological study. It would be very worthwhile to provide special flexibility in graduate-training programs for those persons who want to combine an interest in anthropology with serious immersion in computer science.

7   The use of computers in data processing does not eliminate the human factor from our research. Rather, the computer must be used to do the drudgery that so often detracts from our human research effectiveness. Tedious routines of data scanning, counting, sorting, and calculating should be made as painless and time saving as possible, so that anthropologists (and their research assistants) can concentrate attention on the important matters of their science.

Bibliography

Aronoff, Joel. 1976. *Psychological Needs and Cultural Systems: A Case Study.* New York: Van Nostrand. 1967, by Litton Educational Publishing, Inc. By permission of Van Nostrand Reinhold Company.

Bacon, Francis. 1960. (First published in 1620.) *The New Organon and Related Writings.* Indianapolis, Ind.: Bobbs-Merrill.

Barker, Roger, and L. Barker. 1961. "Behavior Units for the Comparative Study of Culture." In *Studying Personality Cross-Culturally,* ed. B. Kaplan. Evanston, Ill.: Row Peterson.

Barker, Roger, ed. 1963. *The Stream of Behavior.* New York: Appleton-Century-Crofts.

Barker, Roger G. 1968. *Ecological Psychology.* Stanford, Calif.: Stanford University Press.

Barnes, J. A. 1967. "The Frequency of Divorce." In *The Craft of Social Anthropology,* ed. A. L. Epstein. London: Tavistock, 47-100.

Barnouw, Victor. 1963. *Culture and Personality.* Homewood, Ill.: Dorsey.

Barnett, Homer G. 1956. *Anthropology in Administration.* Evanston, Ill.: Row, Peterson and Co.

Barry, David. 1968. "A Computer Simulation of the Chinese Peasant Land Tenure System." Unpublished M.A. thesis, University of Minnesota.

Bateson, Gregory, and Margaret Mead. 1942. *Balinese Character: A Photographic Analysis.* New York Academy of Sciences Special Publication.

Beattie, John. 1965. *Understanding an African Kingdom: Bunyoro.* New York: Holt, Rinehart and Winston. 1965, by Holt, Rinehart and Winston, Inc. Reprinted by permission of the publisher.

Benfer, Robert A. 1968. "The Desirability of Small Samples for Anthropological Inference." *American Anthropologist,* 70: 949-51.

1972. "Factor Analysis as Numerical Induction: How to Judge a Book by Its Cover." *American Anthropologist,* 74: 530-54.

Bennett, John W. 1944. "The Development of Ethnological Theories as Illustrated by Studies of the Plains Indian Sun Dance." *American Anthropologist,* 46: 162-81.

1956. "The Interpretation of Pueblo Culture: A Question of Values." In *Personal Character and Cultural Milieu,* ed. D. G. Haring. Syracuse: Syracuse University Press.

and Gustav Thaiss. 1967. "Sociocultural Anthropology and Survey Research." In *Survey Research in the Social Sciences,* ed. Charles Y. Glock. New York: Russell Sage Foundation. Pp. 269-314.

Berlin, Brent, and Elois Ann Berlin. 1975. "Aguaruna Color Categories." Special Issue on Intra-cultural Variation. *American Ethnologist,* 2: 61-87.

Berreman, Gerald D. 1962. *Behind Many Masks*. Ithaca, N.Y.: Society for Applied Anthropology, Monograph 4.

1963. *Hindus of the Himalayas*. Berkeley and Los Angeles: University of California Press.

Blalock, Hubert M., Jr. 1964. "Casual Inferences in Non-experimental Research." Chapel Hill: University of North Carolina Press.

Boas, Franz. 1943. "Recent Anthropology." *Science*, 98: 311–14, 334–7.

Boissevain, Jeremy. 1965. *Saints and Fireworks: Religion and Politics in Rural Malta*. London: Athlone Press.

and J. Clyde Mitchell, eds. 1973. *Network Analysis: Studies in Human Interaction*. The Hague: Mouton.

Bolton, Ralph. 1973. "Aggression and Hypoglycemia among the Qolla: A Study in Psychobiological Anthropology." *Ethnology*, 12: 227–57.

Bowen, Elenore. 1954. *Return to Laughter*. London: Gollancz.

Briggs, Jean. 1968. *Utkuhiksalingmuit* Ph.D. dissertation, Harvard University.

Brim, John A., and David H. Spain. 1974. *Research Design in Anthropology: Paradigms and Pragmatics in the Testing of Hypotheses*. New York: Holt, Rinehart and Winston.

Burling, Robbins. 1964. "Cognition and Componential Analysis: God's Truth or Hocuspocus?" *American Anthropologist*, 66: 20–8, 120–2.

Campbell, Donald T. 1957. "Factors Relevant to the Validity of Experiments in Social Settings." *Psychological Bulletin*, 54: 297–312.

Cancian, Frank. 1965. *Economics and Prestige in a Maya Community: The Religious Cargo System in Zinacantan*. Stanford, Calif.: Stanford University Press.

Carneiro, Robert L. 1962. "Scale Analysis as an Instrument for the Study of Cultural Evolution." *Southwestern Journal of Anthropology*, 18: 149–69.

Chagnon, Napoleon. 1974. *Studying the Yanamamö*. New York: Holt, Rinehart and Winston.

Chamberlin, Thomas C. 1890. "The Method of Multiple Working Hypotheses." *Science* (old series), 15: 92–6.

1897. "The Method of Multiple Working Hypotheses." *Journal of Geology*, 5: 837–48.

Child, Irvin L., and L. Siroto. 1965. "Bakwele and American Esthetic Evaluation Compared." *Ethnology*, 4: 349–60.

Clark, Kenneth B. 1965. *Dark Ghetto*. New York: Harper & Row.

Cohen, Ronald. 1971. *Dominance and Defiance*. Anthropological Studies No. 6. American Anthropological Association.

1973. "Warring Epistemologies: Quality and Quantity in African Research." In *Survey Research in Africa*, eds. W. M. O'Barr, D. Spain, and M. Tessler. Evanston, Ill.: Northwestern University Press, 36–47.

Colby, Benjamin N. 1966a "Ethnographic Semantics: A Preliminary Survey." *Current Anthropology*, 7: 3–32.

1966b "Cultural Patterns in Narrative." *Science*, 161: 793–8.

1966c "The Analysis of Culture, Content and the Patterning of Narrative Concern in Text." *American Anthropologist*, 68: 374–88. Reproduced by permission of the American Anthropological Association. 1975.

1975. "Cultural Grammars." *Science*, 187: 913–18.

Collier, John, Jr. 1967. *Visual Anthropology: Photography as a Research Method*. New York: Holt, Rinehart and Winston.

Colson, Elizabeth. 1954. "The Intensive Study of Small Sample Communities." In *Method and Perspective in Anthropology*, ed., R. F. Spencer. Minneapolis: University of Minnesota Press, 43–60.

Conklin, H. C. 1955. "Hanunoo Color Categories." *Southwestern Journal of Anthropology*, 11: 339–44.

Davenport, William. 1960. "Jamaican Fishing: A Game Theory Analysis." *Yale University Publications in Anthropology*, 59: 3–11.

Deetz, James, and Edwin S. Dethlefsen. 1967. "Death's Head, Cherub, Urn and Willow." *Natural History*, 76 (3): 28–37.

DeHavenon, Anna Lou. 1975. "Two Operations for the Video-Analysis of Hierarchical Structures in Domestic Groups." Paper presented at the 74th Annual Meeting of the American Anthropological Association. San Francisco.

Denham, Woodrow W. 1973. "The Detection of Patterns in Alyawara Non-verbal Behavior." Ph.D. Dissertation. University of Washington.

DeVore, I., ed., 1965. *Primate Behavior: Field Studies of Monkeys and Apes*. New York: Holt, Rinehart and Winston.

DeWalt, Billie R. 1975. *Modernization in a Mexican Ejido: Choosing Alternative Adaptive Strategies*. Ph.D. Dissertation. University of Connecticut.

Diamond, Stanley. 1964. "Nigerian Discovery: The Politics of Field Work." In *Reflections on Community Studies*, eds. Vidich, Bensman, and Stein. New York: Wiley.

Diamond, Sydney G., and Muriel D. Schein. 1966. *The Waste Collectors*. New York: Department of Anthropology, Columbia University.

Doob, Leonard W. 1964. "Eidetic Images Among the Ibo." *Ethnology*, 3: 357–63.
　1965. "Exploring Eidetic Imagery Among the Kamba of Central Kenya." *Journal of Social Psychology*, 67: 3–22.

Driver, Harold. 1966. "Geographical-Historical Versus Psycho-Functional Explanations of Kin Avoidances." *Current Anthropology*, 7: 131–82.
　and W. C. Massey. 1957. *Comparative Studies of North American Indians*. Philadelphia: The American Philosophical Society.
　and Karl F. Schuessler. 1967. "Correlational Analysis of Murdock's 1957 Ethnographic Sample." *American Anthropologist*, 69: 322–52.

DuBois, Cora. 1960. (First published 1944). *The People of Alor* (2 vols.). New York: Harper Torchbook.

Edgerton, Robert B. 1965. " 'Cultural' vs. 'Ecological' Factors in the Expression of Values, Attitudes, and Personality Characteristics." *American Anthropologist*, 67: 422–47.
　1971. *The Individual in Cultural Adaptation*. Berkeley and Los Angeles: University of California Press.

Eggan, Fred. 1954. "Social Anthropology and the Method of Controlled Comparison." *American Anthropologist*, 56: 743–63.

Ember, Carol B. 1975. "Residential Variation in Hunter-Gatherers." *Behavior Science Research*, 10: 199–228.

Epstein, A. L. 1967a. "The Case Method in the Field of Law." In *The Craft of Social Anthropology*, ed. A. L. Epstein. London: Tavistock Publications, Ltd.
　1967b. *The Craft of Social Anthropology*. London: Tavistock Publications, Ltd.

Erasmus, Charles. 1961. *Man Takes Control*. Minneapolis: University of Minnesota Press.

Erickson, Frederick. 1976. "Gatekeeping Encounters: A Social Selection Process." In

Anthropology and Public Policy: Fieldwork and Theory, ed. P. Sanday. New York: Academic Press.

Eysenck, H. J. 1965. *Fact and Fiction in Psychology*. Harmonsworth. Middlesex: Penguin Books.

Feigl, Herbert. 1945. "Operationism and Scientific Method." *Psychological Review*, 52: 250–9.

Festinger, Leon, and Daniel Katz. 1953. *Research Methods in the Behavioral Sciences*. New York: Holt, Rinehart and Winston.

Firth, Raymond. 1959. *Social Change in Tikopia*. London: Allen and Unwin.

Ford, Clellan S., T. Prothro, and I. Child. 1966. "Some Transcultural Comparisons of Esthetic Judgment." *Journal of Social Psychology*, 68: 19–26.

Foster, George M. 1969. *Applied Anthropology*. Boston: Little, Brown and Co.

Frake, Charles. 1962. "The Ethnographic Study of Cognitive Systems." In *Anthropology and Human Behavior*, ed. T. Gladwin and W. G. Sturtevant. Washington: Anthropological Society of Washington, pp. 72–85. Reproduced by permission of the Anthropological Society of Washington.

1964a. "A Structural Description of Subanum 'Religious Behavior.' " In *Explorations in Cultural Anthropology*, ed. W. Goodenough. New York: McGraw-Hill, 111–29.

1964b. "Notes on Queries in Anthropology." *American Anthropologist*, 66 (part 2): 132–45.

1964c. "Further Discussion of Burling." *American Anthropologist*, 66: 119.

Freed, Stanley. 1963. "An Objective Method for Determining the Collective Caste Hierarchy of an Indian Village." *American Anthropologist*, 65: 879–91. Reproduced by permission of the American Anthropological Association.

Freeman, Linton C. 1965. *Elementary Applied Statistics: For Students in Behavioral Science*. New York: Wiley.

and Robert F. Winch. 1957. "Societal Complexity: An Empirical Test of a Typology of Societies." *American Journal of Sociology*, 62: 461–6.

Freilich, Morris. 1963. "The Natural Experiment, Ecology and Culture." *Southwestern Journal of Anthropology*, 19: 21–39.

ed. 1970. *Marginal Natives: Anthropologists at Work*. New York: Harper & Row.

French, John R. F., Jr., 1953. "Experiments in Field Settings." In *Research Methods in the Behavioral Sciences*, eds. L. Festinger and D. Katz. New York: Holt, Rinehart and Winston.

Gallaher, Art, Jr. 1961. *Plainville Fifteen Years Later*. New York: Columbia University Press.

Gerlach, Luther. 1964. "Socio-cultural Factors Affecting the Diet of the Northeast Coastal Bantu." Journal of the *American Dietetic Association*, 45: 420–4.

Gilbert, J. P., and E. A. Hammel. 1966. "Computer Simulation and Analysis of Problems in Kinship and Social Structure." *American Anthropologist*, 68: 70–93.

Gladwin, Thomas, and Seymour Sarason. 1953. *Truk: Man in Paradise*. Viking Fund Publications in Anthropology, 20.

Gladwin, T., and W. G. Sturtevant. 1962. Introduction to paper by Frake. *Anthropology and Human Behavior*. Washington: Anthropological Society of Washington, pp. 72–3.

Glascock, Anthony P. and Robert Kimble. Personal communication

Glaser, Barney, and Anselm L. Strauss. 1967. *The Discovery of Grounded Theory*. Chicago: Aldine.

Glock, Charles Y., ed. 1967. *Survey Research in the Social Sciences*. New York: Russell Sage Foundation.

Goffman, Erving. 1959. *The Presentation of Self in Everyday Life*. Garden City, N.Y.: Doubleday.

Golde, Peggy, ed. 1970. *Women in the Field*. Chicago: Aldine.

Goldfrank, Esther. 1945. "Socialization, Personality and the Structure of Pueblo Society." *American Anthropologist*, 47: 516–39.

Goldschmidt, W., et al. 1965. "Variation and Adaptability of Culture: A Symposium." *American Anthropologist*, 67: 400–47. Reproduced by permission of the American Anthropological Association.

van Lawick-Goodall, Jane. 1971. *In the Shadow of Man*. New York: Dell.

Goode, William J., and Paul K. Hatt. 1952. *Methods in Social Research*. New York: McGraw-Hill.

Goodenough, Ward. 1956. "Componential Analysis and the Study of Meaning." *Language*, 32: 195–216.

　1963. "Some Applications of Guttman Scaling Analysis to Ethnography and Culture Theory." *Southwestern Journal of Anthropology*, 19: 235–50.

　1965. "Yankee Kinship Terminology: A Problem in Componential Analysis." *American Anthropologist*, 67 (part 2): 259–87.

Graves, Nancy B. 1970. "Childrearing Patterns and Maternal Perceptions of Locus of Control," paper read at the A.A.A. meetings, San Diego.

Graves, Theodore D. 1967. "Acculturation, Access, and Alcohol in a Tri-ethnic Community." *American Anthropologist*, 69 (3–4): 306–21.

　and Nancy B. Graves and Michael J. Kobrin. 1969. "Historical Inferences from Guttman Scales: The Return of Age-Area Magic?" *Current Anthropology*, 10: 317–38.

Guttman, Louis. 1944. "A Basis for Scaling Qualitative Data." *American Sociological Review*, 9: 139–50.

Hall, Edward T. 1966. *The Hidden Dimension*. Garden City, N.Y.: Doubleday.

　1974. *Handbook for Proxemic Research*. Washington, D.C.: Society for the Anthropology of Visual Communication.

Halpern, Joel. 1958. *A Serbian Village*. New York: Columbia University Press.

Harris, Marvin. 1964. *The Nature of Cultural Things*. New York: Random House. 1964 by Random House, Inc. Reprinted by permission.

　1968. *The Rise of Anthropological Theory*. New York: Crowell.

　1970. "Referential Ambiguity in the Calculus of Brazilian Racial Identity," *Southwestern Journal of Anthropology*, 26: 1–14.

　1974. "Why a Perfect Knowledge of All the Rules One Must Know to Act Like a Native Cannot Lead to the Knowledge of How Natives Act." *Journal of Anthropological Research* 30: 242–51.

Hays, Terence. 1974. "Mauna: Explorations in Ndumba Ethnobotany." Ph.D. dissertation, University of Washington.

Henry, Jules, and Zunia Henry. 1953. "Doll Play of Pilagá Indian Children." In *Personality in Nature, Society and Culture*, eds. C. Kluckhohn, H. A. Murray, and D. M. Schneider. New York: Knopf.

Henry, William E. 1974. *The Thematic Apperception Technique in the Study of Culture-Personality Relations*. Genetic Psychological Monographs, 35.

Hiebert, Paul. 1967. "Structure and Integration in a Central Indian Village." Unpublished Ph.D. dissertation, University of Minnesota.

Hoebel, E. Adamson. 1966. *Anthropology*. Third Edition. New York: McGraw-Hill.

Holmberg, Allan. 1954. "Adventures in Culture Change." In *Method and Perspective in Anthropology*, ed. R. F. Spencer. Minneapolis: University of Minnesota Press: 103–16.

——— 1969. *Nomads of the Long Bow: The Sirionó of Eastern Bolivia*. Garden City, N.Y.: The Natural History Press.

Honigmann, John J. 1973. "Sampling in Ethonographic Field Work." In *A Handbook of Method in Cultural Anthropology*, eds. R. Naroll and R. Cohen. New York: Columbia University Press, 266–81.

Hotchkiss, John C. 1967. "Children and Conduct in a Ladino Community of Chiapas, Mexico." *American Anthropologist*, 69: 711–18.

Hughes, Charles C., et al. 1960. *People of Cove and Woodlot*. New York: Basic Books.

Hymes, Dell. 1965. *The Use of Computers in Anthropology*. The Hague: Mouton.

Iwao, S., and I. Child. 1966. "Comparisons of Aesthetic Judgments by American Experts and by Japanese Potters." *Journal of Social Psychology*, 68: 27–33.

James, Edwin. 1956. (First published 1830.) *Thirty Years of Indian Captivity of John Tanner*. Minneapolis, Minn.: Ross and Haines.

Jessor, Richard, et al. 1968. *Society, Personality, and Deviant Behavior*. New York: Holt, Rinehart and Winston.

Johnson, Allen. 1975. "Time Allocation in a Machiguenga Community." *Ethnology*, 14 (3): 301–10.

Johnson, Orna R. 1975. "Shifting Hierarchies in Polygynous Households Among the Machiguenga of the Peruvian Amazon." Paper presented at the 74th Annual Meeting of the American Anthropological Association. San Francisco.

Jones, Delmos. 1974. "Job Training and Unemployment: Is Southwestern Jiving Me Again?" *Reviews in Anthropology*, 1: 307–12.

Jongmans, D. G., and P. Gutkind, eds. 1967. *Anthropologists in the Field*. New York: Humanities Press.

Kaplan, Abraham. 1964. *The Conduct of Inquiry*. San Francisco: Chandler Publishing Co.

Kaplan, Bert. 1955. *A Study of Rorschach Responses in Four Cultures*. Cambridge: Peabody Museum of Harvard University Papers, 42 (2).

Kay, Paul. 1964. "A Guttman Scale Model of Tahitian Consumer Behavior." *Southwestern Journal of Anthropology*, 20: 160–7.

Keiser, Lincoln L. 1969. *Vice Lords: Warriors of the Streets*. New York: Holt, Rinehart and Winston.

Kilbride, Philip L., Michael C. Robbins, and Robert B. Freeman, Jr. 1968. "Pictorial Depth Perception and Education Among Baganda School Children." *Perceptual and Motor Skills*, 26: 1116–8.

Klecka, William R., Norman H. Nie, and C. Hadlai Hull. 1975. *Statistical Package for the Social Sciences Primer*. New York: McGraw-Hill.

Klopfer, Bruno. 1956. *Developments in the Rorschach Technique*. Vol. 2, *Fields of Application*. New York: Harcourt, Brace & World.

Köbben, Andre J. 1967. "Participation and Quantification; Field Work Among the Djuka (Bush Negroes of Surinam)." In *Anthropologists in the Field*, eds. D. G. Jongmans and P. Gutkind. New York: Humanities Press.

Kuhn, Thomas S. 1962. *The Structure of Scientific Revolutions*. Chicago: University of Chicago Press.

Kummer, Hans. 1971. *Primate Societies: Group Techniques of Ecological Adaptation.* Chicago: Aldine Publishing Co.

Kunstadter, Peter, et al. 1963. "Demographic Variability and Preferential Marriage Patterns." *American Journal of Physical Anthropology*, 22: 511–19.

Landy, David. 1965. (First published 1959.) *Tropical Childhood: Cultural Transmission and Learning in a Puerto Rican Village.* New York: Harper Torchbooks.

Langness, L. L. 1965. *The Life History in Anthropological Science.* (Series of studies in anthropological method.) New York: Holt, Rinehart and Winston.

Leach, Edmund. 1967. "An Anthropologist's Reflections on a Social Survey." In *Anthropologists in the Field*, eds. D. G. Jongmans and P. Gutkind. New York: Humanities Press.

Leeds, Anthony, and Andrew P. Vayda, eds. 1965. *Man, Culture and Animals: The Role of Animals in Human Ecological Adjustment.* Washington: American Association for the Advancement of Science.

Leighton, Alexander. 1959. *My Name is Legion.* New York: Basic Books.

Leighton, Dorothea, et al. 1963. *The Character of Danger.* New York: Basic Books.

Leslie, Charles. 1960. *Now We Are Civilized.* Detroit, Mich.: Wayne State University Press.

Lewis, Oscar. 1963. (First published 1951.) *Life in a Mexican Village: Tepoztlán Restudied.* Urbana: University of Illinois Press.

Li An-Che. 1937. "Zuni: Some Observations and Queries." *American Anthropologist*, 39: 62–76.

Lieberman, Dena and William Dressler. 1977. "Bilingualism and Cognition of St. Lucian Disease Terms." *Medical Anthropology*, 1: 81–110.

Lowie, Robert H. 1937. *The History of Ethnological Theory.* New York: Rinehart.

Maccoby, M., N. Modiano, and P. Lander. 1964. "Games and Social Character in a Mexican Village." *Psychiatry*, 27: 150–62.

Madge, John. 1965. (Originally published 1953.) *The Tools of Social Science.* Garden City, N.Y.: Doubleday Anchor.

Mahar, Pauline. 1960. "A Ritual Pollution Scale for Ranking Hindu Castes." *Sociometry*, 23: 292–306. By permission of the author and the American Sociological Association.

Malinowski, Bronislaw. 1961. (First published 1922.) *Argonauts of the Western Pacific.* New York: E. P. Dutton. Reprinted by permission of E. P. Dutton & Co., Inc.

Mandelbaum, David G., ed. 1949. *Selected Writings of Edward Sapir in Language, Culture, and Personality.* Berkeley: University of California Press.

Marchione, Thomas. In press. "Factors Associated with Malnutrition in the Children of Western Jamaica." In *Nutritional Anthropology*, eds. N. Jerome, R. Kandel, and G. Pelto. New York: Marcel Dekker.

Marshall, Mac, and Mark Borthwick, 1974. "Consensus, Dissensus, and Guttman Scales: The Namoluk Case." *Journal of Anthropological Research*, 30: 252–70.

Maxwell, Robert J. 1970. "A Comparison of Field Research in Canada and Polynesia." In *Marginal Natives: Anthropologist at Work*, ed. Morris Freilich. New York: Harper & Row.

Mayer, Adrian. 1966. "The Significance of Quasi-Groups in the Study of Complex Societies." In *The Social Anthropology of Complex Societies*, ed. M. Banton. A.S.A. Monograph 4. London: Tavistock Publications, Ltd.

Mead, Margaret, and Francis Cooke MacGregor. 1951. *Growth and Culture: A Photo-*

graphic Study of Balinese Childhood. (Based upon photographs by Gregory Bateson.) New York: Putnam.

Meehl, Paul. 1967. "Theory-Testing in Psychology and Physics: A Methodological Paradox." *Philosophy of Science,* 34 (2): 103–15.

Menzel, Herbert. 1953. "A New Coefficient for Scalogram Analysis." *Public Opinion Quarterly,* 17: 268–80.

Metzger, Duane, and G. Williams. 1963. "A Formal Ethnographic Analysis of Tenejapa Ladino Weddings." *American Anthropologist,* 65: 1076–1101.

    1966. "Some Procedures and Results in the Study of Native Categories: Tzeltal 'Firewood.' " *American Anthropologist,* 68: 389–407. Reproduced by permission of the American Anthropological Association.

Miles, Helen Lynn. 1976. "Chimpanzee Linguistic Capacity and the Acquisition of the American Sign Language for the Deaf." Ph.D. dissertation, University of Connecticut.

Miller, Frank B. 1973. *Old Villages and a New Town: Industrialization in Mexico.* Menlo Park, Calif.: Cummings.

Minturn, Leigh, and W. W. Lambert. 1965. *Mothers in Six Cultures.* New York: Wiley.

Mitchell, J. Clyde. 1954. *African Urbanization in Ndola and Luanshya.* Rhodes-Livingstone Communication, 6.

    1967. "On Quantification in Social Anthropology." In *The Craft of Social Anthropology,* ed. A. L. Epstein. London: Tavistock, 17–46.

Mitchell, Robert C. 1973. "Using Aerial Photographs to Select Samples." In *Survey Research in Africa,* eds. W. M. O'Barr, D. Spain, and M. Tessler. Evanston, Ill.: Northwestern University Press, 100–6.

Morgan, Christiana D., and Henry A. Murray. 1935. "A Method for Investigating Fantasies: The Thematic Apperception Test." *Archives of Neurology and Psychiatry,* 34: 289–306.

Murdock, George P. 1940. "The Cross-Cultural Survey." *American Sociological Review,* 5: 369–70.

    1949. *Social Structure.* New York: Macmillan.

    1950. *Outline of Cultural Materials.* 4th ed. Behavior Science Outlines 1. New Haven, Conn.: Human Relations Area Files.

    1967. "Ethnographic Atlas." *Ethnology,* 6 (and other issues of this journal).

Murray, H. A., et al. 1938. *Explorations in Personality.* New York: Oxford University Press.

Nadel, S. F. 1952. "Witchcraft in Four African Societies: An Essay in Comparison." *American Anthropologist,* 54: 18–29.

Nader, Laura. 1964. *Talea and Juquila.* Berkeley and Los Angeles: University of California Publications in American Archaeology and Ethnology, 48.

Nagel, Ernest. 1961. *The Structure of Science.* New York: Harcourt, Brace & World.

Naroll, Raoul. 1961. "Two Solutions to Galton's Problem." In *Readings in Cross-Cultural Methodology,* ed. P. W. Moore. New Haven, Conn.: HRAF Press: 217–42.

    1962. *Data Quality Control: A New Research Technique.* Glencoe, Ill.: Free Press.

    1964. "A Fifth Solution to Galton's Problem." *American Anthropologist,* 66: 863–67.

    1968. "Some Thoughts on Comparative Method in Cultural Anthropology." In *Methodology in Social Research,* ed. H. M. Blalock. New York: McGraw-Hill: 236–77.

    and Ronald Cohen, eds. 1970. *A Handbook of Method in Cultural Anthropology.* Garden City, N.Y.: The Natural History Press.

Nash, Dennison. 1963. "The Ethnologist as Stranger: An Essay in the Sociology of Knowledge." *Southwestern Journal of Anthropology,* 19: 149–67.

Nash, Manning. 1958. *Machine Age Maya.* American Anthropological Association Memoir, 87.

Ness, Robert. 1975. "Illness and Adaptation in a Newfoundland Outport." Paper presented at the 74th Annual Meeting of the American Anthropological Association. San Francisco.

Newman, Philip. 1965. *Knowing the Gururumba.* New York: Holt, Rinehart and Winston.

Nie, Norman H., et al., 1975. *SPSS: Statistical Package for the Social Sciences.* 2nd ed. New York: McGraw-Hill.

Osgood, Charles. 1964. "Semantic Differential Technique in the Comparative Study of Cultures." In *Transcultural Studies in Cognition,* ed. A. K. Romney and R. G. D'Andrade. *American Anthropologist,* special number.

Padfield, Harland, and Roy Williams. 1973. *Stay Where You Were: A Study of Unemployables in Industry.* Philadelphia: J. B. Lippincott Co.

Paine, Robert. 1957. *Coast Lapp Society I.* Tromso Museums Skrifter IV.

1965. *Coast Lapp Society II.* Tromso Museums Skrifter IV, 2.

Paredes, J. Anthony. 1976. "New Uses for Old Ethnography: A Brief Social History of a Research Project with the Eastern Creek Indians, or How to Be an Applied Anthropologist Without Really Trying." *Human Organization* 35: 315–20.

Peattie, Lisa. 1968. *The View from the Barrio.* Ann Arbor: University of Michigan Press.

Pehrson, Robert. 1957. *The Bilateral Network of Social Relations in Konkama Lapp Parish.* Bloomington, Ind.: University Publications, Slavic and East European Series, No. 5.

Pelto, Gretel. 1967. "Personality and Social Integration in a Chippewa Community." Paper read at the 66th annual meeting of the American Anthropological Association, Washington D.C.

Pelto, Pertti J. 1962. *Individualism in Skolt Lapp Society.* Kansatieteellinen Arkisto 16 (Finnish Antiquities Society), Helsinki.

1968. "The Differences Between 'Tight' and 'Loose' Societies." *Transaction,* 5 (5): 37–40.

1970. "Research in Individualistic Societies." In *Marginal Natives,* ed. M. Freilich. New York: Harper & Row.

1972. "Research Strategies in the Study of Complex Societies: The 'Ciudad Industrial' Project." In *Human Organization Monograph,* No. 11, eds. Thomas Weaver and Douglas White.

and Gretel H. Pelto 1973. "Ethnography: The Fieldwork Enterprise." In *Handbook of Social and Cultural Anthropology,* ed. J. J. Honigmann. Chicago: Rand McNally.

Phillips, Bernard S. 1966. *Social Research.* New York: Macmillan.

Pike, Kenneth. 1954. *Language in Relation to a Unified Theory of the Structure of Human Behavior,* Vol. 1. Calif.: Summer Institute of Linguistics.

Platt, John R. 1966. *The Step to Man.* New York: Wiley.

Poggie, John J., Jr. 1968. "The Impact of Industrialization on a Mexican Intervillage Network." Ph.D. thesis, University of Minnesota.

Pollnac, Richard B. 1975. "Intracultural Variability in the Structure of the Subjective Color Lexicon in Buganda." *American Ethnologist* (Special Issue), 2 (1): 89–109.

and John M. Hickman 1975. "Abduction and Statistical Inference of Interaction Patterns: An Analysis of Data from Peru, Uganda, and Iron Age France." *Sociologus*, 25 (1): 28–61.

Powdermaker, Hortense. 1966. *Stranger and Friend*. New York: W. W. Norton.

Radin, Paul. 1920. *The Autobiography of a Winnebago Indian*. Berkeley: University of California Publications in Anthropology, Archaeology, and Ethnology, 16: 381–473.

Rappaport, Roy A. 1967. *Pigs for the Ancestors*. New Haven, Conn.: Yale University Press.

Redfield, Robert. 1941. *Folk Cultures of the Yucatan*. Chicago: University of Chicago Press.

Richards, A. I. 1939. *Land, Labor and Diet in Northern Rhodesia*. London: O.U.P. for the International African Institute.

1940. *Bemba Marriage and Present Economic Conditions*. Rhodes-Livingston Paper, 4.

Rivers, W. H. R. 1910. "The Genealogical Method of Anthropological Inquiry." *Sociological Review*, 3: 1–12.

Robbins, Michael C., and Philip L. Kilbride. 1968. "Time Estimation and Acculturation Among the Baganda." *Perceptual and Motor Skills*, 26: 1010.

eds. 1973. *Psychocultural Change in Modern Buganda*. Nkanga Editions. Kampala: Makerere Institute of Social Research.

Robbins, Michael C., et al. 1969. "Factor Analysis and Case Selection in Complex Societies." *Human Organization*, 28: 227–34.

Roberts, John M., M. J. Arth, and R. R. Bush. 1959. "Games in Culture." *American Anthropologist*, 61: 597–605.

Roberts, John M., and Brian Sutton-Smith. 1962. "Child Training and Game Involvement." *Ethnology*, 1: 167–85.

Rohner, Ronald P., and Pertti J. Pelto. 1970. "Sampling Methods: Chaney and Ruiz Revilla: Comment." *American Anthropologist*, 72 (6): 1453–6.

Romney, A. Kimball, and Roy G. D'Andrade. 1964. "Cognitive Aspects of English Kin Terms." In *Transcultural Studies in Cognition*. *American Anthropologist*, 66: 146–70.

Rosenthal, Robert. 1966. *Experimenter Effects in Behavioral Research*. New York: Appleton-Century-Crofts.

Rowe, J. Howland. 1953. "Technical Aids in Anthropology: A Historical Survey." In *Anthropology Today*, ed. A. L. Kroeber. Chicago: Chicago University Press.

Royal Anthropological Institute. 1951. *Notes and Queries on Anthropology*, 6th ed. London: Routledge.

Rubel, Arthur J. 1960. "Concepts of Disease in Mexican-American Culture." *American Anthropologist*, 62: 795–814.

Rummel, R. J. 1968. "Understanding Factor Analysis." *Journal of Conflict Resolution*, 11 (4): 444–79.

Sahlins, Marshall. 1958. *Social Stratification in Polynesia*. Seattle: The American Ethnological Society.

Sanjek, Roger. 1971. "Brazilian Racial Terms: Some Aspects of Meaning and Learning." *American Anthropologist*, 73: 1126–43.

1972. "Ghanaian Networks: An Analysis of Interethnic Relations in Urban Situations." Ph.D. dissertation, Columbia University.

1975. "Cognitive Maps of the Ethnic Domain in Urban Ghana." Paper presented at the 74th Annual Meeting of the American Anthropological Association. San Francisco.

Sankoff, Gillian. 1971. "Quantitative Analysis of Sharing and Variability in a Cognitive Model." Ethnology, 10: 389—408.

Sarkar, N. K., and S. J. Tambiah. 1957. *The Disintegrating Village*. Colombo, Ceylon.

Sarmela, Matti. 1970. *Perinneaineiston Kvantitatiivisesta Tutkimuksesta*. Tietolipas 65. Helsinki: The Finnish Literature Society.

Sawyer, Jack, and Robert A. Levine. 1966. "Cultural Dimensions: A Factor Analysis of the World Ethnographic Sample." *American Anthropologist*, 68: 708–31. Reproduced by permission of the American Anthropological Association.

Schensul, Stephen. 1969. "Marginal Rural Peoples: Behavior and Cognitive Models Among Northern Minnesotans and Western Ugandans." Ph.D. dissertation, University of Minnesota.

    1973. "Action Research: The Applied Anthropologist in a Community Mental Health Program." In *Anthropology Beyond the University*, ed. A. Redfield. Athens: University of Georgia Press.

    and J. A. Paredes and P. J. Pelto. 1968. "The Twilight Zone of Poverty." *Human Organization*, 27: 30–40.

    and Mary Bakszysz-Bymel. 1975. "The Role of Applied Research in the Development of Health Services in a Chicano Community in Chicago." In *Topias and Utopias in Health*, eds. S. Ingman and A. Thomas. The Hague: Mouton.

Schofield, William. 1964. *Psychotherapy: The Purchase of Friendship*. Englewood Cliffs, N.J.: Prentice-Hall.

Schwab, William B. 1960. "An Experiment in Methodology in a West African Urban Community." In *Human Organization Research*, eds. Richard N. Adams and Jack J. Preiss. Homewood, Ill.: Dorsey, 408–21.

Science. 1967. Volume 162. American Association for the Advancement of Science.

Scudder, Thayer, and Elizabeth F. Colson. 1972. "The Kariba Dam Project: Resettlement and Local Initiative." In *Technology and Social Change*, eds. H. R. Bernard and P. J. Pelto. New York: Macmillan, pp. 39–70.

Sebeok, A. Thomas. 1965. "The Computer as a Tool in Folklore Research." In *The Use of Computers in Anthropology*, ed. D. Hymes. The Hague: Mouton.

Segall, Marshall H., Donald T. Campbell, and Melville J. Herskovits. 1966. *The Influence of Culture on Visual Perceptions*. Indianapolis, Ind.: Bobbs-Merrill.

Siegel, Sidney. 1956. *Nonparametric Statistics for the Behavioral Sciences*. New York: McGraw-Hill.

Silverberg, James. 1975. "Eyewitnessing Versus Hearsay Evidence in Participant Observation: The Case for Actonic Ethnology." Paper presented at the 74th Annual Meeting of the American Anthropological Association. San Francisco.

Silverman, Sydel F. 1966 (also 1975). "An Ethnographic Approach to Social Stratification: Prestige in a Central Italian Community." *American Anthropologist*, 68 (4): 899–921. Reproduced by permission of the American Anthropological Association.

Simić, Androi. 1973. *The Peasant Urbanites*. New York: Seminar Press.

Simon, Barbara. 1972. "Power, Privilege and Prestige in a Mexican Town." Ph.D. dissertation, University of Minnesota.

Sommer, Robert. 1969. *Personal Space*. Englewood Cliffs, N.J.: Prentice-Hall.

Sorenson, E. Richard, and D. Carleton Gajdusek. 1966. *The Study of Child Behavior and Development in Primitive Cultures*. Supplement to *Pediatrics* 37 (no. 1, pt. II).

Spindler, George. 1955. *Socio-Cultural and Psychological Processes in Menominee Acculturation*. Berkeley and Los Angeles: University of California Publications in Cultural Sociology 5.

——— 1970. *Being an Anthropologist*. New York: Holt, Rinehart and Winston.

Spindler, Louise, and George Spindler. 1958. "Male and Female Adaptations in Culture Change." *American Anthropologist*, 60: 217–33.

Stands-in-Timber, John, and Margot Liberty. 1967. *Cheyenne Memories*. New Haven, Conn., and London: Yale University Press.

Straus, Murray. 1968. "Communication, Creativity, and Problem-Solving Ability of Middle- and Working-Class Families in Three Societies." *American Journal of Sociology*, 73 (4): 417–30.

——— and Jacqueline Straus. 1968. "Family Roles and Sex Differences in Creativity of Children in Bombay and Minneapolis." *Journal of Marriage and the Family*, 30: 46–53.

Sturtevant, William G. 1964. "Studies in Ethnoscience." *American Anthropologist*, 66 (part 2): 99–131.

Thomas, David Hurst. 1976. *Figuring Anthropology: First Principles of Probability and Statistics*. New York: Holt, Rinehart and Winston.

Thompson, Richard A. 1974. *The Winds of Tomorrow: Social Change in a Maya Town*. Chicago: The University of Chicago Press.

Thompson, Richard W. 1975. "Gratification Patterns in Buganda: An Explanation of Intra-Cultural Diversity." *American Ethnologist* (special issue) 2: 193–206.

Thrasher, Frederic M. 1927. *The Gang*. Chicago: University of Chicago Press.

Turnbull, Colin. 1962. *The Forest People*. Garden City, N.Y.: Doubleday.

Tylor, E. B. 1889. "On a Method of Investigating the Development of Institutions." Reprinted in 1961 in *Readings in Cross-Cultural Methodology*, ed. Frank W. Moore. New Haven, Conn.: Human Relations Area Files, pp. 1–28.

Valentine, Charles. 1968. *Culture and Poverty*. Chicago: University of Chicago Press.

Van Lawick-Goodall, Jane. 1971. *In the Shadow of Man*. Boston: Houghton Mifflin.

Wallace, A. F. C. 1965. "The Problem of the Psychological Validity of Componential Analysis." *American Anthropologist*, 67 (part 2): 229–48.

——— and John W. Atkins. 1960. "The Meaning of Kinship Terms." *American Anthropologist*, 62: 58–80.

Walker, Marshall. 1963. *The Nature of Scientific Thought*. Englewood Cliffs, N.J.: Prentice-Hall.

Warner, W. Lloyd. 1959. *The Living and the Dead*. New Haven, Conn.: Yale University Press.

——— and Marcia Meeker and Kenneth Eels. 1960. (First published 1949.) *Social Class in America: A Manual of Procedure for the Measurement of Social Status*. New York: Harper Torchbooks.

Watson, James B. 1968. *The Double Helix*. New York: The New American Library.

Watson, O. Michael. 1970. *Proxemic Behavior: A Cross-Cultural Study*. The Hague: Mouton.

——— 1972. *Symbolic and Expressive Uses of Space: An Introduction to Proxemic Behavior*. Reading, Mass.: Addison-Wesley.

——— and Theodore D. Graves. 1966. "Quantitative Research in Proxemic Behavior." *American Anthropologist*, 68: 971–85.

Wax, Rosalie H. 1960a. "Reciprocity in Field Work." In *Human Organization Research*, ed. Richard N. Adams and Jack J. Preiss. Homewood, Ill.: Dorsey.

    1960b. "Twelve Years Later: An Analysis of Field Experience." In *Human Organization Research*, ed. Richard N. Adams and Jack J. Preiss. Homewood, Ill.: Dorsey.

Webb, Eugene J., et al. 1966. *Unobtrusive Measures: Non-reactive Research in the Social Sciences.* Chicago: Rand McNally.

Weidman, Hazel. 1973. "Implications of the Culture-Broker Concept for the Delivery of Health Care." Paper presented at the Annual Meeting of the Southern Anthropological Society, Wrightsville Beach, N.C.

White, Douglas R. 1967. "Concomitant Variation in Kinship Structures." Unpublished M.A. thesis, University of Minnesota.

Whiting, Beatrice, ed. 1963. *Six Cultures: Studies in Child Rearing.* New York: Wiley.

Whiting, Beatrice B., and John W. M. Whiting. 1975. *Children of Six Cultures: A Psycho-Cultural Analysis.* Cambridge, Mass.: Harvard University Press.

Whiting, John M., Irvin L. Child, W. W. Lambert, and associates. 1966. *Field Guide for the Study of Socialization.* New York: Wiley.

Whitten, Norman A., Jr. 1965. *Class, Kinship and Power in an Ecuadorian Town.* Stanford: Stanford University Press.

Williams, Thomas Rhys. 1967. Field Methods in the Study of Culture. (Series of studies in anthropological method.) New York: Holt, Rinehart and Winston.

Winter, W. 1964. "Recent Findings from the Application of Psychological Tests to Bushman." *Psychogram*, 6: 42–55.

Wintrob, Ronald. 1969. "An Inward Focus: A Consideration of Psychological Stress in Field Work." In *Stress and Response to Fieldwork*, eds. F. Henry and S. Saberwal. New York: Holt, Rinehart and Winston.

Woods, Clyde, and Theodore Graves. 1973. *The Process of Medical Change in a Highlands Guatemalan Town.* Los Angeles: Latin American Center, University of California.

Young, Frank W. 1965. *Initiation Ceremonies: A Cross-Cultural Study of Status Dramatization.* Indianapolis, Ind.: Bobbs-Merrill.

    and Ruth C. Young. 1960. "Social Integration and Change in Twenty-four Mexican Villages." *Economic Development and Cultural Change*, 8: 366–77.

    and Ruth C. Young. 1961. "Key Informant Reliability in Rural Mexican Villages." *Human Organization*, 20 (3): 141–48.

Zubrow, Ezra B. W. 1976. "Stability and Instability: A Problem in Long-Term Regional Growth." In *Demographic Anthropology: Quantitative Approaches.* E. B. Zubrow, ed. Albuquerque: University of New Mexico Press.

Index

325